American Government

American Government

Readings and Cases

Karen O'Connor
Emory University

Allyn and Bacon

Boston   London   Toronto   Tokyo   Sydney   Singapore

Senior Editor: Stephen Hull
Marketing Manager: Karon Bowers
Production Administrator: Marjorie Payne
Cover Administrator: Linda Knowles
Composition/Prepress Buyer: Linda Cox
Manufacturing Buyer: Megan Cochran

Copyright © 1995 by Allyn and Bacon
A Simon & Schuster Company
Needham Height, Massachusetts 02194

Library of Congress Cataloging-in Publication Data

O'Connor, Karen, 1952-
    American government : readings and cases / Karen O'Connor.
      p. cm.
    Includes index.
    ISBN 0-02-388900-4
    1. United States—Politics and government. 2. United States—
Constitutional history. I. Title.
JK21.025 1994
320.473—dc20   94-38283
                                          CIP

This book is printed on acid-free, recycled paper.

Printed in the United States of America
10 9 8 7 6 5 4 3 2 1   99 98 97 96 95 94

❖ CONTENTS ❖

of the First Amendment's free speech protection are
examined.

❖ RELATED TOPICS ❖

❖ PREFACE ❖

Numerous readers are available to supplement American politics texts or to serve as core readings for courses in an American government or national politics course or for any introductory course in national government. Why another? In twenty years of teaching courses including "National Politics," "Constitutional Law," "Women and Politics," "Interest Groups Politics" I have found that students like the study of politics better when they see its real-life applications. Constitutional cases, which allow students to see how the system has responded (or failed to respond) to the needs of an individual, society, or even the national interest, are often an excellent way to get students interested in other (what they often see as more "boring") aspects of politics, especially when classic readings in political science are introduced.

To elevate their study of American politics above the level of a high-school civics course, however, students should begin to learn that political science is the study of politics. To that end, the readings in *American Government: Cases and Readings* are designed to allow instructors to explain the roots of our government and to highlight what political scientists and other commentators have said about that process. Livelier readings are also included, as are more excerpts from U.S. Supreme Court cases than appear in other such compilations. And because we live in a demographically and politically changing country, a special effort was made to include readings about women and other traditionally disadvantaged groups.

American Government: Cases and Readings is divided into four parts that correspond to many American government texts, this book therefore can be used as a companion reader with most textbooks on the market. The four parts are I. "The Roots of the American Political System"; II. "The Institutions of Government"; III. "Political Behavior and the Political Processes of Government"; and IV. "Public Policy".

Each part consists of several chapters that also correspond to traditional American government text chapters. Part II, for example, contains chapters on the Congress (6), the Presidency (7), the Bureaucracy (8), and the Judiciary (9). The opening text in each part discusses what is to come and offers questions to guide the reader. The learning objectives of each part are stressed in the section openers.

Following Chapter 1, each chapter begins with a short excerpt from *The Federalist Papers* and one or two "classic" readings. Each chapter also contains articles or commentary on more current issues in American politics. And, where appropriate, nearly every chapter includes one or more constitutional law cases to illustrate points made in the chapter.

Interspersed throughout the part and chapter readings are questions designed to facilitate class discussion and to encourage critical thinking about the readings and about the American political system generally. It is hoped that these questions will enliven class discussion and engender more student interest in politics and political science.

As with any work, *American Government: Cases and Readings* could not have been completed without help. As a graduate student at Emory University, Laura van Assendelft (now of Mary Baldwin College) helped by obtaining permissions and locating materials. Most of all, she was and continues to be a supportive friend. Another Emory graduate student, Bernadette Nye, assisted in preparing the manuscript and helped edit the readings, proving that two heads are, once more, better than one. This project could not have been completed without her help.

At Macmillan, Robert Miller encouraged this project and pushed me to keep it going. Steve Hull of Allyn and Bacon saw it through to completion.

I am also indebted to several individuals in the profession who took the time to read and comment on this manuscript in various stages of its preparation. In particular, I would like to thank

MaryAnne Borrelli, Connecticut College

David L. Cingranelli, SUNY-Binghamton

Vicki M. Kraft, Ithaca College

Claude Pomerleau, University of Portland

Ronald E. Pynn, University of North Dakota

Howard L. Reiter, University of Connecticut

R. D. Sloan Jr., University of Colorado

John W. Winkle III, University of Mississippi

❖ PART ONE ❖

The Roots of the American Political System

The roots of the American political system are as old as those of the giant redwoods in California. The American political system didn't miraculously spring into being; it is the product of many forces, ideas, individuals, and circumstances. Throughout the five chapters in Part I, the important role of individuals and their ideas in the shaping of the United States of today are discussed. From the basic notions elegantly articulated in the Declaration of Independence by the brilliant Thomas Jefferson to a variety of landmark Supreme Court cases involving ordinary men and women (who proved not to be so ordinary), individuals with the strength of character to forge a new nation, fashion an inventive federal system, or challenge the Supreme Court to interpret the U.S. Constitution and the Bill of Rights have all contributed in significant ways to the United States of America you live in today.

What were the forces and ideas that provided the impetus for colonists to break with Great Britain? Once a break was made and the Revolutionary War fought, how did those ideas affect the drafting and ratification of the U.S. Constitution, the basic framework created to govern the new nation? What rights were left out of the original document that forced the quick addition of the Bill of Rights? And how have those rights been interpreted over time? Keep these questions in mind as you read the chapters and readings in Part I.

"The Roots of a New Nation" are the focus of Chapter 1. The question of what kinds of rights one must give up to any government in order to allow it to maintain order has plagued political philosophers for centuries. Why do we need government? How do individuals' perceptions of men and women in their natural state (without formal governmental structures) affect the kinds of governments they create? And how did those notions affect the colonists' decision to break with Great Britain and to enumerate their reasons for declaring their independence? These are questions you should ask as you read this short chapter.

"The Constitution, the Fight for Ratification, and the Amendment Process" are considered in Chapter 2. As James Madison argued in *Federalist Nos. 47* and *48*, the Founders were always concerned with notions of power, questions that permeate many chapters throughout this book.

Madison believed that a nation could not be strong unless it had a strong national government. Yet, the system of checks and balances constructed in the Constitution were carefully designed to make sure that no one branch of government had too much power. But what is meant by "too much power"? As times have changed and circumstances have produced "new" interpretations of the Constitution, lawmakers, judges, and scholars have argued over what was the actual intent of the Framers. Sometimes, however, even the Constitution has proved not to be sufficiently elastic to accommodate itself to new situations. Then, the option often has been to amend the Constitution, a process also discussed in this chapter.

"Federalism" and the ramifications of the Founders' creation of a federal system are the focus of Chapter 3. In all likelihood, even the far-sighted drafters of the Constitution did not envision a national government whose powers would continue to grow faster than its population. Over the years, the federal courts have been key players in the national government's extension of its activities into areas originally within the domain of the states. The resultant tensions between the states and the national government and how those tensions affect the citizenry are central elements of this chapter.

"Civil Liberties" are discussed in Chapter 4. Although many Federalists argued against a Bill of Rights, many Americans strongly supported the notion that the national government be limited in its ability to interfere with the civil liberties of its citizens. Over the years, the U.S. Supreme Court has played a major role in how the civil liberties guarantees contained in the Bill of Rights are applied both to the states and the national government. The balance between the right of an individual to practice his or her religion or to speak or act out in protest are questions that have vexed the Court and lawmakers for years and continue to do so, as the readings in Chapter 4 make clear.

"Civil Rights" the rights of African Americans, women, homosexuals, and other politically disadvantaged groups, are the subjects of Chapter 5. Originally, slaves were counted for purpose of representation as only three-fifths of a white person. Today, questions continue to rage about how far the government should go to remedy the pervasive forms of discrimination that African Americans suffered. Other groups, too, clamor for rights. In a society where "equal protection of the law" is guaranteed to all citizens, what is equality?

By the time you finish reading the chapters in Part I, you should understand some of the philosophical underpinnings of the founding of the United States and how those ideas were reflected in the Declaration of Independence, the Constitution, and the Bill of Rights. Just as important, you should understand how the role of government has evolved and how the various liberties and rights contained in the Constitution have been interpreted and applied.

CHAPTER 1

♦ ♦ ♦

The Roots of Government

You have undoubtedly learned of the role that the thoughts of political philosophers such as Aristotle and Montesquieu played in the founding of the new nation. Ideas about what kinds of governments should be created, however, are predicated on a common belief that governments are necessary. Families, for example, are usually not organized into formal governmental structures. But once societies reach a certain size, some forms of government are generally created. In the excerpts that follow from John Locke and Thomas Hobbes, try to understand that, while they saw governments as a necessity, their perspectives on the nature of man and, therefore, on the nature of government, were quite different.

Think about the various national governments in the world today. Some are monarchies; some are socialist states. Others are based on communist or even totalitarian models. At the heart of many of these forms of government are basic assumptions about the nature of people and how people act in certain situations. As you read Readings 1 and 2 by John Locke and Thomas Hobbes, respectively, ask yourself with which author you agree. Try not to be put off by the old English of Hobbes's *Leviathan.* Remember, it was these words that many colonists read. It was these thoughts that influenced the Framers as they drafted a new Constitution and a new federal form of government. As you read both pieces, think about what forms of government logically flow from Locke and Hobbes's respective philosophies.

After you think about Locke and Hobbes, read Reading 3, The Declaration of Independence. Of course, most Americans have heard of the Declaration of Independence. But how many actually read it from start to finish? If you have read it, when was the last time you thought about it? July 4th, American Independence Day, commemorates the official reading of the Declaration from the steps of Independence Hall in Philadelphia. It is this document—and its contents—that are celebrated every year as it continues to ground Americans' basic notions of government.

• 1 •

Of the Beginning of Political Societies, from The Second Treatise of Government

JOHN LOCKE

John Locke was not only a political philosopher but also a creator of governments. He drafted the first constitution that governed Carolina in 1669 (it wasn't separated into North and South Carolina until 1691). Ironically, he devised for Carolina a government much more archaic and hierarchical than he was to advocate in later writings. In *Two Treatises of Government* (1690), Locke argues that individuals were endowed with certain inalienable natural rights to life, liberty, and property. He argues further that the very legitimacy of governments rested on the consent of the governed. In *The Second Treatise of Government* he discusses man's inadequacies in the state of nature and his need to unite in a community, or government, for personal security. Individuals, says Locke, turn to government to improve their lot; but the power of government must rest on the will of the majority and must be limited in form and scope of activity in order to protect individual rights.

Men being, as has been said, by nature all free, equal, and independent, no one can be put out of this estate and subjected to the political power of another without his own consent. The only way whereby any one divests himself of his natural liberty and puts on the bonds of civil society is by agreeing with other men to join and unite into a community for their comfortable, safe, and peaceable living one amongst another, in a secure enjoyment of their properties and a greater security against any that are not of it. . . . For when any number of men have, by the consent of every individual, made a community, they have thereby made that community one body, with a power to act as one body, which is only by the will and determination of the majority; . . . which the consent of every individual that united into it agreed that it should; and so every one is bound by that consent to be concluded by the majority.

SOURCE: John Locke, "Of the Beginning of Political Societies," from *The Second Treatise of Government,* Thomas P. Peardon, ed. (New York: Macmillan Publishing Company), pp. 54–57.

. . . And thus every man, by consenting with others to make one body politic under one government, puts himself under an obligation to every one of that society to submit to the determination of the majority and to be concluded by it; or else this original compact, whereby he with others incorporates into one society, would signify nothing, and be no compact, if he be left free and under no other ties than he was in before in the state of nature.

. . . And thus that which begins and actually constitutes any political society is nothing but the consent of any number of freemen capable of a majority to unite and incorporate into such a society. And this is that, and that only, which did or could give beginning to any lawful government in the world.

. . . But to conclude, reason being plain on our side that men are naturally free, and the examples of history showing that the governments of the world that were begun in peace had their beginning laid on that foundation, and were made by the consent of the people, there can be little room for doubt either where the right is, or what has been the opinion or practice of mankind about the first erecting of governments.

TOWARD CRITICAL THINKING

1. According to Locke, what kinds of obligations do individuals have toward their government? What kinds of powers do citizens relinquish to governments?

2. What role, if any, do women seem to play in Locke's views on government and individual rights?

· 2 ·

On the Natural Conditions of Mankind, from Leviathan

THOMAS HOBBES

Hobbes, who wrote in an era earlier than Locke, was not nearly so optimistic about the nature of man. In his classic words, men's lives in the state of nature are "solitary, poor, nasty, brutish, and short." In his comprehensive and sweeping treatise on the nature of man and his relationship to God and government, *Leviathan* (1651), Hobbes argued that individuals must give up more to governments as a trade-off in order to maintain an ordered society. Without a single, strong leader, Hobbes sees little hope for humankind.

Nature hath made men so equall, in the faculties of body, and mind; as that though there bee found one man sometimes manifestly stronger in body, or of quicker mind then another; yet when all is reckoned together, the difference between man, and man, is not so considerable, as that one man can thereupon claim to himselfe any benefit, to which another may not pretend, as well as he. For as to the strength of body, the weakest has strength enough to kill the strongest, either by secret machination, or by confederacy with others, that are in the same danger with himselfe.

And as to the faculties of the mind, . . . I find yet a greater equality amongst men, than that of strength. For Prudence, is but Experience; which equall time, equally bestowes on all men, in those things they equally apply themselves unto. . . .

From this equality of ability, ariseth equality of hope in the attaining of our Ends. And therefore if any two men desire the same thing, which neverthelesse they cannot both enjoy, they become enemies; and in the way to their End, . . . endeavour to destroy, or subdue one an other. And from hence it comes to passe, that where an Invader hath no more to feare, than an other mans single power; if one plant, sow, build, or possesse a convenient Seat, others may probably be expected to come prepared with forces united, to dispossesse, and deprive him, not only of the fruit of his

SOURCE: Thomas Hobbes, "On the Natural Conditions of Mankind and the Rights of Sovereigns," from *Leviathan,* Richard Tuck, ed. *Cambridge Texts in the History of Political Thought.* Cambridge: Cambridge University Press, 1989, pp. 86–89.

labour, but also of his life, or liberty. And the Invader again is in the like danger of another.

And from this diffidence of one another, there is no way for any man to secure himselfe, so reasonable, as Anticipation; that is, by force, or wiles, to master the persons of all men he can, so long, till he see no other power great enough to endanger him: And this is no more than his own conservation requireth, and is generally allowed. Also because there be some, that taking pleasure in contemplating their own power in the acts of conquest, which they pursue farther than their security requires; if others, that otherwise would be glad to be at ease within modest bounds, should not by invasion increase their power, they would not be able, long time, by standing only on their defence, to subsist. And by consequence, such augmentation of dominion over men, being necessary to a mans conservation, it ought to be allowed him. . . .

So that in the nature of man, we find three principall causes of quarrell. First, Competition; Secondly, Diffidence; Thirdly, Glory.

. . . For WARRE [war], consisteth not in Battell [battle] onely, or the act of fighting; but in a tract of time, wherein the Will to contend by Battell is sufficiently known: and therefore the notion of *Time,* is to be considered in the nature of Warre; as it is in the nature of Weather. For as the nature of Foule weather, lyeth not in a showre or two of rain; but in an inclination thereto of many dayes together: So the nature of War, consisteth not in actual fighting; but in the known disposition thereto, during all the time there is no assurance to the contrary. All other times is PEACE.

Whatsoever therefore is consequent to a time of Warre, where every man is Enemy to every man; the same is consequent to the time, wherein men live without other security, than what their own strength, and their own invention shall furnish them withall. In such condition, there is no place for Industry; because the fruit thereof is uncertain: and consequently no Culture of the Earth; no Navigation, nor use of the commodities that may be imported by Sea; no commodious Building; no Instruments of moving, and removing such things as require much force; no Knowledge of the face of the Earth; no account of Time; no Arts; no Letters; no Society; and which is worst of all, continuall feare, and danger of violent death; And the life of man, solitary, poore, nasty, brutish, and short. . . . No more are the Actions, that proceed from those Passions, till they know a Law that forbids them: which till Lawes be made they cannot know: nor can any Law be made, till they have agreed upon the Person that shall make it.

. . . It is therefore in vain to grant Soveraignty by way of precedent Covenant. The opinion that any Monarch receiveth his Power by Covenant, that is to say on Condition, proceedeth from want of understanding this easie truth, that Covenants being but words, and breath, have no force to oblige, contain, constrain, or protect any man, but what it has from the publique Sword; that is, from the untyed hands of that Man, or Assembly of men that hath the Soveraignty, and whose actions are avouched by them all, and performed by the strength of them all, in him united.

. . . But the Rights, and Consequences of Soveraignty, are the same in both. His Power cannot, without his consent, be Transferred to another: He cannot Forfeit it: He cannot be Accused by any of his Subjects, of Inquiry: He cannot be Punished by them. He is Judge of what is necessary for Peace; and Judge of Doctrines: He is Sole Legislator; and Supreme Judge of Controversies; and of the Times, and Occasions of Warre and Peace: to him it belongeth to choose Magistrates, Counsellours, Commanders, and all other Officers, and Ministers; and to determine of Rewards, and Punishments, Honour, and Order. The reasons whereof, are the same which are alledged in the precedent Chapter, for the same Rights, and Consequences of Soveraignty by Institution.

TOWARD CRITICAL THINKING

1. Without government, what sorts of problems does Hobbes envision?

2. Hobbes notes three principle reasons for men to quarrel. How do these factors continue to effect the success of the national government today?

• 3 •

The Declaration of Independence

The Declaration of Independence, now on display in the National Archives in Washington, DC, is probably the most famous document in American political history. We don't celebrate "Constitution Day"; we do, however, as a nation celebrate our independence from Great Britain, which formally came with the signing of the Declaration of Independence.

Thomas Jefferson was charged with writing the document for the Continental Congress. When he was finished, it was edited by a committee and adopted by the Second Continental Congress. It is a short, succinct statement of specific reasons for the colonists' break with their mother country.

In CONGRESS, July 4, 1776

THE UNANIMOUS DECLARATION of the thirteen united STATES OF AMERICA,

When in the Course of human events, it becomes necessary for one people to dissolve the political bands which have connected them with another, and to assume, among the powers of the earth, the separate and equal station to which the Laws of Nature and of Nature's God entitle them, a decent respect to the opinions of mankind requires that they should declare the causes which impel them to the separation.

We hold these truths to be self-evident, that all men are created equal, that they are endowed by their Creator with certain unalienable Rights, that among these are Life, Liberty, and the pursuit of Happiness.—That to secure these rights, Governments are instituted among Men, deriving their just powers from the consent of the governed,—that whenever any Form of Government becomes destructive of these ends, it is the Right of the People to alter or to abolish it, and to institute new Government, laying its foundation of such principles and organizing its powers in such form, as to them shall seem most likely to effect their Safety and Happiness. Prudence, indeed will dictate that Governments long established should not be changed for light and transient causes; and accordingly all experience hath shown, that mankind are more disposed to suffer, while evils are sufferable, than to right themselves by abolishing the forms to which they are accustomed. But when a long train of abuses and usurpations, pursuing invariably the same Object evinces a design to reduce them under absolute Despotism, it is their right, it is their duty, to throw off such Government, and to provide new Guards for their future security.—Such has been the patient sufferance of these Colonies; and such is now the necessity which constrains them to alter their former System of Government. The history of the present King of Great Britain is a history of repeated injuries and usurpations, all having in direct object the establishment of an absolute Tyranny over these States. To prove this, let Facts be submitted to a candid world.

He has refused to Assent to Laws, the most wholesome and necessary for the public good.

He has forbidden his Governors to pass Laws of immediate and pressing importance, unless suspended in their operation till his Assent should be obtained; and when so suspended, he has utterly neglected to attend to them.

He has refused to pass other Laws for the accommodation of large districts of people, unless those people would relinquish the right of Representation in the Legislature, a right inestimable to them and formidable to tyrants only.

He has called together legislative bodies at places unusual, uncomfortable, and distant from the depository of Public Records, for the sole purpose of fatiguing them into compliance with his measures.

He has dissolved Representative Houses repeatedly, for opposing with manly firmness his invasions on the rights of the people.

He has refused for a long time, after such dissolutions, to cause others to be elected; whereby the Legislative powers, incapable of Annihilation, have returned to the People at large for their exercise; the State remaining in the mean time exposed to all dangers of invasion from without, and convulsions within.

He has endeavored to prevent the population of these States; for that purpose obstructing the Laws for Nationalization of Foreigners; refusing to pass others to encourage their migration hither, and raising the conditions to new Appropriations of Lands.

He has obstructed the Administration of Justice, by refusing his Assent to Law for establishing Judiciary Powers.

He has made Judges dependent on his Will alone, for the tenure of their offices, and the amount and payment of their salaries.

He has erected a multitude of New Offices, and sent hither swarms of Officers to harass our People, and to eat out their substance.

He has kept among us, in times of peace, Standing Armies without the Consent of our legislatures.

He has affected to render the Military independent of and superior to the Civil Power.

He has combined with others to subject us to a jurisdiction foreign to our constitution, and unacknowledged by our laws; giving his Assent to their Actions of pretended Legislation.

For Quartering large bodies of armed troops among us:

For protecting them, by a mock Trial, from punishments for any Murders which they should commit on the Inhabitants of these States:

For cutting off our Trade with all parts of the world:

For imposing Taxes on us without our Consent:

For depriving us in many cases, of the benefits of Trial by jury:

For transporting us beyond Seas to be tried for pretended offenses:

For abolishing the free System of English Laws in a neighboring Province, establishing therein an Arbitrary government, and enlarging its Boundaries so as to render it at once an example and fit instrument for introducing the same absolute rule into these Colonies:

For taking away our Charters, abolishing our most valuable Laws, and altering fundamentally the Forms of our Government:

For suspending our own Legislatures, and declaring themselves invested with powers to legislate for us in all cases whatsoever.

He has abdicated Government here, by declaring us out of his Protection and waging Ware against us.

He has plundered our seas, ravaged our Coasts, burnt our towns, and destroyed the lives of our people.

He is at this time transporting large Armies of foreign Mercenaries to compleat the works of death, desolation and tyranny, already begun with circumstances of Cruelty & Perfidy scarcely paralleled in the most barbarous ages, and totally unworthy the Head of a civilized nation.

He has constrained our fellow Citizens taken Captive on the high Seas to bear Arms against their Country, to become the executioners of the friends and Brethren, or to fall themselves by their Hands.

He has excited domestic insurrections amongst us, and has endeavored to bring on the inhabitants of our frontiers the merciless Indian Savages, whose known rule of warfare, in an undistinguished destruction of all ages, sexes and conditions.

In every Stage of these Oppressions We have Petitioned for Redress in the most humble terms: Our repeated Petitions have been answered only by repeated injury. A Prince, whose character is thus marked by every act which may define a Tyrant, is unfit to be the ruler of a free people.

Nor have We been wanting in attentions to our British brethren. We have warned them from time to time of attempts by their legislature to extend an unwarrantable jurisdiction over us. We have reminded them of the circumstances of our emigration and settlement here. We have appealed to their native justice and magnanimity; and we have conjured them by the ties of our common kindred to disavow these usurpations, which would inevitably interrupt our connections and correspondence. They too have been deaf to the vice of justice and of consanguinity. We must, therefore, acquiesce in the necessity, which denounces our Separation, and hold them, as we hold the rest of mankind, Enemies in War, in Peace Friends.

WE, THEREFORE, the Representatives of the UNITED STATES OF AMERICA, in General Congress, Assembled, appealing to the Supreme Judge of the world for the rectitude of our intentions, do, in the Name, and the Authority of the good People of these Colonies, solemnly publish and declare, that these United Colonies are, and of Right ought to be Free and Independent States; that they are Absolved from all Allegiance to the British Crown, and that all political connection between them and the State of Great Britain, is and ought to be totally dissolved; and that as Free and Independent States, they have full Power to levy War, conclude Peace, contract Alliances, establish Commerce, and to do all other Acts and Things which Independent States may of right do.—And for the support of the Declaration, with a firm reliance on the protection of divine Providence, we mutually pledge to each other our Lives, our Fortunes and our sacred honor.

TOWARD CRITICAL THINKING

1. What reasons were offered for the colonists' separation from England? Could less drastic measures have been taken?

2. Compare the Declaration of Independence to the U.S. Constitution in Appendix A. How many of the specific charges made against King George III found their way into the Constitution? The Bill of Rights?

THINKING ABOUT THE ROOTS OF THE AMERICAN POLITICAL SYSTEM

1. How were Thomas Jefferson and members of the Second Continental Congress influenced by the writings of John Locke and Thomas Hobbes? Can you see the imprint of one English theorist more clearly than the other? In what areas?

2. What does the Declaration say about Americans' perspective on the role of government? About notions of equality? How have these ideas changed over the years?

CHAPTER 2

◆ ◆ ◆

The Constitution, The Fight for Ratification, and the Amendment Process

Once the Declaration of Independence was signed, the questions then confronting the colonists were how to govern themselves as well as how to conduct a war with a major power. At first, they agreed on a confederate form of government, which was no more than a loose union of thirteen sovereign states. But once the Revolutionary War with Great Britain was won, several problems with the new national government as created by the Articles of Confederation became apparent. Eventually, many of the problems became so great—especially those dealing with commerce and the conduct of international relations—that the Founders chose to throw out the Articles of Confederation and create an entirely new form of government called a federal system (see Chapter 3).

The Federalist Papers are a set of essays penned by ardent supporters of the proposed Constitution (see Appendix A)—Alexander Hamilton, James Madison, and John Jay. In individual essays (known by their numbers) these Federalists, as the authors were called because they favored a stronger national government, tried to convince the electorate that the newly drafted Constitution was a wise thing and not something to be feared. In Reading 3, *Federalist No. 47,* for example, James Madison sets forth his arguments for a strong national government and for ratification of the proposed Constitution. Drawing on ideas of the French political philosopher Montesquieu, Madison and the Framers settled on a national government with three ostensibly equal branches of government. In such an arrangement, power could be "checked with power" as "an essential precaution in favor of liberty."

In Reading 5, the editors of *The Economist* look back on the conditions leading up to the adoption of the Constitution and point out the lessons that other nations can learn from our constitutional experience. Again, the workability and longevity of a system with an executive and a judiciary with the power to hear all controversies arising under the national Constitution in addition to a legislative branch of government are noted as examples for the European Community, now called the European Union.

The role of the judiciary, especially the United States Supreme Court, in interpreting what the U.S. Constitution was intended to mean is a question that continues to vex scholars. In Reading 6, "The Framers, the Supreme Court, and Notions of Original Intent," prominent constitutional historian Leonard W. Levy notes that even James Madison, who was present at the Constitutional Convention and made copious notes, was unsure of how the document was to be read. Madison himself refused to rely on his recordings of the proceedings in Philadelphia to ascertain its meaning, proclaiming that "the debates and incidental decisions of the Constitution can have no authoritative character."*

Over the years, in spite of Madison's admonitions, some scholars have argued that the Framers' "intentions" must be construed strictly; others have argued that the Constitution must be a flexible document. But at times, the Constitution has proved to be inadequate for changing times and circumstances, and amendments have been necessary. The first set of amendments to the Constitution was the Bill of Rights (see Appendix A). Since then, seventeen additional amendments have been added to the Constitution.

As discussed in Reading 7 by John R. Vile, "Proposals to Amend the Constitution," many successful amendments have dealt with the structure or workings of government. Most of those have been fairly uncontroversial. For example, the 22nd Amendment limited presidents to two terms; this had been an informal convention in place until Franklin Delano Roosevelt's unprecedented election to four terms. Other amendments involving the structure of government, such as the proposed amendment to give statehood to the District of Columbia, simply die because the states seem to respond with a collective yawn to their ratification. Other proposed amendments, generally involving public policy or expanded rights, are more controversial. Sometimes they are simply too controversial to gain ratification by three-quarters of the states—the percentage mandated by the Constitution before an amendment can be added to the Constitution. That was the case with the proposed Equal Rights Amendment, which fell three states short of ratification.

---

*Letter to Thomas Ritchie, September 15, 1821, in *Letters and Other Writings of James Madison,* William C. Rives and Philip R. Fendall, eds. (New York: Worthington, 1884, 4 volumes) III, p. 228.

· 4 ·

Federalist No. 47

JAMES MADISON

In *Federalist No. 47,* Madison examines the structure of the new national government and tries to convince those people who were suspicious of a stronger national government that the creation of separate and distinct legislative, executive, and judicial departments will distribute national power to the satisfaction of most. Power checks power in the new government in order to avoid the tyranny of any one branch or person so feared by the citizenry.

To the People of the State of New York: . . .

One of the principal objections inculcated by the more respectable adversaries to the Constitution, is its supposed violation of the political maxim, that the legislative, executive, and judiciary departments ought to be separate and distinct. . . .

The oracle who is always consulted and cited on this subject is the celebrated Montesquieu. . . .

The British Constitution was to Montesquieu what Homer has been to the didactic writers on epic poetry. . . .

On the slightest view of the British Constitution, we must perceive that the legislative, executive, and judiciary departments are by no means totally separate and distinct from each other. . . .

From these facts, by which Montesquieu was guided, it may clearly be inferred that, in saying "There can be no liberty where the legislative and executive powers are united in the same person, or body of magistrates.". . . His meaning . . . can amount to no more than this, that where the *whole* power of one department is exercised by the same hands which possess the *whole* power of another department, the fundamental principles of a free constitution are subverted. . . .

. . . [S]ays he, "there can be no liberty, because apprehensions may arise lest *the same* monarch or senate should *enact* tyrannical laws to *execute* them in a tyrannical manner."

If we look into the constitutions of the several States, we find that, notwithstanding the emphatical and, in some instances, the unqualified terms in which this axiom has been laid down, there is not a single instance in which the several departments of power have been kept absolutely separate and distinct. New Hampshire, whose constitution was the last formed, seems to have been fully aware of the impossibility and inexpediency of avoiding any mixture whatever of these departments, and has qualified the doctrine by declaring "that the legislative, executive, and judiciary powers ought to be kept as separate from, and independent of, each other *as the nature of a free government will admit; or as is consistent with that chain of connection that binds the whole fabric of the constitution in one indissoluble bond of unity and amity*" [*sic*]. Her constitution accordingly mixes these departments in several respects. The Senate, which is a branch of the legislative department, is also a judicial tribunal for the trial of impeachments. The President, who is the head of the executive department, is the presiding member also of the Senate; and, besides an equal vote in all cases, has a casting vote in case of a tie. The executive head is himself eventually elective every year by the legislative department, and his council is every year chosen by and from the members of the same department. Several of the officers of state are also appointed by the legislature. And the members of the judiciary department are appointed by the executive department. . . .

According to the constitution of Pennsylvania, the president, who is the head of the executive department, is annually elected by a vote in which the legislative department predominates. In conjunction with an executive council, he appoints the members of the judiciary department, and forms a court of impeachment for trial of all officers, judiciary as well as executive. The judges of the Supreme Court and justices of the peace seem also to be removable by the legislature; and the executive power of pardoning in certain cases, to be referred to the same department. The members of the executive council are made EX-OFFICIO justices of peace through the State. . . .

In South Carolina, the constitution makes the executive magistracy eligible by the legislative department. It gives to the latter, also, the appointment of the members of the judiciary department, including even justices of the peace and sheriffs; and the appointment of officers in the executive department, down to captains in the army and navy of the State.

In the constitution of Georgia, where it is declared "that the legislative, executive, and judiciary departments shall be separate and distinct, so that neither exercise the powers properly belonging to the other," we find that the executive department is to be filled by appointments of the legislature; and the executive prerogative of pardon to be finally exercised by the same authority. Even justices of the peace are to be appointed by the legislature.

In citing these cases in which the legislative, executive, and judiciary departments have not been kept totally separate and distinct, I wish not to be regarded as an advocate for the particular organizations of the several State governments. . . . What I have wished to evince is, that the charge brought against the proposed Constitution, of violating the sacred maxim of free government, is warranted neither by the real meaning annexed to that maxim by its author, nor by the sense in which it has hitherto been understood in America.

TOWARD CRITICAL THINKING

1. Why did the drafters of the Constitution believe it wise to create three independent branches of government? Was this idea original to them?

2. Why was it a good idea for Madison to note examples from the states to support the Framers' adoption of a system of checks and balances?

• 5 •

If You Sincerely Want to Be a United States

THE ECONOMIST

Rarely do nations have the opportunity to completely devise new forms of government or to completely reformulate how their governments work. Today, in the aftermath of the breakup of the Soviet Union and at a time when many nations in western Europe seek to form alliances and overarching governmental structures, the editors of *The Economist* note the many lessons that can be learned from the American experience. After the original union of states created under the Articles of Confederation proved unworkable, a completely new form of government was created to govern the struggling nation. And, with only minor alterations, the basic framework for a national government created by the Framers has endured.

♦ What the New World Can Teach the Old about Making One out of Many

Imagine a hot summer in Paris. By grace of a kindly time-warp, a group of European eminences have assembled for a conference. Charles de Gaulle is their chairman. Among those attending are John Maynard Keynes (who has a continent-wide reputation, though he is still only 29) and Albert Einstein. Bertrand Russell is not there—he is holidaying on Cape Cod—but he barrages the proceedings by fax. Russell is kept abreast of things by young King Juan Carlos of Spain, who, with Keynes, provides the driving force of the conference.

Impossible, except in one of those rosy early-morning dreams. Now remember the men who gathered at Philadelphia in the summer of 1787. George Washington was the chairman. Alexander Hamilton, whose short life never knew a dull moment, was there, as was James Madison, a pragmatic man of principle who would later become president. Together, they directed the conference. Benjamin Franklin was there too, though somewhat in his dotage. Thomas Jefferson (compared with whom Ber-

SOURCE: The Economist (March 23,1991):21–24. © 1991 The Economist Newspaper Group, Inc. Reprinted with permission.

trand Russell was a startlingly narrow fellow) was not there, but kept an eye on things from Paris.

. . . Might the most mature and successful constitutional settlement in the world have some lessons for these European parvenus?

◆ They Were One, and They Knew It

Start with two great differences between America then and Europe now. The America that declared its independence from Britain in 1776 was, except for its black slaves, an extraordinarily homogeneous society.

Think of those huge distances, and those primitive communications, and wonder at the early Americans' sense of cohesion. Although North and South already showed the difference that had to be bridged by war in 1861–65, Americans shared some essential attributes. A few German and Dutch dissenters apart, their stock was solidly British. Their intellectual heroes (a nod to Montesquieu notwithstanding) were from the British tradition: Hobbes and Locke, Smith and Hume. Their language was English; their law was English law; their God an English God.

Wherever on the coast they settled, they had originally had to win the land by backbreaking struggle (even in the Carolinas, whose plantations were far bigger than New England farms). Three thousand perilous miles from England, they had all learnt the same self-sufficiency. Most of them, or their fathers, had fought Indians.

And those who did not leave for Canada after the break with Britain had a second thing in common: they had all won their independence from an external power, by force of arms. Their successful war of liberation made them feel more clearly "American" than ever before.

Yet that war had been prosecuted by thirteen states, not one; and it did not forge anything that, to modern eyes, looks like a nation-state. Indeed, this absence of unity was made explicit by the articles of confederation, which the thirteen states signed in 1781. Article 2 said that the states retained their "sovereignty, freedom and independence". They merely (article 3) entered into a "firm league of friendship with each other".

After only six years, the articles of 1781 were deemed unsatisfactory enough to warrant revision. The result—today's constitution—provided a system of government that was federal in form, but with a much stronger central government than had existed before. So, if Europe wants to learn from America, it had better start with a look at the supposed defects of those articles.

In broad terms, critics of the confederation argued that it was unstable, an awkward half-way house between a collection of independent states and a truly single country. Their criticisms concentrated on two things:

economics, in particular the internal market of the thirteen states; and foreign policy, the ability of the states to fend off foreign dangers.

Take economics first. The monetary and fiscal policy of the America that had just chucked out the British was chaotic. Congress (the body of delegates that had, so far as possible, directed the war against Britain, and whose position was formalised by the articles) could not pay off its creditors. It had no taxing power, and could only issue "requisitions" (in effect, requests for money) to the states. Some paid; some did not. Some states took over the responsibility for the part of the national debt that was owed to their own citizens, and then paid this in securities they issued themselves. There was a shortage of sound money (coin). Some states issued paper money themselves; much of it soon lost its face value. The currency of one state was not normally legal tender in another.

Tariff policy was a particular bugbear. States with small towns and a few ports, such as New Jersey and Connecticut, were at the mercy of big states like Pennsylvania and New York, through whose ports America's imports flowed. Tariffs levied by New York would be paid by consumers in (say) Connecticut; but Connecticut's treasury derived no benefit from these tariffs. In short, the internal barriers to trade were big.

Abroad, the thirteen states faced a ring of dangers. Britain still held Canada and a string of forts to the west of the United States. If it wished, it could have encircled the 13 states; its troops burnt Washington in 1812. Spain controlled Florida and—worse—it presided over navigation on the Mississippi.

Americans with a sense of where history was taking them (meaning most Americans of the time) well knew that, in Europe, loose confederations were vulnerable to their enemies. Some members of Congress compared that body to the Polish parliament, whose every member had a veto. The comparison hurt: at that time, Poland was being divided three ways by its enemies. The German confederation, or Holy Roman Empire, was notoriously feeble. It was characterised, said Madison, by "the licentiousness of the strong and the oppression of the weak"—a "nerveless" body "agitated with unceasing fermentation in its bowels."

The Americans decided they wanted calmer bowels and a better circulation. In the Federalist Papers—the collection of essays written by Hamilton, Madison and John Jay after the convention of 1787—Hamilton was to weave together the economic and political arguments. Trade wars between the states, he suggested, would sooner or later turn into shooting wars. Given the lack of unity of the American states, European powers (with their "pernicious labyrinths of politics and wars") would divide and rule. The destiny to which God had pointed America would vanish in the ensuing strife. . . .

◆ The Three Big Things of 1787

... Hamilton and the others who wanted a stronger central government won the day in Philadelphia. The convention's report was adopted by the states, though not without a few close shaves. And America got the constitution it still has. How has it lasted so long? For three main reasons that should interest today's Europeans.

The first was that the constitution created an executive—the president— where none had existed before. The president embodied a response to those external threats. He was to be the commander-in-chief of the armed forces. Although Congress had the power to declare war (and jealously preserves it), the president, with the advice and consent of the Senate, could conclude treaties and appoint ambassadors. He was to be the instrument of a unified foreign policy. This was made explicit by the constitution's first article, which prohibited any of the states from entering into any treaty, alliance or confederation, and from keeping troops, and from engaging in war unless it was invaded or was in imminent danger.

Second, the constitution was a document of limited powers. It gave to the central government (or so went the theory) only those powers specifically allocated to it. The tenth amendment made plain what Hamilton and Madison thought implicit: "The powers not delegated to the United States by the Constitution," it says, "nor prohibited to it by the states, are reserved to the states respectively, or to the people."

Third, the constitution recognised a "judicial power," and established a Supreme Court. The court, among other things, was to have jurisdiction over all cases arising "under the constitution" (and the constitution itself was declared to be "the supreme law of the land"). It also had jurisdiction over disputes between any one of the states and the United States, and between two or more states themselves. Members of the Supreme Court had no date of retirement. In other words, the Supreme Court was to be charged with deciding whether the practice of government conformed with the theory as laid down in the constitution.

How might modern Europe use the American experience? ...

... [L]ate twentieth-century Europeans share the eighteenth-century American desire to create a single-market and remove barriers to internal trade. Here the Americans found it necessary to make the states cede some sovereignty, and to grant the union some powers it had not previously possessed. The states were forbidden to levy their own external tariffs. In the so-called "commerce clause" of the constitution, the federal government was given the exclusive power to "regulate commerce with foreign nations, and among the several states."

In much the same way, Project 1992 is designed to realise the Community's dream of a single market, free of all internal impediments.

European federalists would argue that the goal of monetary union is all of a piece with this. If a single trading block has twelve national currencies, the transactions' costs of trade will always be higher than if there was but one. Americans at the 1787 convention would have recognised the force of this; the constitution they wrote forbids states to coin their own money. (Still, it was not until 1913 that America established a stable system for guiding national monetary policy.)

But that is not the whole of the American lesson. Those Europeans who doubt whether the American experience of federalism can be applied to Europe will find Americans ready to argue their case for them. One argument of America's own anti-federalists (still around, two centuries later) strikes a particular chord.

American's anti-federalists say the combination of a broad commerce clause and a powerful Supreme Court has been disastrous. It is a simple matter to show that almost anything is a matter of "inter-state commerce." Even if a company does almost all its business within one state, for instance, it may still use the federal postal service. Once interstate commerce has been proved, the central government can easily decide that such commerce is within its regulatory competence. . . . As early as 1870 the Supreme Court held that Congress could insist on the inspection of steamships travelling entirely within the waters of one state, if other vessels on those waters carried goods bound for other states.

According to the anti-federalists, the breadth of the commerce clause means that an activist Supreme Court, given an inch, takes a mile. The power of states to regulate their own affairs has been diminished, and the power of the central government has been allowed to increase excessively.

Non-Americans living in America, wrapped in the red tape of federalism (try working out where to get your car exhaust tested each year if you bought the car in Virginia, live in Maryland and work in the District of Columbia), may think the argument over-done; they usually pray for less power for the individual states, not more. But many Americans still worry about excessive centralisation. So do people on the other side of the Atlantic. . . .

◆ The Right to Opt Out

Europe's anti-federalists can draw further succour from America. The part of a future Europe that most Europeans find it hardest to picture clearly is the idea of Europe acting towards the outside world with a united mind, a single will. . . .

This has a direct constitutional implication. Recall how important foreign policy, the threat abroad, was to Madison and Hamilton. They would have considered a union without a single foreign and defence policy to be a nonsense on stilts. So they created a powerful executive, independent of the states, to take control of that policy. Even those Europeans who want a single foreign policy shy away from a European equivalent of the American presidency. Yet without a president, embodying within his person a common will towards the world outside, it is hard to see how Europeans can create what Americans would regard as a federal Europe.

The non-homogeneity, and the hesitation about a European president as powerful as America's, will not necessarily remain as influential as they are today. But one awkward lesson from America is permanent. This is the fact that America did not take its final political shape in 1787; three-quarters of a century later, the founding fathers' structure blew up.

Most non-Americans do not realise how large the civil war of 1861–65 looms in America's collective memory. It killed more than 600,000 people, foreshadowing the efficient slaughter that Europe did not experience until Verdun and the Somme fifty years later. In its last year, when the North's armies under Grant and Sherman marched into the South's heartland, it became unbearably brutal. If you are going to have a constitution linking several states that cherish their sovereignty, it is worth making sure in advance that it does not lead to the kind of war America's constitution led to.

Unfair! yell Northern historians, for whom it is an article of faith that the civil war was fought not over a constitutional principle (the right of states to secede from the union) but over a social injustice (slavery). The Northerners have a case, even though—as Southerners never tire of pointing out—the abolition of slavery was not formally an original aim of the war: the fact is that, without slavery, the Southerners would not have wanted to secede. Since Europe's federalists would argue that nothing divides European countries from each other as passionately as slavery divided North and South, they may feel justified in ignoring the terrible warning of the civil war.

They would be wrong. Nobody knows what explosive arguments the future of Europe will bring. Some countries may see relations with Russia as the right centrepiece for Europe's foreign policy; others may put relations with America in that place; still others will focus on the Arab world to Europe's south. Some Europeans may want far more restrictive immigration policies than others, which could lead to some sharp intra-European border tensions. Country X will favour fewer controls on arms sales abroad than Country Y. Europe's capacity to speak and act as one is still almost entirely theoretical. If Europeans are genuinely interested in learning from the American experience, this lesson should be taken to heart: make it clear in advance that, whatever union is to be forged, states can leave it, unhindered, at will.

TOWARD CRITICAL THINKING

1. What factors facilitated the drafting of the Constitution? How might the eastern or western European experiences differ?

2. What are the main features in the U.S. Constitution that might be of interest to other nations looking to adopt a new form of government? Are there any features of the American system that might not serve other nations as well?

· 6 ·

The Framers, the Supreme Court, and Notions of Original Intent

LEONARD W. LEVY

" 'Tis funny about th' constitution,' said Mr. Dooley, the philosophic Irish bartender who was created by Finley Peter Dunne. 'It reads plain, but no wan can underherstant it without an interpreter.' "[*] Truer words were never spoken. As Leonard W. Levy points out in this excerpt from his longer work on the same topic,[**] the U.S. Supreme Court has often invoked what it took to be the original intent of the Framers when interpreting various provisions of the Constitution or the Bill of Rights. Vague clauses invite interpretation. But the question often is, whose judgement or interpretation should be controlling?

The Supreme Court is the official and final interpreter of the U.S. Constitution, but from the beginning of its history, disputes have raged about how it should interpret that document. In its very first constitutional decision the Court provoked a controversy on the question whether its judgment faithfully adhered to the intentions of the Framers of the Constitution. For several decades after the ratification of the Constitution the fading memories of those who had attended the Philadelphia Constitutional Convention supplied the main evidence of the Framers' intent. Even when those memories were fresh, the Framers disagreed vehemently about what the Convention had meant or intended, as the controversy in 1791 over the chartering of the Bank of the United States showed. Not until the publication of Madison's "Notes of Debates in the Federal Convention" in 1840 did a source become available [to foster the efforts of those who advocate what is called] original intent analysis.

SOURCE: Excerpted with permission of Macmillan Publishing Company from Preface and Chapter 1 of *Original Intent and the Framers' Constitution* by Leonard W. Levy. Copyright © by Macmillan Publishing Company.

[*] Leonard Levy, *Original Intent and the Framers' Constitution,* (New York: Macmillan Publishing Company, 1988), p. ix.
[**] Ibid.

The Court has professed to favor a constitutional jurisprudence of original intent since the first decade of its history. More accurately, the Court has invoked the authority or intent of the Framers whenever it suited the Justices. . .

The term "original intent" (or "original intention") stands for an old idea that the Court should interpret the Constitution according to the understanding of it by its Framers. In most cases original intent should be followed when clearly discernible, and it is always entitled to the utmost respect and consideration as an interpretive guide. . . .

Liberty and equality are the underpinnings of the Constitution, the essential ingredients of the philosophy of natural rights that the Framers passed on to posterity and, alas, no longer has the respect it once mustered. Much that is part of original intent still commands our loyalties, our admiration, and our affection: government by consent of the governed; majority rule under constitutional restraints that limit majorities; a bill of rights that applies to all branches of the government; a federal system; a tripartite system of government with a single executive, a bicameral legislature, and an independent judiciary; an elaborate system of checks and balances that limits the separation of powers; representative government; and elections at fixed intervals. . . .

Original intent as constitutional theory is rarely if ever at issue in real cases decided by the Supreme Court. When the Court employs original intent, it refers to the understanding of the Framers respecting a particular provision of the Constitution that is imprecise. In real cases the meaning of the provisions involved in litigation is not clear. Indeed the Constitution tends to be least clear when most involved in litigation; that is especially true of rights as compared with matters of structure. Some of the most important clauses of the Constitution are vague, ambiguous, or, paradoxically, too specific in meaning. The most important evidence of original intent is the text of the Constitution itself, which must prevail whenever it surely embodies a broader principle than can be found in the minds or purposes of its Framers. For example, they had political and religious expression in mind when they framed the First Amendment, but its language contains no restriction. They probably did not mean to extend the rights protected by the Sixth Amendment to "all" criminal prosecutions, but the text says "all" and deserves obedience. They had black Americans uppermost in mind when they designed the Fourteenth Amendment, but its expansive expression applies to all, not only to all races but to people of all religions, creeds, and national or ethnic backgrounds, regardless of legitimacy, sex, or alienage. . .

Until [the 1980s], original intent had no political coloration. Both liberals and conservatives, especially among judges, . . . relied on original intent to add respectability to their opinions. But, constitutional historians, among others, do not respect judicial versions of history. Clinton Rossiter, a great constitutional scholar of conservative proclivities, censured politicians and scholars as well as judges when he said that most talk about original intent "is as irrelevant as it is unpersuasive, as stale as it is strained, as rhetorically absurd as it is historically unsound." He added that "men of power who know least about 'the intent of the Framers' are most likely to appeal to it for support of their views." Perhaps because original intent has severe limitations as an instrument of constitutional adjudication in real cases and ought not be taken too seriously, [in 1985] the *Encyclopedia of the American Constitution* has no article on the subject. . . .

At that time, . . . Edwin Meese III, then attorney general of the United States, castigated the Supreme Court in a sensational speech before the American Bar Association for opinions that he disliked, and he demanded that the Court abandon decisions based on its views of sound public policy. The Court, Meese declared, should give "deference to what the Constitution—its text and intention—may demand." . . . In 1986 Robert H. Bork, then a judge of the United States Court of Appeals for the District of Columbia, argued that judges who do not construe the Constitution in accordance with the original intent of its Framers "will, in truth, be enforcing their own morality upon the rest of us and calling it the Constitution." The present Chief Justice of the United States, William H. Rehnquist, has professed similar views. . . .

◆ The Framers and Original Intent

James Madison, Father of the Constitution and of the Bill of Rights, rejected the doctrine that the original intent of those who framed the Constitution should be accepted as an authoritative guide to its meaning. . . . The fact that Madison, the quintessential Founder, discredited original intent is probably the main reason that he refused throughout his life to publish his "Notes of Debates in the Federal Convention," incomparably our foremost source for the secret discussions of that hot summer in Philadelphia in 1787. . . .

Not even James Madison and Alexander Hamilton as the authors of *The Federalist,* writing as "Publius," relied on their authoritative experience as Framers. In their essays they speculated about what the Convention "must have" intended, as if they did not know from first-hand experience. *The Federalist #37,* which purported to "survey . . . the work of the Convention," did not mention or ascribe to the Framers any intentions or understandings of any significance. Rather, Madison predicated his essay on the principle that the meaning of the Constitution must emerge in the course of time and as a result of experience, however difficult the inherent ambiguities of language made that task. . . .

. . . The founders of the national government and its early officers simply did not think in terms of the original intent at Philadelphia. . . .

Given the differences of opinion among Framers on [the charting of a national] bank issue, original intent may not have been as discernible as it seemed in this case, or it may not have mattered significantly. More likely, the constitutional text lent itself to reinterpretation in the light of policy preferences by the administration in power. When the bank's charter expired twenty years later, and the United States fought the War of 1812 at considerable cost, without its financial services, experience taught new constitutional lessons. In 1816 Congress chartered a second Bank of the United States, at the instigation and support of the Madison administration. Three years later, in the monumental case of *McCulloch* v. *Maryland,* [see pp. 44–47] the Supreme Court sustained the constitutionality of the act in an opinion by Chief Justice John Marshall (who had been a ratifier of the Constitution). Once again, original intent counted for nothing. If Marshall had consulted the Journal of the Convention, he would have had to explain his way around it. He ignored it. Indeed, he never cited the Journal. In *McCulloch* his astoundingly broad interpretation of congressional powers dismayed even Madison, who declared that the Constitution would not have been ratified if the people had known that the United States possessed nearly illimitable powers. . . .

One must be familiar with Madison's thought to understand that when he spoke of "the intentions of the parties" to the Constitution or the supremacy of the views of those who gave the Constitution its "stamp of authority," he meant the people of the United States acting through their state conventions; when he spoke of the intention of "those who made the Constitution" or of its "authors," he meant those who ratified it, not those in Philadelphia who framed it. So too, one must be familiar with his thought to understand that when he spoke of the supremacy of their views, he did not mean that one turned to those views for an explanation of specific or particular clauses of the Constitution. When he said that the debates of the Convention could have "no authoritative character," he did not mean that the debates lacked significance when one construed the meaning of the Constitution; he intended, rather, that as a matter of fundamental political theory, the consent of the governed, who alone were sovereign, was the force that legitimated the Constitution. As he put the point: "But whatever respect may be thought due to the intention of the Convention, which prepared & proposed the Constitution, as presumptive evidence of the general understanding at the time of the language used, it must be kept in mind that the only authoritative intentions were those of the people of the States, as expressed thro' the Conventions which ratified the Constitution." . . . .

How then was the meaning of the Constitution to be fathomed? Madison believed that experience fixed meaning in doubtful cases but that meaning was not fixed forever. He would have preferred a static Constitution, and he resisted, even deplored, certain changes in meaning. He probably had in mind the Hamiltonian financial system, the Sedition Act, and overbroad judicial opinions such as those in *McCulloch* v. *Maryland* and *Cohens* v. *Virginia* when he said that deviations from the "fair construction of the instrument have always given me a pain," and he wished that innovations based on overbroad constructions would cease; but he knew that change was inevitable. He would have preferred to believe that the Constitution speaks for itself according to the usual and established rules of interpretation, for which intention cannot be substituted. And he advocated that whenever possible the language of the Constitution should be construed according to the people's understanding as evidenced by "contemporaneous expositions."

But he understood that just as words changed in meaning, so did the Constitution. "It could not but happen, and was foreseen at the birth of the Constitution," he declared, "that difficulties and differences of opinion might occasionally rise in expounding terms and phrases necessarily used in such a charter," especially as to the powers in the federal system. Practice would settle some doubtful matters, and the meaning of the Constitution, to the extent that it depended upon judicial interpretations, would emerge from decisions over a period of time. Madison conceded that experience had caused him to change strong opinions on some matters. For example, he once thought that the Constitution prohibited Congress from chartering a bank, but he had been compelled to change his mind, because the sovereign will had expressed itself by acquiescence in a course of exposition that altered the original meaning of the Constitution. Popular understanding simply had overruled his previous views of the matter. When an authoritative, uniform, and sustained course of decision or practice received "public sanction," Madison believed that the Constitution evolved in meaning, and the old must give way to the new. When the words that composed a text altered in their meaning, "it is evident that the shape and attributes of the Government must partake of the change to which the words and phrases of all living languages are constantly subject. . . . [O]ur Constitution is already undergoing interpretations unknown to its founders. . . . " Similarly, he observed: "Some of the terms of the Federal Constitution have already undergone perceptible deviations from their original import." Those were not facts that he applauded; rather, he personally disapproved but understood and acquiesced.

TOWARD CRITICAL THINKING

1. What position did James Madison take about the intentions of the Framers as a guide for constitutional interpretation? What circumstances surrounding the Constitutional Convention might indicate that the Framers did not want their intentions to control future generations?

2. According to Levy, what were the basic underpinnings of the Constitution and how did the new debate over original intent occur? How does the acceptance of the notion of judicial interests relate to judicial interpretation? Is judicial interpretation just another form of constitutional amendment?

· 7 ·

Proposals to Amend the Constitution

JOHN R. VILE

The Framers didn't want their work tampered with lightly. The document they produced was designed to endure with only slight modification or change. Thus, not only do potential constitutional amendments require a two-thirds vote in both houses of Congress, but they also must be popular enough to convince a *majority* of legislators in *three-fourths* of the states of their appropriateness for inclusion in the Constitution. As the supporters of the proposed Equal Rights Amendment,—as well as other amendments—have found, this can be a daunting task, especially when controversy surrounds an amendment.

John R. Vile notes that more than 10,000 amendments to the Constitution have been proposed since 1789. Only a few have ever even been sent to the states for their approval. And his review of these proposed amendments reveals that in spite of the large number of amendments that were suggested to reverse unpopular Supreme Court decisions, few actually would have limited individual rights.

Almost from the time scientific polling began, scholars have attempted to gauge public support for the Bill of Rights.[1] . . . Such surveys often suggest that while elites are generally committed to such freedoms, the general public, however supportive of the concept of a Bill of Rights, is less knowledgeable about and supportive of the individual guarantees of liberty found in the first 10 amendments.[2]

Related to concerns about general public support for individual civil rights and liberties are periodic fears . . . about the possibility that

SOURCE: John R. Vile, "Proposals to Amend the Bill of Rights: Are Fundamental Rights in Jeopardy?" *Judicature* 75, no. 2 (August–September 1991): 62–67. Reprinted by permission.

[1] For such a recent survey examining attitudes toward the First Amendment, see Wyatt, *Free Expression and the American Public* (Murfreesboro, Tennessee: for the American Society of Newspapers Editors, 1991)

[2] Based on such surveys, one historian has concluded that "the Bill of Rights has captured the loyalty of Americans even if they do not know exactly what it contains." See Hall, *Introduction, By and for the People: Constitutional Rights in American History* 1 (Arlington Heights, Illinois: Harlan Davidson, Inc., 1991). On a similar point, see Mead, *The United States Constitution: Personalities, Principles, and Issues* (Columbia: University of South Carolina Press, 1987), p. 214.

the Bill of Rights might be repealed or some other horrible calamity initiated.[3] . . .

Are the rights found in the first 10 amendments, whose bicentennial is now being celebrated, jeopardized by the amending process? . . . In an attempt to cast some light on this question, however, I have reviewed amendments that members of Congress have introduced that would have modified the Bill the Rights or other significant civil rights and liberties. . . . If such rights are in serious jeopardy, this danger will surely be evident by a review of the more than 10,000 proposals that have been submitted in what is arguably the nation's most representative branch of government. . . .

Although the need for a Bill or Rights had been hotly debated,[4] once ratified there were few proposals that would indicate that the Bill of Rights—which was then limited in its application to the national government alone—[5] was in serious jeopardy during the first 100 years of American history. Indeed, with the example of the three post-Civil War amendments before him, [Herman] Ames noted that, "[t]he proposed amendments of the last half century have . . . been directed rather to the increase and protection of personal rights and privileges than to their abridgement."[6]. . .

There were, of course, many proposals that were eventually incorporated into Amendments Thirteen through Fifteen, which served respectively to abolish slavery, guarantee citizenship rights to all Americans, and prohibit voting discrimination on the basis of race. With the ratification of these amendments, which certainly marked significant expansion of the guarantees of the Bill of Rights, Ames perhaps overly optimistically argued that, "[t]he freedom of the individual is now completely assured, and the thirteenth, fourteenth, and fifteenth amendments stand as unalterable statements of the fact."[7]

◆ The Populist and Progressive Eras

M. A. Musmanno wrote a second survey of proposed amendments that covered the period from the end of Ames's study until 1926, a time encompassing the years usually associated with the Populists and Progressives. Given the reform sentiment generally connected with both move-

---

[3] *See, for example,* Kean, *A Constitutional Convention Would Threaten Rights We Have Cherished for 200 Years,* 4 Det. C. L. Rev. 1087 (Winter, 1986), and Rovere, *Affairs of State,* The New Yorker, March 19, 1979, at 136–143.

[4] For a short summary of this debate, see Storing, *What the Anti-Federalists Were For 64–70* (Chicago: The University of Chicago Press, 1981), pp. 64–70.

[5] See the Supreme Court's decision in *Barron* v. *Baltimore,* 7 Peters 243 (1833).

[6] Ames, *The Proposed Amendments to the Constitution of the United States during the First Century of Its History* (New York: Burt Franklin, 1970 reprint), at 190.

[7] *Id.* at 239.

ments, it may not be surprising that approximately the same number of amending proposals, about 1,300, was introduced during this shorter period as in the previous 100 years.[8] A number of amending proposals during this period would have expanded or restricted individual liberties as guaranteed in the Bill of Rights and elsewhere in the Constitution. One proposed amendment, probably unnecessary to accomplish its purpose, would have modified the Second Amendment so as to give Congress the power to restrict the carrying of concealed weapons in the District of Columbia and the territories.[9]

A number of proposal, many generated by Utah's entrance into the Union, would have prohibited polygamy and or divorce and/or sought to guarantee uniform marriage laws. Amendments establishing a national eight-hour day and prohibiting child labor[10] would have added an economic component to the political rights guaranteed in the Bill of Rights. Other than the amendments actually ratified, the child labor amendment appears to be the only one from this time period that came up for a vote on the House or Senate floor; although it was approved by the necessary congressional majorities in 1924, it was not subsequently ratified by the states and was arguably unneeded after the Supreme Court upheld congressional powers in this area.[11]

Some amendments would have denied rights to aliens, especially Japanese; one amendment so phrased as to limit citizenship to "white persons, Africans, American Indians, or their descendants."[12] Another amendment would have applied the religion clauses of the First Amendment to the states and prohibited aid to sectarian schools.[13] Other proposed amendments would have extended equal rights to women[14] or have added an acknowledgement of God in the Constitution. . . .

The only amendments actually ratified during the period of Musmanno's study were amendments Sixteen through Nineteen.[15] Of these,

---

[8] Musmanno, *Proposed Amendments to the Constitution,* 70th Congress, 2d Session, House Document No. 551 (Washington: United States Government Printing Office, 1929). A study by Charles C. Tansill roughly covers the same time period, albeit in somewhat different fashion. See *Proposed Amendments to the Constitution of the United States Introduced in Congress From December 4, 1889, to July 2, 1926, 69th Congress, 1st Sess.,* Document No. 93 (Washington: Government Printing Office, 1926).

[9] Musmanno, *id.* at 100.

[10] *Id.* at135–139.

[11] For text of this amendment, see Anastaplo, *The Constitution of 1787: A Commentary 299* (Baltimore: The Johns Hopkins University Press, 1989).

[12] Musmanno, *supra* n. 8, at 181.

[13] *Id.* at 181.

[14] *Id.* at 213.

[15] *See* Grimes. *Democracy and the Amendments to the Constitution* 65–100 (Lexington, Massachusetts: Lexington Books, 1978). For further discussion of this period, see Vile, *American Views of the Constitutional Amending Process: An Intellectual History of Article V,* 35 Am. J. Legal Hist. (January 1991): 57–61.

the Eighteenth (establishing national alcoholic prohibition), could certainly be viewed as a restriction of personal liberty, while the Seventeenth (providing for direct election of Senators) and the Nineteenth (extending the suffrage to women) were significant expansions of civil liberties. The Sixteenth Amendment (constitutionalizing a national income tax) was only indirectly relevant to this topic.

◆ From the Roaring Twenties to the Eisenhower Fifties

The period from 1926 to 1957, during which the nation underwent a constitutional revolution symbolized the Supreme Court's so-called "switch in time that saved nine,"[16] is covered in a report issued in 1957.[17] Altogether there were 1,541 separate, albeit often redundant, proposals introduced. More than in any previous survey, quite a number of these proposals would have affected the Bill of Rights. . . .

. . . Of the amendments proposed and ratified in this time period, however, none significantly affected individual rights other than the Twenty-First Amendment repealing prohibition. The Twentieth Amendment was directed to the problem of lame duck representation, while the Twenty-Second limited the president to two full terms.

◆ A Time of Transition

The next treatment of proposed constitutional amendments overlaps with the previous one.[18] . . . Again there were many requests, well over 200, for equal rights for men and women. There were continuing resolutions to insert references to Christianity into the Constitution, two more proposals for abolishing capital punishment, and about 70 proposals (undoubtedly stimulated by the Supreme Court's decision in *Engel* v. *Vitale* striking down the use of a prayer composed for school students by the New York State Board of Regents)[19] to permit prayer in public schools and buildings. Other proposals would have abolished the poll tax, extended

---

[16] This switch in interpretation is often associated with the cases of *West Coast Hotel Co.* v. *Parrish*, 300 U.S. 379 (1937) and *N.L.R.B.* v. *Jones & Laughlin Steel Corporation*, 301 U.S. 1 (1937). *See* Abraham, *Freedom and the Court*, 4th ed. (New York: Oxford University Press, 1982).

[17] Johnston and Hupman, *Proposed Amendments to the Constitution of the United States Introduced in Congress from the 69th Congress, 2d Session through the 84 Congress, 2d Session, December 6, 1926, to January 3, 1957, 85th Congress, 1st Sess.*, Document No. 65 (Washington: United States Government Printing Office, 1957).

[18] Johnston and Hupman, *Proposed Amendments to the Constitution of the United States of America Introduced in Congress from the 69th Congress, 2d Session through the 87th Congress, 2d Session, December 6, 1926 to January 3, 1963, 87th Congress, 2d Session*, Document No. 163 (Washington: U.S. Government Printing Office, 1969).

[19] 370 U.S. 421 (1962).

voting rights to eighteen year olds, and redefined treason. The poll tax amendment was voted on by Congress during this time period.

Apart from prayer in schools and the equal rights amendment, one or both of which could be considered to be an expansion of rights, no other amendment that would have affected the Bill of Rights appears to have had widespread support. The only amendment proposed and ratified during this time was the Twenty-Third, expanding the rights of residents in the District of Columbia by granting them electoral votes equal to that of the smallest states.

◆ The Great Society Years

From 1963–1969, during which Lyndon Johnson proposed his Great Society programs,[20] 1,548 congressional amending proposals were introduced. There were an increasing number of proposed amendments that would have modified interpretations of the Bill of Rights during this period. For the most part, however, these seem to be less a product of opposition to such rights as originally understood than reactions to the Warren Court's increased judicial intervention in this field and the increasing number of rights the Court incorporated into the due process clause of the Fourteenth Amendment and now applied to limit state action.

Proposals related to apportionment (of which more than 100 were introduced), while they dealt more directly with the Fourteenth Amendment than with the first 10, were but one indication of the interplay between proposed amendments and judicial decisions relative to human rights during this time period.[21] . . . There were over 250 proposals related to the equal rights amendment (the Senate of the 89th Congress voted for this amendment by an insufficient vote of 55 to 38)[22] and over 150 proposals relative to prayer in public schools.

Amendments were proposed to permit voluntary confessions and to modify judicial decisions relating to the employment of subversives and to the conduct of police interrogations. There were proposals for legalizing "voluntary" segregation and prohibiting use of the mail by subversives as

---

[20] Valeo, Hupman, and Haley, *Proposed Amendments to the Constitution of the United States of America Introduced in Congress from the 88th Congress, 1st Session through the 90th Congress, 2d Session, January 9, 1963, to January 3, 1969*, 91st Congress, 1st sess., Document No. 91–38 (Washington: Government Printing Office, 1969).

[21] These resolutions, as well as requests from the state legislatures for another constitutional convention, were stimulated by the Supreme Court's decisions in *Baker* v. *Carr,* 369 U.S. 186 (1962) and *Reynolds* v. *Sims,* 377 U.S. 533 (1964). The first case declared apportionment to be a justiciable issue; the second applied the one person, one vote standard to apportionment of both houses of state legislatures.

[22] Valeo, Hupman, and Haley, *supra* n. 20, at 93.

well as numerous proposals that would soon bear fruit in regard to eighteen year olds' right to vote. The Twenty-Fourth Amendment limiting poll taxes and the Twenty-Fifth Amendment relating to presidential disability were, however, the only ones to be ratified during the Johnson years.

◆ From Nixon to Reagan

The last published survey of proposed constitutional amendments covers the period from 1969 through 1984.[23] . . . Once again, there were more proposals that would affect the Bill of Rights, but, as in the previous period, most were responses to innovative Supreme Court decisions expanding interpretations of rights rather than attempts to pare these rights as traditionally understood.

There were numerous proposals . . . responding to the Supreme Court decision in *Roe* v. *Wade.*[24] The proposals were designed either to protect unborn children, prohibit abortion, or return this matter to state control. There were proposals related to the display and handling of the flag (these dramatically increased and almost resulted in a congressionally proposed amendment[25] in the wake of *Texas* v. *Johnson* and *U.S.* v. *Eichman,* which overturned convictions for flag-burning),[26] to regulation of pornography, to permitting voluntary participation in the pledge of allegiance. There were several proposals to alter the provision against self-incrimination in the Fifth Amendment and to limit school busing, and there were well over 100 proposals to provide equal access for religious groups in public schools, a feat that was eventually accomplished without the ratification of an amendment.[27]

. . . The only three proposals affecting rights that made it through the congressional hurdles, however, were the Twenty-Sixth Amendment lowering the voting age to eighteen, the equal rights amendment, and the

---

[23] Davis, *Proposed Amendments to the Constitution of the United States of America Introduced in Congress from the 91st Congress, 1st Session, through the 98th Congress, 2nd Session, January 1969–December 1984* Report No. 85–36 (Washington: Congressional Research Service, February 1, 1985). For a study focusing on congressional responses to prayer, busing, and abortion during this period, see Keynes with Miller, *The Court vs. Congress: Prayer, Busing, and Abortion* (Durham: Duke University Press, 1989).

[24] 410 U.S. 113 (1973).

[25] For a pessimistic account of the flag-burning controversy and what it says about the commitment of Americans to fundamental liberties, see Goldstein, *The Great 1989–1990 Flag Flap: An Historical, Political, and Legal Analysis,* 45 *U. Miami L. Rev.* (September 1990): 19–106.

[26] 57 U.S.L.W. 4770 (1989), 58 U.S.L.W. 4744 (1990).

[27] See *Board of Education of Westside Community Schools* v. *Mergens,* 110 L. Ed 2d 191 (1990).

proposal for congressional representation for the District of Columbia. Neither of the last two measures were subsequently ratified by the necessary number of states, although the equal rights amendment fell only three states short of this goal.[28]

◆ Polling Evidence

. . . Austin Ranney . . . reviewed polling data on eleven proposed amendments that were on the national agenda about the time of the constitutional bicentennial. Ranney found that the public was substantially more receptive to such amendments than was the Congress; the public expressed apparent support for nine of the eleven proposals. These nine items were:

> ERA, balanced budgets, school prayer, direct election of presidents, regional presidential primaries, a national presidential primary, national initiative, limiting terms of senators and representatives, and [the] presidential item veto.[29]

Of these proposal, the ERA would presumably have expanded the Bill of Rights, and the prayer amendment would have arguably tilted the balance of First Amendment interpretation from the establishment to the free exercise clause. However positively or negatively these amendments may be viewed, neither would have resulted in massive changes in the Bill of Rights as currently understood. Moreover, Ranney found support to be lacking for a proposed amendment to outlaw abortion, such an amendment potentially having a far more drastic effect on existing practices. As Ranney viewed his findings, the proposals that a majority of the people most generally favored were "all intended to limit the reach and power of the national government in one way or another."[30] In large part, this was the primary purpose of the Bill of Rights itself.

◆ Conclusion

Based on Ranney's finding, on proposals to rewrite the Constitution and on individual amendments proposed to Congress, as well as on the extreme difficulty of successfully utilizing the constitutional amending

---

[28] For explanations of this failure, see Mansbridge, *Why We Lost the ERA* (Chicago: University of Chicago Press, 1986) and Berry, *Why ERA Failed* (Bloomington: Indiana University Press, 1986).

[29] Ranney, *What Constitutional Changes Do Americans Want?*, in *This Constitution* 285 (Washington, D.C.: Congressional Quarterly, 1986).

[30] *Id.* at 286.

process,[31] it would not appear that there is great cause to fear that the Bill of Rights will be significantly diminished through the amending mechanism. The whole force of amendments in American history has indeed been, "a pattern of successive extensions of democracy."[32] These extensions have almost all expanded the scope of individual civil liberties. It is, of course, always possible that one or another Supreme Court interpretation of the Bill of Rights might one day be reversed; but reversals seem far more likely to come from the Court itself than from amendments proposed by two-thirds majorities of both houses of Congress and ratified by three-fourths of the states. Amendments relating to flag burning, prayer in schools, abortion, or the rights of criminal defendants are certainly not inconceivable. Each such proposal would, of course, have to be examined on its own merits, but none either singly or taken together appears to reveal a general desire to eliminate the Bill of Rights.

FIGURE 2.1
Methods of ammending the Constitution

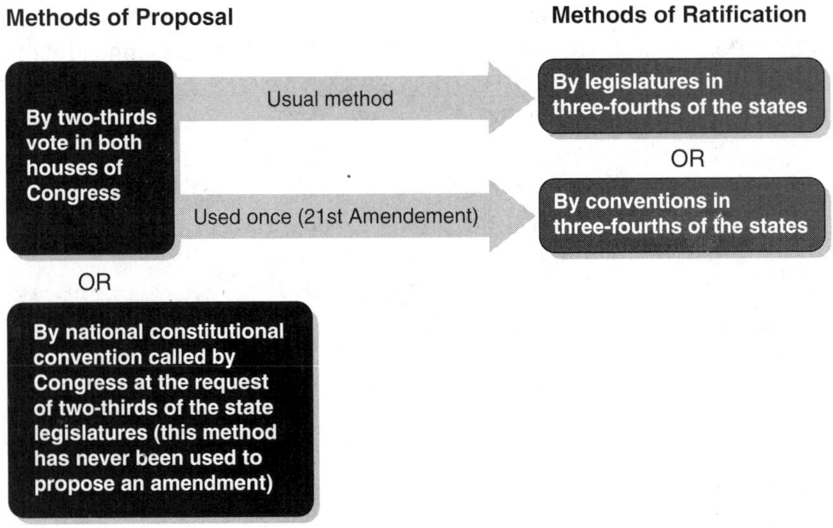

Methods of Proposal   **Methods of Ratification**

By two-thirds vote in both houses of Congress

Usual method → By legislatures in three-fourths of the states

OR

Used once (21st Amendement) → By conventions in three-fourths of the states

OR

By national constitutional convention called by Congress at the request of two-thirds of the state legislatures (this method has never been used to propose an amendment)

---

[31] Berry, "How Hard It Is to Change," *The New York Times Magazine* (September 13, 1987), at 93–98. Constitutional amendments require proposal by two-thirds of both houses of Congress and ratification by three-fourths of the states. Alternatively, amendments may be proposed in a convention called by Congress after applications from two-thirds of the states; such amendments would not become law until approved by three-fourths of the states.

[32] Grimes, *supra* n. 15 at 163.

TOWARD CRITICAL THINKING

1. The Framers clearly wanted to make it difficult to amend the Constitution. Given Americans' belief in the protection of minority rights, however, are the supermajority requirements for ratification of amendments problematic? (See Figure 2.1.)

2. What kinds of amendments are most likely to win ratification?

THINKING ABOUT THE CONSTITUTION, THE FIGHT FOR RATIFICATION, AND THE AMENDMENT PROCESS

1. What would John Locke or Thomas Hobbes say about the system of checks and balances created in the new Constitution? Would they have agreed on the need for a Bill of Rights?

2. Given the supermajorities required for ratification of constitutional amendments, how likely do you think ratification of the Bill of Rights would be today?

3. Is protection of minority rights or the redress of structural problems in the Constitution best left to judicial interpretation of the existing document? Should constitutional interpretation be effected by the nature of the times?

CHAPTER 3

◆ ◆ ◆

Federalism

When the Founders created a federal system, they settled on a new form of government in which the powers of the national government were specifically enumerated. Before the thirteen states entered into the new union, each basically considered itself a sovereign state. Thus, their powers did not need enumeration; the states believed that they would be able to claim all those powers that were not given to the national government by the Constitution. But as the readings in this chapter highlight, it is highly unlikely that the states (or the people) ever would have consented to place so much power in the hands of the central government, especially in view of how those powers have evolved and expanded over time.

As Alexander Hamilton, an ardent proponent of a strong federal government, notes in *Federalist No. 17* (Reading 8), many of the Framers sincerely believed that it would "always be far more easy for the State governments to encroach upon the national authorities than for the national government to encroach upon the State authorities." How wrong he was. In Reading 9, *McCulloch* v. *Maryland* (1819), Federalist Chief Justice John Marshall made it clear that the states were not to "encroach" on the powers of the national government. And just five years later in *Gibbons* v. *Ogden* (1824), the Court broadly interpreted Congress's powers under the commerce clause contained in Article I, section 8 of the Constitution to include the ability to regulate any commerce that took place between two states. *Gibbons* thus ushered in a new era of national commerce largely unfettered by state law. Together, *McCulloch* and *Gibbons* substantially increased the powers of the national government just a few decades after the Constitution was ratified.

The struggle between the national and state governments is the focus of Cass R. Sunstein's thoughts on the nature of government in Reading 10 as he discusses *The Rediscovery of American Federalism,* a book by noted political scientist Samuel H. Beer. Especially critical to the Founders' ideas of a sound national government was the creation of a government with substantial commercial powers—those powers underscored by the Marshall opinions in *McCulloch* and *Gibbons.*

Over the years, as the powers of the national government increased, often, many people argued, at the expense of the states, various presidents tried to involve the states in a variety of so-called plans to return power and control to the states over a variety of functions that some believed best left in their hands. In Reading 11, political scientist Aaron Wildavsky argues that political scientists, politicians, and pundits have spent too much time thinking of labels to describe the federal system. Whether it's layer cake, marble cake, or fruitcake federalism, Wildavsky believes that the citizenry is best served not by worrying about which level of government has the power; the United States would be better served by worrying about the growth of government.

John Kincaid does not necessarily view federalism as a growth problem, as revealed in Reading 12. In "Constitutional Federalism," Kincaid points out the key role the U.S. Supreme Court has played in usurping power from the states. He notes the Court's role in striking down state racial segregation in public schools and its reapportionment rulings as sweeping decisions that brought individuals into the political process and undermined the power of the states. The unprecedented rise in national programs designed to assist individuals has also enlarged the role of the national government in local and individual affairs. Collectively, these rulings have fundamentally altered the balance of power between the national and state governments.

A new direction in federalism is suggested by the U.S. Supreme Court's decision in *Webster* v. *Reproductive Health Services* (1989) (Reading 13). In *Webster,* a majority of the states-rights-minded Court appeared to issue an open invitation to the states to begin legislating to restrict abortions as they saw fit under their police powers. State legislators took that cue from the Supreme Court, and in forty-eight of the fifty states, abortion-curbing proposals were introduced, although not necessarily passed.

· 8 ·

Federalist No. 17

ALEXANDER HAMILTON

In *Federalist No. 17* Alexander Hamilton argues earnestly for a
strong national government while recognizing and heralding the closeness of state governments to the people. He believed that the kinds of issues that states were best concerned with were not "desirable" objects of
national legislation. Nor did Hamilton believe that the police powers reserved to the states would ever offer any "temptation" to "persons intrusted with the administration of the general [national] government."

To the People of the State of New York:

. . . It may be said that it would tend to render the government of the
Union too powerful, and to enable it to absorb those residuary authorities
which it might be judged proper to leave with the States for local purposes. Allowing the utmost latitude to the love of power which any
reasonable man can require, I confess I am at a loss to discover what
temptation the persons intrusted with the administration of the general
government could ever feel to divest the States of the authorities of that
description. The regulation of the mere domestic police of a State appears
to me to hold out slender allurement to ambition. Commerce, finance,
negotiation, and war seem to comprehend all the objects which have
charms for minds governed by that passion; and all the power necessary
to those objects ought, in the first instance, to be lodged in the national
depository. The administration of private justice between the citizens of
the same State, the supervision of agriculture and of other concerns of a
similar nature, all those things, in short, which are proper to be provided
for by local legislation, can never be desirable cares of a general jurisdiction. It is therefore improbable that there should exist a disposition in the
federal councils to usurp the powers with which they are connected;
because the attempt to exercise those powers would be as troublesome as
it would be nugatory; and the possession of them, for that reason, would
contribute nothing to the dignity, to the importance, or to the splendor of
the national government.

. . . It will always be far more easy for the State governments to
encroach upon the national authorities than for the national government
to encroach upon the State authorities. . . .

. . . Upon the same principle that a man is more attached to his family than to his neighborhood, to his neighborhood than to the community at large, the people of each State would be apt to feel a stronger bias towards their local governments than towards the government of the Union; unless the force of that principle should be destroyed by a much better administration of the latter.

TOWARD CRITICAL THINKING

1. What kind of "local" activities did Hamilton envision to be within the proper scope of state police powers? How many of these activities are still considered "local" in nature today?

2. What support did Hamilton offer to prove his assertions that it would be much easier for states to encroach on the powers of the central government? Hamilton is often described as brilliant. How could he have been so wrong?

McCulloch *v.* Maryland
4 Wheat. 316 (1819)

McCulloch was the first major decision of the Marshall Court to attempt to define the federal/state relationship. In 1816 Congress created what was called the Second Bank of the United States. In 1818 the Maryland legislature enacted a statute imposing a tax on all banks not chartered by the legislature. James McCulloch, a clerk of the U.S. bank, issued bank notes without the stamps required by the Maryland law, the stamps being proof that the state tax had been paid. He was promptly arrested, tried, and convicted for violating the Maryland statute. Not surprisingly, his conviction was upheld by the highest Maryland state court. McCulloch then appealed his conviction to the U.S. Supreme Court. While most commentators had expected him to lose his case in the Maryland courts, the issue presented in his case posed important questions about the nature of the federal system and the respective powers of the state and national governments. The basic question for the U.S. Supreme Court to answer, however, was: Was the Maryland statute valid or was it "repugnant to the constitution of the United States" or to the act of Congress that chartered the bank?

Chief Justice Marshall delivered the opinion of the Court:

The constitution of our country, in its most interesting and vital parts, is to be considered; the conflicting powers of the government of the Union and of its members, as marked in that constitution, are to be discussed; and an opinion given, which may essentially influence the great operations of the government. No tribunal can approach such a question without a deep sense of its importance, and of the awful responsibility involved in its decision. But it must be decided peacefully, or remain a source of hostile legislation, perhaps of hostility of a still more serious nature; and if it is to be so decided, by this tribunal alone can the decision be made. On the Supreme Court of the United States has the constitution of our country devolved this important duty.

The first question . . . is, has Congress power to incorporate a bank? . . .

This government is acknowledged by all to be one of enumerated powers. The principle, that it can exercise only the powers granted to it, would seem too apparent to have required to be enforced by all those arguments which its enlightened friends, while it was depending before the people, found it necessary to urge. That principle is now universally admitted. But the question respecting the extent of the powers actually granted, is perpetually arising, and will probably continue to arise, as long as our system shall exist. . . .

Although, among the enumerated powers of government, we do not find the word "bank" or "incorporation," we find the great powers to lay and collect taxes; to borrow money; to regulate commerce; to declare and conduct a war; and to raise and support armies and navies. The sword and the purse, all the external relations, and no inconsiderable portion of the industry of the nation, are entrusted to its government. . . . [I]t may with great reason be contended, that a government, entrusted with such ample powers, on the due execution of which the happiness and prosperity of the nation so vitally depends, must also be entrusted with ample means for their execution. The power being given, it is the interest of the nation to facilitate its execution. It can never be their interest, and cannot be presumed to have been their intention, to clog and embarrass its execution by withholding the most appropriate means. . . .

. . .

But the constitution of the United States has not left the right of Congress to employ the necessary means, for the execution of the powers conferred on the government, to general reasoning. To its enumeration of powers is added that of making "all laws which shall be necessary and proper, for carrying into execution the foregoing powers, and all other powers vested by this constitution, in the government of the United States, or in any department thereof."

. . .

The argument on which most reliance is placed, is drawn from the peculiar language of this clause. Congress is not empowered by it to make all laws, which may have relation to the powers conferred on the government, but such only as may be *"necessary and proper"* for carrying them into execution. The word *"necessary,"* is considered as controlling the whole sentence, and as limiting the right to pass laws for the execution of the granted powers, to such as are indispensable, and without which the power would be nugatory. That it excludes the choice of means, and leaves to Congress, in each case, that only which is most direct and simple.

Is it true, that this is the sense in which the word "necessary" is always used? Does it always import an absolute physical necessity, so strong, that one thing, to which another may be termed necessary, cannot exist without that other? We think it does not. If reference be had to its use, in the common affairs of the world, or in approved authors, we find that it frequently imports no more than that one thing is convenient, or useful, or essential to another. To employ the means necessary to an end, is generally understood as employing any means calculated to produce the end, and not as being confined to those single means, without which the end would be entirely unattainable. Such is the character of human language, that no word conveys to the mind, in all situations, one single definite idea; and nothing is more common than to use words in a figurative sense. Almost all compositions contain words, which, taken in their rigorous sense, would convey a meaning different from that which is obviously intended. . . .

. . . [W]ere its necessity less apparent, none can deny its being an appropriate measure; and if it is, the degree of its necessity, as has been very justly observed, is to be discussed in another place. Should Congress, in the execution of its powers, adopt measures which are prohibited by the Constitution; or should Congress, under the pretext of executing its powers pass laws for the accomplishment of objects not entrusted to the government, it would become the painful duty of this tribunal, should a case requiring such a decision come before it, to say that such an act was not the law of the land. But where the law is not prohibited, and is really calculated to effect any of the objects entrusted to the government, to undertake here to inquire into the degree of its necessity, would be to pass the line which circumscribes the judicial department, and to tread on legislative ground. This court disclaims all pretensions to such a power. . . .

After the most deliberate consideration, it is the unanimous and decided opinion of this court that the act to incorporate the bank of the United States is a law made in pursuance of the Constitution, and is a part of the supreme law of the land. . . .

It being the opinion of the court that the act incorporating the bank is constitutional, . . . we proceed to inquire:

Whether the state of Maryland may, without violating the Constitution, tax that branch?

That the power of taxation is one of vital importance; that it is retained by the states; that it is not abridged by the grant of a similar power to the government of the Union: that it is to be concurrently exercised by the two governments: are truths which have never been denied. But, such is the paramount character of the Constitution that its capacity to withdraw any subject from the action of even this power, is admitted. The states are expressly forbidden to lay any duties on imports or exports, except what may be absolutely necessary for executing their inspection laws. If the obligation of this prohibition must be conceded—if it may restrain a state from the exercise of its taxing power on imports and exports—the same paramount character would seem to restrain, as it certainly may restrain, a state from such other exercise of this power, as is in its nature incompatible with, and repugnant to, the constitutional laws of the Union. . . .

This great principle is, that the Constitution and the laws made in pursuance thereof are supreme; that they control the constitution and laws of the respective states, and cannot be controlled by them.

. . .

That the power to tax involves the power to destroy; that the power to destroy may defeat and render useless the power to create; that there is a plain repugnance, in conferring on one government a power to control the constitutional measures of another, which other, with respect to those very measures, is declared to be supreme over that which exerts the control, are propositions not to be denied. . . .

If the states may tax one instrument, employed by the government in the execution of its powers, they may tax any and every other instrument. They may tax the mail; they may tax the mint; they may tax patent-rights; they may tax all the means employed by the government, to an excess which would defeat all the ends of government. This was not intended by the American people. . . .

The question is, in truth, a question of supremacy; and if the right of the states to tax the means employed by the general government be conceded, the declaration that the constitution, and the laws made in pursuance thereof, shall be the supreme law of the land, is empty and unmeaning declaration. . . .

But the two cases are not on the same reason. The people of all the states have created the general government, and have conferred upon it the general power of taxation. . . .

The court has bestowed on this subject its most deliberate consideration. The result is a conviction that the states have no power, by taxation or otherwise, to retard, impede, burden, or in any manner control the operations of the constitutional laws enacted by Congress to carry into execution the powers vested in the general government. This is, we think, the unavoidable consequence of that supremacy which the Constitution has declared.

We are unanimously of the opinion that the law passed by the legislature of Maryland, imposing a tax on the Bank of the United States, is unconstitutional and void.

This opinion does not deprive the states of any resources which they originally possessed. It does not extend to a tax paid by the real property of the bank, in common with the other real property within the state, nor to a tax imposed on the interest which the citizens of Maryland may hold in this institution, in common with other property of the same description throughout the state. But this is a tax on the operations of the bank, and is, consequently, a tax on the operation of an instrument of the Union to carry its powers into execution. Such a tax must be unconstitutional. . . .

TOWARD CRITICAL THINKING

1. *McCulloch* v. *Maryland* is renowned for Chief Justice Marshall's expansive interpretation of the powers of the national government. What sources or specific powers did he look to in the Constitution to justify the authority of Congress to charter a national bank?

2. Why is the power to tax also the power to destroy? How does this sweeping proclamation relate to federalism?

· *10* ·

Founders, Keepers

CASS R. SUNSTEIN

In *To Make a Nation: The Rediscovery of American Federalism,*
Samuel H. Beer posits his belief that the views of Montesquieu and
James Madison are in a constant state of tension. This tension, says University of Chicago Law School professor Cass R. Sunstein, comprises
"the Great drama of American constitutional thought." Chief Justice John
Marshall and other Federalists took one view of the federal system. Eventually, Madison took another. In "Founders, Keepers," Sunstein highlights some of the practical and political dilemmas that federalism creates.

. . . Americans revere their Constitution, but it is not clear that it
speaks directly to us. To be sure, we are aware of the basic structures of
federalism, of checks and balances, of the Bill of Rights, of the power of
the Supreme Court. But we no longer have much sense of the concrete
struggles and dilemmas that gave the Constitution its dimensions and its
shape. We are entirely unlike the citizens described by Thomas Paine, who
carried the Constitution in their pockets and frequently consulted it for
guidance on the issues of the day. Sometimes the Constitution seems too
abstract, too old, too distant, even a bit too sterile. Its authors do not seem
like real people addressing concrete problems. . . .

For [Samuel] Beer, the great drama of American constitutional
thought, still very much with us today, involves a concrete struggle between two sets of ideas. On the one side are the heirs of Montesquieu,
believing that a republic can flourish only if it is small and homogeneous.
On this view heterogeneity and difference pose great risks to stability and
social peace. A large nation must be a kind of confederacy, allowing a
large degree of autonomy for self-governing subunits. On the other side
are the heirs of James Madison, Montesquieu's great critic, arguing that
heterogeneity is an affirmative good, that it promotes social deliberation
and that a large unified republic, not a confederacy, is best able to combat
the risks of factionalism, or what we would now call interest-group
pressures.

SOURCE: Cass R. Sunstein, "Founders, Keepers," *The New Republic* (May 24,
1993):38–41. Reprinted by permission of The New Republic.

. . . "Government by discussion" is Beer's term for a system in which deliberation among the diverse and the heterogeneous would encourage the emergence of general truths. . . .

Equipped with this notion, Beer vigorously rejects the idea that the American constitutional project was to disable government. On the contrary, he sees the Framers' project as expansive, enabling and facilitative—as an effort to establish positive constitutionalism suitable for a "strong democracy" with the broad powers sufficient to meet both domestic and foreign challenges. Beer reminds us that a serious problem with the Articles of Confederation was a weak state, unable to engage in the tasks that were necessary for a commercial republic. The Framers wanted to strengthen government, not to paralyze it.

Finally, Beer shows that Americans rejected Montesquieu's recommendation of a confederate republic in favor of a new entity altogether: the "compound republic." Montesquieu thought that a large republic would be subject to self-destructive tumult. The only possible remedy was a kind of confederacy in which each local unit would have significant autonomy. In such a system, differences would be diminished and self-government would be more likely. The appropriate institution was therefore a kind of convention or agreement among separate states, in which secession was an acknowledged right. We might think of the European Community as a modern example. As Beer shows, Madison turned Montesquieu's teaching on its head. Madison argued that a large republic would be freer from tumult, and that heterogeneity could be turned to a large nation's advantage. In a combined republic, the source of authority was the people, not the states, and the national government would be supreme over the states. And in a large republic, the various factions would counteract each other, and national representatives, operating above the fray, would be more likely to consult the public good. Rights would be more rather than less secure. Moreover, the parochial interests of the states could be overcome to everyone's benefit. This was the great advantage over Montesquieu's confederacy, in which each state, following its own self-interest, would contribute to the collective disadvantage and eventually its own.

The American systems of national representation, separation of powers and federalism would furnish "Auxiliary precautions." National representation would enable better deliberation; the system of separation of powers would be an efficient division of labor and also improve general discussion. Madison made two arguments for maintaining a significant role for the states. The first was efficiency. Because people had different desires and tastes, it was important to allow the states basic governing authority, for they could respond to local interests. But Madison also urged that states exert a check on the federal government, allowing a vertical as well as horizontal system of checks and balances. In this way, the existence of states could help counteract the spirit of faction. But under the Founders' system, there was no question that in the end the national government, backed by the sovereignty of the people, would be supreme. Federalism was hardly a means of limiting the system of self-rule. It was part and parcel of the democratic faith of the early Americans. . . .

But Beer shows that the Framers cannot fairly be characterized as aristocratic enemies of popular rule. They insisted that sovereignty lay with the people, not with their representatives, and much of their thought was associated with this rejection of their monarchical heritage. Where they distrusted pure democracy, it was not because they sought to entrench class privilege or existing distributions of wealth, but because they wanted to ensure institutions that would benefit from the best kind of public deliberation, and to offer constraints against its absence. . . .

Beer also offers an important corrective to the view that the American founders were hostile to government. On the contrary, their Constitution was designed to enable public action. Thus the great sources of national power—commerce, taxation, spending for the general welfare—were intended to confer the kind of government authority necessary for a commercial republic. This was hardly the project of people who sought to stifle the activities of the new government. . . .

TOWARD CRITICAL THINKING

1. How and in what manner do the views of Montesquieu and Madison diverge about the nature and size of government? What are the pluses and minuses of the respective systems advocated by each writer?

2. According to Sunstein, which presidents pushed the boundaries of federalism to their own ends?

· *11* ·

Birthday Cake Federalism

AARON WILDAVSKY

Political scientist Martin Grodzins once characterized the American federal system as a "marble cake." Instead of each level of government—national, state, and local—having separate and distinct spheres of activity that could be characterized as akin to a "layer cake," he identified the system that had evolved as best likened to a "marble cake," in which functions were not discrete nor clearly defined. Aaron Wildavsky argues that by the 1980s, we had "fruitcake" federalism. In this kind of system, with so many layers and pressure points, political "plums" (benefits) could be had by all who understood the system. He also makes serious comments about the nature of the federal system and suggestions for reform that still are timely.

Individualism, diversity, variety in government. Pro-federalists, anti-federalists, and "picket fence" federalism. Revenue sharing. Rich states and poor states. The demarcation criterion. The fifty-first state.

Parallel play—room for states, room for national government, and room for them together—was once the neat theory of the American federal system. Under the prevailing image of the layer cake, the parts never overlapped except when constitutionally mandated. When it was observed that the parallel lines had really intermingled to become a marble instead of a layer cake, there was confusion but not consternation. As Daniel Elazar had demonstrated, cooperative federalism was the norm virtually from the outset; so there remained the good feeling that American pragmatism had apparently triumphed over arid theory. The question of what exactly to call this compound of national and state rules, was for a time, superseded by calling it good. So long as a few bands of dark were still visible against the light, there was sufficient resolution to say it was something. But as government grew from the mid-1960s, bands of marble collapsed every which way and became so crisscrossed that no one could say what was up or down or who was (simultaneously?) on top or bottom. Big government (large numbers of large programs taking a larger propor-

SOURCE: Aaron Wildavsky, "Birthday Cake Federalism," in *American Federalism: A New Partnership for the Republic,* Robert E. Hawkins (ed.) (New Brunswick, NJ: Transaction Books, 1982), pp. 181–190. Reprinted by permission of Transaction Books.

tion of national income) had made the division of powers between governments unrecognizable; it was hard to tell one level apart from another or (say, with the federal government's supporting local libraries) to discern any difference in principle between them.

◆ Fruitcake Federalism

What kind of federal cake is this? Apparently, the layer cake and the marble cake have been succeeded by the fruitcake. Dual federalism (the layer cake) and cooperative federalism (the marble cake) now give way to "fruitcake" federalism.

At [federal] budget time it is always Christmas. . . . There are plums to be had for the picking. The closer one approaches the brandy-soaked cake, the more intoxicated one becomes with the rising fumes. One is sober enough to pick out the goodies but too drunk to notice how much one is eating. What has happened to these fruits of government spending?

If Americans do not want to get stuck in the congealed mass of this fruitcake, they might try changing the cook, but in my opinion they would be better advised to change the ingredients of their federal system to find a more individualistic cake, favoring a diversity of governments and a variety of programs.

What kind of federal cake would that be? In "birthday cake federalism," mature men and women would be allowed to choose how many candles and calories fit their self-image. Birthday cakes are individualized. Each person chooses the one he wants. Those who overeat pay the penalty. In any case, they do not eat other people's cakes and others do not eat theirs; birthdays come at different times and are celebrated in different ways. I always though that was what federalism was supposed to be about—diversity, variety, and not a little competition.

What has happened to make the old-time glory of the American political system—its openness, its variety, its very unity in diversity—appear to be its principle defect?. . . It is well to remind ourselves of what the argument over federalism used to be about. The old argument was that federalism did not work well because it created numerous veto points that frustrated majority will: by the time the impetus for change gathered sufficient steam to mobilize support in all the necessary places, it had exhausted its reformist ardor. And even if there was policy, it had been so compromised in passage and so exhausted in administration that the confused child of implementation hardly resembled the sturdy parents of conception. The opposing position was that the modern anti-federalists mistook opportunities for obstacles. Their veto points, pro-federalists argued, were actually "multiple cracks" enhancing access to the political process. Federalism facilitated majority building out of minority interests. Federalism therefore meant more legislation, not less.

Who was right? Neither and both. There were more vetoes of proposals, but there was actually more legislation. Compromises cumulated almost always in the direction of larger size. The more big programs, it turned out, the greater the incoherence among them. Both sides had been arguing about the quantities of good legislation; both were swamped with quantities, simply.

The result is federal structure without federalism. The existence of federal structure enhances entrepreneurship in program development. Every officeholder and bureaucrat, wherever situated, is encouraged to catch up with and surpass every other. . . . Thus federalism as a doctrine for assigning functions to areal entities, or as a process of diversification through competition, goes by the boards. Competition for the same subsidies in substantive spheres of policy—"picket fence" federalism, as it has been called—increases uniformity. In this "mishmash" that I call "fruitcake federalism" (that is, being bogged down in governmental plums and puddings), federal structure serves to multiply the offices and opportunities for increasing the quantity but not the quality of public policy.

Slowly the suspicion dawns that the old divisions may not be the new ones. As the states, the cities, and the "feds" fight over policies and payments, the people observe that they all grow larger. Perhaps what they have in common as governments is more important than what separates them. Perhaps the proper division is citizens versus government or the public versus the private sector. The growth of governments rather than the growth of *which* government thus becomes a major public issue.

The first clue to the appearance of a fruitcake federalism is the difficulty everyone has in deciding whether states, localities, or the "feds" have gained or lost power vis-à-vis each other in the era of big government. All possible answers, it turns out, are true in regard to some policies at some times but not in regard to others at other times. Can the federal government do without the states or vice versa? Not really. Will states and localities refuse federal funds? Hardly likely. Will the federal government be able to cut the states out? No. . . .

My first thesis is that the size of all governments is more important than what they do. My second thesis is that citizens may be better served if we ask how to improve their choices, rather than worrying over which level of big government should monopolize a service. Students of federalism should look not only at the balance between levels of government but, more important today, at the relative proportions of the public and private sectors. If federalism is institutionalized competition among governments, increasing rather than limiting citizen choice among service providers is its contemporary key (Wildavsky 1980). . . . When the fruitcake gives way to the birthday cake designed for individual expression, when citizen choice characterizes federalism, the taste will differ state by state—which is as it should be if we want government to adjust to individual taste rather than for people to adjust to their government.

. . .

◆ The Two Virtues

The virtue of the central government is uniformity; its laws would be loathsome if they were to treat citizens differently depending on where they lived. The virtue of state governments is diversity; their laws would be procrustean if they repeated themselves regardless of locale. Stamping out carbon copies is something the center should do but states should not. What can we say about the conditions for these two virtues? Each one's maintaining its own style is a condition for attaining the virtue of the other. If states maintain diversity, this gives the center a stronger rationale for sticking to uniformity—its lack is being made up elsewhere. And as long as some things are done on a uniform basis, there is a stronger rationale for varying others.

Thus it is all right for the central government to limit expenditures, which facilitates a uniform rate of spending, but not for the states to do likewise as a class. For some states it is desirable to impose limits, but not for all; and even for those who do so, it is preferable that they choose different levels (higher and lower) and different modes (limits as proportions of national product or personal income, or as balanced budget requirements, etc.). By stressing diversity among states, lessons may be learned that would otherwise not be possible. By maintaining diversity, citizens may sort themselves so they live with the kind of government they want. . . .

Still, some states are able to spend more than others. Since some states have oil, gas, and coal that others lack, the resource-rich are going to be better off in many ways, among them the ability to collect taxes paid, in effect, by consumers in other states. Should that be considered a problem? Some people are born beautiful, others ugly—such are the breaks. Even so, states have alternatives other than holding out the tin cup to the federal government. Resource-poor states can acquire synthetic fuel or nuclear energy plants. Yet, it will be objected, these are dirty and may be dangerous. Does the equal protection clause protect each state against unpleasantness? The answer, of course, is no; but states can choose to be poor and pleasant and people can decide whether they want to live under such circumstances.

What would happen to poor people under regimes of stronger state competition? The news is good and bad. Under the good fairy, the poor go where the jobs are and those who cannot work go where states are best able to afford high levels of welfare. The system is self-regulating: the rich support the poor, as states choose to be richer with fewer environmental amenities or poor with a more pleasant physical environment, and people with low income are treated to what they really need most—money.

Now for the wicked fairy. The richer states may be more individualistic, in which case they may lower welfare. Poor people may be left in poor states. Should that happen, the federal government might pay poor states a subsidy for each person on welfare. Would people rather have jobs? Then there are states that provide work.

This vision of variety might not be so bad: the federal government learns to perform a narrower range of tasks better. States learn to live with widely varying styles of life. People vote with their feet for the kind of life they would like to live. In our time, perhaps that kind of active personal choice among life-styles may be as good as we can get from government.

◆ Distinguishing Federal from State Activities

Where is the philosopher's stone of federalism, the demarcation principle between central and state functions, that would rationalize a division of labor within the American federal system? The answer is: nowhere. Every effort to specify what is local and what is national, I believe, will founder on these facts of life: every national activity has its local aspects and every local activity a national perspective; any two incompatible objectives may be reconciled by a third to which they contribute, and any two that are complementary may be made contradictory in reference to their contributions to a third. It follows that no criteria of choice can be consistent in regard to all the legitimate political perspectives that may be brought to bear on them.*

The philosophical problem previews the political dilemma. Failure to specify a demarcation line suggests a lack of principle. Yet efforts to operate under such a criterion admit of so many exceptions that the cure is worse than the disease; government grows larger without any more rhyme or reason than before.

Consider the case of income security or family assistance or income maintenance, known in Reagan parlance as the "social safety net." Financed by the federal government, perhaps in the Friedmanite form of a negative income tax, a floor under income would be huge. Millions more

---

*The extensive and inconclusive literature on the idea of a demarcation separating science from nonscience should serve as a warning to enthusiasts.

people would participate than are presently on welfare. The pressure to push benefits up would be difficult to resist. Yet these modest amounts of money could hardly cover catastrophic illness or even the everyday costs of medical care. Fattening the floor to cover medical insurance, energy, food, or whatever else is deemed to be beyond the purchasing power of the individual would raise the program totals by billions, preempting the major tax base for federal use. Why begin "supply-side" federalism by increasing the federal share?

Any knowledgeable person can make a good (though not, of course, conclusive) case for federal assumption of a favored activity. The costs of medical care could be limited, for example, by exclusive federal financing, ruling out private or state and local activity. The reason is that a lump sum, by limiting inputs into the medical system, would more effectively ration resources. . . . The relative priorities of different programs are bound to cause continuous disagreement.

What, then, should be done if one desires a federal system that stresses variety, diversity, and competition? As usual, negative knowledge comes earlier than positive—big government is antithetical to federalism because it preempts resources for the national government and because it causes virtually every activity to mix the levels of government. Variety in programs suffers as the central controllers seek as much conformity as possible.

The point I wish to pursue about positive knowledge is that we do not need what we should not have. A cognitive approach through a formula for demarcation suggests that there is some general theory, known by some particular people, to which government activity should be subject. This idea should be rejected, for that would mean there must be activities not now ensconced at the federal level that should be there. Let us turn instead to setting up conditions for social interaction most likely to produce outcomes that can retrospectively be described as diverse, varied, and competitive—i.e., federal.

◆ The Federal Government as the Fifty-First State

The first thing is to reduce the federal tax take to a considerably lower proportion of national income. This reduction is permissive; it allows states room into which they can expand. (Putting tax reduction first, by the way, allows advocates of smaller government to gain control of the balanced budget issue; once taxes have been cut, the way to balance can only be through reduction of expenditure.) The second thing is to proportionately whittle down . . . block grants, and such. Current programs may be maintained but they need not be kept constant in purchasing power. The less the states are enticed into federal programs by the prospect of largesse, the more they think of what they can do with their own resources and the more varied their responses are likely to be.

The third thing is not to prejudge the issue; when you do not know what to do, why do anything? Let the states pick up what they wish; let the "feds" give up what they can. And may the best government win.

Is "interaction" a synonym for inactivity? Not necessarily. The federal government can act as the "fifty-first" state by encouraging variety through competition whenever it judges that another alternative ought to be offered to the people directly (such as competitive medical plans) or to the states (better service delivery).

TOWARD CRITICAL THINKING

1. Why does Wildavsky believe that the "size of all governments is more important than what they do?" How does that fact relate to the delivery of individual services?

2. If the virtue of state government is diversity, then how can individual rights be protected? In what areas could state diversity be considered a plus? A minus? How do Wildavsky's comments support the notion that the states provide the national government with laboratories for experiment?

· 12 ·

Constitutional Federalism
Displacing Places to Benefit Persons

JOHN KINCAID

No matter how Aaron Wildavsky or other writers characterize the federal system, it has changed over time. And from the earliest days of the Republic, the Supreme Court has played a key role in defining the relationship between the national government and the states. As John Kincaid points out, the Court's interpretation of various laws as well as of the U.S. Constitution has also altered basic ideas about what individuals could *expect* from the national government. And, says Kincaid, organized labor unions, which draw their membership *nationally,* have been at the forefront of litigation designed to nationalize federal protections for workers, a power originally considered to be an exclusive function of the states under the Tenth Amendment.

During the 1980s, federalism was significantly altered by a defining contest between persons and places over the nature of the federal union. . . .

The decisive action occurred in the 1980s, in part, because battle lines were drawn starkly. On one side, President Ronald Reagan and soon-to-be Chief Justice William H. Rehnquist, among others, adhered to the view of federalism expressed in Reagan's first inaugural address: "the Federal Government did not create the States; the States created the Federal Government." On the other side were adherents to the view expressed by Senator William H. Seward in 1850: "The States are not parties to the Constitution as States; it is the Constitution of the people of the United States.". . .

The debate became acrimonious in 1985 when U.S. Attorney General Edwin Meese III suggested to the American Bar Association that the Court had violated the "original intent" of the federal Constitution by selectively applying provisions of the U.S. Bill of Rights to the states via

SOURCE: John Kincaid, "Constitutional Federalism: Labor's Role in Displacing Places to Benefit Persons," *PS: Political Science & Politics* 26, no. 2 (June 1993): 172–177. Reprinted by permission.

the Fourteenth Amendment. This provoked an unusual public rebuke from Justices William J. Brennan, Jr., and John Paul Stevens.

✦ Displacing Places to Benefit Persons

The basis of federalism finally shifted, therefore, from places to persons. Federal policy making focused decidedly on individual rights and benefits under assumption of virtually plenary power vis-à-vis places; interest groups representing classes of persons across jurisdictions proliferated to secure federal rights and benefits, at times competing with state and local officials; and state and local governments were themselves defined as interest groups in policy making and as administrative agencies in policy implementation.

A major vehicle for the shift to persons has been the Fourteenth Amendment (1868), holding that no state shall "deprive any *person* of life, liberty, or property, without due process of law; nor deny to any *person* within its jurisdiction the equal protection of the laws." The Supreme Court was the first to use this vehicle after World War II to protect the rights of real persons, rather than corporate persons, against state action. In principle, the reach of the Fourteenth Amendment to persons could have been extensive, while its disturbance of state powers could have been limited; however, the Court set out to reform state and local institutions as well. Of the Court's extensive rights, jurisprudence, desegregation, and reapportionment were especially important for setting the constitutional as well as political stage for the emergence of persons over places in the federal system.

By striking down racial segregation in public schools (*Brown* v. *Board of Education,* 1954), the Court swung open the door to civic participation for persons excluded under state law, signaling that state and local governments must fairly include and represent all persons within their jurisdictions. . . .

In its reapportionment rulings (*Wesberry* v. *Sanders,* 1964; *Reynolds* v. *Sims,* 1964), the Court shifted the basis of representation in the U.S. House and state legislatures from place to persons by substituting its "one person, one vote" rule for the "one place, one legislative vote" rules used in many states. Implementation of these decisions undercut the political bases of rural bosses and fragmented the political bases of urban bosses who had defended state and local powers even while often supporting increased federal spending and economic regulation.

Thus, for federalism, the long-run import of these decisions lay in their political consequences for state-federal relations. In principle, the Court's institutional reform jurisprudence could have produced a "resurgence of the states" (Bowman and Kearney 1986) as stronger co-sovereigns; instead, it reduced the states to interest groups even while enhancing their ability to administer national policies and innovate in the absence of national policy.

... As the Court became more conservative after 1969, the states won more Fourteenth Amendment cases. In explicit federalism cases, however, the states did no better, and even did slightly worse in 1981–89 than in 1953–80 (Kearney and Sheenan 1992).

These outcomes reflected, in part, the reorientation of the political branches from places to persons, which enabled the Congress especially to surpass the Court in extending benefits to persons during the 1980s and, thereby, expand federal powers over state powers. . . .

One of the most telling measures of federal power is preemption because it actually displaces state law (Zimmerman 1991). Although Congress enacted approximately 123 statutes explicitly preempting state powers in 1933–69 compared to about 83 from 1789 through 1932, it enacted some 233 explicit preemptions in the short twenty-two-year period, 1970–1981—fully 53 percent of all preemptions enacted in 203 years (ACIR 1992).

... [Moreover], the Supreme Court struck down as unconstitutional 525 state laws and local ordinances in 1789–1932 (3.6 per year), 330 in 1933–69 (9.2 per year), and 361 in 1970–90 (17.2 per year). The number of acts of Congress held unconstitutional were 58 in 1789–1932 (0.4 per year), 40 in 1933–69 (1.1 per year), and 37 in 1970–90 (1.8 per year) (Congressional Research Service, 1987). Conditions attached to grants-in-aid, direct federal regulation (e.g., mandates) of state and local governments, and federal court orders superintending state and local institutions . . . also increased significantly since the late 1960s (ACIR 1993; Kincaid 1993). By these measures, federal encroachments on state powers since 1969 have far exceeded those of the New Deal-to-Great Society era, and flowed well beyond commerce to encompass direct interests of persons.

Organized labor was one of the first major interests representing a class of persons across jurisdictions to gain significant influence on federal policy making in this century. . . .

... Its bases were cities and mining communities. . . . Cities were under-represented in most legislatures; labor had socialist leanings; and many political bosses were hostile to unions. . . . Labor was . . . not seeking direct subsidies, but rather protections—especially for wage, hour, health, and collective bargaining rights—against employers regulated by state and local governments. Consequently, . . . federal attention to labor entailed potential clashes with state Tenth Amendment interests. . . .

Congress, however, softened the clash with state powers. The FLSA [(Federal Fair Labor Standards Act)], like the National Labor Relations

Act of 1935, barred direct federal regulation of the states. Happily for state and local political bosses, the FLSA did not cover their government workers. . . .

◆ Fair Labor vs. Urban Fiscal Stress

In 1974, Congress extended the FLSA's wage-and-hour rules to nearly all employees of state and local governments. The National League of Cities—joined by the National Governors' Conference, nineteen states, and four cities—challenged the extension.

The Supreme Court, by a 5–4 vote, . . . held that the 1974 FLSA amendments represented an assertion of power which, unchecked, would permit the federal government to "devour the essentials of state sovereignty" (*National League of Cities* v. *Usery, [NLC]* 1976) . . .

◆ 1985 Was *1984* for the States

For state powers, George Orwell missed the arrival of Big Brother by one year. Events culminated in 1985 to effect a substantial, perhaps irrevocable, change in the federal system.

By the late 1970s, private-sector unions were in steep decline, and public-sector unions were losing members. In the early 1980s, President Reagan fired striking air-traffic controllers, and the recession further eroded union membership. Reagan also advocated a "new federalism,". . . posed federalism as a Tenth Amendment issue, and sought to disentangle federal-state relation in an almost dual federalist fashion. . . . With a Republican majority in the Senate in 1981–1986, he achieved some of his objectives.

In 1979, however, the U.S. Department of Labor had issued an opinion that *NLC* did not bar application of the FLSA's wage-and-hour rules to employees of the San Antonio Metropolitan Transit Authority. On appeal, in 1985, the Supreme Court, in another 5–4 decision (*Garcia*), reversed *NLC* and sustained the FLSA extension, holding that the "sovereign interests" of the states "are more properly protected by procedural safeguards inherent in the structure of the federal system than by judicially created limitations on federal power." In *South Carolina* v. *Baker* (1988), the Court made it even more clear that the states must look to the national political process, not to judicial enforcement of the Tenth Amendment, to protect their interests. . . .

In 1985, Congress enacted the National Minimum Drinking Age Act. Reagan, unable to resist the popular appeal of Mothers Against Drunk Drivers, signed the law, which required reductions in federal highway funds to states failing to raise to twenty-one the legal age for purchasing alcoholic beverages. In 1987, the Court, in a decision (*South Dakota* v.

Dole) possibly more significant than *Garcia,* held that even though Congress lacks authority to regulate drinking ages, it can attach an age requirement to a grant program because state participation in aid programs is voluntary. Given the virtual political and fiscal impossibility of withdrawing from such programs as highway aid and Medicaid, the decision greatly expanded Congress's ability to reach core state powers through its spending power. . . .

◆ Conclusion

The shift of federalism from places to persons during the 1980s seems to signal an end to the type of cooperative federalism, characterized by place-benefitting aid and place-sensitive legislation, that prevailed from the New Deal to the Great Society. . . .

The shift from places to person has also produced a certain revival of independent state powers: "the new judicial federalism" (Kincaid 1988). As the U.S. Supreme Count turned conservative, state courts began in the 1970s to extend greater rights to persons under state declarations of rights than the federal Court recognizes under the U.S. Bill of Rights. If based on "independent and adequate" state constitutional grounds, such decisions are immune from Supreme Court review. Similarly, in many areas of regulation (e.g., environmental protection), states can exceed federal standards. These powers, however, are exercised above minimal national standards, which can, under current doctrine, be made ever more maximal by the federal courts and Congress.

REFERENCES

Bowman, Ann O'M. and Richard Kearney. 1986. *The Resurgence of the States.* Englewood Cliffs, NJ: Prentice-Hall.

Brown v. *Board of Education of Topeka,* 347 U.S. 483 (1954).

Congressional Research Service. 1987. *The Constitution: Analysis and Interpretation.* Washington, DC: U.S. Government Printing Office.

FERC v. *Mississippi,* 456 U.S. 742 (1982).

Garcia v. *San Antonio Metropolitan Transit Authority,* 469 U.S. 528 (1985).

Kearney, Richard C. and Reginold S. Sheehan. 1992. "Supreme Court Decision Making: The Impact of Court Composition on State and Local Government Litigation." *Journal of Politics* 54 (November): 1008–25.

Kincaid, John. 1988. "State Court Protections of Individual Rights Under State Constitutions: The New Judicial Federalism." *Journal of State Government* 61 (Sept./Oct.): 163–69.

Kincaid, John. 1993. "From Cooperation to Coercion in American Federalism: Housing, Fragmentation, and Preemption, 1789–1992." *Journal of Law and Politics* 9 (Winter): 333–430.

National League of Cities v. *Usery,* 426 U.S. 833 (1976).

Reynolds v. *Sims,* 377 U.S. 533 (1964).

South Carolina v. *Baker,* 485 U.S. 505 (1988).

South Dakota v. *Dole,* 483 U.S. 203 (1987).

U.S. Advisory Commission on Intergovernmental Relations (ACIR). 1992a. *Federal Statutory Preemption of State and Local Authority.* Washington, DC: ACIR.

U.S. Advisory Commission on Intergovernmental Relations. 1993. *Federal Regulation of State and Local Governments: The Mixed Record of the 1980s.* Washington, DC: ACIR.

Wesberry v. *Sanders,* 376 U.S. 1 (1964).

Zimmerman, Joseph F. 1991. *Federal Preemption: The Silent Revolution.* Ames: Iowa State University Press.

TOWARD CRITICAL THINKING

1. What factors led to the Supreme Court's taking a greater interest in the individual's place in the federal system? What is the long-term consequence of this phenomenon for federal-state relationships?

2. In *Gibbons* v. *Ogden* (1824) the Supreme Court broadly interpreted the commerce clause to allow Congress wide leeway to regulate business matters. What role should the Court have in defining the nature of the federal system? Will Clinton appointees change the direction of the Court toward federal/state relations?

· *13* ·

Webster *v.* Reproductive Health Services
492 U.S. 490 (1989)

In 1973 in *Roe* v. *Wade,*[*] the United States Supreme Court interpreted the U.S. Constitution as protecting a woman's right to terminate her pregnancy. Over the years, various states attempted to limit the scope of that decision by enacting laws to restrict abortion rights. As more and more conservative Justices were added to the Supreme Court by Republican presidents Ronald Reagan and George Bush, many people believed that Roe might be overturned.

Webster involved a challenge to a Pennsylvania statute that included four contested sections: (1) a preamble, which declared that the "life of each human being begins at conception"; (2) a prohibition on the use of public facilities or employees to perform abortions; (3) a ban on public funding of abortion counseling; and (4) required that a doctor, prior to performing an abortion on a woman whom he or she believes to be twenty or more weeks pregnant, ascertain whether the fetus is "viable" by performing such examinations and tests as are necessary to determine the gestational age, weight, and lung maturity of the fetus.

Several health care professionals providing abortion services brought suit against the Attorney General of the State of Missouri challenging the constitutionality of the Missouri statute. A federal district court struck down each of these provisions as unconstitutional. This judgment was subsequently affirmed by a federal appeals court on the grounds that these regulations were incompatible with the Supreme Court's ruling in *Roe* v. *Wade*. *Roe* essentially guaranteed a woman's right to an abortion free from state interference prior to fetal viability, which the Court decided occurred around a woman's seventh month of pregnancy. The Attorney General of Missouri appealed the state's loss to the U.S. Supreme Court. The Court was badly divided in *Webster,* with several justices announcing their belief that *Roe* v. *Wade* should be overruled. As to the contested preamble, the Court declined to rule since it had not been enforced by the state. The Court's conclusions about the other sections of the Missouri law are set out below.

Opinion: Chief Justice Rehnquist
Vote: 5 to 4

---

[*]410 U.S. 113 (1973).

. . . Section 188.210 provides that "[i]t shall be unlawful for any public employee within the scope of his employment to perform or assist an abortion, not necessary to save the life of the mother," while Section 188.215 makes it "unlawful for any public facility to be used for the purpose of performing or assisting an abortion not necessary to save the life of the mother." The Court of Appeals held that these provisions contravened this Court's abortion decisions. . . . We take a contrary view.

As we said earlier . . . "our cases have recognized that the Due Process Clauses generally confer no affirmative right to governmental aid, even where such aid may be necessary to secure life, liberty, or property interests of which the government itself may not deprive the individual." In *Maher* v. *Roe,* the Court upheld a Connecticut welfare regulation under which Medicaid recipients received payments for medical services related to childbirth, but not for nontherapeutic abortions. The Court rejected the claim that this unequal subsidization of childbirth and abortion was impermissible under *Roe* v. *Wade.*

. . . As in those cases, the State's decision here to use public facilities and staff to encourage childbirth over abortion "places no governmental obstacle in the path of a woman who chooses to terminate her pregnancy." . . . Missouri's refusal to allow public employees to perform abortions in public hospitals leaves a pregnant woman with the same choices as if the State had not chosen to operate any public hospitals at all.

. . . Thus we uphold the Act's restrictions on the use of public employees and facilities for the performance or assistance of nontherapeutic abortions.

The Missouri Act contains three provisions relating to "Encouraging or counseling a woman to have an abortion not necessary to save her life." Section 188.205 states that no public funds can be used for this purpose; Section 188.210 states that public employees cannot, within the scope of their employment engage in such speech; and Section 188.215 forbids such speech in public facilities. The Court of Appeals . . . held that all three of these provisions were unconstitutionally vague, and that "the ban on using public funds, employees, and facilities to encourage or counsel a woman to have an abortion is an unacceptable infringement of the woman's Fourteenth Amendment right to choose an abortion after receiving medical information necessary to exercise the right knowingly and intelligently."

Missouri has chosen only to appeal the Court of Appeals' invalidation of the public funding provision, Section 188.205. A threshold question is whether this provision reaches primary conduct, or whether it is simply an instruction to the State's fiscal officers not to allocate funds for abortion counseling. We accept, for purposes of decision, the State's claim that Section 188.205 "is not directed at the conduct of any physician or health care provider, private or public," but "is directed solely at those persons responsible for expending public funds."

Appellees contend that they are not "adversely" affected under the State's interpretation of Section 188.205, and therefore that there is no longer a case or controversy before us on this question. We accordingly direct the Court of Appeals to vacate the judgment of the District Court with instructions to dismiss the relevant part of the complaint.

Section 188.029 of the Missouri Act provides:

"Before a physician performs an abortion on a woman he has reason to believe is carrying an unborn child of twenty or more weeks gestational age, the physician shall first determine if the unborn child is viable by using and exercising that degree of care, skill, and proficiency commonly exercised by the ordinarily skillful, careful, and prudent physician engaged in similar practice under the same or similar conditions. In making this determination of viability, the physician shall perform or cause to be performed such medical examinations and tests as are necessary to make a finding of the gestational age, weight, and lung maturity of the unborn child and shall enter such findings and determination of viability in the medical record of the mother."

. . . The viability testing provision of the Missouri Act is concerned with promoting the State's interest in potential human life rather than in maternal health. Section 188.029 creates what is essentially a presumption of viability at twenty weeks, which the physician must rebut with tests indicating that the fetus is not viable prior to performing an abortion. It also directs the physician's determination as to viability by specifying consideration, if feasible, of gestational age, fetal weight, and lung capacity.

. . . In *Roe* v. *Wade,* the Court recognized that the State has "important and legitimate" interests in protecting maternal health and in the potentiality of human life. During the second trimester, the State "may, if it chooses, regulate the abortion procedure in ways that are reasonably related to maternal health." After viability, when the State's interest in potential human life was held to become compelling, the State "may, if it chooses, regulate, and even proscribe, abortion except where it is necessary, in appropriate medical judgment, for the preservation of the life or health of the mother."

. . . *Stare decisis* is a cornerstone of our legal system, but it has less power in constitutional cases, where, save for constitutional amendments, this Court is the only body able to make the needed changes. We have not refrained from reconsideration of a prior construction of the Constitution that has proved "unsound in principle and unworkable in practice." *Garcia* v. *San Antonio Metropolitan Transit Authority.* We think the *Roe* trimester framework falls into that category.

. . . We do not see why the State's interest in protecting potential human life should come into existence only at the point of viability, and that there should therefore be a rigid line allowing state regulation after viability but protecting potential human life should come into existence only at the point of viability, and that there should therefore be a rigid line allowing state regulation after viability but prohibiting it before . . .

. . . The tests that Section 188.029 requires the physician to perform are designed to determine viability. The State here has chosen viability as the point at which its interest in potential human life must be safeguarded . . . It is true that the tests in question increase the expense of abortion, and regulate the discretion of the physician in determining the viability of the fetus. Since the tests will undoubtedly show in many cases that the fetus is not viable, the tests will have been performed for what were in fact second-trimester abortions. But we are satisfied that the requirement of these tests permissibly furthers the State's interest in protecting potential human life, and we therefore believe Section 188.029 to be constitutional.

TOWARD CRITICAL THINKING

1. What justification did Chief Justice Rehnquist offer to uphold the constitutionality of the Missouri regulations? Why did this Court opt to give states greater leeway in setting the rights of individuals and the unborn?

2. *Webster's* allowance of a variety of state abortion restrictions was sometimes viewed by many as a direct invitation to the states to begin to restrict access to abortion. All fifty states considered, and many adopted, some form of new abortion laws. Did the Framers intend for the Supreme Court to suggest to the states that they legislate in certain areas?

THINKING ABOUT FEDERALISM

1. In Reading 11, Aaron Wildavsky appears to celebrate differences among states. Is it reasonable in a federal system to have diverse laws concerning drunk driving, the death penalty, labor laws, or reproductive rights?

2. Are there any rights that are particularly well suited for state versus national government protections or enforcement?

3. Given the so-called three co-equal branches of government created by the Framers, is it appropriate for the Supreme Court to play such an important role in defining the federal system?

CHAPTER 4

◆ ◆ ◆

Civil Liberties

Many of the people in attendance at the Constitutional Convention in Philadelphia saw no need for a Bill of Rights or for the national government to guarantee certain liberties. Those fundamental liberties, said staunch Federalist Alexander Hamilton in *Federalist No. 84,* (Reading 14), were well protected by state constitutions. Moreover, any attempt by the Framers to enumerate specific rights would undoubtedly result in certain rights being left out. Better not to have an all-inclusive list than to allow some people to speculate that some liberties were not retained by the people.

Even though the Constitution was adopted by the states without a Bill of Rights, the sentiments of Anti-Federalists such as Samuel Bryan were uppermost in the minds of the men elected to the First Congress. As noted in Reading 15, fears that the national government would fail to safeguard basic civil liberties led to the drafting of a Bill of Rights to add to the new Constitution.

James Madison, the architect of the Bill of Rights, originally viewed their writing as "a nauseous project." [*] As highlighted in Table 4-1 on page 76, the various rights and liberties it guaranteed, however, continue to shape Americans' ideas about the proper role and scope of government. Like John Locke, most citizens recognize that some rights must be sacrificed for the sake of an orderly society. The Bill of Rights, however, contains the basic core of liberties cherished by most Americans.

Most Americans probably first think of the guarantees contained in the First Amendment when they think about the Bill of Rights. Even the U.S. Supreme Court has found that those rights are so fundamental and cherished that they must be accorded the highest level of protection from unwarranted governmental restriction. But as originally written, the first ten Amendments were but guarantees from the actions of the national government. As pointed out by Fred W. Friendly and Martha J. H. Elliot in "Seventeen Words: The Quiet Revolution of the Fourteenth Amendment" (Reading 16), after ratification of the Fourteenth Amendment in 1866, the Supreme Court gradually moved to make most of the protections contained in the Bill of Rights applicable to the states. Through this

---

[*] Quoted in Jack N. Rakove, "Madison Won Passage of the Bill of Rights But Remained a Skeptic," *Public Affairs Report* (March 1991), p. 6.

process of selective incorporation, the states, too, must take special pains to guarantee the liberties contained in the Bill of Rights to their citizens.

Historically, most cases that have come to the U.S. Supreme Court alleging the denial of liberties contained in the Bill of Rights have centered on the several protections contained in the First Amendment or the procedural protections guaranteed to criminal defendants in the Fourth, Fifth, Sixth, or Eighth Amendments. As illustrated in *Lee* v. *Weisman* (1992) and *Church of the Lukumi Babalu Aye* v. *City of Hialeah* (1993) (Readings 17a and 17b), questions surrounding the scope of the First Amendment's free exercise and establishment clauses continue today. Just how far governments can go to accommodate diverse religious beliefs without penalizing citizens for their beliefs or practices are issues that the U.S. Supreme Court is called on to answer every term.

The First Amendment also guarantees freedom of speech and of the press. Since the early years of the United States, both the national and state governments have often run afoul of these guarantees. The Alien and Sedition Acts, for example, were enacted by Congress in 1798 to outlaw political criticism. Although their constitutionality was never addressed by the Supreme Court because they were quickly repealed, in all likelihood, they would have been ruled unconstitutional.

Throughout history the Supreme Court and society at large have grappled also with a variety of thorny, free-speech issues. Although Amendment I of the Bill of Rights of the U.S. Constitution guarantees freedom of speech, that freedom is not absolute. In *R.A.V.* v. *City of St. Paul* (Reading 18a) and Paul McMasters's "Free Speech versus Civil Discourse: Where Do We Go From Here?" (Reading 18b) two similar speech issues are presented. In *R.A.V.,* the U.S. Supreme Court ruled on the constitutionality of a city ordinance that prohibited the display of symbols designed to anger or alarm others based on their race, color, creed, religion or gender. McMasters discusses the propriety of college speech codes, many of which were enacted in the late 1980s as part of what some people term the "politically correct" or "PC" movement. Through 1994, the constitutionality of these codes had yet to be addressed by the U.S. Supreme Court.

Other amendments found in the Bill of Rights also give rise to important civil liberties questions. Many of them even involve life or death issues. The cases presented here in Readings 19a and 19b—*Gideon* v. *Wainwright* (1963) and *McCleskey* v. *Kemp* (1987)—represent very different types of issues decided by very different Supreme Courts. The earlier Warren Court (1953–1969) was much more liberal than the current Rehnquist Court (1986–   ),[*] and the basic philosophies of each Court regarding the civil liberties protections due convicted criminals are strikingly illustrated by these rulings.

---

[*] Courts are known by the name of the Chief Justice who presides over them.

Federalist No. 84

ALEXANDER HAMILTON

Much of the debate surrounding ratification of the U.S. Constitution concerned the fears of many citizens not only that the proposed new form of government—a federal system—would place too much power in the hands of the national government at the expense of the states, but also that a powerful national government would rob the citizenry of numerous fundamental liberties not specifically guaranteed in the new Constitution. In *Federalist No. 84,* Alexander Hamilton tries to quell those fears by underscoring that the language of the Constitution itself guarantees to "THE PEOPLE" the rights not set out in the document itself. Moreover, argues Hamilton, the specific enumeration of rights in a Constitution is "not only unnecessary," but "dangerous."

To the People of the State of New York.

The most considerable of the remaining objections is that the plan of the convention contains no bill of rights. . . .

. . . Here, in strictness, the people surrender nothing; and as they retain every thing they have no need of particular reservation. "WE THE PEOPLE of the United States, to secure the blessings of liberty to ourselves and our posterity, do *ordain* and *establish* this Constitution for the united States of America" [sic]. Here is a better recognition of popular rights than volumes of those aphorisms which make the principal figure in several of our State bills of rights, and which would sound much better in a treatise of ethics than in a constitution of government.

But a minute detail of particular rights is certainly far less applicable to a Constitution like that under consideration, which is merely intended to regulate the general political interests of the nations, than to a constitution which has the regulation of every species of personal and private concerns. . . .

I go further, and affirm that bills of rights, in the sense and to the extent in which they are contended for, are not only unnecessary in the proposed Constitution, but would even be dangerous. They would contain various exceptions to powers not granted; and, on this very account, would afford a colorable pretext to claim more than were granted. For why declare that things shall not be done which there is no power to do? Why, for instance, should it be said that the liberty of the press shall not be restrained, when no power is given by which restrictions may be imposed? I will not contend that such a provision would confer a regulating power; but it is evident that it would furnish, to men disposed to usurp, a plausible pretense for claiming that power. They might urge with a semblance of reason, that the Constitution ought not to be charged with the absurdity of providing against the abuse of an authority which was not given, and that the provision against restraining the liberty of the press afforded a clear implication, that a power to prescribe proper regulations concerning it was intended to be vested in the national government. This may serve as a specimen of the numerous handles which would be given to the doctrine of constructive powers by the indulgence of an injudicious zeal for bills of rights. . . .

There remains but one other view of this matter to conclude the point. The truth is, after all the declamations we have heard, that the Constitution is itself, in every rational sense and to every useful purpose, A BILL OF RIGHTS. The several bills of rights in great Britain form its Constitution, and conversely the constitution of each State is its bill of rights. And the proposed Constitution, if adopted, will be the the bill of rights of the Union. Is it one object of a bill of rights to declare and specify the political privileges of the citizens in the structure and administration of the government? This is done in the most ample and precise manner in the plan of the convention; comprehending various precautions for the public security, which are not to be found in any of the State constitutions. Is another object of a bill of rights to define certain immunities and modes of proceeding, which are relative to personal and private concerns? This we have seen has also been attended to, in a variety of cases, in the same plan. Adverting therefore to the substantial meaning of a bill of rights, it is absurd to allege that it is not to be found in the work of the convention. It may be said that it does not go far enough, though it will not be easy to make this appear; but it can with no propriety be contended that there is no such thing. It certainly must be immaterial what mode is observed as to the order of declaring the rights of the citizens, if they are to be found in any part of the instrument which establishes the government. And hence it must be apparent that much of what has been said on this subject rests merely on verbal and nominal distinctions, entirely foreign from the substance of the thing.

Another objection which has been made, and which, from the frequency of its repetition, it is to be presumed is relied on, is of this nature: "It is improper . . . to confer such large powers, as are proposed, upon the national government; because the seat of that government must of necessity be too remote from many of the States to admit of a proper knowledge on the part of the constituent, of the conduct of the representative body." This argument, if it proves anything, proves that there ought to be no general government whatever. . . . But there are satisfactory reasons to show that the objection is in reality not well founded.

TOWARD CRITICAL THINKING

1. Given that ratification without a Bill of Rights at times appeared in jeopardy, why do you think that Hamilton and other Federalists remained so adamantly opposed to their inclusion in the original document? Why did he think their inclusion was dangerous?

2. Hamilton strongly believed that a Bill of Rights was unnecessary because the enumeration of some rights and liberties would in all likelihood mean that some important rights were omitted. As you look at Table 4-1 on page 76, can you think of any important rights not mentioned? What about the right to privacy, which has come to be the constitutional foundation for the right to abortion? (See Reading 13, *Webster* v. *Reproductive Health Services*).

· *15* ·

Centinel, *No. 1*

SAMUEL BRYAN

Taking strong exception to Hamilton's admonitions, Samuel Bryan and other Anti-Federalists argued vehemently for inclusion of a Bill of Rights before adoption of the new Constitution. Anti-Federalists were very concerned that the new system of checks and balances devised by the Framers would prove inadequate to protect individuals and individual liberties from the tyranny of a strong national government. In this letter, widely reprinted in newspapers and flyers at the time, Bryan praises the virtues of a simple governmental structure, one closer to the people. Any other form of government, says Bryan, is likely to overlook such basic liberties as freedom of the press, trial by jury in civil cases, and essential basic "personal rights" already included in many state constitutions.

I ✦

Friends, Countrymen and Fellow Citizens,

. . . Mr. Adams' *sine qua non* of a good government is three balancing powers, whose repelling qualities are to produce an equilibrium of interests, and thereby promote the happiness of the whole community. He asserts that the administrators of every government, will ever be actuated by views of private interest and ambition, to the prejudice of the public good; that therefore the only effectual method to secure the rights of the people and promote their welfare, is to create an opposition of interests between the members of two distinct bodies, in the exercise of the powers of government, and balanced by those of a third. This hypothesis supposes human wisdom competent to the task of instituting three co-equal orders in government, and a corresponding weight in the community to enable them respectively to exercise their several parts, and whose views and interests should be so distinct as to prevent a coalition of any two of them for the destruction of the third. . . .

. . . The highest responsibility is to be attained, in a simple structure of government, for the great body of the people never steadily attend to

---

SOURCE: Samuel Bryan, "Centinel," no. 1 (October 5, 1787) in *The Anti-Federalist Papers and the Constitutional Convention Debates* (New York: New American Library, 1986), pp. 227–237.

the operations of government, and for want of due information are liable to be imposed on—If you complicate the plan by various orders, the people will be perplexed and divided in their sentiments about the source of abuses or misconduct, some will impute it to the senate, others to the house of representatives, and so on, that the interposition of the people may be rendered imperfect or perhaps wholly abortive. . . . This tie of responsibility will obviate all the dangers apprehended from a single legislature, and will the best secure the rights of the people. . . .

If one general government could be instituted and maintained on principles of freedom, it would not be so competent to attend to the various local concerns and wants, of every particular district, as well as the peculiar governments, who are nearer the scene, and possessed of superior means of information; besides, if the business of the *whole* union is to be managed by one government, there would not be time. Do we not already see, that the inhabitants in a number of larger states, who are remote from the seat of government, are loudly complaining of the inconveniences and disadvantages they are subjected to on this account, and that, to enjoy the comforts of local government, they are separating into smaller divisions. . . .

From this investigation into the organization of this government, it appears that it is devoid of all responsibility or accountability to the great body of the people, and that so far from being a regular balanced government, it would be in practice a *permanent* ARISTOCRACY.

The framers of it, actuated by the true spirit of such a government, which ever abominates and suppresses all free enquiry and discussion, have made no provision for the *liberty of the press,* that grand *palladium of freedom,* and *scourge of tyrants;* but observed a total silence on that head. It is the opinion of some great writers, that if the liberty of the press, by an institution of religion, or otherwise, could be rendered *sacred,* even in *Turkey,* that despotism would fly before it. And it is worthy of remark, that there is no declaration of personal rights, premised in most free constitutions; and that trial by *jury* in *civil* cases is taken away; for what other construction can be put on the following, viz. Article III. Sect. 2d. "In all cases affecting ambassadors, other public ministers and consuls, and those in which a State shall be party, the Supreme Court shall have *original* jurisdiction. In all the other cases above mentioned, the Supreme Court shall have *appellate* jurisdiction, both as to *law and fact?*" It would be a novelty in jurisprudence, as well as evidently improper to allow an appeal from the verdict of a jury, on the matter of fact; therefore, it implies and allows of a dismission of the jury in civil cases, and especially when it is considered, that jury trial in criminal cases is expressly stipulated for, but not in civil cases.

But our situation is represented to be so *critically* dreadful, that, however reprehensible and exceptionable the proposed plan of government may be, there is no alternative, between the adoption of it and absolute ruin.—My fellow citizens, things are not at that crisis, it is the argument of tyrants; the present distracted state of Europe secures us from injury on that quarter, and as to domestic dissensions, we have not so much to fear from them, as to precipitate us into this form of government, without it is a safe and proper one. For remember, of all *possible* evils, that of *despotism* is the *worst* and the most to be *dreaded.*

TOWARD CRITICAL THINKING

1. If fundamental rights were already secured by most state constitutions, why were they such an important issue for Anti-Federalists?

2. Why did the Anti-Federalists fear the tyranny of a strong central government so much? Did all of the liberties specifically noted by Bryan ultimately find their way into the Bill of Rights?

TABLE 4-1
The Bill of Rights

First Amendment	Freedom of religion, speech, press, and assembly
Second Amendment	The right to bear arms
Third Amendment	Prohibition against quartering of troops in private homes
Fourth Amendment	Prohibition against unreasonable searches and seizures
Fifth Amendment	Rights guaranteed to the accused: requirement for grand jury indictment; protections against double jeopardy, self-incrimination; guarantee of due process
Sixth Amendment	Right to a speedy and public trial before an impartial jury, to cross-examine witnesses, and to have counsel present
Seventh Amendment	Right to trial by jury in civil suits
Eighth Amendment	Prohibition against excessive bail and fines, and cruel and unusual punishments
Ninth Amendment	Rights not listed in the Constitution retained by the people
Tenth Amendment	States or people reserve those powers not denied to them by the Constitution or delegated to the national government

· *16* ·

Seventeen Words
The Quiet Revolution of the Fourteenth Amendment

FRED W. FRIENDLY and MARTHA J. H. ELLIOT

The Constitution was adopted without a Bill of Rights. But one of the first actions of the First Congress was passage of the Bill of Rights, which, in turn, was quickly ratified by the states. The Bill of Rights was a directive to the national government—not to the states—to protect a variety of liberties. The question of whether the Bill of Rights applied to the states did not even arise until forty-four years after they had been added to the U.S. Constitution. In *Barron* v. *Baltimore* (1833),[*] however, the U.S. Supreme Court definitively concluded that the first ten amendments to the Constitution constrained *only* the national government. Thus, individuals aggrieved by state actions must look to state constitutions for protections of their civil and political liberties.

Ratification of the Fourteenth Amendment in 1866 signalled the beginning of the end of that view. As Friendly and Elliot discuss, over the years the Supreme Court moved to apply various sections of the Bill of Rights to the states through language in that amendment that bars any state from depriving *"any person of life, liberty, or property without the due process of law."* This incorporation of some of the guarantees in the Bill of Rights into the protections of what is called the due process clause of the Fourteenth Amendment has been gradual. Nevertheless, it has fundamentally altered the balance of power between the national and state governments and at the same time expanded the scope of civil liberties constitutionally protected from governmental infringement.

. . . If *Barron* were still the ruling opinion, then the individual states might be free to censor newspapers or inflict cruel and unusual punishments or deny a person the right to a jury trial.[1] Not only is this not the case, but the Supreme Court today spends more than half its time wrestling with questions related to the fundamental liberties guaranteed by the

SOURCE: Fred W. Friendly and Martha J. H. Eliot, *The Constitution: That Delicate Balance* (New York: McGraw-Hill, Inc., 1984), pp. 17–29. Reproduced with permission of McGraw-Hill.

[*] 7 Pet. (32 U.S.) 243 (1833).

[1] Of course, some state constitutions also prohibit these encroachments of liberty. However, under *Barron,* if a state constitution did not guarantee these protections, the federal government was powerless to enforce them.

Bill of Rights. How, then, did the situation change so dramatically? The answer is a complicated combination of the Civil War, the Fourteenth Amendment, and the Supreme Court itself. . . .

The Fourteenth Amendment was a direct result of the Civil War, a war many statesmen had tried to avoid. . . .

When the military battles ended in 1865, the political battles continued in Congress. . . .

. . . What emerged from this effort was the Fourteenth Amendment of 1866, which stated that "All persons born or naturalized in the United States, and subject to the jurisdiction thereof, are citizens of the United States and of the State wherein they reside." The part of the Amendment that would eventually lead to the overturning of *Barron* was at the end of Section 1:

> No State shall make or enforce any law which shall abridge the privi-leges or immunities of citizens of the United States; *nor shall any State deprive any person of life, liberty, or property, without due process of law;* nor deny to any person within its jurisdiction the equal protection of the laws. (Emphasis added.)

It is impossible now to look back and conclusively prove what exactly the framers of the Fourteenth Amendment had in mind when they those words. What did they mean by "privileges or immunities" or "due process of law" or "equal protection"? Twentieth-century legal scholars and historians have debated the intention of the authors, of the Congress, and of the states that eventually ratified the measure. . . .

Whatever their intent, the framers of the amendment could not have foreseen the impact that those seventeen words of the due process clause would have on the Bill of Rights and the future balance of power between the federal and state governments. It was as if the Congress had held a second constitutional convention, and created a federal government of vastly expanded proportions. The concern of the framers in 1787 had been to protect the people and the states from intrusion by the central government, and the Bill of Rights had been drafted to insure protection of those fundamental liberties. The Fourteenth Amendment and its later interpretation by the Supreme Court changed that balance; now the federal government—and especially the judiciary—would protect the people from arbitrary action by state governments. It was the beginning of a new era in constitutional development, in which the federal government would play a much larger role. . . .

◆ Giving Meaning to the Fourteenth Amendment

In 1871, three years after the Fourteenth Amendment was ratified, Congressman Bingham, its primary architect, had an opportunity to explain what the amendment's framers had intended. In a debate on a bill designed to enforce the amendment, Bingham attempted to convince his fellow congressmen that the amendment had been designed to "vest in Congress a power to protect the rights of citizens against the States, and individuals in States, never before granted." Bingham said that he had written the first section with the counsel of John Marshall "who, though departed this life still lives among us in his immortal spirit, and still speaks to us from the reports of the highest judicial tribunal on earth." He explained that in February of 1866 he had reread Marshall's decision in *Barron* and "apprehended as I never did before certain words in the opinion." Bingham told his colleagues that Marshall had been powerless to enforce the Bill of Rights in the state of Maryland. As Marshall had said, if the framers of the Bill of Rights "intended them to be limitations on the State governments, they would have . . . expressed that intention." In other words, since the Bill of Rights amendments did not specify that their guarantees of rights applied against the states, Marshall felt he could not read that interpretation into them.

Bingham explained that he considered that problem seriously when writing the language of the Fourteenth Amendment. He wanted to make sure that his intention to grant those protections against the states was absolutely clear. Although he did not mention the due process clause in his oration to his colleagues, Bingham did assert that the privileges and immunities of a citizen were defined in the first eight amendments.[2] He had, he claimed, tried to give the Supreme Court the power it didn't have at the time of *Barron:* the power to apply the Bill of Rights to the states.

Whatever Bingham had intended when he drafted the amendment, his explanation was planting a new idea—that the Constitution as now amended went beyond setting up the federal government and protecting citizens from the potential abuses of the central government. It was the beginning of an era in which, ever so slowly, the federal government would begin scrutinizing the activities of state governments—although initially in areas involving property, not individual rights.

Bingham's sentiments were echoed in 1873 by the plaintiffs' attorneys in the *Slaughterhouse Cases.* That litigation began when the carpetbag Louisiana state legislature passed laws that gave the exclusive privilege to operate slaughterhouses to one butcher firm. The adversely affected butchers sued, alleging that their "privileges and immunities" as

---

[2] The Ninth and Tenth Amendments were not relevant. The Ninth Amendment says that "The enumeration in the Constitution, of certain rights, shall not be construed to deny or disparage others retained by the people." The Tenth reads "The powers not delegated to the United States by the Constitution, nor prohibited by it to the States, are reserved to the States, respectively, or to the people."

citizens—specifically the right to operate a business—had been violated. In a 5 to 4 vote, the Supreme Court disagreed, and with that decision the "privileges and immunities" clause of the Fourteenth Amendment was all but nullified.

However, Justice Field's dissent argued for the absolute right of a man to be engaged in a given business or profession. Field insisted that the Fourteenth Amendment protects "the citizens of the United States against the deprivation of their common rights by state legislation." He explained that the amendment had been enacted "to place the common rights of American citizens under the protection of the national government." Those rights, he stated, were "inalienable rights, rights which are the gift of the creator; which the law does not confer, but only recognizes."

Thus, although the Court had reaffirmed the notion put forth in *Barron* that the Bill of Rights did not apply to the states, Justice Field's dissent was the beginning of the concept that liberty had, with the Fourteenth Amendment, taken on a new constitutional and national meaning. Under that broader definition, states must meet a national standard in their legislation and administration of justice, and the federal government had the duty to see that the standard was enforced.

Field's view of the Fourteenth Amendment would not be the prevailing sentiment of the Supreme Court for some time. However, it lived on in dissenting opinions. In 1884, Justice John Marshall Harlan took a slightly different tack, advocating the incorporation of the entire Bill of Rights via the due process clause of the Fourteenth Amendment. In his dissent in *Hurtado* v. *California* Harlan argued that Joseph Hurtado's murder conviction was unconstitutional because he had been indicted by "information" rather than by a grand jury. Harlan felt that the lack of a grand jury proceeding was a violation of the due process guarantees in the Fifth and Fourteenth Amendments. Subsequently, Harlan never failed "in appropriate cases—of which there really were not very many—to write impassioned opinions in dissent, urging his associates to accept the principle of the nationalization of the Bill of Rights."

While Harlan argued for personal liberties, a majority of the Court developed this broader concept of liberty into a legal framework designed to protect property. It was an outgrowth of an era of laissez-faire economics in which business and industry resisted the efforts of government to regulate the economy. Known as "substantive due process," the theory held that the Fourteenth Amendment's due process clause incorporated the protections of property vested in the Fifth Amendment's guarantee that no person shall "be deprived of life, liberty, or property without due process of law." Due process came to mean more than a procedural guarantee—that a person would have his day in court. It came to mean that the substance of an act of a legislature could in and of itself be a violation of rights. Thus legislation was now scrutinized not just in terms of *how* it was administered, but *what* it was controlling. Out of the substantive due process theory came the notion of "liberty of contract" or "Lochnerizing," as it was called, through which the Court overturned progressive economic legislation enacted by the states. The Lochner case of 1905 is an example of this process.

Lochner, a bakery owner, was convicted of violating a New York State law that limited the hours of bakery workers to 10 hours a day and 60 hours a week. He appealed, and the Supreme Court overturned his conviction and voided the statute because the state of New York had engaged in "meddlesome interferences with the rights of the individual." The Court explained, "The general rights to make a contract in relation to his business is part of the liberty of the individual protected by the Fourteenth Amendment of the Federal Constitution." If bakery workers wanted to work more hours—or perhaps if their employers demanded it—the state could not interfere. Child labor was another area which the Supreme Court, in 1905, felt could not be regulated.

However, it was also in the Lochner case that Justice Holmes first blasted the notion of a constitutionally guaranteed "liberty of contract": "This case is decided upon an economic theory which a large part of the country does not entertain. . . . But a constitution is not intended to embody a particular economic theory, whether of paternalism . . . or of *laissez faire.*"

The principle of substantive due process prevailed throughout the first quarter of the twentieth century, but it slowly fell into discredit when economic conditions, worsened by the Depression, called for more experimentation by the states in economic legislation.

◆ From Contracts to Fundamental Liberties

First in dissents, Justices Holmes and Brandeis maintained a steadfast and pervasive pressure against the concept of substantive due process, viewing it as a subversion of the original purpose of the Fourteenth Amendment by the very institution charged with its preservation, the Supreme Court. At the same time these justices were willing to use the Amendment as a vehicle to nullify state laws that they believed fettered essential individual rights of political expression. In this way, the Court began to give closer scrutiny to those liberties which were written into the Bill of Rights. And as the membership of the Court gradually changed, its view of what the Fourteenth Amendment meant shifted.

Starting, in 1925, with the free speech guarantee of the First Amendment, the Court began to accept the Harlan-Brandeis-Holmes theory that many of the fundamental liberties written into the Bill of Rights were enforceable on the states. In a piecemeal fashion began another phase of constitutional interpretation, in which certain personal liberties were taken under the protective umbrella of the Constitution. From freedom of speech to freedom of press to the right to counsel, the list grew.

Finally, in 1937, Justice Benjamin Cardozo spelled the Court's position on the relationship between the Bill of Rights and the states in *Palko* v. *Connecticut.* Frank Palko had been tried for killing two policemen and convicted of second-degree murder with a sentence of life imprisonment. The state of Connecticut had appealed the verdict and sentence, and after a new trial, Palko was convicted of first-degree murder and sentenced to death. He appealed on the ground that his second trial was an instance of double jeopardy, prohibited by the Fifth Amendment.

Although Cardozo rejected Palko's claim that his Fifth Amendment rights against double jeopardy could not be violated by the state, the Justice did set up an "Honor Roll" of rights. In Cardozo's view there were certain rights enumerated in the Bill of Rights which were "the very essence of a scheme of ordered liberty" and must be protected from state infringement. Others were not ranked as being fundamental; "justice would not perish" without them. Double jeopardy, the right to trial by jury, the right of indictment by grand jury were not part of "the concept of ordered liberty." Freedom of speech and press and religion, in contrast, did fall within that framework.

Thus by the time of *Palko,* the role of the federal government through the judiciary had undergone another metamorphosis; it was now to protect actively certain fundamental civil liberties of the citizens of the states against state action. This mandate was expressed a year later in a famous footnote written in an otherwise insignificant case, *United States* v. *Carolene Products Company.* While first asserting that economic legislation would be given less constitutional scrutiny (and thus signaling the end of "liberty of contract"), Justice Harlan Fiske Stone announced a new double standard of what legislation the Court would give close attention. Laws that threatened basic liberties were to receive a close scrutiny by the Court; economic legislation would not.[3]

For much of the last half century, the Court as been spending the majority of its time on questions concerning the Fourteenth Amendment and its relationship to the Bill of Rights. Some justices have relied on the

---

[3] 1. There may be narrower scope for operation of the presumption of constitutionality when legislation appears on its face to be within a specific prohibition of the Constitution, such as those of the first ten Amendments, which are deemed equally specific when held to be embraced within the Fourteenth. . . . 2. It is unnecessary to consider now whether legislation which restricts those political processes which can ordinarily be expected to bring about repeal of undesirable legislation, is to be subject to more exacting judicial scrutiny under the general prohibitions of the Fourteenth Amendment than are most other types of legislation.

Cardozo concept; others, such as Justice Hugo Black, have insisted that the entire Bill of Rights must be incorporated. Another judicial interpretation of the Fourteenth Amendment, known as "selective incorporation plus," would guarantee that states must not violate most of the rights specified in the first eight amendments as well as certain other fundamental rights. Under this interpretation, the Court has recognized a "right of privacy" and other "natural" and "fundamental" rights. It was this theory that led to the Court's ruling on abortion. . . .

Thus, in this century the Supreme Court has given new meaning to the Bill of Rights, a meaning probably never imagined by John Marshall or James Madison or Thomas Jefferson. . . .

TOWARD CRITICAL THINKING

1. How much weight should the intent of the primary architect of the Fourteenth Amendment have on its interpretation?

2. Do you think that Alexander Hamilton would have approved of the Court's protection of certain fundamental liberties from state action? What are fundamental rights or liberties?

· *17* ·

Freedom of Religion

The First Amendment contains some of the most famous language in the Bill of Rights: "Congress shall make no law respecting an establishment of religion, or prohibiting the free exercise thereof. . . ." But what constitutes "establishment of religion" or its "free exercise" are questions that continue to vex the Supreme Court as well as local, state, and national legislators. Just how high should the wall between church and state be? Some constitutional scholars would argue that it should be an impenetrable fortress; others argue for only a picket fence.

Religious establishment and free exercise cases usually offer interesting facts as well as important legal issues. In recent years, for example, the Supreme Court has decided cases involving the rights of Native Americans to use peyote—a hallucinogenic drug—in religious services, the right of a state to require the Amish to comply with highway safety laws, and state support of Nativity scenes at Christmas time. *Lee* v. *Weisman* and *Church of the Lukumi Babalu Aye* v. *City of Hialeah* are only two of the more interesting and thought-provoking religion cases the Court has decided in recent years.

· *17a* ·

Lee *v.* Weisman

112 S. Ct. 2649 (1992)

The school board allowed principals in the public middle and high schools of Providence, Rhode Island, to invite clergy members to deliver invocations and benediction prayers at school graduation ceremonies. Daniel Weisman brought suit on behalf of his daughter after his objections to this practice at her middle school failed to produce a change in policy. The federal district court denied Weisman's motion for a temporary restraining order. Deborah Weisman attended her graduation, prayers were recited, and her father sought a permanent injunction, to bar future prayers at public school graduations. The District Court granted the injunction, finding that the prayers were in violation of the First Amendment; its judgement was affirmed by the U.S. Court of Appeals. The school board then appealed that decision to the U.S. Supreme Court. The U.S. Solicitor General, on behalf of the United States, filed an *amicus curiae* (friend of the court) brief on the side of the school board urging the Court to overrule several previous decisions in order to allow it to uphold the constitutionality of school prayer.
    Opinion: Justice Anthony Kennedy
    Vote: 5 to 4

. . . The question before us is whether including clerical members who offer prayers as part of the official school graduation ceremony is consistent with the Religion Clauses of the First Amendment, provisions the Fourteenth Amendment makes applicable with full force to the States and their school districts. . . .

The principle that government may accommodate the free exercise of religion does not supersede the fundamental limitations imposed by the Establishment Clause. It is beyond dispute that, at a minimum, the Constitution guarantees that government may not coerce anyone to support or participate in religion or its exercise, or otherwise act in a way which "established a [state] religion or religious faith, or tends to do so." . . . The State's involvement in the school prayers challenged today violates these central principles.

That involvement is as troubling as it is undenied. A school official, the principal, decided that an invocation and a benediction should be given; this is a choice attributable to the State, and from a constitutional perspective it is as if a state statute decreed that the prayers must occur. The principal chose the religious participant, here a rabbi, and that choice is also attributable to the State. The reason for the choice of a rabbi is not disclosed by the record, but the potential for divisiveness over the choice of a particular member of the clergy to conduct the ceremony is apparent.

. . . The potential for divisiveness is of particular relevance here though, because it centers around an overt religious exercise in a secondary school environment where . . . subtle coercive pressures exist and where the student had no real alternative which would have allowed her to avoid the fact or appearance of participation.

The State's role did not end with the decision to include a prayer and with the choice of clergyman. Principal Lee provided Rabbi Gutterman with a copy of the "Guidelines for Civic Occasions," and advised him that his prayers should be nonsectarian. . . . It is a cornerstone principle of our Establishment Clause jurisprudence that "it is no part of the business of government to compose official prayers for any group of the American people to recite as a part of a religious program carried on by government," and that is what the school officials attempted to do.

Petitioners argue, and we find nothing in the case to refute it, that the directions for the content of the prayers were a good-faith attempt by the school to ensure that the sectarianism which is so often the flashpoint for religious animosity be removed from the graduation ceremony. The concern is understandable, as a prayer which uses ideas or images identified with a particular religion may foster a different sort of sectarian rivalry than an invocation or benediction in terms more neutral. The school's explanation, however, does not resolve the dilemma caused by its participation. The question is not the good faith of the school in attempting to make the prayer acceptable to most persons, but the legitimacy of its undertaking that enterprise at all when the object is to produce a prayer to be used in a formal religious exercise which students, for all practical purposes, are obliged to attend. . . .

The First Amendment's Religion Clauses mean that religious beliefs and religious expression are too precious to be either proscribed or prescribed by the State. The design of the Constitution is that preservation and transmission of religious beliefs and worship is a responsibility and a choice committed to the private sphere, which itself is promised freedom to pursue that mission. It must not be forgotten then, that while concern must be given to define the protection granted to an objector or a dissenting nonbeliever, these same Clauses exist to protect religion from government interference. James Madison, the principal author of the Bill of Rights, did not rest his opposition to a religious establishment on the sole ground of its effect on the minority. A principal ground for his view was: "[E]xperience witnesseth that ecclesiastical establishments, instead of maintaining the purity and efficacy of Religion, have had a contrary operation." . . .

The First Amendment protects speech and religion by quite different mechanisms. Speech is protected by insuring its full expression even when the government participates, for the very object of some of our most important speech is to persuade the government to adopt an idea as its own. . . . The method for protecting freedom of worship and freedom of conscience in religious matters is quite the reverse. In religious debate or expression the government is not a prime participant, for the Framers deemed religious establishment antithetical to the freedom of all. The Free Exercise Clause embraces a freedom of conscience and worship that has close parallels in the speech provisions of the First Amendment, but the Establishment Clause is a specific prohibition on forms of state intervention in religious affairs with no precise counterpart in the speech provisions. . . . The explanation lies in the lesson of history that was and is the inspiration for the Establishment Clause, the lesson that in the hands of government what might begin as a tolerant expression of religious views may end in a policy to indoctrinate and coerce. A state-created orthodoxy puts at grave risk that freedom of belief and conscience which are the sole assurance that religious faith is real, not imposed.

The lessons of the First Amendment are as urgent in the modern world as in the Eighteenth Century when it was written. One timeless lesson is that if citizens are subjected to state-sponsored religious exercises, the State disavows its own duty to guard and respect that sphere of inviolable conscience and belief which is the mark of a free people. To compromise that principle today would be to deny our own tradition and forfeit our standing to urge others to secure the protections of that tradition for themselves.

As we have observed before, there are heightened concerns with protecting freedom of conscience from subtle coercive pressure in the elementary and secondary public schools. . . .

Our decisions . . . recognize, among other things, that prayer exercises in public schools carry a particular risk of indirect coercion. The concern may not be limited to the context of schools, but it is most pronounced there. . . . What to most believers may seem nothing more than a reasonable request that the nonbeliever respect their religious practices, in a school context may appear to the nonbeliever or dissenter to be an attempt to employ the machinery of the State to enforce a religious orthodoxy.

We need not look beyond the circumstances of this case to see the phenomenon at work. The undeniable fact is that the school district's supervision and control of a high school graduation ceremony places public pressure, as well as peer pressure, on attending students to stand as a group or, at least, maintain respectful silence during the Invocation and Benediction. This pressure, though subtle and indirect, can be as real as any overt compulsion. Of course, in our culture standing or remaining silent can signify adherence to a view or simple respect for the views of others. And no doubt some persons who have no desire to join a prayer have little objection to standing as a sign of respect for those who do. But for the dissenter of high school age, who has a reasonable perception that she is being forced by the State to pray in a manner her conscience will not allow, the injury is no less real. There can be no doubt that for many, if not most, of the students at the graduation, the act of standing or remaining silent was an expression of participation in the Rabbi's prayer. That was the very point of the religious exercise. It is of little comfort to a dissenter, then, to be told that for her the act of standing or remaining in silence signifies mere respect, rather than participation. What matters is that, given our social conventions, a reasonable dissenter in this milieu could believe that the group exercise signified her own participation or approval of it.

Finding no violation under these circumstances would place objectors in the dilemma of participating, with all that implies, or protesting. We do not address whether that choice is acceptable if the affected citizens are mature adults, but we think the State may not, consistent with the Establishment Clause, place primary and secondary school children in this position. Research in psychology supports the common assumption that adolescents are often susceptible to pressure from their peers towards conformity, and that the influence is strongest in matters of social convention. . . . To recognize that the choice imposed by the State constitutes an unacceptable constraint only acknowledges that the government may no more use social pressure to enforce orthodoxy than it may use more direct means. . . .

We do not hold that every state action implicating religion is invalid if one or a few citizens find it offensive. People may take offense at all manner of religious as well as nonreligious messages, but offense alone does not in every case show a violation. We know too that sometimes to endure social isolation or even anger may be the price of conscience or nonconformity. But, by any reading of our cases, the conformity required of the student in this case was too high an exaction to withstand the test of the Establishment Clause. The prayer exercises in this case are especially improper because the State has in every practical sense compelled attendance and participation in an explicit religious exercise at an event of singular importance to every student, one the objecting student had no real alternative to avoid. . . .

For the reasons we have stated, the judgment of the Court of Appeals is Affirmed.

TOWARD CRITICAL THINKING

1. The Supreme Court has ruled that it is constitutional for Congress to open each session with a prayer and to have its own chaplain. Why are public school graduation ceremonies treated differently?

2. How did the principal's actual guidelines and advice to the rabbi cross the barrier mandated by the Constitution between church and state? Did the principal's actions constitute governmental "establishment" of religion?

· *17b* ·

Church of the Lukumi Babalu Aye *v.* City of Hialeah

113 S. Ct. 2217 (1993)

The Church of the Lukumi Babalu Aye and its followers were members of the Santeria faith, a somewhat mysterious religion that took root among slaves brought to Cuba from eastern Africa in the eighteenth and nineteenth centuries. Members were persecuted in Cuba, and the religion was brought to the United States by Cuban exiles, many of whom settled in South Florida. The religion claims more than one million members worldwide. One of its principle forms of devotion is animal sacrifice. According the U.S. Supreme Court:

> Sacrifices are performed at birth, marriage, and death rites, for the cure of the sick, for the initiation of new members and priests, and during an annual celebration. Animals sacrificed in the Santeria rituals include chickens, pigeons, doves, ducks, guinea pigs, goats, sheep, and turtles. The animals are killed by the cutting of the carotid arteries in the neck. The sacrificed animal is cooked and eaten, except after health and death rituals[*]

When the Church of the Lukumi Babalu Aye leased land in Hialeah, Florida, to establish a church there, the city council held an emergency public session. It quickly passed several ordinances noting "concern" with religious practices inconsistent with public morals, peace, and safety. The City Council also expanded state cruelty to animal laws in order to punish anyone who "unnecessarily kill[s] . . . an animal in a . . . ritual . . . not for the primary purpose of food." It also banned the "possession, sacrifice, or slaughter" of any animal in "any type of ritual."

The church and its president filed suit, alleging that the ordinances violated their right to free exercise of their religion as guaranteed by the First Amendment. The federal district court upheld the ordinances, concluding that the city had a compelling governmental interest in preventing public health risks and cruelty to animals, which justified the absolute prohibition on animal sacrifices. The U.S. Court of Appeals affirmed, and the Church sought review from the Supreme Court.

Opinion: Justice Anthony Kennedy
Vote: 9 to 0

---

[*] 1993 U.S. Lexis 4022 at 11.

. . .

II ✦

[T]he city does not argue that Santeria is not a "religion" within the meaning of the First Amendment. Nor could it. Although the practice of animal sacrifice may seem abhorrent to some, "religious beliefs need not be acceptable, logical, consistent, or comprehensible to others in order to merit First Amendment protection." . . .

The Free Exercise Clause protects against governmental hostility which is masked, as well as overt. . . .

The record in this case compels the conclusion that suppression of the central element of the Santeria worship service was the object of the ordinances. First, though use of the words "sacrifice" and "ritual" does not compel a finding of improper targeting of the Santeria religion, the choice of these words is support for our conclusion. There are further respects in which the text of the city council's enactments discloses the improper attempt to target Santeria. Resolution 87–66, adopted June 9, 1987, recited that "residents and citizens of the City of Hialeah have expressed their concern that certain religions may propose to engage in practices which are inconsistent with public morals, peace or safety," and "reiterate[d]" the city's commitment to prohibit "any and all [such] acts of any and all religious groups." No one suggests, and on this record it cannot be maintained, that city officials had in mind a religion other than Santeria.

It becomes evident that these ordinances target Santeria sacrifice when the ordinances' operation is considered. . . .

The subject at hand does implicate, of course, multiple concerns unrelated to religious animosity, for example, the suffering or mistreatment visited upon the sacrificed animals, and health hazards from improper disposal. But the ordinances when considered together disclose an object remote from these legitimate concerns. . . .

The legitimate governmental interests in protecting the public health and preventing cruelty to animals could be addressed by restrictions stopping far short of a flat prohibition of all Santeria sacrificial practice. If improper disposal, not the sacrifice itself, is the harm to be prevented, the city could have imposed a general regulation on the disposal of organic garbage. It did not do so. Indeed, counsel for the city conceded at oral argument that, under the ordinances, Santeria sacrifices would be illegal even if they occurred in licensed, inspected, and zoned slaughterhouses. . . . Thus, these broad ordinances prohibit Santeria sacrifice even when it does not threaten the city's interest in the public health. The District Court accepted the argument that narrower regulation would be unenforceable because of the secrecy in the Santeria rituals and the lack of any central religious authority to require compliance with secular disposal regulations. . . . It is difficult to understand, however, how a prohibition of the sacrifices themselves, which occur in private, is enforceable if a ban on improper disposal, which occurs in public, is not. The neutrality of a law is suspect if First Amendment freedoms are curtailed to prevent isolated collateral harms not themselves prohibited by direct regulation. . . .

. . . Narrower regulation would achieve the city's interest in preventing cruelty to animals. With regard to the city's interest in ensuring the adequate care of animals, regulation of conditions and treatment, regardless of why an animal is kept, is the logical response to the city's concern, not a prohibition on possession for the purpose of sacrifice. The same is true for the city's interest in prohibiting cruel methods of killing. Under federal and Florida law and Ordinance 87–40, which incorporates Florida law in this regard, killing an animal by the "simultaneous and instantaneous severance of the carotid arteries with a sharp instrument"—the method used in Kosher slaughter—is approved as humane. . . . The District Court found that, though Santeria sacrifice also results in severance of the carotid arteries, the method used during sacrifice is less reliable and therefore not humane. . . . If the city has a real concern that other methods are less humane, however, the subject of the regulation should be the method of slaughter itself, not a religious classification that is said to bear some general relation to it. . . .

2 ◆

That the ordinances were enacted " 'because of,' not merely 'in spite of,' " their suppression of Santeria religious practice . . . is revealed by the events preceding enactment of the ordinances. . . . The city council made no attempt to address the supposed problem before its meeting in June 1987, just weeks after the Church announced plans to open. The minutes and taped excerpts of the June 9 session, both of which are in the record, evidence significant hostility exhibited by residents, members of the city council, and other city officials toward the Santeria religion and its practice of animal sacrifice. . . .

3 ◆

. . . The ordinances had as their object the suppression of religion. The pattern we have recited discloses animosity to Santeria adherents and their religious practices; the ordinances by their own terms target this religious exercise; the texts of the ordinances were gerrymandered with care to proscribe religious killings of animals but to exclude almost all secular killings; and the ordinances suppress much more religious conduct than is necessary in order to achieve the legitimate ends asserted in their defense. These ordinances are not neutral, and the court below committed clear error in failing to reach this conclusion.

. . .

III ◆

A law burdening religious practice that is not neutral or not of general application must undergo the most rigorous of scrutiny. To satisfy the commands of the First Amendment, a law restrictive of religious practice must advance "'interests of the highest order'" and must be narrowly tailored in pursuit of those interests. . . . It follows from what we have already said that these ordinances cannot withstand this scrutiny. . . .

IV ◆

The Free Exercise Clause commits government itself to religious tolerance, and upon even slight suspicion that proposals for state intervention stem from animosity to religion or distrust of its practices, all officials must pause to remember their own high duty to the Constitution and to the rights it secures. Those in office must be resolute in resisting importunate demands and must ensure that the sole reasons for imposing the burdens of law and regulation are secular. Legislators may not devise mechanisms, overt or disguised, designed to persecute or oppress a religion or its practices. The laws here in question were enacted contrary to these constitutional principles, and they are void. . . .

It is only in the rare case that a state or local legislature will enact a law directly burdening religious practice as such. . . . Because the respondent here does single out religion in this way, the present case is an easy one to decide.

A harder case would be presented if petitioners were requesting an exemption from a generally applicable anti-cruelty law. The result in the case before the Court today, and the fact that every Member of the Court concurs in that result, does not necessarily reflect this Court's views of the strength of a State's interest in prohibiting cruelty to animals. This case does not present, and I therefore decline to reach, the question whether the Free Exercise Clause would require a religious exemption from a law that sincerely pursued the goal of protecting animals from cruel treatment.

TOWARD CRITICAL THINKING

1. What kind of ordinance (if any) could the city enact to curb the Santeria practice of animal sacrifice? What kind of test does the Court apply to restrictions
   that infringe on freedom of religion?

2. In 1879, The U.S. Supreme Court upheld state laws that outlawed the Mormon
   practice of polygamy. How would practices such as multiple marriage not warrant constitutional protection while those involving animal sacrifice do?

· *18* ·

Freedom Of Speech

Freedom of speech was one of the freedoms deemed fundamental to colonists. Not surprisingly, then, it found its way into the First Amendment. Although the Constitution guarantees freedom of speech (and as interpreted by the Supreme Court what is called "symbolic speech"), that right is not absolute. Obscenity, for example, has been found to be beyond the protection of the free speech (or freedom of the press) clauses. In *Chaplinsky* v. *New Hampshire* (1942) as discussed in Reading 18a, the Court concluded that certain "well defined and narrowly limited" categories of speech fell outside of constitutional protection. Thus, "the lewd and obscene, the profane, the libelous," and what were termed "fighting words"—those intended to provoke a reasonable person to violence or illegal action—can be regulated by the states or the national government.

Since *Chaplinsky,* which was decided during World War II at a time when the Court feared disastrous consequences if individuals were allowed to speak out routinely against the war or public officials, the Justices have given less latitude to the states to restrict any forms of speech. As revealed in *R.A.V.* v. *City of St. Paul,* Reading 18a, in 1992 the Supreme Court refused to uphold a conviction based on a city ordinance that made it a crime for anyone to display symbols that would anger or arouse other citizens on the basis of race among other grounds.

Around the same time cities such as St. Paul were enacting ordinances designed to discourage racial or other forms of intolerance, a move took place on college campuses across the country to ban a variety of forms of speech that might make some groups uncomfortable or the subject of ridicule. This politically correct movement is the subject of Paul McMaster's essay (Reading 18b).

R.A.V. *v.* City of St. Paul, Minnesota

112 S. Ct. 2538 (1992)

After allegedly burning a cross on a black family's lawn, Robert A. Viktora, known in court as R.A.V., because he was only seventeen at the time the crime was committed, was charged under the St. Paul, Minnesota, Bias-Motivated Crime Ordinance.* That hate speech ordinance prohibited the display of any symbols that "one knows or has reason to know arouses anger, alarm or resentment in others on the basis of race, color, creed, religion or gender." The trial court dismissed this charge finding that the ordinance was too broad in its coverage and that it was impermissibly content-based, but the State Supreme Court reversed. The Minnesota high court rejected the overbreadth claim. It concluded that the phrase, "arouses anger, alarm or resentment in others," had been construed in earlier state cases to limit the ordinance's reach to "fighting words," which an earlier U.S. Supreme Court decision had found to be a category of expression unprotected by the First Amendment (*Chaplinsky v. New Hampshire* [1942]). The state court also concluded that the ordinance was not impermissibly content-based because it was narrowly tailored to serve a compelling governmental interest in protecting the community against bias-motivated threats to community safety and order. R.A.V.'s court-appointed attorney then appealed the conviction to the U.S. Supreme Court. He wasn't representing a particularly appealing defendant—R.A.V. was a "skin head" and numerous liberal groups including People for the American Way, the National Association for the Advancement of Colored People, and the attorneys general of seventeen states urged the Court to uphold the ordinance and the conviction.

Opinion: Justice Antonin Scalia
Vote: 9–0

In the predawn hours of June 21, 1990, petitioner and several other teenagers allegedly assembled a crudely made cross by taping together broken chair legs. They then allegedly burned the cross inside the fenced yard of a black family that lived across the street from the house where petitioner was staying. Although this conduct could have been punished

---

*For more on *R.A.V.* see Edward J. Cleary, *Beyond The Burning Cross: The First Amendment and the Landmark R.A.V. Case.* New York: Random House, 1994.

under any of a number of laws, one of the two provisions under which [the] city of St. Paul chose to charge petitioner (then a juvenile) was the St. Paul Bias-Motivated Crime Ordinance . . . which provides:

"Whoever places on public or private property a symbol, object, appellation, characterization or graffiti, including, but not limited to, a burning cross or Nazi swastika, which one knows or has reasonable grounds to know arouses anger, alarm or resentment in others on the basis of race, color, creed, religion or gender commits disorderly conduct and shall be guilty of a misdemeanor."

Petitioner moved to dismiss this count on the ground that the St. Paul ordinance was substantially overbroad and impermissibly content-based and therefore facially invalid under the First Amendment. The trial court granted this motion, but the Minnesota Supreme Court reversed. That court rejected petitioner's overbreadth claim because, as construed in prior Minnesota cases, . . . the modifying phrase "arouses anger, alarm or resentment in others" limited the reach of the ordinance to conduct that amounts to "fighting words," i.e., "conduct that itself inflicts injury or tends to incite immediate violence . . . ," and therefore the ordinance reached only expression "that the first amendment does not protect." The court also concluded that the ordinance was not impermissibly content-based because, in its view, "the ordinance is a narrowly tailored means toward accomplishing the compelling governmental interest in protecting the community against bias-motivated threats to public safety and order." . . .

I ◆

In construing the St. Paul ordinance, we are bound by the construction given to it by the Minnesota court. . . . Accordingly, we accept the Minnesota Supreme Court's authoritative statement that the ordinance reaches only those expressions that constitute "fighting words" within the meaning of *Chaplinsky.* . . . Petitioner and his amici urge us to modify the scope of the Chaplinsky formulation, thereby invalidating the ordinance as "substantially overbroad." We find it unnecessary to consider this issue. Assuming, arguendo, that all of the expression reached by the ordinance is proscribable under the "fighting words" doctrine, we nonetheless conclude that the ordinance is facially unconstitutional in that it prohibits otherwise permitted speech solely on the basis of the subjects the speech addresses.

The First Amendment generally prevents government from proscribing speech, see, e.g., *Cantwell* v. *Connecticut* (1940), or even expressive conduct, see, e.g., *Texas* v. *Johnson* (1989), because of disapproval of the ideas expressed. Content-based regulations are presumptively invalid. . . .

From 1791 to the present, however, our society, like other free but civilized societies, has permitted restrictions upon the content of speech in a few limited areas, which are "of such slight social value as a step to truth that any benefit that may be derived from them is clearly outweighed by the social interest in order and morality." We have recognized that "the freedom of speech" referred to by the First Amendment does not include a freedom to disregard these traditional limitations. See, e.g., *Roth* v. *United States* (1957) (obscenity); *Beauharnais* v. *Illinois* (1952) (defamation); *Chaplinsky* v. *New Hampshire* (1942) ("fighting words"). . . .

We have sometimes said that these categories of expression are "not within the area of constitutionally protected speech," . . . or that the "protection of the First Amendment does not extend" to them. . . . What they mean is that these areas of speech can, consistently with the First Amendment, be regulated because of their constitutionally proscribable content (obscenity, defamation, etc.)—not that they are categories of speech entirely invisible to the Constitution, so that they may be made the vehicles for content discrimination unrelated to their distinctively proscribable content. Thus, the government may proscribe libel; but it may not make the further content discrimination of proscribing only libel critical of the government. We recently acknowledged this distinction in *Ferber,* 458 U.S., at 763, where, in upholding New York's child pornography law, we expressly recognized that there was no "question here of censoring a particular literary theme. . . ."

. . .

In other words, the exclusion of "fighting words" from the scope of the First Amendment simply means that, for purposes of that Amendment, the unprotected features of the words are, despite their verbal character, essentially a "nonspeech" element of communication. Fighting words are thus analogous to a noisy sound truck: Each is, as Justice Frankfurter recognized, a "mode of speech," both can be used to convey an idea; but neither has, in and of itself, a claim upon the First Amendment. As with the sound truck, however, so also with fighting words: The government may not regulate use based on hostility—or favoritism—towards the underlying message expressed.

. . .

II ◆

Applying these principles to the St. Paul ordinance, we conclude that, even as narrowly construed by the Minnesota Supreme Court, the ordinance is facially unconstitutional. Although the phrase in the ordinance, "arouses anger, alarm or resentment in others," has been limited by the

Minnesota Supreme Court's construction to reach only those symbols or displays that amount to "fighting words," the remaining, unmodified terms make clear that the ordinance applies only to "fighting words" that insult, or provoke violence, "on the basis of race, color, creed, religion or gender." Displays containing abusive invective, no matter how vicious or severe, are permissible unless they are addressed to one of the specified disfavored topics. Those who wish to use "fighting words" in connection with other ideas—to express hostility, for example, on the basis of political affiliation, union membership, or homosexuality—are not covered. The First Amendment does not permit St. Paul to impose special prohibitions on those speakers who express views on disfavored subjects. . . . In its practical operation, moreover, the ordinance goes even beyond mere content discrimination, to actual viewpoint discrimination. Displays containing some words—odious racial epithets, for example—would be prohibited to proponents of all views. But "fighting words" that do not themselves invoke race, color, creed, religion, or gender—aspersions upon a person's mother, example—would seemingly be usable ad libitum in the placards of those arguing in favor of racial, color, etc. tolerance and equality, but could not be used by that speaker's opponents. One could hold up a sign saying, for example, that all "anti-Catholic bigots" are misbegotten; but not that all "papists" are, for that would insult and provoke violence "on the basis of religion." St. Paul has no such authority to license one side of a debate to fight freestyle, while requiring the other to follow Marquis of Queensbury Rules.

What we have here, it must be emphasized, is not a prohibition of fighting words that are directed at certain persons or groups (which would be facially valid if it met the requirements of the Equal Protection Clause); but rather, a prohibition of fighting words that contain (as the Minnesota Supreme Court repeatedly emphasized) messages of "bias-motivated" hatred and in particular, as applied to this case, messages "based on virulent notions of racial supremacy." . . . One must wholeheartedly agree with the Minnesota Supreme Court that "it is the responsibility, even the obligation, of diverse communities to confront such notions in whatever form they appear," but the manner of that confrontation cannot consist of selective limitations upon speech. . . . The point of the First Amendment is that majority preferences must be expressed in some fashion other than silencing speech on the basis of its content.

The content-based discrimination reflected in the St. Paul ordinance comes within neither of the specific exceptions to the First Amendment prohibition we discussed earlier, nor within a more general exception for content discrimination that does not threaten censorship of ideas. It assuredly does not fall within the exception for content discrimination based on the very reasons why the particular class of speech at issue (here, fighting words) is proscribable. As explained earlier, . . . the reason why fighting words are categorically excluded from the protection of the First Amendment is not that their content communicates any particular idea, but that their content embodies a particularly intolerable (and socially unnecessary) mode of expressing whatever idea the speaker wishes to convey. St. Paul has not singled out an especially offensive mode of expression—it has not, for example, selected for prohibition only those fighting words that communicate ideas in a threatening (as opposed to a merely obnoxious) manner. Rather, it has proscribed fighting words of whatever manner that communicate messages of racial, gender, or religious intolerance. Selectivity of this sort creates the possibility that the city is seeking to handicap the expression of particular ideas. That possibility would alone be enough to render the ordinance presumptively invalid, but St. Paul's comments and concessions in this case elevate the possibility to a certainty.

St. Paul argues that the ordinance comes within another of the specific exceptions we mentioned, the one that allows content discrimination aimed only at the "secondary effects" of the speech. . . . According to St. Paul, the ordinance is intended, "not to impact on [sic] the right of free expression of the accused," but rather to "protect against the victimization of a person or persons who are particularly vulnerable because of their membership in a group that historically has been discriminated against." . . . Even assuming that an ordinance that completely proscribes, rather than merely regulates, a specified category of speech can ever be considered to be directed only to the secondary effects of such speech, it is clear that the St. Paul ordinance is not directed to secondary effects within the meaning of [previous cases.] . . .

It hardly needs discussion that the ordinance does not fall within some more general exception permitting all selectivity that for any reason is beyond the suspicion of official suppression of ideas. The statements of St. Paul in this very case afford ample basis for, if not full confirmation of, that suspicion.

Finally, St. Paul and its amici defend the conclusion of the Minnesota Supreme Court that, even if the ordinance regulates expression based on hostility towards its protected ideological content, this discrimination is nonetheless justified because it is narrowly tailored to serve compelling state interests. Specifically, they assert that the ordinance helps to ensure the basic human rights of members of groups that have historically been subjected to discrimination, including the right of such group members to live in peace where they wish. We do not doubt that these interests are compelling, and that the ordinance can be said to promote them. But the "danger of censorship" presented by a facially content-based statute . . . requires that that weapon be employed only where it is "necessary to serve the asserted [compelling] interest." The existence of adequate content-neutral alternatives thus "undercuts significantly" any defense of such a statute . . . , casting considerable doubt on the government's protestations that "the asserted justification is in fact an accurate description of the purpose and effect of the law." . . . The dispositive question in this case, therefore, is whether content discrimination is reasonably-necessary to achieve St. Paul's compelling interests; it plainly is not. An ordinance not limited to the favored topics, for example, would have precisely the same beneficial effect. In fact the only interest distinctively served by the content limitation is that of displaying the city councils special hostility towards the particular biases thus singled out. That is precisely what the First Amendment forbids. The politicians of St. Paul are entitled to express that hostility—but not through the means of imposing unique limitations upon speakers who (however benightedly) disagree.

. . .

Let there be no mistake about our belief that burning a cross in someone's front yard is reprehensible. But St. Paul has sufficient means at its disposal to prevent such behavior without adding the First Amendment to the fire.

The judgment of the Minnesota Supreme Court is reversed, and the case is remanded for proceedings not inconsistent with this opinion.

TOWARD CRITICAL THINKING

1. Justice Hugo Black adopted what is called an absolutist approach maintaining that the First Amendment's language, "Congress shall make no law," must be interpreted literally to prohibit any governmental infringements on speech. Historically, a majority of the Court has never adopted his view. Given the Court's unambigious, unanimous decision in *R.A.V.,* can you think of any kinds of speech codes that might withstand judicial scrutiny?

2. Could St. Paul have come up with another way to punish this conduct without resorting to prosecution under its Bias-Motivated Crime statute?

· *18b* ·

Free Speech versus Civil Discourse: Where Do We Go from Here?

PAUL McMASTERS

Since the founding period, freedom of speech and the press have been particularly volatile areas of the law. Over the years, the Supreme Court has usually given greater protection to speech than to deeds. At no time, however, have free speech rights ever been absolute.

In the late 1980s, new restrictions on speech began to appear on college campuses throughout the United States. The move toward speech codes on campuses has caused a nationwide uproar, often pitting both conservatives and some liberals against these codes. Paul McMasters, national president of the Society of Professional Journalists, discusses the "politically correct movement" (PC) and offers advice to individuals on both sides of the debate.

The call from the nation's university campuses for a society more sensitive to its diverse elements—labeled the "politically correct" movement in recent years—has provoked heated debate both on and off campus. Coincident with the arrival of an increasingly diverse faculty, staff, and student body, . . . the imperative of political correctness has spread far beyond the humanities departments and law schools where it was born. In many ways—the panic among some politicians and pundits notwithstanding—it has been a good thing, despite flights of excess and episodes of downright silliness.

The clash of ideas sparked by this movement has produced a philosophical furor over whether the group should be elevated over the individual, whether equality should take priority over freedom of expression, whether the sensibilities of the oppressed should prevail over robust discourse. . . .

While the debate rages, change creeps in.

SOURCE: Paul McMasters, "Free Speech versus Civil Discourse: Where Do We Go from Here? *Academe* (January/February 1994):8–13. Reprinted by permission.

The Clinton administration has made diversity a priority in appointments and policies. The workplace, movies and television, the news media, magazines, books, and our educational system all reflect a multicultural awareness not thought possible even a decade ago. Laws and court rulings against discrimination and harassment undergird that awareness.

The movement has forced us to sound the true depth of hate that haunts our society. Both individuals and institutions have been sensitized not only to acts of bigotry and bias, but also to words that hurt and harm. It has moved us to compassion. It has moved us to act. Innovative and creative ideas have poured forth, challenging long-held tradition and provoking long-needed change.

Unfortunately the hate keeps coming. Women, racial and ethnic minorities, gays and lesbians, the disabled, and a host of others who have yet to claim their rightful standing in our society are being assaulted by acts and words. Hate crimes and hurtful speech are rampant. . . .

In its zeal to right wrongs, the politically correct movement has developed a troubling impulse to restrict words, images, symbols, even ideas. That infectious impulse has spread, too, only partly because the need for remedy is so urgent.

As a result, political and academic leaders . . . proffer reckless solutions to seemingly intractable problems. They would tie the federal funding of art to whether it is acceptable to a majority; they would censor rap music to raise the status of women and protect them from harm; they would curb violence on the streets by banning its depiction on television, in the movies, and in video games.

. . . Censorship is not a shield but a double-edged sword. A notable example is instructive: In 1992, Canada's Supreme Court adopted the theories on pornography developed by Catharine MacKinnon as a way to protect women from assaultive speech. The Canadian government then employed the new tool to suppress feminist, lesbian, and gay material trying to make its way across the border. Customs agents seized two works by Andrea Dworkin, MacKinnon's partner in developing the theories. Copies of *Black Looks: Race and Representation,* by feminist scholar bell hooks [sic], popular in women's studies courses, also were confiscated. That was not the aim but the result of restricting certain kinds of speech. . . .

Unfortunately, that is the mood on campus these days; traditionally protected forms of expression are regularly assaulted. Courses deemed impolitic in this politically correct milieu are excised from the catalog. Professors are hounded from the classroom for "incorrect" words and lectures or for failure to warn students of possibly offensive material. Law school students, watched by witnesses, sign diversity pledges proclaiming their sensitivity. Entire editions of college newspapers that for some reason have failed to meet the standards of offended individuals or groups are stolen, trashed, or burned.

One of the more popular manifestations of this censorship impulse on campus has been speech codes that punish those deemed politically incorrect. Those who advocate speech codes often prevail because of their passion and ingenuity if not for their reason. Speech codes, they say, are essential in any meaningful struggle for true equality and to establish an environment conducive to study and learning. . . .

Interestingly, the political far right came late to the defense of free speech. Taking time out from attempts to censor textbooks, to eviscerate the National Endowment for the Arts, and to put prayer in school, they have swarmed to the speech code debate, often making heroes of scoundrels and leaving untended the victims of hate speech. So, too, have ardent defenders of free expression come late to the conversation, intimidated, no doubt, by the pedantry and the self-righteousness in much of the politically correct debate. Who would not be reluctant to leap into that bog? Who would not be reluctant to champion the right of bigots to spew their bitter bile? . . .

Speech codes have not stopped hate speech. Speech codes are used all too frequently to prosecute and persecute those they would protect. Rather than encourage education, they have enforced a form of ignorance. They have diverted the dialogue from a focus on a fair society to a preoccupation with censorship. They have failed to draw a definitive line between acceptable speech and unacceptable speech. They have trivialized the debate.

They risk exacerbating racial tensions rather than calming them. They have yet to pass constitutional muster, so say the courts. And more.

Speech code advocates fail to see the irony and contradictions in their own positions. They would entrust, for example, fair enforcement of speech codes to the very individuals and institutions they have labeled racist, sexist, and other-ist. . . .

Then there is the practical matter of drafting a speech code that is enforceable by even the most fair-minded of systems. While some sort of consensus might be reached on the most extreme forms of hate speech, the defining process begins to break down when the discussion turns to "insensitive" speech, "harassment," and symbols, images, and ideas. Further problems develop as the process moves to who can be guilty of hate speech. Finally, the drafters have to accommodate exempted forums: news articles, satire, editorial cartoons, controversial speakers, rap groups, and comedians invited to perform on campus. . . .

Those who would halt the spread of speech codes and stay the censor's hand have to develop meaningful solutions. Those solutions must

BOX 4.1

Speech Regulations at Public Colleges and Universities

ARATI R. KORWAR

In a recently completed study under the auspices of the Freedom Forum's First Amendment Center, Ms. Korwar inventories speech proscriptions in 384 campus handbooks and student guides. Omitted from her study were separate statements of equal opportunity, affirmative action, and nondiscrimination, as well as specific policies on sexual harassment. Following is her discussion of [some] current campus rules with potential First Amendment implications.

Advocacy of offensive or outrageous viewpoint

Included in this category are rules against incitement to violence, incitement to riot, advocacy of the commission of illegal acts, advocacy of the overthrow of the government, and advocacy of biased ideas. About 28 percent of institutions in the survey had advocacy rules. Here are two examples of rules against advocacy of biased ideas. The Fashion Institute of Technology prohibits "any behavior that implicitly or explicitly carries messages of racism, stereotyping, or discrimination of any kind." The State University of New York College of Agriculture and Technology at Cobleskill has a harsh-sounding policy that states, "students found diminishing the dignity of other members of the community . . . racial, sexual, religious, or ethnic disparagement, which are unlawful and inconsistent with the College's aspiration to produce citizens respectful and tolerant of the diversity of people, will be dismissed and will not receive degrees from Cobleskill College.

Advocacy of offensive ideas, such as the notion that Caucasians are generally superior to all other races, is protected by the First Amendment. The two rules quoted above appear to punish protected expression. Regulation of advocacy of law violation must follow the *Brandenburg* incitement test to be constitutional.

Verbal abuse or verbal harassment directed at members of specific groups

Some institutions have the general harassment codes discussed above, which include verbal harassment, and also have special codes that make harassment based on particular group status punishable. For example, the University of Southern Maine prohibits "harassment or intimidation of another person."

focus on affirming the strength and independence of some targets of hate speech and on building the strengths of others to cope with hate speech in and outside the campus cocoon.

Where do we go from here? Officials at the University of Pennsylvania apparently have already decided. They have dropped the speech code and are seeking better ways to address the problem of racism, sexism, and other-isms on campus. Across the nation, university officials are taking another look at speech codes. Fortunately, some courses of action move the debate beyond the simple regulation of speech.

The challenge in this vital undertaking is to achieve civility in discourse without imposing conformity in thought. The approach should be censureship, not censorship. . . .

Such a program might include a university statement of principle about diversity and multiculturalism that students would see during the application process; a discussion of civil discourse and sensitivity during student orientation; adoption of statements of principle by campus organizations; student government candidates who promote tolerance in the campus community; faculty workshops that help professors deal with the problems of hate speech; student publications that deal fairly and frankly with racism and sexism; a way for victims of hate speech to report it, to address a forum within which to decry it. . . .

What the critics of speech codes have discovered in this whole process is that simply waving the First Amendment flag and walking away will not win the day. They have to stay and debate. They have to match the creativity and passion of the speech code advocates. They must dare to defend bad words for good principles.

They must show that the First Amendment does not take sides. They must show that all sides can march under the First Amendment banner. All sides must heed its mandate for tolerance, understanding, and a search for common ground. In it, there is hope. It may well be the only hope.

TOWARD CRITICAL THINKING

1. Are campus speech codes denials of basic First Amendment rights? The Supreme Court has ruled that speech that might incite violence can be regulated or banned by the states. Does the kind of speech regulated by speech codes fall into the same category?

2. Irrespective of their constitutionality, what are good arguments against speech codes? For them?

· *19* ·

The Rights of Criminal Defendants

Criminal defendants are also given significant protections in the Bill of Rights. During the liberal Warren Court era (1953–1969) the Court for the first time made many of the guarantees contained in the Bill of Rights applicable to the states, including the right to be free from unreasonable searches and seizures[*]; the right to counsel, as illustrated in *Gideon* v. *Wainwright* (1963) (Reading 19a); the right to confront witnesses[**]; and the right to a trial by jury.[†] As many liberal justices have retired and were replaced by more conservative justices, several Warren Court and even Burger Court decisions were modified or overruled. *McCleskey* v. *Kemp* (1987) (Reading 19b) illustrates how far the Rehnquist Court has altered principles enunciated by earlier courts.

---

[*] *Mapp* v. *Ohio,* 367 U.S. 643 (1961).
[**] *Pointer* v. *Texas,* 380 U.S. 400 (1965).
[†] *Duncan* v. *Louisiana,* 391 U.S. 145 (1968).

· *19a* ·

Gideon *v.* Wainwright

372 U.S. 335 (1963)

Clarence Earl Gideon was arrested for breaking into a pool hall. At his trial, he represented himself; the state of Florida did not have to supply him with a lawyer because Gideon was not charged with a capital offense. Gideon, a poor, uneducated man, was no match for the local prosecutor, and he was found guilty of the charges against him.

Once in prison, Gideon became something of a jail-house lawyer. He used all of his free time to study law in the prison library, and he filed a number of unsuccessful lower court actions challenging the constitutionality of his incarceration. He got lucky when he sent a handwritten petition to the U.S. Supreme Court. Not only did the Justices accept his case for review, but the Court also appointed Abe Fortas, a prominent Washington, D.C., lawyer (and future Supreme Court Justice) to represent Gideon. Twenty-two states signed on to an *amicus curiae* brief written by the Attorney General of Minnesota, Walter Mondale (who later was to be elected vice president of the United States), in support of Gideon. Those states already guaranteed their citizens who were too poor to afford an attorney legal representation in non-capital offenses.

Opinion: Justice Hugo Black
Vote: 9 to 0

. . .

Since 1942, when *Betts* v. *Brady* was decided by a divided Court, the problem of a defendant's federal constitutional right to counsel in a state court has been a continuing source of controversy and litigation in both state and federal courts. To give this problem another review here, we granted *certiorari*. Since Gideon was proceeding *in forma pauperis,* we appointed counsel to represent him and requested both sides to discuss in their briefs and oral arguments the following: "Should this Court's holding in *Betts* v. *Brady* be reconsidered?"

The facts upon which Betts claimed that he had been unconstitutionally denied the right to have counsel appointed to assist him are strikingly like the facts upon which Gideon here bases his federal constitutional claim. . . . Since the facts and circumstances of the two cases are so nearly indistinguishable, we think the *Betts* v. *Brady* holding if left standing would require us to reject Gideon's claim that the Constitution guarantees him the assistance of counsel. Upon full reconsideration we conclude that *Betts* v. *Brady* should be overruled.

The Sixth Amendment provides, "In all criminal prosecutions, the accused shall enjoy the right . . . to have the Assistance of Counsel for his defence." We have construed this to mean that in federal courts counsel must be provided for defendants unable to employ counsel unless the right is competently and intelligently waived. Betts argued that this right is extended to indigent defendants in state courts by the Fourteenth Amendment. In response the Court stated that, while the Sixth Amendment laid down "no rule for the conduct of the states, the question recurs whether the constraint laid by the amendment upon the national courts expresses a rule so fundamental and essential to a fair trial, and so, to due process of law, that it is made obligatory upon the states by the Fourteenth Amendment." In order to decide whether the Sixth Amendment's guarantee of counsel is of this fundamental nature, the Court in *Betts* set out and considered "[r]elevant data on the subject . . . afforded by constitutional and statutory provisions subsisting in the colonies and the states prior to the inclusion of the Bill of Rights in the national Constitution, and in the constitutional, legislative, and judicial history of the states to the present date." On the basis of this historical data the Court concluded that "appointment of counsel is not a fundamental right, essential to a fair trial." . . .

We accept *Betts* v. *Brady*'s assumption, based as it was on our prior cases, that a provision of the Bill of Rights which is "fundamental and essential to a fair trial" is made obligatory upon the States by the Fourteenth Amendment. We think the Court in *Betts* was wrong, however, in concluding that the Sixth Amendment's guarantee of counsel is not one of these fundamental rights. Ten years before *Betts* v. *Brady,* this Court, after full consideration of all the historical data examined in *Betts,* had unequivocally declared that "the right to the aid of counsel is of this fundamental character." . . . Several years later, in 1936, the Court reemphasized what it had said about the fundamental nature of the right to counsel in this language:

> "We concluded that certain fundamental rights, safeguarded by the first eight amendments against federal action, were also safeguarded against state action by the due process of law clause of the Fourteenth Amendment, and among them the fundamental right of the accused to the aid of counsel in a criminal prosecution." . . .

In light of these and many other prior decisions of the Court, it is not surprising that the *Betts* Court, when faced with the contention that "one charged with crime, who is unable to obtain counsel, must be furnished counsel by the state," conceded that "[e]xpressions in the opinions of this court lend color to the argument. . . ." The fact is that in deciding as it did—that "appointment of counsel is not a fundamental right, essential to a fair trial"—the Court in *Betts* v. *Brady* made an abrupt break with its own well-considered precedents. In returning to these old precedents sounder we believe than the new, we but restore constitutional principles established to achieve a fair system of justice. Not only these precedents but also reason and reflection require us to recognize that in our adversary system of criminal justice, any person haled into court, who is too poor to hire a lawyer, cannot be assured a fair trial unless counsel is provided for him. This seems to us to be an obvious truth. Governments, both state and federal, quite properly spend vast sums of money to establish machinery to try defendants accused of crime. Lawyers to prosecute are everywhere deemed essential to protect the public's interest in an orderly society. Similarly, there are few defendants charged with crime, few indeed, who fail to hire the best lawyers they can get to prepare and present their defenses. That government hires lawyers to prosecute and defendants who have the money hire lawyers to defend are the strongest indications of the widespread belief that lawyers in criminal courts are necessities, not luxuries. The right of one charged with crime to counsel may not be deemed fundamental and essential to fair trials in some countries, but it is in ours. From the very beginning, our state and national constitutions and laws have laid great emphasis on procedural and substantive safeguards designed to assure fair trials before impartial tribunals in which every defendant stands equal before the law. This noble ideal cannot be realized if the poor man charged with crime has to face his accusers without a lawyer to assist him, A defendant's need for a lawyer is nowhere better stated than in the moving words of Mr. Justice Sutherland in *Powell* v. *Alabama*:

> "The right to be heard would be, in many cases, of little avail if it did not comprehend the right to be heard by counsel. Even the intelligent and educated layman has small and sometimes no skill in the science of law. If charged with a crime, he is incapable, generally, of determining for himself whether the indictment is good or bad. He is unfamiliar with the rules of evidence. Left without the aid of counsel he may be put on trial without a proper charge, and convicted upon incompetent evidence, or evidence irrelevant to the issue or otherwise inadmissible. He lacks both the skill and knowledge adequately to prepare his defense, even though he have a perfect one. He requires the guiding hand of counsel at every step in the proceedings against him. Without it, though he be not guilty, he faces the dangers of conviction because he does not know how to establish his innocence."

The Court in *Betts* v. *Brady* departed from the sound wisdom upon which the Court's holding in *Powell* v. *Alabama* rested. Florida, supported by two other States, has asked that *Betts* v. *Brady* be left intact. Twenty-two States, as friends of the Court, argue that Betts was "an anachronism when handed down" and that it should now be overruled. We agree.

The judgment is reversed and the cause is remanded to the Supreme Court of Florida for further actions not inconsistent with this opinion.

TOWARD CRITICAL THINKING

1. Precedents are prior decisions of the Court that are usually given great weight. In expanding the rights of criminal defendants in state court proceedings under the Sixth and Fourteenth Amendments, Justice Black noted several precedents. Which ones seemed to influence this Court the most? Why?

2. Anti-Federalists were very concerned that the national government would not give citizens the liberties they enjoyed in the states. In the case of rights of criminal defendants, the liberal Warren Court forced national norms on the states. What do you think Samuel Bryan or other Anti-Federalists would say about that development?

· 19b ·

McCleskey *v.* Kemp

481 U.S. 279 (1987)

In 1972, in *Furman* v. *Georgia,*[*] the U.S. Supreme Court for the first time struck down imposition of the death penalty under the "cruel and unusual punishment" clause of the Eighth Amendment. A Georgia jury had convicted Furman of murder, and two other juries had convicted two other defendants of rape. All three juries imposed the death penalty without having been given any specific guidelines by their trial court judges. All three convicted men were African Americans. *Furman*'s five-justice majority ruled that allowing juries wide discretion produced random results. This randomness was cruel and unusual punishment and as such violated the Eighth Amendment. In a separate opinion, Justice William O. Douglas went on to conclude that the death penalty was disproportionately applied to the poor and socially disadvantaged.

After *Furman,* several states enacted new laws to provide instructions to judges and juries concerning the kinds of crimes that could be subject to the death penalty. In 1976, in *Gregg* v. *Georgia,*[**] the U.S. Supreme Court upheld Georgia's new bifurcated system (a separate hearing is held on the sentence after the conviction and new evidence can be introduced) as effectively preventing disproportionate and arbitrary death sentences.

Since 1976 the death penalty has been available in most states, and death sentences are becoming more and more common as a clear majority of the Court finds no constitutional problem with the death penalty. But one issue that continued to be litigated was the question of whether the apparent disproportionate number of African Americans who were "death sentenced" violated the Eighth and/or Fourteenth Amendments. In *McCleskey* v. *Kemp* the Supreme Court first discusses whether Georgia's capital punishment statute violated the equal protection clause of the Fourteenth Amendment.

A study conducted by law professor David Baldus that was introduced at trial found that the death penalty was imposed in 11 percent of the cases when a defendant was charged with killing a white person compared with only 1 percent of the cases in which a defendant was charged with killing an African American. Moreover, the death penalty was imposed in 22 percent of the cases involving African-American defendants and white victims and in only 8 percent of the cases involving white defendants and white victims. Black-on-black crime resulted in only

---

[*] 408 U.S. 238 (1972).
[**] 428 U.S. 153 (1976).

1 percent of the defendants being given a death sentence. Warren McCleskey was a black man who had killed a white police officer.

In analyzing McCleskey's claims, the Supreme Court first turned to his allegation that his death sentence violated the equal protection clause of the Fourteenth Amendment. The Court found that the Baldus study did not establish that the administration of the Georgia capital punishment system was discriminatory. The justices then turned to consider McCleskey's Eighth Amendment claim.

Majority Opinion: Justice Lewis Powell
Dissenting Opinion: Justice William Brennan
Vote: 5 to 4

. . .

McCleskey also argues that the Baldus study demonstrates that the Georgia capital sentencing system violates the Eighth Amendment. . . .

. . . [O]ur decisions since *Furman* have identified a constitutionally permissible range of discretion in imposing the death penalty. First, there is a required threshold below which the death penalty cannot be imposed. In this context, the State must establish rational criteria that narrow the decisionmaker's judgment as to whether the circumstances of a particular defendant's case meet the threshold. . . . Second, States cannot limit the sentencer's consideration of any relevant circumstance that could cause it to decline to impose the penalty. In this respect, the State cannot channel the sentencer's discretion, but must allow it to consider any relevant information offered by the defendant.

. . .

IV ◆

In light of our precedents under the Eighth Amendment, McCleskey cannot argue successfully that his sentence is "disproportionate to the crime in the traditional sense." . . . He does not deny that he committed a murder in the course of a planned robbery, a crime for which this Court has determined that the death penalty constitutionally may be imposed. . . . His disproportionality claim "is of a different sort." . . . McCleskey argues that the sentence in his case is disproportionate to the sentences in other murder cases.

On the one hand, he cannot base a constitutional claim on an argument that his case differs from other cases in which defendants *did* receive the death penalty. On automatic appeal, the Georgia Supreme Court found that McCleskey's death sentence was not disproportionate to other death sentences imposed in the State. . . .

. . . [A]bsent a showing that the Georgia capital punishment system operates in an arbitrary and capricious manner, McCleskey cannot prove a constitutional violation by demonstrating that other defendants who may be similarly situated did *not* receive the death penalty. . . .

Because McCleskey's sentence was imposed under Georgia sentencing procedures that focus discretion "on the particularized nature of the crime and the individual defendant," . . . we lawfully may presume that McCleskey's death sentence was not "wantonly and freakishly" imposed, . . . and thus that the sentence is not disproportionate within any recognized meaning under the Eighth Amendment.

Although our decision in *Gregg* as to the facial validity of the Georgia capital punishment statute appears to foreclose McCleskey's disproportionality argument, he further contends that the Georgia capital punishment system is arbitrary and capricious in *application,* and therefore his sentence is excessive, because racial considerations may influence capital sentencing decisions in Georgia. . . .

To evaluate McCleskey's challenge, we must examine exactly what the Baldus study may show. Even Professor Baldus does not contend that his statistics *prove* that race enters into any capital sentencing decisions or that race was a factor in McCleskey's particular case. Statistics at most may show only a likelihood that a particular factor entered into some decisions. There is, of course, some risk of racial prejudice influencing a jury's decision in a criminal case. There are similar risks that other kinds of prejudice will influence other criminal trials. . . . The question "is at what point that risk becomes constitutionally unacceptable . . . ." McCleskey asks us to accept the likelihood allegedly shown by the Baldus study as the constitutional measure of an unacceptable risk of racial prejudice influencing capital sentencing decisions. This we decline to do. . . .

At most, the Baldus study indicates a discrepancy that appears to correlate with race. Apparent disparities in sentencing are an inevitable part of our criminal justice system. The discrepancy indicated by the Baldus study is "a far cry from the major systemic defects identified in *Furman*". . . . As this Court has recognized, any mode for determining guilt or punishment "has its weaknesses and the potential for misuse." . . .

Specifically, "there can be 'no perfect procedure for deciding in which cases governmental authority should be used to impose death,'" . . . Where the discretion that is fundamental to our criminal process is involved, we decline to assume that what is unexplained is invidious. In light of the safeguards designed to minimize racial bias in the process, the fundamental value of jury trial in our criminal justice system, and the benefits that discretion provides to criminal defendants, we hold that the Baldus study does not demonstrate a constitutionally significant risk of racial bias affecting the Georgia capital-sentencing process.

McCleskey's arguments are best presented to the legislative bodies. It is not the responsibility—or indeed even the right—of this Court to determine the appropriate punishment for particular crimes. It is the legislatures, the elected representatives of the people, that are "constituted to respond to the will and consequently the moral values of the people." . . . Capital punishment is now the law in more than two-thirds of our States. It is the ultimate duty of courts to determine on a case-by-case basis whether these laws are applied consistently with the Constitution. Despite McCleskey's wide-ranging arguments that basically challenge the validity of capital punishment in our multi-racial society, the only question before us is whether in his case, . . . the law of Georgia was properly applied. . . .

Accordingly, we affirm the judgment of the Court of Appeals for the Eleventh Circuit.

It is so ordered.

Justice Brennan with whom Justice Marshall joins, and with whom Justice Blackmun and Justice Stevens join . . . dissenting.

I ✦

Adhering to my view that the death penalty is in all circumstances cruel and unusual punishment forbidden by the Eighth and Fourteenth Amendments, I would vacate the decision below insofar as it left undisturbed the death sentence imposed in this case.

Even if I did not hold this position, however, I would reverse the Court of Appeals, for petitioner McCleskey has clearly demonstrated that his death sentence was imposed in violation of the Eighth and Fourteenth Amendments. . . .

III ✦

It is important to emphasize at the outset that the Court's observation that McCleskey cannot *prove* the influence of race on any particular sentencing decision is irrelevant in evaluating his Eighth Amendment claim [Emphasis supplied]. Since *Furman* v. *Georgia* . . . the Court has been concerned with the *risk* of the imposition of an arbitrary sentence, rather than the proven fact of one. *Furman* held that the death penalty "may not be imposed under sentencing procedures that create a substantial risk that the punishment will be inflicted in an arbitrary and capricious manner." . . . This emphasis on risk acknowledges the difficulty of divining the jury's motivation in an individual case. In addition, it reflects the fact that concern for arbitrariness focuses on the rationality of the system as a whole, and that a system that features a significant probability that sentencing decisions are influenced by impermissible considerations cannot be regarded as rational. As we said in *Gregg* v. *Georgia* . . . "the petitioner looks to the sentencing system as a whole (as the Court did in *Furman* and we do today)": a constitutional violation is established if a plaintiff demonstrates a "*pattern* of arbitrary and capricious sentencing." . . .

Evaluation of McCleskey's evidence cannot rest solely on the numbers themselves. We must also ask whether the conclusion suggested by those numbers is consonant with our understanding of history and human experience. Georgia's legacy of a race-conscious criminal justice system, as well as this Court's own recognition of the persistent danger that racial attitudes may affect criminal proceedings, indicate that McCloskey's claim is not a fanciful product of mere statistical artifice.

For many years, Georgia operated openly and formally precisely the type of dual system the evidence shows is still effectively in place. The criminal law expressly differentiated between crimes committed by and against blacks and whites, distinctions whose lineage traced back to the time of slavery. During the colonial period, black slaves who killed whites in Georgia, regardless of whether in self-defense or in defense of another, were automatically executed. . . .

By the time of the Civil War, a dual system of crime and punishment was well established in Georgia. . . . The state criminal code contained separate sections for "Slaves and Free Persons of Color" . . . and for all other persons. . . . The code provided, for instance, for an automatic death sentence for murder committed by blacks, . . . but declared that anyone else convicted of murder might receive life imprisonment if the conviction were founded solely on circumstantial testimony *or* simply if the jury so recommended. . . . The code established that the rape of a free white female by a black "shall be" punishable by death. . . . However, rape by anyone else of a free white female was punishable by a prison term not less than two nor more than twenty years. The rape of *blacks* was punishable "by fine and imprisonment, at the direction of the court." . . . A black convicted of assaulting a free white person with intent to murder could be put to death at the discretion of the court, . . . but the same offense committed against a black, slave or free, was classified as a "minor" offense whose punishment lay in the discretion of the court, as long as such punishment did not "extend to life, limb or health."

This historical review of Georgia criminal law is not intended as a bill of indictment calling the State to account for past transgression. Citation of past practices does not justify the automatic condemnation of current ones. But it would be unrealistic to ignore the influence of history in assessing the plausible implications of McCleskey's evidence. . . .

History and its continuing legacy thus buttress the probative force of McCleskey's statistics. Formal dual criminal laws may no longer be in effect, and intentional discrimination may no longer be prominent. Nonetheless, as we acknowledged in *Turner,* "subtle, less consciously held racial attitudes" continue to be of concern, 476 U.S., at ____, 106 S.Ct., at 1687, and the Georgia system gives such attitudes considerable room to operate. The conclusions drawn from McCleskey's statistical evidence are therefore consistent with the lessons of social experience.

The majority thus misreads our Eighth Amendment jurisprudence in concluding that McCleskey has not demonstrated a degree of risk sufficient to raise constitutional concern. The determination of the significance of his evidence is at its core an exercise in human moral judgment, not a mechanical statistical analysis. It must first and foremost be informed by awareness of the fact that death is irrevocable, and that as a result "the qualitative difference of death from all other punishments requires a greater degree of scrutiny of the capital sentencing determination." *California* v. *Ramos.* For this reason, we have demanded a uniquely high degree of rationality in imposing the death penalty. A capital-sentencing system in which race more likely than not plays a role does not meet this standard. It is true that every nuance of decision cannot be statistically captured, nor can any individual judgment be plumbed with absolute certainty. Yet the fact that we must always act without the illumination of complete knowledge cannot induce paralysis when we confront what is literally an issue of life and death. Sentencing data, history, and experience all counsel that Georgia has provided insufficient assurance of the heightened rationality we have required in order to take a human life.

TOWARD CRITICAL THINKING

1. What factors led a majority of the Court to conclude that the death penalty—as imposed in Georgia—did not violate the guarantees contained in the Eighth Amendment? What role, if any, do you think public opinion played in the Court's decision?

2. In 1994, in a case involving the constitutionality of Texas's use of intravenous fluids to carry out a death sentence, soon-to-retire Justice Harry Blackmun noted in his lone dissent that he would no longer "coddle the court's delusion" that capital punishment can be fair, saying that the system used to implement the death penalty is "arbitrary and biased against poor and black defendants."[*] Not long thereafter, it was reported that former Justice Powell, the author of *McCleskey,* would change all of his votes in capital cases because capital punishment "serves no useful purpose."[**] Given that the Fourteenth Amendment was used to make the Eighth Amendment applicable to the states, should evidence of some discrimination in the administration of the system be grounds for finding the death penalty unconstitutional? Should the purpose of the penalty be considered in evaluating its constitutionality, as suggested by Justice Powell?

---

[*] *Callins* v. *Collins,* 114 S. Ct. 1127 (1994).
[**] "Powell Recants Death Penalty View," *The National Law Journal,* June 13, 1994, p. A12.

THINKING ABOUT CIVIL LIBERTIES

1. What would Anti-Federalists think about expansion of the Bill of Rights to include protections from state governmental action?

2. Think about the four cases included in this section. Would any of them be decided differently if Samuel Bryan and other Anti-Federalists were on the Court?

3. What kinds of speech did Madison intend the First Amendment to protect? Should only political speech be given special protection? What other civil liberties should be included in that category?

CHAPTER 5

◆ ◆ ◆

Civil Rights

When the Framers were drafting the Constitution, most were intent on creating a workable structure of government. Others, particularly Anti-Federalists, were concerned about governmental interference with civil liberties. Little attention, if any, however, was given to the notion of what we today term "civil rights." As illustrated in *Federalist No. 42* (Reading 20), even the most onerous of civil rights deprivations—slavery—was discussed only in terms of how to regulate it—*not* how to eliminate it.

The failure of the Framers to come to terms with the issue of slavery contributed to the Civil War. One immediate outcome of that war, however, was passage of the Thirteenth, Fourteenth, and Fifteenth Amendments. Despite the civil rights guarantees in those amendments, throughout the South numerous restrictions on the civil rights of African Americans were implemented. It wasn't until much later, as highlighted in Reading 16, that the passage of the Fourteenth Amendment was used effectively to end the onerous Jim Crow laws and practices that kept African Americans as second-class citizens. Not until 1954, in fact, did the U.S. Supreme Court act to shake the foundations of segregation by ruling that the "separate but equal doctrine" announced by an earlier Court had no place in education. *Brown* v. *Board of Education of Topeka* (1954) (Reading 21) truly began a second constitutional and societal revolution, of which the Civil Rights Act of 1964, which barred discrimination in employment based on race, color, or sex, was just one part.

In spite of *Brown* and subsequent legislation, segregation continues to exist, as highlighted by William Celis 3d in "Forty Years After *Brown*, Segregation Persists." (Reading 22). Other inequities also continue, as underscored by Readings 25 and 26 which deal with affirmative action.

African Americans have not been the only "out" group to encounter discrimination in the United States. Women, as well as a variety of other groups at various points in time, also have experienced discrimination. It wasn't until after African Americans made significant legal inroads, however, that discrimination against women was even considered to be impermissible under the Fourteenth Amendment, as discussed in Reading 23. And there are indications that the addition of a second woman to the U.S. Supreme Court has stopped the Court's conservative drift on issues of civil rights as they affect women, as illustrated in *J.E.B.* v. *Alabama* (1994) (Reading 24).

Because some vestiges of race and sex discrimination continue, affirmative action programs have been implemented or suggested as a way to compensate or make up for those inequities. But the equal protection clause is not phrased in a race- or gender-conscious way. The question therefore arises whether affirmative action programs, although designed to help people who have suffered discrimination, actually violate the constitutional rights of others who cannot benefit from those programs. Seymour Martin Lipset explains the dilemma this creates in Reading 26.

· 20 ·

Federalist No. 42

JAMES MADISON

The Framers gave little, if any, thought to the civil rights of most citizens. As early as the Second Continental Congress, Abigail Adams had urged her husband John (later to be the second president of the United States) to "remember the ladies . . . in any new code of laws." Her admonitions did little good. Neither women nor slaves could find much comfort in the new Constitution. In fact, although even the idea of slavery was repugnant to many in attendance at the Constitutional Convention, attendees feared any real discussion of it would have doomed the meeting and the fragile alliances that were needed there. Thus, in *Federalist No. 42*, slavery is mentioned, but it is done only in the context of duties (taxes) to be placed on slaves to discourage their importation into the United States.

The second class of powers lodged in the general government consist of those which regulate the intercourse with foreign nations, to wit: to make treaties; to send and receive ambassadors, other public ministers, and consuls; to define and punish piracies and felonies committed on the high seas, and offenses against the law of nations; to regulate foreign commerce, including the power to prohibit, after the year 1808, the importation of slaves, and to lay an intermediate duty of ten dollars per head, as a discouragement of such importations.

This class of powers forms an obvious and essential branch of the federal administration. If we are to be one nation in any respect, it clearly ought to be in respect to other nations. . . .

It ought to be considered as a great point gained in favor of humanity that a period of twenty years may terminate forever, within these States, the traffic which has so long and so loudly been given by so great a majority of the Union. Happy would it be for the unfortunate Africans if an equal prospect lay before them of being redeemed from the oppression of their European brethren!

. . . The powers included in the third class are those which provide for the harmony and proper intercourse among the States. . . . Were these at liberty to regulate the trade between State and State, it must be foreseen that ways would be found out to load articles of import and export, during passage through their jurisdiction, with duties which would fall on the makers of the latter and the consumers of the former. . . .

Nothing which tends to facilitate intercourse between the States can be deemed unworthy of the public care.

TOWARD CRITICAL THINKING

1. Slavery, the issue that the Framers wished to avoid, ultimately almost destroyed the nation when the Civil War was fought. Do you think the original reticence of the Framers to deal in any great detail with this issue was justified?

2. What did the ban on the importation of slaves after 1808 accomplish?

· *21* ·

Brown *v.* Board of Education of Topeka

347 U.S. 483 (1954)

In the aftermath of the Civil War, the Thirteenth, Fourteenth, and Fifteenth Amendments were added to the Constitution, as discussed in Reading 16, "Seventeen Words: The Quiet Revolution of the Fourteenth Amendment." The Thirteenth Amendment abolished slavery, the Fourteenth Amendment guaranteed all citizens equal protection and due process of the laws, and the Fifteenth Amendment gave all newly freed male slaves the right to vote.

In spite of those civil rights guarantees, the Southern states, in particular, ingeniously passed all types of laws to deprive African Americans of the rights to vote, to use public facilities, to live in certain sections of town, and to attend quality public schools, colleges, and universities. *Brown* v. *Board of Education of Topeka* (1954) (Reading 21) was the culmination of a legal strategy adopted by the National Association for the Advancement of Colored People's Legal Defense and Education Fund (LDF) to overrule an earlier Supreme Court decision—*Plessy* v. *Ferguson.*[*] In *Plessy,* the Court ruled that a state's maintenance of separate facilities for blacks and whites was permitted under the equal protection clause. The LDF, under the directorship of Thurgood Marshall (later the first African American to be appointed to the U.S. Supreme Court), first challenged in court state failure to provide equal law school and graduate school educations to African Americans before tackling the much more controversial issue of the desegregation of elementary and secondary schools.

Brown was actually four cases—one each from Kansas, South Carolina, Virginia, and Delaware—that were consolidated by the Court under a single name. Each state required that separate schools be provided for black and white children. The plaintiff in the lead case was Linda Brown, whose father, a local minister, agreed to act as an LDF plaintiff. He was angry that his eleven-year old was required to walk to an all-black school twenty-one blocks from her home, passing a school reserved for white children just five blocks away. *Brown* presented the Supreme Court with issues, the resolution of which could cause major social change, a fact not lost on the justices. The case was actually argued twice before the Court; the second time the justices asked lawyers on both sides to provide the Court with more information on the question of whether

---

[*]163 U.S. 537 (1896).

the Fourteenth Amendment was intended to prohibit educational discrimination.

Opinion: Chief Justice Earl Warren

Vote: 9 to 0

These cases come to us from the States of Kansas, South Carolina, Virginia, and Delaware. They are premised on different facts and different local conditions, but a common legal question justifies their consideration together in this consolidated opinion.

In each of the cases, minors of the Negro race, through their legal representatives, seek the aid of the courts in obtaining admission to the public schools of their community on a nonsegregated basis. In each instance, they had been denied admission to schools attended by white children under laws requiring or permitting segregation according to race. This segregation was alleged to deprive the plaintiffs of the equal protection of the laws under the Fourteenth Amendment. In each of the cases other than the Delaware case, a three-judge federal district court denied relief to the plaintiffs on the so-called "separate but equal" doctrine announced by this Court in *Plessy* v. *Ferguson*. . . . Under that doctrine, equality of treatment is accorded when the races are provided substantially equal facilities even though these facilities be separate. In the Delaware case, the Supreme Court of Delaware adhered to that doctrine, but ordered that the plaintiffs be admitted to the white schools because of their superiority to the Negro schools.

The plaintiffs contend that segregated public schools are not "equal" and cannot be made "equal," and that hence they are deprived of the equal protection of the laws. Because of the obvious importance of the question presented, the Court took jurisdiction. Argument was heard in the 1952 Term, and reargument was heard this Term on certain questions propounded by the Court.

Reargument was largely devoted to the circumstances surrounding the adoption of the Fourteenth Amendment in 1868. It covered exhaustively consideration of the Amendment in Congress, ratification by the states, then existing practices in racial segregation, and the views of proponents and opponents of the Amendment. This discussion and our own investigation convince us that, although these sources cast some light, it is not enough to resolve the problem with which we are faced. At best, they are inconclusive. The most avid proponents of the post-War Amendments undoubtedly intended them to remove all legal distinctions among "all persons born or naturalized in the United States." Their opponents, just as certainly were antagonistic to both the letter and the spirit of the Amendments and wished them to have the most limited effect. What others in Congress and the state legislatures had in mind cannot be determined with any degree of certainty.

An additional reason for the inconclusive nature of the Amendment's history, with respect to segregated schools, is the status of public education at that time. In the South, the movement toward free common schools, supported by general taxation, had not yet taken hold. Education of white children was largely in the hands of private groups. Education of Negroes was almost nonexistent, and practically all of the race were illiterate. In fact, any education of Negroes was forbidden by law in some states. Today, in contrast, many Negroes have achieved outstanding success in the arts and sciences as well as in the business and professional world. It is true that public education had already advanced further in the North, but the effect of the Amendment on Northern States was generally ignored in the congressional debates. Even in the North, the conditions of public education did not approximate those existing today. The curriculum was usually rudimentary; ungraded schools were common in rural areas; the school term was but three months a year in many states; and compulsory school attendance was virtually unknown. As a consequence, it is not surprising that there should be so little in the history of the Fourteenth Amendment relating to its intended effect on public education.

In the first cases in this Court construing the Fourteenth Amendment, decided shortly after its adoption, the Court interpreted it as proscribing all state-imposed discriminations against the Negro race. The doctrine of "separate but equal" did not make its appearance in this Court until 1896 in the case of *Plessy* v. *Ferguson, supra,* involving not education but transportation. American courts have since labored with the doctrine for over half a century. In this Court, there have been six cases involving the "separate but equal" doctrine in the field of public education. In *Cumming* v. *County Board of Education* . . . and *Gong Lum* v. *Rice* . . . , the validity of the doctrine itself was not challenged. In more recent cases, all on the graduate school level, inequality was found in that specific benefits enjoyed by white students were denied to Negro students of the same educational qualifications. *Missouri* ex rel. *Gaines* v. *Canada; Sipuel* v. *Oklahoma; Sweatt* v. *Painter; McLaurin* v. *Oklahoma State Regents.* In none of these cases was it necessary to reexamine the doctrine to grant relief to the Negro plaintiff. And in *Sweatt* v. *Painter, supra,* the Court expressly reserved decision on the question whether *Plessy* v. *Ferguson* should be held inapplicable to public education.

In the instant cases, that question is directly presented. Here, unlike *Sweatt* v. *Painter,* there are findings below that the Negro and white schools involved have been equalized, or are being equalized, with respect to buildings, curricula, qualifications and salaries of teachers, and other "tangible" factors. Our decision, therefore, cannot turn on merely a comparison of these tangible factors in the Negro and white schools involved in each of the cases. We must look instead to the effect of segregation itself on public education.

In approaching this problem, we cannot turn the clock back to 1868 when the Amendment was adopted, or even to 1896 when *Plessy* v. *Ferguson* was written. We must consider public education in the light of its full development and its present place in American life throughout the Nation. Only in this way can it be determined if segregation in public schools deprives these plaintiffs of the equal protection of the laws.

Today, education is perhaps the most important function of state and local governments. Compulsory school attendance laws and the great expenditures for education both demonstrate our recognition of the importance of education to our democratic society. It is required in the performance of our most basic public responsibilities, even service in the armed forces. It is the very foundation of good citizenship. Today it is a principal instrument in awakening the child to cultural values, in preparing him for later professional training, and in helping him to adjust normally to his environment. In these days, it is doubtful that any child may reasonably be expected to succeed in life if he is denied the opportunity of an education. Such an opportunity, where the state has undertaken to provide it, is a right which must be made available to all on equal terms.

We come then to the question presented: Does segregation of children in public schools solely on the basis of race, even though the physical facilities and other "tangible" factors may be equal, deprive the children of the minority group of equal educational opportunities? We believe that it does.

In *Sweatt* v. *Painter, supra,* in finding that a segregated law school for Negroes could not provide them equal educational opportunities, this Court relied in large part on "those qualities which are incapable of objective measurement but which make for greatness in a law school." In *McLaurin* v. *Oklahoma State Regents, supra,* the Court, in requiring that a Negro admitted to a white graduate school be treated like all other students, again resorted to intangible considerations: " . . . his ability to study, to engage in discussions and exchange views with other students, and, in general, to learn his profession." Such considerations apply with added force to children in grade and high schools. To separate them from others of similar age and qualifications solely because of their race generates a feeling of inferiority as to their status in the community that may affect their hearts and minds in a way unlikely ever to be undone. The effect of this separation on their educational opportunities was well stated by a finding in the Kansas case by a court which nevertheless felt compelled to rule against the Negro plaintiffs:

> Segregation of white and colored children in public schools has a detrimental effect upon the colored children. The impact is greater when it has the sanction of the law; for the policy of separating the races is usually interpreted as denoting the inferiority of the Negro group. A

sense of inferiority affects the motivation of a child to learn. Segregation with the sanction of law, therefore, has a tendency to retard the educational and mental development of Negro children and to deprive them of some of the benefits they would receive in a racially integrated school system.

Whatever may have been the extent of psychological knowledge at the time of *Plessy* v. *Ferguson,* this finding is amply supported by modern authority. Any language in *Plessy* v. *Ferguson* contrary to this finding is rejected.

We conclude that in the field of public education the doctrine of "separate but equal" has no place.* Separate educational facilities are inherently unequal. Therefore, we hold that the plaintiffs and others similarly situated for whom the actions have been brought are, by reason of the segregation complained of, deprived of the equal protection of the laws guaranteed by the Fourteenth Amendment. This disposition makes unnecessary any discussion whether such segregation also violates the Due Process Clause of the Fourteenth Amendment.

Because these are class actions, because of the wide applicability of this decision, and because of the great variety of local conditions, the formulation of decrees in these cases presents problems of considerable complexity. On reargument, the consideration of appropriate relief was necessarily subordinated to the primary question—the constitutionality of segregation in public education. We have now announced that such segregation is a denial of the equal protection of the laws. In order that we may have the full assistance of the parties in formulating decrees, the cases will be restored to the docket, and the parties are requested to present further argument. . . .

TOWARD CRITICAL THINKING

1. By all accounts, Chief Justice Earl Warren struggled with some of his brethren to make certain that *Brown* was a unanimous decision. He knew that the Southern states would look for any opportunity to avoid the ruling. Do you think his was a proper assessment?

2. In *Brown,* the Court ruled that "separate but equal in education" was unconstitutional. Why do you think that the Court didn't go farther and outlaw legal, or what is called *de jure,* discrimination in all other situations such as employment or housing?

---

* At this point, in what is called Footnote Eleven, the Justices cite works by prominent psychiatrists psychologists, and other social scientists describing the harmful effects of segregation on the emotional and mental health of African-American school children.

· 22 ·

Forty Years after Brown, Segregation Persists

WILLIAM CELIS 3D

In 1955, just one year after *Brown,* the Supreme Court ruled that school desegregation must be accomplished "with all deliberate speed."[*] In 1994, the fortieth anniversary of the decision was marked around the United States with mixed feelings as report after report revealed that large numbers of schools or school systems remain segregated. Nearly 70 percent of all African-American students, in fact, attended segregated schools. "It was unrealistic to expect that we could overcome all these entrenched problems, even in forty years," said one NAACP official. "But it's not too late to turn this around. The question is whether the commitment is there."[**] William Celis 3d surveys the "progress" made toward reversing years of segregation and notes the role that segregated housing patterns play in this continuing problem.

Topeka Boulevard, a nine-mile-long stretch of commerce, fulfills most needs of the 120,000 people in this city on the plains. But the four-lane thoroughfare also serves an unintended purpose: dividing the races. Whites live to the west, blacks to the east.

Therein lies the problem for the city's public school system. The elementary schools, which were once deliberately segregated on school board orders, are segregated still, only now it results from housing patterns, not laws.

Those housing patterns have proved to be the implacable foe of school desegregation here and in some 1,200 school districts nationwide that are under Federal court desegregation orders. Such patterns have withstood busing programs that transported black children into predominantly white schools; they have withstood the creation of theme or "magnet" schools designed to lure white students from the suburbs to inner-city

SOURCE: William Celis 3d, "Forty Years After Brown, Segregation Persists," *The New York Times* (May 18, 1994): A1. Copyright © 1994 by The New York Times Company. Reprinted by permission.

[*] 349 U.S. 294 (1955)

[**] Quoted in William Celis 3d, "Forty Years After Brown, Segregation Persists," *The New York Times,* May 18, 1994: A1.

schools, and they have withstood the one-two punch of school consolidations and closings to achieve racial balance in the classrooms that remain.

Forty years have passed since the United States Supreme Court decided the landmark case, *Brown* v. *Board of Education of Topeka,* that outlawed segregated education and marked this city as the cradle of the school desegregation movement. The board no longer designates which schools white students should attend and which are set aside for blacks. But eleven of Topeka's twenty-six elementary schools, a middle school and one high school are still as segregated as the neighborhoods that feed them.

Nationwide, nearly 70 percent of black students attend segregated schools, that is, schools with mostly black and Hispanic enrollments. In 1968, the first year in which educational data were collected, some 78 percent of black students and 54 percent of Hispanic students attended predominantly minority schools. The only difference the intervening years have made is that minorities are now more likely to attend segregated schools in the Northeast and the Midwest than in the South.

Other forces have also undermined the desegregation of schools: stubborn attitudes about race, and the rampant unemployment and underemployment that condemn many minorities to inner cities. Also blunting the effort, civil rights workers say, is the absence of a national will to embrace aggressive solutions like raising taxes or redistributing tax dollars to bring the budgets of poor districts up to those of rich ones.

"School desegregation was not supposed to be a cure-all," said Gary L. Orfield, director of the Harvard Project on School Desegregation. "There was supposed to be a housing act and job opportunities. Most of them have been beaten down. School desegregation is one of the last legs standing, although it is bruised and beaten." . . .

◆ Topeka: Striving Again for Elusive Goal

In many ways, Topeka's experience is a microcosm of the history of desegregation nationally since 1954. Over the decades, the city became more integrated as employers offered good-paying jobs to black men and women, enabling them to enter the middle class and move their families into traditionally white neighborhoods. But whole neighborhoods were still inhabited by low-wage earners—blacks and, increasingly, other minorities, too.

In 1979, the American Civil Liberties Union (ACLU) reopened the *Brown* suit, asserting that the existence of thirteen racially segregated schools on either side of Topeka Boulevard violated the 1954 High Court ruling. . . .

After years of legal maneuvering, in 1993 a Federal court agreed with the ACLU. Now the Topeka district is proposing to close some of the segregated schools, bus more of its 15,000 students across neighborhood lines and create magnet schools, all in the name of integration.

But while several polls have shown that people support desegregation efforts nationally, they tend to fight it locally. Topeka is no exception. The school superintendent, Jeffrey W. Weaver, says he has received anonymous letters and calls with racial slurs from whites and blacks opposing the proposed plan, which was unveiled earlier this school year. He says the attitude among parents whose children will likely be affected by closings and busing is, "Why me?" . . .

◆ Housing: Tackling Root of Segregation

The Civil Rights Act of 1968 gave members of minority groups the right to buy and sell property wherever they wanted. The notion was that creating integrated neighborhoods would lead to integrated schools.

More than twenty-five years later, the legislation has still not delivered on all its promises, in part because the government has repeatedly subverted the plan. Even as Congress was approving the bill, the Department of Housing and Urban Development was building large public housing projects in inner cities, effectively concentrating huge numbers of minority families there. In the 1980's, the Reagan Administration's Justice Department allowed hundreds of complaints against biased real estate agents and landlords, filed under Federal fair-housing laws, to languish.

Battling against this history, the Palm Beach County [Florida] district decided to attack school segregation at its roots. In 1991, the district unveiled an innovative program, which called on home builders to devise strong advertising campaigns for black newspapers and radio stations, with the aim of selling houses to a greater racial mix. Some of the county's thirty seven incorporated communities also altered their building codes, allowing builders to erect more modestly sized and priced homes in areas that previously restricted housing to large lots and structures.

In return for making these changes and attracting minority families, the school district rewarded builders by letting children living in the new developments attend neighborhood schools rather than be bused to achieve integration.

◆ Progress in South Florida

While twenty-nine of the county's communities have signed agreements with the school district, which has 110,000 students across 2,500 square miles, success has been uneven. "In some communities, it has helped us," said Murray Harris, a district spokesman. "But over all, it has not helped us in the way we thought it would."

The percentage of minority residents in communities has increased, sometimes significantly. In Crestwood, it rose to 12.3 percent in 1994 from 3.1 percent in 1991; in Riverbridge, it increased to 11.5 percent this year from 2.3 percent in 1991. But housing prices in some communities remain too high for many black and Hispanic families.

Palm Beach County, however, is no longer alone in taking aim at segregated housing patterns. The Department of Housing and Urban Development will embark this summer on a $70-million model program, Moving to Opportunity, that will involve 6,200 families in New York City, Baltimore, Boston, Chicago and Los Angeles.

The program will assist families as they search for new housing in suburbs and other neighborhoods where they would ordinarily not look. The intent is to break up concentrations of poverty.

But the program may also be a boon to education, since studies indicate that concentrations of poor families with children place a heavy burden on the local schools that must serve their educational, medical and emotional needs.

◆ Magnets: A Powerful Lure, But Mixed Results

Build a curriculum around a special theme, like math or health. Lure the best teachers in those subjects to that school and invite students from all over the city to enroll in it.

The result is a type of public school, a magnet, that has been widely used to draw white students to predominantly black schools and black students to predominantly white ones. Such magnet schools are increasingly viewed as the most effective means to integration, because they give students and parents the freedom of choice. Still, they have a mixed record.

Kansas City, Mo., ringed by predominantly white suburbs, is struggling to make its magnet attract. By contrast, Montclair, N.J., has successfully used magnets to integrate its school-age population. New York City, the nation's largest school system and the home of the largest constellation of magnets, has also effectively used them as lures. . . .

Charlotte [North Carolina], however, stands apart from much of the nation. Its enrollment mix of 60 percent whites and 40 percent minority members has remained essentially unchanged for two decades, primarily because people can move to urban, rural and suburban areas without ever leaving the school district.

. . .

TABLE 5-1
A Tortuous Path Toward Integration

1954—*Brown* v. *Board of Education* (Topeka, Kan.) The United States Supreme Court rules, 9 to 0, that segregated schools are unconstitutional, overturning an 1896 Supreme Court decision, *Plessy* v. *Ferguson,* that said separate but equal facilities were constitutional.

1957—Gov. Orval Faubus of Arkansas orders the National Guard to prevent black students from enrolling in Central High School in Little Rock. President Dwight D. Eisenhower counters by ordering paratroopers to escort the students.

1964—Civil Rights Act of 1964 is approved by Congress. The legislation includes Title VI, allowing the Federal Government to withhold education money to districts that fail to desegregate schools.

1968—*Green* v. *New Kent County (Va.) Board of Education.* The Supreme Court rules that desegregation applies not only to students but also to faculty assignments, extracurricular activities and transportation.

1968—Civil Rights Act of 1968, or Fair Housing Act, gives minorities the right to buy and sell property where they want.

1971—*Swann* v. *Charlotte-Mecklenburg County (N.C.) Public Schools.* The Supreme Court rules that all approaches to school desegregation, including busing, must be used to integrate schools.

1973—*Keyes* v. *Denver School District.* The Supreme Court applies standards of the Charlotte case to Northern states, ruling that they must desegregate schools when segregation was created by the school board.

1974—*Milliken* v. *Bradley (Milliken I).* In the first substantial defeat for civil rights in more than two decades, the Supreme Court severely limits lower courts' ability to order suburbs to join with inner cities in school desegregation plans.

1977—*Milliken* v. *Bradley (Milliken II).* The Supreme Court rules that if school districts are unable to integrate because of housing patterns, increasing resources to inner-city schools with mostly minority enrollment is a satisfactory remedy.

1978—In Topeka, the American Civil Liberties Union reopens the *Brown* suit, arguing that vestiges of segregation remain.

1990—*Board of Education* v. *Dowell (Oklahoma City).* The Supreme Court rules that districts under desegregation order can be released from court supervision once they have taken all practical steps to eliminate the vestiges of legislated segregation.

1992—*Freeman* v. *Pitts* (DeKalb County, Ga.). In a ruling that civil rights advocates said further eroded the Brown decision, the Supreme Court ruled that Federal judges could stop supervising court-ordered school desegregation that they considered to have been achieved, even though full integration had not been achieved.

TOWARD CRITICAL THINKING

1. Political scientist Gerald R. Rosenberg argues that it wasn't until passage of the Civil Rights Act of 1964 that significant progress was made to end segregation in the United States.[*] Do you agree with his assessment? Or is significant progress yet to be made?

2. What are the major causes of continued segregation? What effect, if any, do you believe that the U.S. Supreme Court's decision in *Freeman* v. *Pitts* (1992) (See Table 5-1) will have on continued efforts to desegregate the schools?

---

[*] Gerald R. Rosenberg, *Hollow Hope* (Chicago: University of Chicago Press, 1991).

· 23 ·

Sex Discrimination and the Supreme Court

KAREN O'CONNOR

Women's inferior legal status was one reason that women came to-gether in Seneca Falls, New York, in 1848 at the first women's rights con-vention. It was another seventy-two years, however, before women won even the most elemental of democratic rights—the right to vote. And it was not until 1971 that the Supreme Court interpreted the equal protec-tion clause of the Fourteenth Amendment to prohibit any kind of state dis-crimination against women. Prior to that time, the Court had upheld a Michigan law that barred women from tending bar unless they were the wives or daughters of bar owners, deferring to the state's special interest in the social and "moral" problems of women."[*] Also, the Court had al-lowed Florida to justify its virtual exclusion of women from juries by ac-cepting the state's offer of traditional sex-role stereotypes as reasons to treat women differently from men.[**] Any "reasonable basis," as O'Con-nor notes, was sufficient to justify state discrimination against women. By 1976, however, the Supreme Court had fashioned a new intermediate "test" by which to evaluate the constitutionality of gender-based claims.

. . .

The Supreme Court is often looked upon as ahead of its time, or at least public opinion, in the expansion of rights of minorities. This has not been the case with the rights to women. Instead, as a general rule, the Court has lagged behind societal mores and realities when it has dealt with issues of concern to women. . . .

. . . Although the Fourteenth Amendment is a pledge of protection against state discrimination, over the years the Court has generally applied a two-tiered level of analysis to claims advanced under its provisions. Classifications based on race or national origin are considered suspect classifications and are entitled to be judged by the severe test of strict scrutiny. As such they are presumed invalid unless the government can

SOURCE: Karen O'Connor, "Gender," in Kermit L. Hall, ed. *The Oxford Companion to the Supreme Court of the United States* (New York: Oxford University Press, 1992), pp. 332–335. Copyright © 1992 by Oxford University Press, Inc. Reprinted by permission.

[*] *Goessaert v. Cleary,* 335 U.S. 464 (1948).
[**] *Hoyt v. Florida,* 368 U.S. 367 (1961).

show that they are "necessary to a compelling state interest" and that there were no less-restrictive alternative ways to achieve those goals. In contrast, when the Court applies the less stringent level of ordinary scrutiny, which until 1976 included all other legislative classifications, a state must show only a conceivable or reasonable basis for its action. . . .

It was not until the dawn of the current women's movement that judicial perspectives on what constitutes reasonable discrimination against women began to change. In 1966, the National Organization for Women (NOW) was founded. Soon after, a plethora of other women's rights groups were created. Most of these groups renewed the call for passage of an equal rights amendment (ERA) to the Constitution. While significant lobbying was carried out on that front, some groups, cognizant of the successes that the National Association for the Advancement of Colored People had in securing additional rights for African-Americans through the courts, began to explore the feasibility of a litigation strategy designed to seek a more expansive interpretation of the Fourteenth Amendment. Although prior forays into the courts had ended unfavorably, some believed that the times had changed enough for the justices (or some of the justices) to recognize that sex-based differential treatment of women was unconstitutional. Many believed that the status of women and the climate for change was sufficiently positive to convince even a conservative Court that some change was necessary.

The American Civil Liberties Union (ACLU), long a key player in the expansion of constitutional rights and liberties, led the planning for a comprehensive strategy to elevate sex to suspect classification status. Its first case was *Reed* v. *Reed* (1971). Ruth Bader Ginsburg, a member of the ACLU board, argued the case before the Supreme Court. Her enthusiasm and interest in the expansion of women's rights via constitutional interpretation led the ACLU to found the Women's Rights Project (WRP).

At issue in *Reed* was the constitutionality of an Idaho statute that required that males be preferred to otherwise equally qualified females as administrators of estates for those who died intestate. NOW, the National Federation of Business and Professional Women, and the Women's Equity Action League all filed *amicus curiae* briefs urging the Court to interpret the Fourteenth Amendment as prohibiting discrimination against women on account of sex. Democratic senator Birch Bayh of Indiana, a major sponsor of the ERA, wrote one of the briefs, in which he attempted to apprise the Court of the glaring legal inequities faced by women and to link those inequities, at least in part, to the Court's own persistent refusal to expand the reach of the Equal Protection Clause to gender discrimination. . . .

Chief Justice Warren Burger writing for a unanimous Court in *Reed,* held that the Idaho statute that provided "different treatment . . . to the applicants on the basis of their sex . . . establishes a classification subject to scrutiny under the Equal Protection Clause." . . . With these simple words, the Supreme Court for the first time concluded that sex-based differentials were entitled to some sort of scrutiny under the Fourteenth Amendment. But what type of scrutiny? According to Burger, . . . the test was whether the differential treatment was "reasonable, not arbitrary" and rested "upon some ground of difference having a fair and substantial relation to the object of the legislation, so that all persons similarly circumstanced will be treated alike". . . . The Court then found that the state's objective of reducing the workload of probate judges was insufficient justification to warrant this kind of sex-based statute. In fact, according to the Court, this was "the very kind of arbitrary legislative choice forbidden by the Equal Protection Clause".

This major breakthrough heartened women's rights activists. It also encouraged the WRP to launch a full-blown test case strategy like that pursued by the NAACP Legal Defense and Education Fund that had culminated successfully in *Brown* v. *Board of Education* (1954). WRP attorneys jumped at the opportunity to assist the Sourthern Poverty Law Center of Alabama with the next major sex-discrimination case to come before the Supreme Court, *Frontiero* v. *Richardson* (1973). At issue in *Frontiero* was the constitutionality of a federal statute that, for the purpose of computing allowances and fringe benefits, required female members of the armed forces to prove that they contributed more than 50 percent of their dependent husbands' support. Men were not required to make any such showing about their wives.

By an 8-to-1 vote, the Court struck down the statute, which gave male members of the armed forces potentially greater benefits than females. More importantly, though, only a plurality of four justices voted to make sex a suspect classification entitled to the strict scrutiny standard of review. While four other justices agreed that the statute violated the Equal Protection Clause, they did not agree that sex should be made a suspect classification. In fact three of them specifically noted the pending ratification of the ERA as a reason to wait—to allow the political process to guide judicial interpretation. This was to be the highwater mark of efforts to include sex, along with race, in the category of suspect classifications.

In *Craig* v. *Boren* (1976) Justice William J. Brennan, author of the plurality opinion in *Frontiero,* formulated a different test, known as "intermediate" or "heightened" scrutiny, to apply to sex-discrimination cases. The case involved a challenge to an Oklahoma law that prohibited the sale of 3.2-percent beer to males under the age of twenty-one and females under the age of eighteen. In determining whether this kind of gender-based differential violated the Equal Protection Clause, Brennan wrote that "classifications by gender must serve important governmental

objectives and must be substantially related to achievement of those objectives." . . . He also specifically identified two governmental interests that would not justify sex discrimination: neither administrative convenience nor "fostering 'old' notions of role typing" . . . would any longer be considered constitutionally adequate rationalizations of sex classifications. Shedding many of the stereotypes that had been at the core of *Muller, Hoyt,* and *Goesaert,* the Court specifically noted that there was no more place for "increasingly outdated misconceptions concerning the role of females in the home rather than in the 'marketplace and world of ideas.' " . . . This new intermediate standard of review was subsequently used to invalidate a wide range of discriminatory practices including some Social Security, welfare, and workmen's compensation programs, alimony laws, age of majority statutes and jury service exemptions.

This is not to say that stereotypes do not still exert influence on the Court. In *Rostker* v. *Goldberg* (1981), for example, the Court considered congressional combat restrictions sufficient to rationalize the exclusion of women from the new draft registration requirements of the Military Selective Service Act. . . . A majority of the Court accepted the government's position that the statutory exclusion of women from combat positions combined with the need for combat-ready troops were sufficiently important justifications to meet the burden of the intermediate standard of review. It did not bother to consider the validity of the combat restrictions themselves. And, in *Michael M.* v. *Superior Court of Sonoma County* (1981), the Court held that California's statutory rape law, which applied only to males, did not violate the Equal Protection Clause. Justice William H. Rehnquist noted that the state's concern about teenage pregnancy was a sufficiently strong state interest to justify the statute. Moreover, Rehnquist's opinion pointedly did not apply intermediate scrutiny.

In late 1981 the Court was joined by its first female member, Sandra Day O'Connor. It was not long before she and the other justices were faced with another sex-based claim made under the Fourteenth Amendment. *Mississippi University for Women* v. *Hogan* (1982) involved a state policy that restricted enrollment in one state-supported nursing school to females. Writing for a five-member majority, O'Connor noted that when the purpose of a statute was to "exclude or 'protect' members of one gender because they are presumed to suffer from an inherent handicap or to be innately inferior, the objective itself is illegitimate." . . . As one commentator noted, "she out-Brennaned Justice Brennan." For example, O'Connor went even further than Brennan (long the Court's foremost liberal) by suggesting in a footnote that sex might best be treated by the Court as a suspect classification.

O'Connor's strong opinion in *Hogan* again brought to four the number of justices on the Court who apparently favored some sort of strict

standard of review for sex-based classifications. It is unlikely, however, that sex will soon be measured, at least formally, with anything more than heightened scrutiny. . . . [T]he contrast is clear: race is a suspect classification, sex is not.

Recognizing the fragile nature of even the middle tier of review and the Court's uneven application of its standards, women's rights groups again are seeking passage of an equal rights amendment to the Constitution. Most see such an amendment as the only way to guarantee that women will ever be recognized as fully equal under the Constitution. Some see passage of an amendment as especially important given the kinds of sex-based discrimination cases that the Court is likely to address in the future. Although most of these involve challenges under Title VII of the Civil Rights Act of 1964 and its prohibition against discrimination in employment, Court watchers fear that without the force of an equal rights amendment to overshadow interpretation of the law, the Court's decisions could grow increasingly adverse to women's full equality. In spite of the absence of an ERA, however, even the Rehnquist Court has revealed a reluctance to go back to pre-*Reed* days, when sex-discrimination claims never found a favorable audience with the Court. Its decisions clearly have added to a climate that frowns on blatant discrimination. Given the increasingly conservative nature of the Court, however, and the increasingly complex patterns of discrimination that are being presented to it, it is unlikely that the scope of constitutional protections for women will grow unless other societal changes take place. The active-combat roles played by women in the Gulf War in early 1991, for example, could prompt the Court to uphold a new challenge to the discriminatory provisions of the Military and Selective Service Act previously held constitutional in *Rostker.*

Fewer and fewer constitutional cases involving sex discrimination come before the Court each year, perhaps because women's rights groups are using their time and money to fend off challenges to *Roe* v. *Wade* (1973) and to keep abortion legal. Moreover, most of the "easy" cases have been decided, and there is fairly uniform application of the intermediate standard of review in the lower courts. Thus, most gender cases that the Court now chooses to hear involve employment discrimination and the scope of bona fide occupational qualifications permissible under Title VII. During its 1990 term, for example, the Court heard arguments in *International Union, UAW* v. *Johnson Controls, Inc.* (1991), which involved a company fetal-protection policy that required women in certain hazardous positions be sterilized as a condition of their employment. Many women's rights activists argued that a judicial finding in support of the company policy would inevitably lead to the exclusion of women in all types of lucrative positions and to the resurrection of the paternalism

of *Muller* v. *Oregon.*[*] Their fears, however, proved to be unfounded. In *Johnson Controls* the Court ruled unanimously that the company's policies did not constitute bona fide occupational qualifications and thus violated Title VII. Many commentators now take this as an omen that the Court will continue to build on existing precedents and not retreat to earlier decisions more "protective" of women.

TOWARD CRITICAL THINKING

1. What are the different tests that the Court has developed to analyze equal protection claims? Why is gender-based discrimination accorded a less stringent test, making it easier for states to discriminate against women?

2. Consider how similar in facts are *Mississippi University for Women (MUW)* v. *Hogan* and *Brown* v. *Education.* Yet, *Brown,* involving race discrimination in education, was a 9-to-0 decision; *MUW,* involving sex discrimination, was a 5-to-4 decision. Why was *MUW* only a 5-to-4 decision?

---

[*] In *Muller* (1908) the Court upheld state maximum hours of work for women (but not men) noting women's "physical structure and the performance of maternal functions place her at a disadvantage in the struggle for subsistence."

· 24 ·

J.E.B. *v.* Alabama
114 S. Ct. 1419 (1994)

The appointment of the second woman to the U.S. Supreme Court in 1993 was heralded by women's rights groups. Ruth Bader Ginsburg had pioneered women's rights through her work as head of the American Civil Liberties Union's Women's Rights Project (WRP). As head of the WRP, Ginsburg frequently urged the Supreme Court to treat sex discrimination with the same degree of scrutiny it used when determining the constitutionality of race-based claims of discrimination. Would Ginsburg's addition to the conservative Court make the rest of the Court more likely to elevate sex to a suspect classification?

In *J.E.B.* v. *Alabama,* the state's attorney used nine of his ten peremptory (discretionary) challenges to remove male jurors. The trial court then empaneled an all-female jury to hear a complaint brought by Alabama on behalf of a woman and her child to establish paternity and child support against J.E.B. Even before the jury found him to have fathered the child and ordered him to pay child support, J.E.B.'s lawyer objected to the composition of the jury. He argued that an all-female jury would be much more sympathetic to the state's claims than would a jury that contained males. On appeal, he argued that the state had challenged male jurors solely on the basis of gender, in violation of the equal protection clause of the Fourteenth Amendment.

Opinion: Justice Harry Blackmun

Vote: 6 to 3

In *Batson* v. *Kentucky* (1986), this Court held that the Equal Protection Clause of the Fourteenth Amendment governs the exercise of peremptory challenges by a prosecutor in a criminal trial. The Court explained that although a defendant has "no right to a 'petit jury composed in whole or in part of persons of his own race,'" . . . the "defendant does have the right to be tried by a jury whose members are selected pursuant to nondiscriminatory criteria." . . . Since Batson, we have reaffirmed repeatedly our commitment to jury selection procedures that are fair and nondiscriminatory. . . .

. . . Today we are faced with the question whether the Equal Protection Clause forbids intentional discrimination on the basis of gender, just as it prohibits discrimination on the basis of race. We hold that gender, like race, is an unconstitutional proxy for juror competence and impartiality. . . .

Today we reaffirm what, by now, should be axiomatic: Intentional discrimination on the basis of gender by state actors violates the Equal Protection Clause, particularly where, as here, the discrimination serves to ratify and perpetuate invidious, archaic, and overbroad stereotypes about the relative abilities of men and women.

. . .

II ◆

Discrimination on the basis of gender in the exercise of peremptory challenges is a relatively recent phenomenon. Gender-based peremptory strikes were hardly practicable for most of our country's existence, since, until the nineteenth century, women were completely excluded from jury service. So well-entrenched was this exclusion of women that in 1880 this Court, while finding that the exclusion of African-American men from juries violated the Fourteenth Amendment, expressed no doubt that a State "may confine the selection [of jurors] to males." . . .

Many States continued to exclude women from jury service well into the present century, despite the fact that women attained suffrage upon ratification of the Nineteenth Amendment in 1920. States that did permit women to serve on juries often erected other barriers, such as registration requirements and automatic exemptions, designed to deter women from exercising their right to jury service. . . .

In 1975, the Court finally repudiated the reasoning of *Hoyt* and struck down, under the Sixth Amendment, an affirmative registration statute nearly identical to the one at issue in *Hoyt.* . . . We explained: "Restricting jury service to only special groups or excluding identifiable segments playing major roles in the community cannot be squared with the constitutional concept of jury trial." . . . The diverse and representative character of the jury must be maintained "partly as assurance of a diffused impartiality and partly because sharing in the administration of justice is a phase of civic responsibility." . . .

III ◆

Taylor relied on Sixth Amendment principles, but the opinion's approach is consistent with the heightened equal protection scrutiny afforded gender-based classifications. Since *Reed* v. *Reed* (1971), this Court consistently has subjected gender-based classifications to heightened scrutiny in recognition of the real danger that government policies that professedly are based on reasonable considerations in fact may be reflective of "archaic and overbroad" generalizations about gender, . . . or based on "outdated misconceptions concerning the role of females in the home rather than in the 'marketplace and world of ideas.'" . . .

Despite the heightened scrutiny afforded distinctions based on gender, respondent argues that gender discrimination in the selection of the petit jury should be permitted, though discrimination on the basis of race is not. Respondent suggests that "gender discrimination in this country . . . has never reached the level of discrimination" against African-Americans, and therefore gender discrimination, unlike racial discrimination, is tolerable in the courtroom. . . .

While the prejudicial attitudes toward women in this country have not been identical to those held toward racial minorities, the similarities between the experiences of racial minorities and women, in some contexts, "overpower those differences." . . .

"Throughout much of the nineteenth century the position of women in our society was, in many respects, comparable to that of blacks under the pre-Civil War slave codes. Neither slaves nor women could hold office, serve on juries, or bring suit in their own names, and married women traditionally were denied the legal capacity to hold or convey property or to serve as legal guardians of their own children. . . . And although blacks were guaranteed the right to vote in 1870, women were denied even that right—which is itself 'preservative of other basic civil and political rights'—until adoption of the Nineteenth Amendment half a century later."

Certainly, with respect to jury service, African-Americans and women share a history of total exclusion, a history which came to an end for women many years after the embarrassing chapter in our history came to an end for African-Americans.

We need not determine, however, whether women or racial minorities have suffered more at the hands of discriminatory state actors during the decades of our Nation's history. . . . Thus, the only question is whether discrimination on the basis of gender in jury selection substantially furthers the State's legitimate interest in achieving a fair and impartial trial. In making this assessment, we do not weigh the value of peremptory challenges as an institution against our asserted commitment to eradicate invidious discrimination from the courtroom. Instead, we consider whether peremptory challenges based on gender stereotypes provide substantial aid to a litigant's effort to secure a fair and impartial jury.

Far from proffering an exceptionally persuasive justification for its gender-based peremptory challenges, respondent maintains that its decision to strike virtually all the males from the jury in this case "may reasonably have been based upon the perception, supported by history, that men otherwise totally qualified to serve upon a jury might be more sympathetic and receptive to the arguments of a man alleged in a paternity action to be the father of an out-of-wedlock child, while women equally qualified to serve upon a jury might be more sympathetic and receptive to the arguments of the complaining witness who bore the child." . . .

We shall not accept as a defense to gender-based peremptory challenges "the very stereotype the law condemns." . . . Respondent's rationale, not unlike those regularly expressed for gender-based strikes, is reminiscent of the arguments advanced to justify the total exclusion of women from juries. Respondent offers virtually no support for the conclusion that gender alone is an accurate predictor of juror's attitudes; yet it urges this Court to condone the same stereotypes that justified the wholesale exclusion of women from juries and the ballot box. Respondent seems to assume that gross generalizations that would be deemed impermissible if made on the basis of race are somehow permissible when made on the basis of gender.

Discrimination in jury selection, whether based on race or on gender, causes harm to the litigants, the community, and the individual jurors who are wrongfully excluded from participation in the judicial process. The litigants are harmed by the risk that the prejudice which motivated the discriminatory selection of the jury will infect the entire proceedings. . . . The community is harmed by the State's participation in the perpetuation of invidious group stereotypes and the inevitable loss of confidence in our judicial system that state-sanctioned discrimination in the courtroom engenders.

When state actors exercise peremptory challenges in reliance on gender stereotypes, they ratify and reinforce prejudicial views of the relative abilities of men and women. Because these stereotypes have wreaked injustice in so many other spheres of our country's public life, active discrimination by litigants on the basis of gender during jury selection "invites cynicism respecting the jury's neutrality and its obligation to adhere to the law." . . . The potential for cynicism is particularly acute in cases where gender-related issues are prominent, such as cases involving rape, sexual harassment, or paternity. Discriminatory use of peremptory challenges may create the impression that the judicial system has acquiesced in suppressing full participation by one gender or that the "deck has been stacked" in favor of one side. . . . ("The verdict will not be accepted or understood [as fair] if the jury is chosen by unlawful means at the outset.")

. . . All persons, when granted the opportunity to serve on a jury, have the right not to be excluded summarily because of discriminatory and stereotypical presumptions that reflect and reinforce patterns of historical discrimination. Striking individual jurors on the assumption that they hold particular views simply because of their gender is "practically a brand upon them, affixed by law, an assertion of their inferiority." . . . It denigrates the dignity of the excluded juror, and, for a woman, reinvokes a history of exclusion from political participation. The message it sends to all those in the courtroom, and all those who may later learn of the discriminatory act, is that certain individuals, for no reason other than gender, are presumed unqualified by state actors to decide important questions upon which reasonable persons could disagree.

TOWARD CRITICAL THINKING

1. Race and gender were considered to be equally wrong reasons for the state to discriminate in *J.E.B.* What standard of review does the Court appear to be applying?

2. Not surprisingly, Justice Ginsburg (and Justice O'Connor) voted with the majority. In an earlier case involving sexual harassment, Justice Ginsburg suggested, "It remains an open question whether classifications based on gender are inherently suspect."[*] What do you think it will take for the Court to consider violations of women's civil rights on the same plane as those of African Americans?

---

[*]*Harris* v. *Forklift Systems,* 520 U.S. (1993).

· 25 ·

Regents of the University of California *v.* Bakke

438 U.S. 265 (1978)

Affirmative action programs, while seemingly a relatively new idea, have their origins in presidential executive orders. As early as the 1940s, President Harry S Truman ordered that expanded employment opportunities be made available for African Americans. Later, in 1965, President Lyndon B. Johnson issued another executive order requiring all employers doing business with the federal government to recruit minority workers in order to redress the past discrimination that had occurred prior to the Civil Rights Act of 1964. These plans were strengthened over the years. And if employers failed to comply with affirmative action guidelines, they risked the loss of their valuable government contracts. Soon, state and local governments also adopted such programs to aggressively redress race and gender inequities in their workforces. Private and public colleges and universities also created affirmative action programs in order to enroll more students from minority groups that were underrepresented in their student bodies.

Potential legal problems to race- or gender-conscious programs, called "affirmative action" programs, stem from two sources. If state action is involved, the equal protection clause of the Fourteenth Amendment, which guarantees all citizens "equal protection of the laws," may be violated. Or a private employer or even state or local government may run afoul of the Civil Rights Act of 1964. That Act reads in part:

> It shall be an *unlawful* employment practice for an employer . . . to limit, segregate, or classify his employees or applicants for employment in any way which would deprive or tend to deprive any individual of employment opportunities or otherwise adversely affect his status as an employee, because of such individual's race, color, religion, sex, or national origin. (Emphasis added.)

The most significant and most talked about affirmative action case continues to be *Regents of the University of California* v. *Bakke.* Because a state university was involved, *Bakke* was an equal protection challenge to the University of California at Davis's affirmative action program that set aside sixteen places each year in its incoming medical class, leaving eighty-four places for students admitted through the regular admission process.

Allan Bakke was a white male student who graduated with honors from the University of Minnesota. He was also a veteran of the Vietnam War. After receiving a master's degree in engineering from Stanford University, he developed an interest in medicine, took extra science courses to qualify him for medical school admission, and worked as a volunteer at a local hospital. At age thirty-three he applied to medical school and was rejected. He was rejected again in 1974. When he learned that applicants admitted under the special admissions program at UC Davis were statistically less qualified than he was, he sued for admission, alleging that the university's program violated the equal protection clause (see the table below).

The trial court held that the state's program was unconstitutional but refused to order Bakke admitted to the school. The California Supreme Court then also found the program unconstitutional and ordered Bakke admitted to the medical school. But his admission was stayed, pending the university's appeal to the U.S. Supreme Court, which accepted the case for review.

As you can probably imagine, the stakes were high on both sides of the case as national attention focused on it as a symbol of affirmative action. For opponents of affirmative action, the case was an opportunity to reverse a costly and philosophically abhorrent program set up to redress wrongs committed by other people in another era. For civil rights groups, the possibility of a loss declaring affirmative action programs unconstitutional could bring educational and employment opportunities to a grinding halt. Not surprisingly, then, this case produced the largest number of *amicus curiae* briefs to date submitted to the Supreme Court on behalf of various organizations and interested individuals in a single case—fifty-seven.

Just as society was badly divided over not only the legality but also the appropriateness of affirmative action programs, so was the Supreme Court. Four justices strongly supported the program, four others voiced strong reservations about the constitutionality of affirmative action in general and the UC Davis program in particular. Justice Lewis Powell, a Southerner who had been appointed by Republican Richard M. Nixon, found himself in the middle. Since the four supporters of affirmative action agreed with some portions of his opinion, his became the "swing"

Admissions Data for the UC Davis Medical School Entering Class 1974

| | | | | *Class Entering in 1974* MCAT (Percentiles) | | |
	SGPA[a]	OGPA[b]	Verbal	Quantitative	Science	Gen. Infor.
Allan Bakke	3.44	3.46	96	94	97	72
Average of regular admittees	3.36	3.29	69	67	82	72
Average of special admittees	2.42	2.62	34	30	37	18

SOURCE: Regents of the University of California v. Bakke (1978).
Notes: a. Science grade point average.
b. Overall grade point average.

vote in upholding some race-based programs. But Powell also believed
that strict quotas were unconstitutional in the absence of a showing of
prior discrimination. Thus, portions of his opinion, when joined with the
four opponents of affirmative action, resulted in a finding that UC
Davis's strict quotas were unconstitutional. Powell's opinion, in essence,
thus defined what the Court would consider permissible efforts to reduce
the effects of prior discrimination.

Opinion: Justice Lewis Powell
Vote: 5 to 4

. . .

Petitioner does not deny that decisions based on race or ethnic origin
by faculties and administrations of state universities are reviewable under
the Fourteenth Amendment. For his part, respondent does not argue that
all racial or ethnic classifications are *per se* invalid. The parties do disagree as to the level of judicial scrutiny to be applied to the special
admissions program. Petitioner argues that the court below erred in applying strict scrutiny, as this inexact term has been applied in our cases. That
level of review, petitioner asserts, should be reserved for classifications
that disadvantage "discrete and insular minorities." Respondent, on the
other hand, contends that the California court correctly rejected the notion
that the degree of judicial scrutiny accorded a particular racial or ethnic
classification hinges upon membership in a discrete and insular minority
and duly recognized that the "rights established [by the Fourteenth
Amendment] are personal rights."

En route to this crucial battle over the scope of judicial review, the
parties fight a sharp preliminary action over the proper characterization of
the special admissions program, Petitioner prefers to view it as establishing a "goal" of minority representation in the Medical School. Respondent, echoing the courts below, labels it a racial quota.

This semantic distinction is beside the point: The special admissions
program is undeniably a classification based on race and ethnic background. To the extent that there existed a pool of at least minimally
qualified minority applicants to fill the 16 special admissions seats, white
applicants could compete only for 84 seats in the entering class, rather
than the 100 open to minority applicants. Whether this limitation is described as a quota or a goal, it is a line drawn on the basis of race and
ethnic status.

The guarantees of the Fourteenth Amendment extend to all persons.
Its language is explicit: "No State shall . . . deny to any person within its
jurisdiction the equal protection of the laws. . . . The guarantee of equal
protection cannot mean one thing when applied to one individual and
something else when applied to a person of another color. If both are not
accorded the same protection, then it is not equal. . . .

Racial and ethnic distinctions of any sort are inherently suspect and thus call for the most exacting judicial examination. . . .

Although many of the Framers of the Fourteenth Amendment conceived of its primary function as bridging the vast distance between members of the Negro race and the white "majority," the Amendment itself was framed in universal terms, without reference to color, ethnic origin, or condition of prior servitude. . . .

We have held that in "order to justify the use of a suspect classification, a State must show that its purpose or interest is both constitutionally permissible and substantial, and that its use of the classification is necessary . . . to the accomplishment of its purpose or the safeguarding of its interest." The special admissions program purports to serve the purposes of: (i) "reducing the historic deficit of traditionally disfavored minorities in medical schools and in the medical profession"; (ii) countering the effects of societal discrimination; (iii) increasing the number of physicians who will practice in communities currently underserved; and (iv) obtaining the educational benefits that flow from an ethnically diverse student body. It is necessary to decide which, if any, of these purposes is substantial enough to support the use of a suspect classification.

If petitioner's purpose is to assure within its student body some specified percentage of a particular group merely because of its race or ethnic origin, such a preferential purpose must be rejected not as insubstantial but as facially invalid. Preferring members of any one group for no reason other than race or ethnic origin is discrimination for its own sake. This the Constitution forbids.

The State certainly has a legitimate and substantial interest in ameliorating, or eliminating where feasible, the disabling effects of identified discrimination. The line of school desegregation cases, commencing with *Brown,* attests to the importance of this state goal and the commitment of the judiciary to affirm all means toward its attainment. . . .

We have never approved a classification that aids persons perceived as members of relatively victimized groups at the expense of other innocent individuals in the absence of judicial, legislative, or administrative findings of constitutional or statutory violations. After such findings have been made, the governmental interest in preferring members of the injured groups at the expense of others is substantial, since the legal rights of the victims must be vindicated. In such a case, the extent of the injury and the consequent remedy will have been judicially, legislatively, or administratively defined. Also, the remedial action usually remains subject to continuing oversight to assure that it will work the least harm possible to other innocent persons competing for the benefit. Without such findings of constitutional or statutory violations, it cannot be said that the government has any greater interest in helping one individual than in refraining from harming one another. Thus, the government has no compelling justification for inflicting such harm. . . .

Hence, the purpose of helping certain groups whom the faculty of the Davis Medical School perceived as victim of "social discrimination" does not justify a classification that imposes disadvantages upon persons like respondent, who bear no responsibility for whatever harm the beneficiaries of the special admissions program are thought to have suffered. . . .

Petitioner identifies, as another purpose of its program, improving the delivery of health-care services to communities currently underserved. It may be assumed that in some situations a State's interest in facilitating the health care of its citizens is sufficiently compelling to support the use of a suspect classification. But there is virtually no evidence in the record indicating that petitioner's special admissions program is either needed or geared to promote that goal. . . .

Petitioner simply has not carried its burden of demonstrating that it must prefer members of particular ethnic groups over all other individuals in order to promote better health-care delivery to deprived citizens. Indeed, petitioner has not shown that its preferential classification is likely to have any significant effect on the problem.

The fourth goal asserted by petitioner is the attainment of a diverse student body. This clearly is a constitutionally permissible goal for an institution of higher education. Academic freedom, though not a specifically enumerated constitutional right, long has been viewed as a special concern of the First Amendment. The freedom of a university to make its own judgments as to education includes the selection of its student body. . . .

Thus, in arguing that its universities must be accorded the right to select those students who will contribute the most to the "robust exchange of ideas" petitioner invokes a countervailing constitutional interest, that of the First Amendment. In this light, petitioner must be viewed as seeking to achieve a goal that is of paramount importance in the fulfillment of its mission. . . .

Ethnic diversity, however, is only one element in a range of factors a university properly may consider in attaining the goal of a heterogeneous student body. Although a university must have wide discretion in making the sensitive judgments as to who should be admitted, constitutional limitations protecting individual rights may not be disregarded. Respondent urges—and the courts below have held—that petitioner's dual admissions program is a racial classification that impermissibly infringes his rights under the Fourteenth Amendment. As the interest of diversity is compelling in the context of a university's admissions program, the question remains whether the program's racial classification is necessary to promote this interest. . . .

It may be assumed that the reservation of a specified number of seats in each class for individuals from the preferred ethnic groups would contribute to the attainment of considerable ethnic diversity in the student body. But petitioner's argument that this is the only effective means of serving the interest of diversity is seriously flawed. In a most fundamental sense the argument misconceives the nature of the state interest that would justify consideration of race or ethnic background. It is not an interest in simple ethnic diversity, in which a specified percentage of the student body is in effect guaranteed to be members of selected ethnic groups, with the remaining percentage an undifferentiated aggregation of students. The diversity that furthers a compelling state interest encompasses a far broader array of qualifications and characteristics of which racial or ethnic origin is but a single though important element. Petitioner's special admissions program, focused *solely* on ethnic diversity, would hinder rather than further attainment of genuine diversity. . . .

In such an admissions program, race or ethnic background may be deemed a "plus" in a particular applicant's file, yet it does not insulate the individual from comparison with all other candidates for the available seats. The file of a particular black applicant may be examined for his potential contribution to diversity without the factor of race being decisive when compared, for example, with that of an applicant identified as an Italian-American if the latter is thought to exhibit qualities more likely to promote beneficial educational pluralism. Such qualities could include exceptional personal talents, unique work or service experience, leadership potential, maturity, demonstrated compassion, a history of overcoming disadvantage, ability to communicate with the poor, or other qualifications deemed important. In short, an admissions program operated in this way is flexible enough to consider all pertinent elements of diversity in light of the particular qualifications of each applicant, and to place them on the same footing for consideration, although not necessarily according them the same weight. Indeed, the weight attributed to a particular quality may vary from year to year depending upon the "mix" both of the student body and the applicants for the incoming class.

This kind of program treats each applicant as an individual in the admissions process. The applicant who loses out on the last available seat to another candidate receiving a "plus" on the basis of ethnic background will not have been foreclosed from all consideration for that seat simply because he was not the right color or had the wrong surname. It would mean only that his combined qualifications, which may have included similar nonobjective factors, did not outweigh those of the other applicant. His qualifications would have been weighed fairly and competitively, and he would have no basis to complain of unequal treatment under the Fourteenth Amendment. . . .

In summary, it is evident that the Davis special admissions program involves the use of an explicit racial classification never before countenanced by this Court. It tells applicants who are not Negro, Asian, or Chicano that they are totally excluded from a specific percentage of the seats in an entering class. No matter how strong their qualifications, quantitative and extracurricular, including their own potential for contribution to educational diversity, they are never afforded the chance to compete with applicants from the preferred groups for the special admissions seats. At the same time, the preferred applicants have the opportunity to compete for every seat in the class.

The fatal flaw in petitioners preferential program is its disregard of individual rights as guaranteed by the Fourteenth Amendment. Such rights are not absolute. But when a State's distribution of benefits or imposition of burdens hinges on ancestry or the color of a person's skin, that individual is entitled to a demonstration that the challenged classification is necessary to promote a substantial state interest. Petitioner has failed to carry this burden. For this reason, that portion of the California court's judgment holding petitioner's special admissions program invalid under the Fourteenth Amendment must be affirmed.

In enjoining petitioner from ever considering the race of any applicant, however, the courts below failed to recognize that the State has a substantial interest that legitimately may be served by a properly devised admissions program involving the competitive consideration of race and ethnic origin. For this reason, so much of the California court's judgment as enjoins petitioner from any consideration of the race of any applicant must be reversed.

With respect to respondent's entitlement to an injunction directing his admission to the Medical School, petitioner has conceded that it could not carry its burden of proving that, but for the existence of its unlawful special admissions program, respondent still would not have been admitted. Hence, respondent is entitled to the injunction, and that portion of the judgment must be affirmed.

TOWARD CRITICAL THINKING

1. In sections of his opinion not produced here, Justice Powell voiced his approval of Harvard University's "goals" that usually resulted in a student body that contained approximately 15 percent minority students. Why would that program be acceptable to him but not the one at UC Davis?

2. In the years since *Bakke,* the Court has decided numerous cases involving affirmative action programs. Some have been upheld; others have not. As society moves farther away from an era in which segregation was often the norm, given Justice Powell's opinion, is there less reason for the Court to uphold the constitutionality of these programs?

· 26 ·

Affirmative Action and the American Creed

SEYMOUR MARTIN LIPSET

Although a national consensus on civil rights was forged in the 1960s, says political scientist Seymour Martin Lipset, race as an issue continues to dominate political debate, especially concerning affirmative action. According to Lipset, affirmative action, as implemented today, sets up a conflict between two enduring yet conflicting American values: egalitarianism and individualism. Lipset calls on policy makers to refocus the affirmative action debate but not to discard it.

No achievement of twentieth-century American politics surpasses the creation of an enduring national consensus on civil rights. This consensus was forged during the past quarter century by a civil-rights movement that compelled Americans finally to confront the wide gap between their treatment of blacks and the egalitarian values of their own cherished national creed.

In recent years, however, the leaders of the civil-rights movement have shifted the focus from the pursuit of equal opportunity to the pursuit of substantive equality through policies of preferential treatment. This has brought matters to a difficult pass, because most Americans, including many blacks, have not shifted with the leaders of the movement. The reason is not hard to find. While the civil-rights movement of the 1960s asked Americans to live up to a single unassailable ideal, today it sets up a conflict between two core American values: egalitarianism and individualism.

Affirmative action was born in 1965 in the spirit of the first civil-rights revolution. Soon thereafter it was formed into a system of racial preferences, and today affirmative action is rapidly polarizing the politics of race in America. The editorial and op-ed pages bristle with affirmative action polemics and analyses. In the 1990 contest for the governorship of California, Republican Pete Wilson focused on the "quota" issue in defeating Diane Feinstein. In the same year, Senator Jesse Helms won

SOURCE: Seymour Martin Lipset, "Affirmative Action and the American Creed," *Wilson Quarterly*. Reprinted by permission of the author.

reelection in North Carolina with the help of the quota issue, and in Louisiana ex-Klansman David Duke exploited it to gain a majority of white votes while losing his bid for a Senate seat. His failed campaign for the governorship last fall became a national drama. When Congress began its 1991 session, the first bill introduced by the Democratic leadership in the House of Representatives was a civil-rights bill described by its opponents as "quota" legislation. Even after a version of that bill became law in November, controversy over its meaning and import continued.

Ugly political campaigns and even uglier racial incidents everywhere from Bensonhurst to Los Angeles sometimes make it appear that there has been a resurgence of racism in America. But the old consensus in favor of civil rights and equality of opportunity remains intact. Americans, including many southern whites, categorically reject the kind of racial discrimination that was common in this country only a few decades ago. A 1991 Gallup-*Newsweek* poll reported that "72 percent of blacks and 52 percent of whites said that they would prefer to live in a neighborhood that was racially 'half and half'—more on both sides than felt that way three years ago." Over two-thirds of whites and four-fifths of blacks claim to "know many members of another race well." Almost no whites (6 percent) report that they would feel "uncomfortable working with members of another race" or "for a boss of another race."

At the same time, most Americans endorse some forms of compensatory action to help blacks and other disadvantaged groups perform at the levels of competition set by the larger society: Head Start and other special educational programs, federal aid for college students, job training, and community development. But a large majority of whites and roughly half of all blacks draw the line at preferential treatment, at suspending standards and adopting quotas or other devices that favor citizens on the basis of their membership in groups.

If most Americans oppose such preferential treatment, who backs it? As it turns out, the support comes largely from a segment of the national leadership class. Indeed, the policy was conceived and is still promoted almost entirely by political and social elites, Republicans as well as Democrats, against the wishes of a majority of the American public. The struggle over preferential treatment is in reality less a conflict between whites and blacks than between people and their leaders. . . .

Americans make a critical distinction between compensatory action and preferential treatment. . . .They will go along with special training programs and financial assistance, enabling the previously shackled to catch up with those who are ahead because of earlier unfair advantages. But they draw the line at predetermining the results of the competition.

In some measure, the distinction between "compensatory action" and "preferential treatment" parallels the distinction drawn between "equality of opportunity" and "equality of results." Compensatory action is probably seen as a way to enhance equality of opportunity. Because blacks have been discriminated against in the past, it is fair to give them special consideration so that they will have a better chance in the future. Preferential treatment, on the other hand, probably sounds to most whites like an effort to predetermine the outcome of the competitive process. . . .

Affirmative action is widely seen as reverse discrimination. Many less-affluent whites believe that the number of jobs available for them has declined as a result of preferences for blacks. Two studies undertaken in 1985 and 1987 by Stanley Greenberg of the Analysis Group for the Michigan Democratic Party indicate that negative reaction to affirmative action has played a major role in the defection of white male blue-collar voters from the party. "Much to the surprise and dismay of both Greenberg and his sponsors," one writer noted, "white fury over affirmative action emerged as a top voter concern in both of his reports. Democratic campaign themes such as 'fairness,' 'equity,' and 'justice' were perceived—not without justification—as code words for quotas."

National polls indicate the same concern. Two surveys, one conducted by the University of Michigan's Institute for Social Research in 1986 and the other by NORC in 1990, found large majorities of whites replying that it is "very likely" (28 percent in both) or "somewhat likely" (48 and 42 percent) "that a white person won't get a job or promotion while an equally or less qualified black person gets one instead." Two-fifths of the whites in the 1986 study believed that they or someone in their family would experience job discrimination. A 1991 report on a poll sponsored by the Leadership Conference on Civil Rights concludes that "civil-rights laws are seen by a substantial number of voters as creating unfair advantages, setting up rank or class privilege in the labor market."

"White Americans . . . do not see themselves as racists, or as opponents of equal opportunity and fundamental fairness," observes columnist William Raspberry. "What they oppose are efforts to provide preferential benefits for minorities. . . . How could we expect them to buy a product we [blacks] have spent 400 years trying to have recalled: race-based advantages enshrined in law?"

Misperceptions have much to do with the polarization of racial politics. The best research shows, for example, that there is in reality little reverse discrimination in the competition for lower-skill jobs. Recently, Urban Institute researchers sent equally qualified whites and blacks to apply for general labor, service, retail, and clerical positions in Chicago and Washington, D.C. Whites were treated better in job interviews in 20 percent of the cases; blacks were treated better 7 percent of the time.

Whites were more likely to be hired. One finding is heartening: There was no discrimination in three-quarters of the interview situations. But blacks are still more likely to suffer from racism in working-class job markets than whites are to experience reverse discrimination.

If whites overestimate the extent of reverse discrimination, whites and blacks alike badly underestimate the extent of black economic progress during the past several decades. The general ignorance of black success is due in part to the reluctance of black leaders to admit it. In opinion polls during the mid-1980s, three-fifths of black leaders told pollsters that blacks were "going backward," while two-thirds of a national black sample said they were "making progress." (Support for the optimistic view declined somewhat in the latter years of the Reagan era. In early July 1990, an NBC News-*Wall Street Journal* poll reported that 60 percent of all blacks said that, compared to 10 years ago, blacks in America are "better off," while 29 percent said "worse off.")

The refusal of some black leaders to admit improvement is understandable. The worse things appear, and the greater the gulf seems between themselves and others, the more they can demand. Yet the repeated emphasis on how little progress has been made also helps sustain the argument that government efforts to benefit blacks simply do not work, that there are factors inherent in the black situation that prevent blacks from getting ahead. And many blacks as well as whites tend to swallow that argument. NORC found that during 1985–89, an average of 62 percent of whites and 36 percent of blacks agreed that the reason blacks on average have worse jobs, incomes, and housing than white people is that "most blacks just don't have the motivation or will power to pull themselves out of poverty." An ABC News-*Washington Post* poll in October 1989 found that 60 percent of both whites and blacks agreed with the statement: "If blacks would try harder, they could be just as well off as whites." . . .

The damage is compounded by the news media's relentless focus on the social pathologies of the ghettos, which creates the impression that most blacks live wretched existences. Yet social scientists estimate that the underclass, both black and white, is actually fairly small. William Julius Wilson, the social scientist most responsible for focusing attention on the question, now identifies one-sixth of the nation's 30 million blacks as ghetto poor, a term he prefers. (These are people who live in "areas of extreme poverty, that is, those in which 40 percent of the people are poor.") An Urban Institute group arrives at a lower estimate of the underclass: two or three million people in 1980, about two-thirds of them black, one-fifth Hispanic.

Meanwhile the total proportion of blacks living in poverty—many not afflicted by the pathologies of the underclass—has declined radically.

While there is a great deal of debate about the definition of poverty, census data indicate that the percentage of blacks living in poverty declined from 55 percent in 1959 to 33.5 percent in 1970. In 1990, a recession year, it was 31.9 percent.

The "invisible man" of the 1990s, to borrow Ralph Ellison's phrase, is the successful black working- and middle-class suburbanite. Living in stable families outside traditional black areas, the new "invisible man" is removed from the experience of ghetto blacks and largely ignored by whites. The black suburban population grew by 70 percent during the 1970s, fed primarily by an exodus from central cities. During the 1980s the number of black suburbanites swelled from 5.4 million to 8.2 million. Between 1986 and 1990, 73 percent of black population growth occurred in the suburbs.

Economists James P. Smith and Finis R. Welch, analyzing the changes in the situation of blacks since World War II, concluded in 1986 that "the real story of the last forty years has been the emergence of the black middle class," which "as a group . . . outnumbers the black poor."

The majority of blacks have steady jobs and are either middle class or members of what may be called the yeoman regularly employed working class. They are married or in stable long-term relationships. The income of married blacks is 77 percent that of comparable whites, up from below 60 percent two decades ago. The proportion of blacks who are high school dropouts has fallen, from 31 percent in 1970 to 18 percent in 1988, while that of whites (14 percent) has not changed.

These drastic social and economic changes have led to growing differentiation within the black community. . . .

The two largest groups in the black class structure, the authors say, are now "a lower class dominated by female-headed families and a middle class largely composed of families headed by a husband and wife." The problem is that most black adults live in stable family and economic situations, but most black *children* do not. They are the offspring of the large number of black women who are single mothers. The proportion of black children born in female-headed households was 23 percent in 1960, 28 percent in 1969, 45 percent in 1980, and is 62 percent today. Living in such a household frequently guarantees being poor. The poverty rate for black single-parent families with children was 56.3 percent in 1988. That for two-parent black families with children was 12.5 percent. . . .

Whatever the causes of childhood poverty, affirmative action is no remedy. Preference policies or quotas are not much help to the illegitimate black ghetto youth who grows up in poverty and receives an inferior education. As William Julius Wilson writes, they are more likely to benefit "minority individuals from the most advantaged families . . . [who are]

most qualified for preferred positions—such as higher-paying jobs, college admissions, promotions and so forth. Accordingly, if policies of preferential treatment for such positions are conceived not in terms of the actual disadvantages suffered by individuals but rather in terms of race or ethnic group membership, then these policies will further enhance the opportunities of the more advantaged without addressing the problems of the truly disadvantaged."

The conflict between different versions of equality, between an emphasis on the individual and on the group, will continue here and abroad. . . .

To rebuild the national consensus on civil rights and racial justice, affirmative action should be refocused, not discarded. Quotas and special preferences will not help the poorly educated and unskilled secure good jobs. Success in postindustrial society requires a good education. Extending and vastly improving education in the ghettos, establishing very early Head Start programs as well as financial incentives for students, teachers, and successful schools, and expanding apprentice programs, are the directions to be followed. Such programs should be offered to all less-privileged people, regardless of racial and ethnic origins.

The whole society can also learn from the experience of blacks in the military, which has offered blacks career training and a chance for stable employment and upward mobility. That record argues in favor of a large-scale national-service effort. If all American youth are encouraged to volunteer for national service, those with inadequate education and skills can receive job training while they and their peers help rebuild the nation's infrastructure and deliver social services.

Moving away from policies that emphasize special preferences need not—indeed, must not—mean abandoning the nation's commitment to guaranteeing equal opportunity for disadvantaged citizens. The concept of individual rights remains integral to the American Creed, and racial injustice and caste-like divisions blatantly contradict it. The American dilemma is still with us, and it imposes upon us a moral obligation to ensure that race is neither a handicap nor an advantage. Until black Americans are absorbed fully into our nation's economy and society, we should, in Jefferson's words, continue to fear a just God.

TOWARD CRITICAL THINKING

1. In light of *Bakke* and Lipset's thoughts about affirmative action, do you think that a need for race- or gender-based affirmative action programs continues? What kinds of programs can you suggest to help remedy vestiges of discrimination?

2. In general, who supports affirmative action programs? Who opposes them? Why do supporters and opponents feel the way they do?

THINKING ABOUT CIVIL RIGHTS

1. Do African Americans, women, Hispanics, or any other group deserve special protections if it appears their civil rights are violated?

2. Can any programs ever actually prevent discrimination based on race, gender, or national origin?

3. In the 1990s, the Rodney King case attracted a considerable amount of attention. A passerby captured on videotape King apparently being beaten by Los Angeles police officers. Yet, in a state court proceeding, those officers were found not guilty of assaulting King or of using excessive force to subdue him. Later, public outcries led the U.S. government to charge the officers with violations of King's civil rights under federal civil rights statutes. Is the federal government a better watchdog of civil rights than the states?

❖ PART TWO ❖

The Institutions Of Government

Drawing heavily on the theories of the French political philosopher Montesquieu, the Framers created a strong national government of enumerated powers. Three separate branches of government—the legislative, executive and judicial—were given specified roles to play as the powers of each were often dependent on another to "check power with power."

Article I of the U.S. Constitution (see Appendix A) established the legislative branch of government and created a two-house Congress. With each house responsible to different constituencies and elected for terms of different lengths, a further check was created on the power of the new Congress.

In spite of the Framers' fears of a single tyrannical ruler, they agreed that the new nation needed a president, whose powers and duties were defined in Article II. Most of the delegates to the Philadelphia convention had some fears about creating a single executive. Yet they settled on the idea because all believed that George Washington would be the first president under the new Constitution. Undoubtedly, none of the Framers could ever have envisioned how the powers of the president and the scope of his responsibilities would grow. In fact, although the Constitution makes it clear that the Framers recognized that advisors and department heads would be appointed to assist the president in implementing the laws passed by Congress as well as to help him negotiate with foreign nations, none foresaw the creation of a bureaucracy. Today some political observers even refer to the bureaucracy as the fourth branch of government.

Article III created the Supreme Court and authorized Congress to establish any other courts it believe necessary for the proper administration of justice. But as Alexander Hamilton noted in *Federalist No. 78,* most of his contemporaries considered the federal judiciary to have few real powers. The limited attention given to the judiciary in Article III is perhaps an indication that it was perceived as less than a true equal of the other two branches of government.

Thus, Articles I, II, and III set up the basic framework of the new government. Devising a new plan of government is one thing; having it actually work is another. Over the years, as illustrated by the readings in

Part II, the size, scope, and authority of each branch have changed. Yet even in times of constitutional crisis or potential crises, the nation has endured. Chief Justice John Marshall's showdown with Thomas Jefferson in *Marbury* v. *Madison* (Reading 43), the Civil War, and, more recently, the Watergate scandal (Reading 37) all illustrate the nation's ability to weather crises under a constitutional form of government.

How the institutions of government created by the Constitution have evolved and continue to evolve to meet the demands on an increasingly complex and changing society is the focus of the readings in Part II.

"The Congress" is the core of Chapter 6. How has Congress changed over time? How has its membership changed and responded to the increasing complexity of issues with which it deals? And as more and more members seek to make a career in Washington, D.C., how much of their legislative activity is geared toward reelection? These are all questions addressed in Chapter 6.

Chapter 7 examines the nature of "The Presidency" and the men who have held that office. Each man who has occupied that office has come to it with different expectations, experiences, and world views. How can these differences account for individual presidential successes or failures? As you analyze the first 100 days of the Clinton presidency in Reading 32, compare his presidency with those men who have come before him.

The Framers obviously saw no need to create a fourth branch of government. Nevertheless, over the years, a large federal bureaucracy has been created to help the president administer the laws. Members of Congress, equating reelection success with their ability to appease certain groups, have often added to the size of government by expanding "The Bureaucracy"; this notion is explored in Chapter 8.

Another "unelected" branch of government, "The Judiciary," is the focus of Chapter 9. Since Chief Justice John Marshall claimed the right of judicial review for the Court in *Marbury* v. *Madison* (1803) (Reading 43), the powers and role of the Supreme Court and the federal courts in the federal system continue to grow. In spite of the fact that the Rehnquist Court is deciding fewer cases, this Court, as well as the Courts before it, continues to play a major role in the processes of government, as well as in issues involving individual rights and liberties, as discussed in Chapters 4 and 5.

CHAPTER 6

♦ ♦ ♦

The Congress

The year 1992 was not just the "Year of the Woman." It also saw the election of Ben Nighthorse Campbell, an American Indian, to the U.S. Senate and of Carol Moseley-Braun, as the first African-American woman (and only African American) to sit in the Senate.

When the Framers met in Philadelphia to fashion a representative body, they truly had no idea how representative it would ultimately be. While Congress today, according to Box 6.1, "Talks Like a Woman," it's been a long time in coming, if, indeed, that assertion is even true.

In *Federalists No. 52* and *62* (Reading 27), James Madison notes the need for each house of Congress to be responsible to different constituencies. The popularly elected House, with two-year terms was to be more responsive to its constituents; the Senate, with six-year terms, was to be the slower, more deliberative body. The Senate was also entrusted with special duties, especially regarding confirmation of presidential appointments and foreign affairs.

In spite of the Framers' desires to keep politics out of the process and to deemphasize the reelection process, as several of the readings in this chapter highlight, reelection is often on the minds of members of the House or Senate. Although few elected officials who came to the early Congresses, as explained by James Sterling Young (Reading 25), viewed their elections as the first step on the path to a long career in Congress, today, most members are motivated by reelection concerns, as noted by Morris P. Fiorina (Reading 29), Marjorie Margolies-Mezvinsky (Reading 30), and Robert P. Weber (Reading 31).

Reelection and committee behaviors can be closely tied together, as Robert P. Weber illustrates. Ultimately, the demands of both proved too frustrating for the House member whom Weber highlights. Frustrations and the rewards of performing every lawmaker's constitutionally set task—law making—are vividly described by Richard E. Cohen (Reading 32) as he discusses congressional efforts to work with President Clinton in an effort to pass an economic program.

· 27 ·

Federalists No. 52 *and* 62

JAMES MADISON

From the beginning, one problem that vexed the Framers was how to create a legislature. The Virginia Plan, the first formal plan for the creation of the new government presented in Philadelphia, called for a two-house legislature, a suggestion quickly agreed on by the Framers. It also called for representation in each house to be proportionate to the population from each state. The large states liked this proposal; not surprisingly, smaller states were threatened by this notion. New Jersey, a small state, then suggested a one-house legislature with but one vote from each state. The Great Compromise resulted in representation in the lower House, the House of Representatives, being proportional to state population. The upper house, the Senate, was to be a smaller body, with each state having two representatives there, regardless of its population. In *Federalist No. 52* James Madison notes the qualifications of members in the House of Representatives and offers justifications for their frequent election. In *Federalist No. 62,* he explains why the qualifications for members of each house are different and the advantages of a two-house legislature where states are equally represented in one of the two houses.

Federalist No. 52

. . .

. . . A representative of the United States must be of the age of twenty-five years; must have been seven years a citizen of the United States; must, at the time of his election, be an inhabitant of the State he is to represent; and, during the time of his service, must be in no office under the United States. Under these reasonable limitations, the door of this part of the federal government is open to merit of every description, whether native or adoptive, whether young or old, and without regard to poverty or wealth, or to any particular profession of religious faith.

The term for which the representatives are to be elected falls under a second view which may be taken of this branch. . . .

First. As it is essential to liberty that the government in general should have a common interest with the people, so it is particularly essential that the branch of it under consideration should have an immediate dependence on, and an intimate sympathy with, the people. Frequent elections are unquestionably the only policy by which this dependence and sympathy can be effectually secured. But what particular degree of frequency may be absolutely necessary for the purpose does not appear to be susceptible of any precise calculation, and must depend on a variety of circumstances with which it may be connected. . . .

. . . [T]he advantage of biennial elections would secure to them every degree of liberty, which might depend on a due connection between their representatives and themselves.

Let us bring our inquiries nearer home. The example of these States, when British colonies, claims particular attention, at the same time that it is so well known as to require little to be said on it. The principle of representation, in one branch of the legislature at least, was established in all of them. But the periods of election were different. They varied from one to seven years. Have we any reason to infer, from the spirit and conduct of the representatives of the people, prior to the Revolution, that biennial elections would have been dangerous to the public liberties? The spirit which everywhere displayed itself at the commencement of the struggle, and which vanquished the obstacles to independence, is the best of proofs that a sufficient portion of liberty had been everywhere enjoyed to inspire both a sense of its worth and a zeal for its proper enlargement. This remark holds good as well with regard to the then colonies whose elections were less frequent, as to those whose elections were most frequent. Virginia was the colony which stood first in resisting the parliamentary usurpations of Great Britain; it was the first also in espousing, by public act, the resolution of independence. In Virginia, nevertheless, if I have not been misinformed, elections under the former government were septennial. This particular example is brought into view, not as a proof of any peculiar merit . . . I conceive it to be a very substantial proof, that the liberties of the people can be in no danger from *biennial* elections.

Federalist No. 62

. . .

I. The qualifications proposed for senators, as distinguished from those of representatives, consist in a more advanced age and a longer period of citizenship. A senator must be thirty years of age at least; as a representative must be twenty-five. And the former must have been a citizen nine years; as seven years required for the latter. The propriety of these distinctions is explained by the nature of the senatorial trust, which, requiring greater extent of information and stability of character, requires at the same time that the senator should have reached a period of life most likely to supply these advantages; and which, participating immediately in transactions with foreign nations, ought to be exercised by none who are not thoroughly weaned from the prepossessions and habits incident to foreign birth and education. . . .

. . . [I]t may be remarked that the equal vote allowed to each State is at once a constitutional recognition of the portion of sovereignty remaining in the individual States and an instrument for preserving that residuary sovereignty. So far the equality ought to be no less acceptable to the large than to the small States; since they are not less solicitous to guard, by every possible expedient, against an improper consolidation of the States into one simple republic.

Another advantage accruing from this ingredient in the constitution of the Senate is the additional impediment it must prove against improper acts of legislation. No law or resolution can now be passed without the concurrence, first, of a majority of the people, and then of a majority of the States. . . .

. . . It is a misfortune incident to a republican government, though in a less degree than to other governments, that those who administer it may forget their obligations to their constituents and prove unfaithful to their important trust. In this point of view a senate, as a second branch of the legislative assembly distinct from and dividing the power with a first, must be in all cases a salutary check on the government. It doubles the security to the people by requiring the concurrence of two distinct bodies in schemes of usurpation or perfidy, where the ambition or corruption of one would otherwise be sufficient. . . .

. . . The necessity of a Senate is not less indicated by the propensity of all single and numerous assemblies to yield to the impulse of sudden and violent passions, and to be seduced by factious leaders into intemperate and pernicious resolutions. . . .

. . . Every nation, consequently, whose affairs betray a want of wisdom and stability, may calculate on every loss which can be sustained from the more systematic policy of its wiser neighbors. But the best instruction on this subject is unhappily conveyed to America by the example of her own situation. She finds that she is held in no respect by her friends; that she is the derision of her enemies; and that she is a prey to every nation which has an interest in speculating on her fluctuating councils and embarrassed affairs.

The internal effects of a mutable policy are still more calamitous. It poisons the blessings of liberty itself. It will be of little avail to the people that the laws are made by men of their own choice if the laws be so voluminous that they cannot be read, or so incoherent that they cannot be understood; if they be repealed or revised before they are promulgated, or undergo such incessant changes that no man, who knows what the law is today, can guess what it will be tomorrow. Law is defined to be a rule of action; but how can that be a rule, which is little known, and less fixed?

Another effect of public instability is the unreasonable advantage it gives to the sagacious, the enterprising, and the moneyed few over the industrious and uninformed mass of the people. Every new regulation concerning commerce or revenue, or in any matter affecting the value of the different species of property, presents a new harvest to those who watch the change, and can trace its consequences; a harvest, reared not by themselves, but by the toils and cares of the great body of their fellow citizens. This is a state of things in which it may be said with some truth that laws are made for the *few,* not for the *many.*

In another point of view, great injury results from an unstable government. The want of confidence in the public councils damps every useful undertaking, the success and profit of which may depend on a continuance of existing arrangements. What prudent merchant will hazard his fortunes in any branch of commerce when he knows not but that his plans may be rendered unlawful before they can be executed? What farmer or manufacturer will lay himself out for the encouragement given to any particular cultivation or establishment, when he can have no assurance that his preparatory labors and advances will not render him a victim of inconstant government? In a word, no great improvement or laudable enterprise can go forward which requires the auspices of a steady system of national policy.

But the most deplorable effect of all is that diminution of attachment and reverence which steals into the hearts of the people towards a political system which betrays so many marks of infirmity, and disappoints so many of their flattering hopes. No government, any more than an individual, will long be respected without being truly respectable; nor be truly respectable without possessing a certain portion of order and stability.

TOWARD CRITICAL THINKING

1. What were some of the principal reasons offered by Madison to justify different qualifications for members of each house of Congress?
2. How did the different terms of office serve as a check on the power of Congress according to Madison?

· 28 ·

The Washington Community

JAMES STERLING YOUNG

The men who first came to Congress were a diverse lot with little in common save for the fact that most had government experience before coming to Washington and lawyers dominated the group. But unlike today, service in Congress was not considered a long-term career move; in fact, few members set up households in the District of Columbia, and turnover was quite high. Thus, not only was Congress itself "new," but so were its members, and seniority played no role in running the relatively free-wheeling body.

. . .

. . . Life on the Hill imposed upon a crowd of citizen delegates a communal discipline fit for Calvinists or monks. It threw together, under conditions of social intimacy not easily endured even by men long disciplined to it, a group which utterly lacked binding ties of the sort that reinforced, rationalized, and made tolerable the intensely communal life of the New England villagers. Common membership in the legislative institution they had, and common subjection to the ordeal of election: these were binding ties of sufficient strength, apparently, to draw them into a society apart from executives. Career officeholders they were, too. More than four-fifths of the members of one Congress had government experience before coming to Washington . . . and of 439 Senators and Representatives whose careers have been investigated more than two-thirds continued their political careers in other public jobs after leaving the congressional community. But the stability of group membership, the social sameness, the habituation of the members to each other, and the fraternal feelings that usually distinguish congregational communities were conspicuous by their absence in the community on Capitol Hill.

Instead of a stable community membership, one finds a society of transients. Almost none of the members acquired homes in the capital or established year-round residence there. They merely wintered in Washington, spending more time each year with constituents than with each other. Each new Congress, moreover, brought a host of new faces to the com-

SOURCE: The Washington Community 1800–1828, by James Sterling Young, Copyright 1966 © Columbia University Press, New York. Reprinted with permission of the publisher.

munity, drastically reconstituting its membership every two years. For the first four decades of national government between one-third and two-thirds of the congressional community left every two years not to return. . . . New faces appeared and familiar ones departed with considerably greater frequency than in today's Congress: on the average, the biennial turnover was 41.5 percent of the total membership, as compared with 15.8 percent turnover from the 78th to the 79th Congress and 22.4 percent from the 79th to the 80th Congress. While there were a few for whom the Hill was more than a way station in the pursuit of a career, a man's affiliation with the congressional community tended to be brief. Roughly two-thirds of the Representatives on the roster of the 13th Congress, for example, did not serve for more than two terms, and two-thirds of the Senators failed to serve more than one term—quite a few of them resigning before they completed even that. . . .

Thus, for all the forced social intimacy of their community life, the rulers on Capitol Hill were largely strangers to each other. "We never remain long enough together to become personally acquainted." "There are many individuals in this House whom I do not know, for I have never met them in the House or out of it." "Friendships . . . we had few and limited opportunities to cultivate," recalled another legislator, and those "were soon broken by our subsequent separation in different and often far-distant states."

There was, needless to say, the political sectarianism of their different constituency ties, sharpened by the legislators' self-appointed roles as "advocates, retained expressly to support the particular views of particular parties" among their electorates at home. There were differences in occupational background, although lawyers predominated in the same proportion as in the modern House of Representatives. . . .

. . . There were those from the plantation culture and the courthouse politics of the southeast—mercurial, proficient at oratory and duels, "ready to construe contradiction into insult" and "great aristocrats in their . . . habits, if not in their politics." The products of an almost totally different culture and life experience were the New Englanders, cultural aliens in the slaveholding Southland. Austere, moralistic, inner-directed, they "keep to their lodgings," "an unmixed people . . . and used only to see neighbors like themselves."

. . . Social coexistence was insufferable with slaveholders "accustomed to speak in the tone of masters" and with frontiersmen having "a license of tongue incident to a wild and uncultivated state of society. With men of such states of mind and temperament," a Massachusetts delegate protested, "men educated in . . . New England . . . could have little pleasure in intercourse, less in controversy, and of course no sympathy." . . .

TABLE 1
Civil Occupations of Legislators, 9th and 13th Congresses[a]

	Senators		Representatives		Percent of total membership (N = 338)	
Professions						
Law	42		142		54.4[b]	
Other	6	48	34	176	11.8	66.2
Agriculture		9		48		16.9
Trade, commerce, finance		3		45		14.2
Other occupations		1		8		2.7
		61		277		100.0

SOURCE: Biographical sketches appearing in the *Biographical Directory of the American Congress* and the *Dictionary of American Biography.*

[a] The table excludes 64 members whose civil occupations could not be ascertained. A small number of members who served in one chamber in the 9th Congress and the other chamber in the 13th Congress are counted twice.

[b] The proportions of lawyers increased by 13.2 percentage points from the 9th to the 13th Congress, while the proportion of farmers and planters dropped by 8.7 percentage points.

To those who would seek political agreement in an atmosphere of social tensions, the rules of proceeding in Congress offered no aid at all. . . .

. . . There was no Rules Committee of the House to control the legislative proposals that got to the floor, and no other body served that function. . . . Garrulity was the rule, and orations of two or three days length were not uncommon. . . .

Leadership, power to stop or control debate, was nowhere evident. There were no seniority leaders, seniority not being recognized as a basis for rank or prerogative either socially or politically on Capitol Hill. There were no elective or formally recognized party leaders such as are found in the modern Congress: "absolutely no persons holding the station of what are called, in England, Leaders . . . .

With permissiveness of the rules and lack of formally recognized leadership went no spirit of cooperation, conciliation, or deference to the opinions of others. On the contrary, individuation of behavior and opinion was approved and valued, while following the lead of others was scorned as a sign either of weakness of character or of ulterior motives for personal gain. To accommodate was to compromise one's principles. To "disdain the idea of relying . . . [on] any man or set of men" was doctrine; and manifestoes of personal independence so suffused the legislative liturgy that the stenographer reported them in paraphrase for the official record: "He had, he said, a right to his opinion. . . . He held himself responsible for it to no man . . . but at his own will and pleasure. . . . I will express my opinion on this and every other subject, without restraint." Men who agreed on an issue felt constrained to adduce different reasons for arriving at their opinions: "The actual practice is to acknowledge no. . . . guidance; each member taking good care . . . to let [others] . . . see that he is independent." . . .

Outside the chambers themselves the members did not, for all the closeness of their confinement, intermingle freely or associate widely. Instead they segregated into mutually exclusive, closely knit voluntary associations, forming a segmented social structure of face-to-face peer groups. These were the boardinghouse fraternities which almost all legislators joined when they came to Washington—the members who took their meals together, who lived together at the same lodginghouse, and who spent most of their leisure time together. Originating before the move to Washington and continuing at least until the Civil War, the congressional messes, as the members called their fraternities, were the basic social units of the Capitol Hill community. It is likely . . . that they were the basic units of its political structure as well.

. . .

Mess group affiliation was recognized as a mark of identification among legislators. Conversationally members might be referred to as one of innkeeper "Dowson's crowd" or as a member of keeper "Coyle's family." Some boardinghouse groups were given distinctive names, such as the "Washington Mess" (so identified in the *Congressional Directory* for 1809) and the "War Mess," a fraternity of War Hawks in 1810–12. In further recognition of the importance of the boardinghouse groups the early *Congressional Directories,* rather than listing members in alphabetical order or by state, listed them by boardinghouse, each group roster headed by the name of the boardinghouse keeper and the groups listed in order of the proximity of their lodgings to the Capitol. . . .

TOWARD CRITICAL THINKING

1. Why do you think that turnover rates were so high in both houses of Congress?

2. Why did regional and cultural differences seem to make such a difference in early Congresses? What role did congressional "messes" play in deepening these divisions? Were they a substitute for today's numerous specialized caucuses or even for the two political parties?

· 29 ·

The Rise of the Washington Establishment

MORRIS P. FIORINA

Unlike members of the earlier Congresses noted in Reading 28, to-day's members of Congress often wish to make a career out of governmental service in Washington, D.C. As political scientist Morris P. Fiorina notes, key ways for incumbents to maximize their chances of being reelected are through constituency service and bringing home the bacon to their districts in the form of pork barrel legislation. Law making, says Fiorina, can be a risky venture for representatives; after all, someone in the district is usually alienated by the way their representative votes. In contrast, constituency service is often a "win-win" situation.

◆ Dramatis Personae

I assume that most people most of the time act in their own self-interest. This is not to say that human beings seek only to amass tangible wealth but rather to say that human beings seek to achieve their own ends—tangible and intangible—rather than the ends of their fellow men. . . .

. . . I assume that the primary goal of the typical congressman is reelection. Over and above the $57,000 salary plus "perks" and outside money, the office of congressman carries with it prestige, excitement, and power. It is a seat in the cockpit of government. . . . *Even those congressmen genuinely concerned with good public policy must achieve reelection in order to continue their work. Whether narrowly self-serving or more publicly oriented, the individual congressman finds reelection to be at least a necessary condition for the achievement of his goals. . . .

◆ Tammany Hall Goes to Washington

What should we expect from a legislative body composed of individuals whose first priority is their continued tenure in office? We should

SOURCE: Morris P. Fiorina, *Keystone of the Washington Establishment,* copyright © 1989 Yale University Press, New Haven, CT, pp. 37–47. Reprinted by permission of the publisher.

*Salaries in 1994 were $133,600.

170

expect, first, that the normal activities of its members are those calculated to enhance their chances of reelection. And we should expect, second, that the members would devise and maintain institutional arrangements which facilitate their electoral activities. . . .

For most of the twentieth century, congressmen have engaged in a mix of three kinds of activities: lawmaking, pork barreling, and casework. Congress is first and foremost a lawmaking body, at least according to constitutional theory. In every postwar session Congress "considers" thousands of bills and resolutions, many hundreds of which are brought to a record vote. . . . Naturally the critical consideration in taking a position for the record is the maximization of approval in the home district. If the district is unaffected by and unconcerned with the matter at hand, the congressman may then take into account the general welfare of the country. . . .

A second activity favored by congressmen consists of efforts to bring home the bacon to their districts. . . . Congressmen consider new dams, federal buildings, sewage treatment plants, urban renewal projects, etc. as sweet plums to be plucked. Federal projects are highly visible, their economic impact is easily detected by constituents, and sometimes they even produce something of value to the district. The average constituent may have some trouble translating his congressman's vote on some civil rights issue into a change in his personal welfare. But the workers hired and supplies purchased in connection with a big federal project provide benefits that are widely appreciated. The historical importance congressmen attach to the pork barrel is reflected in the rules of the House. That body accords certain classes of legislation "privileged" status: they may come directly to the floor without passing through the Rules Committee, a traditional graveyard for legislation. What kinds of legislation are privileged? Taxing and spending bills, for one: the government's power to raise and spend money must be kept relatively unfettered. But in addition, the omnibus rivers and harbors bills of the Public Works Committee and public lands bills from the Interior Committee share privileged status. The House will allow a civil rights or defense procurement or environmental bill to languish in the Rules Committee, but it takes special precautions to insure that nothing slows down the approval of dams and irrigation projects.

A third major activity takes up perhaps as much time as the other two combined. Traditionally, constituents appeal to their Congressman for myriad favors and services. Sometimes only information is needed, but often constituents request that their congressman intervene in the internal workings of federal agencies to affect a decision in a favorable way, to reverse an adverse decision, or simply to speed up the glacial bureaucratic process. . . .

Actually congressmen are in an almost unique position in our system, a position shared only with high-level members of the executive branch. Congressmen possess the power to expedite and influence bureaucratic decisions. This capability flows directly from congressional control over what bureaucrats value most: higher budgets and new program authorizations. In a very real sense each congressman is a monopoly supplier of bureaucratic unsticking services for his district. . . .

From the standpoint of capturing voters, the congressman's lawmaking activities differ in two important aspects from his pork-barrel and casework activities. First, programmatic actions are inherently controversial. Unless his district is homogeneous, a congressman will find his district divided on many major issues. Thus when he casts a vote, introduces a piece of nontrivial legislation, or makes a speech with policy content he will displease some elements of his district. Some constituents may applaud the congressman's civil rights record, but others believe integration is going too fast. Some support foreign aid, while others believe it's money poured down a rathole. Some advocate economic equality, others stew over welfare cheaters. On such policy matters the congressman can expect to make friends as well as enemies. Presumably he will behave so as to maximize the excess of the former over the latter, but nevertheless a policy stand will generally make some enemies.

In contrast, the pork barrel and casework are relatively less controversial. New federal projects bring jobs, shiny new facilities, and general economic prosperity, or so people believe. Snipping ribbons at the dedication of a new post office or dam is a much more pleasant pursuit than disposing of a constitutional amendment on abortion. Republicans and Democrats, conservatives and liberals, all generally prefer a richer district to a poorer one. Of course, in recent years the river damming and streambed straightening activities of the Army Corps of Engineers have aroused some opposition among environmentalists. Congressmen happily reacted by absorbing the opposition and adding environmentalism to the pork barrel: water treatment plants are currently a hot congressional item.

Casework is even less controversial. Some poor, aggrieved constituent becomes enmeshed in the tentacles of an evil bureaucracy and calls upon Congressman St. George to do battle with the dragon. Again Clapp writes;

> A person who has a reasonable complaint or query is regarded as providing an opportunity rather than as adding an extra burden to an already busy office. The party affiliation of the individual even when known to be different from that of the congressman does not normally act as a deterrent to action. Some legislators have built their reputations and their majorities on a program of service to all constituents irrespec-

tive of party. Regularly, voters affiliated with the opposition in other contests lend strong support to the lawmaker whose intervention has helped them in their struggle with the bureaucracy.

. . . Practicing politicians will tell you that word of mouth is still the most effective mode of communication. News of favors to constituents gets around and no doubt is embellished in the process.

In sum, when considering the benefits of his programmatic activities, the congressman must tote up gains and losses to arrive at a net profit. Pork barreling and casework, however, are basically pure profit.

A second way in which programmatic activities differ from casework and the pork barrel is the difficulty of assigning responsibility to the former as compared with the latter. No congressman can seriously claim that he is responsible for the 1964 Civil Rights Act, the ABM [anti-ballistic missile], or the 1972 Revenue Sharing Act. Most constituents do have some vague notion that their congressman is only one of hundreds and their senator one of an even hundred. . . . The constituent who receives aid believes that his congressman and his congressman alone got results. Similarly, congressmen find it easy to claim credit for federal projects awarded their districts. The congressman may have instigated the proposal for the project in the first place, issued regular progress reports, and ultimately announced the award through his office. Maybe he can't claim credit for the 1965 Voting Rights Act, but he can take credit for Littletown's spanking new sewage treatment plant.

Overall then, programmatic activities are dangerous (controversial), on the one hand, and programmatic accomplishments are difficult to claim credit for, on the other. While less exciting, casework and pork barrelling are both safe and profitable. For a reelection-oriented congressman the choice is obvious.

The key to the rise of the Washington establishment (and the vanishing marginals) is the following observation: *the growth of an activist federal government has stimulated a change in the mix of congressional activities.* Specifically, a lesser proportion of congressional effort is now going into programmatic activities and a greater proportion into pork-barrel and casework activities. As a result, today's congressmen make relatively fewer enemies and relatively more friends among the people of their districts.

To elaborate, a basic fact of life in twentieth-century America is the growth of the federal role and its attendant bureaucracy. . . .

As the years have passed, more and more citizens and groups have found themselves dealing with the federal bureaucracy. They may be seeking positive actions—eligibility for various benefits and awards of government grants. Or they may be seeking relief from the costs imposed by bureaucratic regulations—on working conditions, racial and sexual quotas, market restrictions, and numerous other subjects. While not malevolent, bureaucracies make mistakes, both of commission and omission, and normal attempts at redress often meet with unresponsiveness and inflexibility and sometimes seeming incorrigibility. Whatever the problem, the citizen's congressman is a source of succor. The greater the scope of government activity, the greater the demand for his services.

Private monopolists can regulate the demand for their product by raising or lowering the price. Congressmen have no such (legal) option. When the demand for their services rises, they have no real choice except to meet that demand—to supply more bureaucratic unsticking services—so long as they would rather be elected than unelected. Thus vulnerability to escalating constituency demands is largely academic, though.

. . .

The nature of the Washington system is now quite clear. Congressmen (typically the majority Democrats) earn electoral credits by establishing various federal programs (the minority Republicans typically earn credits by fighting the good fight). The legislation is drafted in very general terms, so some agency, existing or newly established, must translate a vague policy mandate into a functioning program, a process that necessitates the promulgation of numerous rules and regulations and, incidentally, the trampling of numerous toes. At the next stage, aggrieved and/or hopeful constituents petition their congressman to intervene in the complex (or at least obscure) decision processes of the bureaucracy. The cycle closes when the congressman lends a sympathetic ear, piously denounces the evils of bureaucracy, intervenes in the latter's decisions, and rides a grateful electorate to ever more impressive electoral showings. Congressmen take credit coming and going. They are the alpha and the omega.

The popular frustration with the permanent government in Washington is partly justified, but to a considerable degree it is misplaced resentment. *Congress is the linchpin of the Washington establishment.* The bureaucracy serves as a convenient lightning rod for public frustration and a convenient whipping boy for congressmen. But so long as the bureaucracy accommodates congressmen, the latter will oblige with ever larger budgets and grants of authority. Congress does not just react to big government—it creates it. All of Washington prospers. More and more bureaucrats promulgate more and more regulations and dispense more and more money. Fewer and fewer congressmen suffer electoral defeat. Elements of the electorate benefit from government programs, and all of the electorate is eligible for ombudsman services. But the general, long-term welfare of the United States is no more than an incidental by-product of the system.

Exhibit: How the Congressman-as-Ombusman Drums up Business

NEED HELP WITH A FEDERAL PROBLEM?

Please feel free to communicate with me in person, by phone or by mail. Daily from 9 a.m. until 5 p.m. my Congressional District office in Fullerton is open to serve you and your family. The staff will be able to help you with information or assistance on proposed Federal legislation and procedures of Federal agencies. If you are experiencing a problem with Social Security, educational assistance, Veterans Administration, Immigration, Internal Revenue Service, Postal Service, Environmental Protection Agency, Federal Energy Office or any other Federal agency please contact me through this office. If you decide to write to me, please provide a telephone number as many times I can call you with information within a day or two.

CONGRESSMAN CHARLES E. WIGGINS

Brashears Center, Suite 103
1400 N. Harbor Boulevard
Fullerton, Ca 92635 (714) 870-7266

My Washington address is
Room 2445 Rayburn Building, Washington, D.C.
20515. Telephone (202) 225-4111

U.S. House of Representatives
Washington D.C. 80818
Public Document

Official Business

POSTAL CUSTOMER-LOCAL
39th District

CALIFORNIA

TOWARD CRITICAL THINKING

1. Would term limits put an and to the cycle of Congress creating more government in order to enhance individual members' chances of being reelected? Is constituency service a good or bad thing, or both?

2. Why doesn't Fiorina see law making as one of Congress's major functions? How different is the Congress he describes from the one envisioned by the Framers?

· 30 ·

Freshman Rush—First You Run to Get Elected, Then You Just Keep Running

MARJORIE MARGOLIES-MEZVINSKY

In spite of being a former Washington reporter and the wife of a former member of Congress, the politics of committee assignments and power were new to this freshman member of Congress. Elected in 1992 by the narrowest of margins, Margolies-Mezvinsky immediately began to lobby congressional leaders for important committee assignments that would put her in a position to enhance her chances for reelection. But as her first chance encounter with a Republican on an elevator on her way to cast her first vote revealed, Margolies-Mezvinsky consistently voted Democratic—including casting a crucial vote on the president's 1994 economic package. That vote earned her the wrath of many constituents in her district and made her a major target of the national Republican Party leadership in 1994.

It felt like my first time on Capitol Hill. As a television reporter for WRC–TV in the 1980s I had logged many miles in these marble halls. But this was the first time I was coming to Congress not as an outsider but as the newly elected member from the thirteenth district of Pennsylvania.

I approached the security guard, expecting some official greeting. Instead he began the routine check through my purse. "This is Congresswoman-elect Marjorie Margolies-Mezvinsky," my aide explained. The guard gave me back my purse and ushered me through.

It wasn't his fault. I may have known I was elected, but nobody else in Washington did. . . .

Overnight we go from election-night winners to know-nothing freshmen. And whether you are in college or in Congress, being a freshman is like riding a roller coaster—you are moving so fast that you barely have time to savor the highs, survive the lows, and hang on for dear life. . . .

SOURCE: Marjorie Margolies-Mezvinsky, "Freshman Rush," *Washingtonian Magazine* (April 1993). Reprinted by permission.

. . . My election had been so close that I arrived at my November 3 party with only a concession speech in my pocket. In the end, I squeaked into office by 1,300 votes.

I was too busy getting elected to prepare for actually being in Congress. Now I had to make up for lost time by immediately beginning my next campaign—the campaign for support from the coterie of men on the Hill who control assignments to congressional committees.

Committee assignments are like college classes—freshmen have the least seniority and the hardest time getting the ones they want. Some freshmen had started their campaigns for committees as soon as they won their primaries.

Right after the election I called John Murtha, dean of the Pennsylvania Democratic delegation, about committee assignments. He advised me to start lobbying for the ones I wanted.

I had set my sights on the Energy and Commerce Committee. E&C generates much of the critical legislation in the House. Along with Ways and Means and Appropriations, it's where the action is. To get on E&C I would need the support of the entire Pennsylvania delegation, the Ohio-Pennsylvania region, the Democratic leadership, committee chairman John Dingell, and then the Democratic Steering and Policy Committee, which meets behind closed doors to make final selections. It is the equivalent of sorority rush, except that the whole process takes place on the QT. . . .

By the time the Pennsylvania delegation met on December 7, I had met almost every Democrat from my state. At a dinner for new members I caught the only two who had eluded me. One of them said, "Marjorie, I'm not even going to make you grovel for this one." . . .

The Democratic Leadership Conference, a group that numbered the president-elect among its members, held a dinner the same night as the Steering and Policy Committee met to make committee assignments. There was one school of thought that advised standing right outside the committee room during deliberations to remind members of your requests.

I went to the dinner, leaving a staffer outside the committee room with instructions to call on the beeper as soon as she heard. Blanche Lambert, a freshman from Arkansas, was told at the dinner an hour later that she had been assigned to Energy and Commerce. Knowing that she was likely the only woman named to the committee, I felt my heart sink.

As I was walking over to congratulate Blanche, Mike Synar of Oklahoma intercepted me. He extended his hand and said, "Congratulations— you're on E&C." That's how I learned I had gotten my first-choice committee assignment. . . .

I had met some members of my class during the campaign. Nineteen ninety-two was the year of the woman, and the "New Female Network" had brought women candidates together for fund-raising and strategy sessions. We knew that our class would change the face of the House— 24 of the 110 freshmen are women and 27 are minorities. In fact, of the 13 class officers, 11 are women, minorities, or both. . . .

There is no question that a grounding in journalism helps on the Hill. It isn't just the importance of the media in winning elections. As a reporter, I was a trained fact-finder, which is helpful in committee work. I was also accustomed to moving fast to follow a story, always knowing where the exits and the bathrooms are, and carrying everything I might need in an emergency—all useful habits for a new member of Congress. . . .

From the start, I realized that I was luckier than many of my fellow freshmen. After working for more than fifteen years as a television reporter in Washington, I knew Northeast from Northwest, and where to get a good haircut. One of my campaign volunteers had worked for retiring Congressman Harley Staggers, and she wangled use of an office from her old boss. Other freshmen were operating out of work stations in the basement of the Rayburn Building.

Having a district fairly close to the capital is another advantage. I planned to commute daily by train—as Senator Joe Biden does between Wilmington and DC—while my husband, Ed, stayed in Philadelphia with the family. During particularly heavy weeks, I planned to stay with friends in Bethesda or Alexandria and return home on Thursday night. . . .

It takes an extraordinary family to accommodate a long-distance commuting mother—and my family is that. As a single reporter in New York I had adopted two little girls from Asia, my daughters Lee Heh and Holly. In 1975 four stepdaughters came into our lives, mainly on weekends, when I married Ed Mezvinsky, then a congressman from Iowa. We've had two boys of our own—Marc, 15, and Andrew, 10—and become legal guardians for three boys from Southeast Asia—Hai, Dang, and Vu. This brings the grand total to eleven kids. . . .

In mid-December, the House held a lottery for offices. Members draw for office space the same way college students draw for dormitory rooms. Freshmen draw last. Out of the 110 freshman numbers, my staff drew 97. I expected to find myself in a broom closet.

On January 4, one day before swearing-in ceremonies, I saw my lovely little office for the first time. It is a three-room suite on the fifth floor of the Longworth Building, with a view of a gravel court. Longworth looked like a dorm just before the start of fall semester. Paint fumes lingered from touch-ups the night before. Stacks of cartons, unmatched furniture, and assorted paraphernalia lined the corridors; jeans-clad staffers carrying boxes filled every elevator.

Elevators take on an unexpected importance in Congress. Waiting for elevators, some programmed to stop at every floor, costs precious minutes when you are racing to the House floor for a vote—that's why freshmen end up with offices on the fifth, sixth, or seventh floors of Longworth. . . .

On January 5, the morning the 103rd Congress would be sworn in . . . the day started before dawn for a dozen members of the freshman class. We were guests on "CBS This Morning." . . .

After the CBS show, I rushed back to my office for two local broadcast interviews and then to a meeting of the Democratic Caucus. . . .

At noon I stood on the House floor to take the oath of office. . . .

From the House floor, I ran back to the Rayburn Building and the thousand people gathered to celebrate with me. . . .

No sooner had I been sworn in again than the bells sounded for the first vote of the 103rd Congress. . . . I jumped into the elevator with another freshman, a Republican.

"How are you voting?" I said.

"Aye," he said.

"That means I vote nay."

TOWARD CRITICAL THINKING

1. How could the system be changed to prevent members from beginning to seek reelection before they even arrive in Washington, D.C.?

2. Do you think Margolies-Mezvinsky's experiences are typical? Do new members need more "training" before coming to Capitol Hill? Are neophyte politicians better than the governmental "careerists" described by Young (Reading 28) and Fiorina (Reading 29)?

BOX 6.1

Congress Learns to Talk Like a Woman

DAVID SARASOHN

When Patty Murray became a U.S. senator three months ago, her greatest adjustment wasn't the workload or the contrast with the Washington state Legislature or even the fact that she couldn't wear her tennis shoes on the Senate floor.

What really hung her up was the language barrier. "Senators speak in a different language, about baselines, CBOs, charts and graphs," Sen. Murray says. "Women talk about the effects of that piece of paper on their communities."

Sen. Murray, of course, has only been in the Senate three months; after five years—or ten or twenty—she may be talking about FY97 out-years and M-1 projections with the best of them. But for now, new voices in Congress are speaking not only in a different pitch, but in a different language.

This is the year after the Year of the Woman, and there are now six women in the Senate and forty-seven in the House. You could see how things might sound a little different.

"It was just mind-boggling to have a parental-leave debate," says Celinda Lake, a Washington pollster specializing in female candidates, "and have a U.S. senator say that 'When I had my first baby I had to leave my job.'"

"People think that we are changing the form of the debate" when women senators talk about their lives, Sen. Murray says. "People are stopped. They don't know how to debate that. I was debating (Texas Republican) Phil Gramm, and he answered that I made an eloquent argument, and then went back to talking baselines and statistics."

According to Ms. Lake, even that response reflects a change.

"Male politicians used to answer with the moral equivalent of 'The little lady doesn't get it,'" Ms. Lake recalls, "Now they can't say that, so they say she's made an eloquent argument."

SOURCE: David Sarasohn, "Congress Learns to Talk Like a Woman," Reprinted by permission of the author.

· *31* ·

Home Style and Committee Behavior: The Case of Richard Nolan

ROBERT P. WEBER[*]

The relationship between what members of Congress do in Washington and back home in their districts is complex. Political scientist Richard F. Fenno Jr. argues that members develop a "home style" to enhance their electability and thus their congressional careers in an institution where seniority is key. Home styles differ, based on a variety of factors, but the important question is this: Does an understanding of those behaviors help us understand a member's behavior in Washington, D.C.? Political scientist Robert P. Weber concludes that it does. His thoughtful analysis of the behaviors of Rep. Richard Nolan (D.-Minn.) shows that Nolan was often torn between what the voters back home wanted and what he viewed as his broader responsibilites as a legislator.

Both the members of Congress and their constituencies are complex phenomena. So too are the relationships between what representatives do in their districts and what they do in Washington. Members of the House work hard at maintaining the support of their constituents, developing what Richard Fenno terms a "home style" to win and to hold sufficient support to continue a congressional career (Fenno 1978). As a concept, home style includes a combination of allocative, presentational, and explanatory activities that congressmen undertake in relation to their perceptions of their constituencies. Members make verbal and nonverbal presentations to their various constituencies, Fenno argues, attempting to elicit support and legitimacy from their audiences. Though homes styles may differ depending upon personal, contextual, and strategic factors, each representative seeks to achieve a degree of constituent trust that affords both leeway in Washington and survival in the district.

SOURCE: Robert P. Weber, "Home Style and Committee Behavior," in *Home Style and Washington Work,* Morris Fiorina and David Rohde (eds.) (Ann Arbor: The University of Michigan Press, 1991), pp. 71–95. Reprinted by permission of the publisher.

[*] I am grateful to Joseph Farry and Richard F. Fenno, Jr., for their many helpful comments on an earlier draft of this essay.

181

Does understanding a member's home style help us to understand his or her behavior in Washington? . . . If students of Congress are to build upon Fenno's pioneering work, then questions about the linkage between behavior in the district and behavior in Washington ultimately must be addressed.

This study relies upon research in the district and research in Washington to examine the correspondence between one member's home style and his behavior on the Agriculture Committee. The subject of this essay [is] Richard Nolan (D-Minnesota). . . .

◆ The Geographical District: ". . . Conservative and Republican"

Richard Nolan's view of his geographical district began with an emphasis upon its size. It was a district that was "large and spread out, twenty-two counties running from the Iowa border to Central Minnesota." It was also a district that in demographic characteristics was "basically rural, mostly farmers, small towns entirely dependent upon an agricultural economy, and a couple of medium-sized cities." From these cryptic observations he moved rapidly to a political description of his district, a description that emphasized its marginality and partisanship. Both objectively and subjectively he represented a highly competitive district, "the most marginal in the state—the most sought after district in Minnesota by Republicans." He pointed with pride to his "rather handsome 5 percent margin" in the last election, a figure that "is good for a district as competitive as the Sixth District." Though he emphasized the district's marginality, party competition did not produce extreme feelings of electoral vulnerability. He knew that he might lose this district, but he also believed that "Nobody can take it away from me, if I really want it."

To the highly competitive character of his geographical district, Nolan added an ideological dimension. District voters were inclined, he believed, to be "conservative and Republican in their basic tendencies." His district had "quite a large number of conservatives" and "they make a lot of noise." . . .

As an avowed liberal Democrat, Nolan had little sense of policy congruence with his "basically conservative and Republican" geographical district. On one occasion he observed that:

> Not only do I represent the most marginal district in the State, but I'm on the far left of the political spectrum and most of my constituents are to the right of center. I'm faced with representing a marginal district where I'm always running against the tide of public opinion.

Nolan recognized that this gulf between his positions and those of his district required an adjustment, but he also believed that he was not compelled to modify his views in order to be reelected. To compensate for the absence of a policy fit with his geographical district, he returned frequently to his district. "I have to go back home every weekend," he claimed, "and sometimes I even find myself jumping on the airplane and going back to Minnesota during the middle of the week." He had to go home often, he insisted, "to show my constituents that I don't have any horns."

The frequency of trips back to his district as well as the opportunities they imply served as Nolan's major defense against a successful Republican challenge. He returned not to convert his critics, but to buttress and maintain the support of his primary and reelection coalition. His fear was that "If people don't know me personally, they'd be inclined to believe some of the things that the right-wingers say about me." It was to his reelection coalition that he primarily devoted his time and attention, a personal and strategic allocation that produced a measure of electoral well-being within a highly competitive situation. . . .

◆ "My Reelection Depended an Whether I Got a Seat on the Committee"

The concept of home style, largely because of its constituency orientation, provides at most a partial guide to Washington behavior. By observing Richard Nolan in his district we saw him concentrating almost exclusively on a reelection goal. Yet, as Fenno notes, "when we speak of Washington careers, we speak primarily of the goals of influence in the House and the making of good public policy" (Fenno 1978, 215). Though members may incorporate aspects of these goals into their home styles, a district perspective yields only limited information about the mix of goals that an individual holds. To gather information about the relative weights that a member assigns to these different goals requires that we combine a Washington perspective with our view from the district. In addition, just as some aspects of a member's home style are contextually defined, his or her Washington performance also occurs within a particular context. Prudential judgments about how well or how poorly Richard Nolan's Washington behavior corresponded to his home style cannot be made unless we make an effort to learn something of the milieu in which he functioned.

To recognize that members of Congress pursue different goals in different contexts serves to remind us that Congress is an extraordinarily complex institution. And to recognize this complexity at the outset is probably a useful antidote to premature judgments about the usefulness of the concept of home style as an aide to understanding Washington behavior. These caveats should not, however, lead us to conclude that home styles and Washington behavior are entirely unrelated phenomena. It is the philosophy of representative government that links behavior in the district with choices in Washington and it is the activity of the member in both places that imparts concrete meaning to this abstract idea. It is to an examination of the relationship between Richard Nolan's Washington behavior and his home style that we now turn.

As a newly elected member, Nolan immediately turned his attention to serving his primary constituency and to securing his own reelection to office. His decision to seek a seat on the Agriculture Committee reflected these concerns, a choice of committee assignments that served both purposes. "After my first election," he said, "I went on the Agriculture Committee out of a sense of obligation to the farmers in my district." If freed from the constraints imposed by his own reelection coalition, Nolan's own policy predilections might well have prompted him to seek a committee assignment that offered an opportunity to draft "good policy.". . .

Nolan's sense of obligation to the farmers in his district, as well as his own campaign pledge to seek this assignment, encouraged him to apply for this position. But it was also his own instinct for survival in a competitive and ideologically hostile district that offered equally compelling reasons for serving on this committee. He aggressively sought a position on the committee, personally lobbying the members of the Steering and Policy Committee:

> I got on the Agriculture Committee by request. I wanted it. I lobbied most of the Steering and Policy Committee and I told them that I really needed to be on that Committee—that my reelection to Congress depended on whether I got a seat on the Committee.

Nolan's assessment of the relationship between committee assignment and enhanced reelection prospects, it should be noted, did not distinguish him from the vast majority of colleagues on the committee. . . .

. . .

◆ "Most of the Committee Really Represented Large-Scale Farmers . . ."

Judgments about good policy and what the individual can do to realize that policy objective involve complex calculations about relationships between means and ends. In Nolan's case his judgments about these relationships rested upon two key perceptions: his view of his colleagues on the committee and his view of the House as an institution. In both instances there is a good deal of similarity between Nolan's Washington behavior and the posture he assumed in his district.

Nolan could point to a handful of committee members, mostly young Democrats, with whom he felt a special camaraderie. Almost without exception, these were individuals who shared similar policy views. Almost entirely lacking, however, was much sense of a policy fit with the great majority of his committee colleagues. He had won the support of his farmers by pledging to seek 100 percent parity for farm prices. Now, however, he found himself on a committee where he soon discovered that "not all farmers or all committee members want 100 percent parity for their commodities." . . .

Nolan recognized that positions taken in the district, particularly on agricultural issues, restricted his flexibility on the committee. It was not, however, flexibility that he valued. He found, for example, little attractiveness in the idea that flexibility might offer maximum opportunity for maneuver within the committee. Nolan's posture, consistent with his home style, was instead one of early commitment to extreme positions, especially the positions that he had taken in his district. As he explained, "I liked to always stake out a strong and generally what was considered an extreme position, one that I thought was right." . . .

◆ "I Just Got Burned Out"

After six years in the House and at the age of thirty-six, Richard Nolan retired from the House of Representatives. It was a decision that came as a complete surprise to all but one of his Washington staff. Young, physically energetic, in good health, with sufficient seniority to hold a subcommittee chairmanship—all of these factors seemed to argue for a continued congressional career. And yet Richard Nolan retired from the House, one of several so-called premature retirements. It was a decision that terminated both his career in the district and in the House, a decision that represented the final linkage between his home style and his Washington behavior.

Nolan, as he devoted more of his energies to the pursuit of his policy goals on the Hill, also devoted less time in his district to the cultivation of his reelection coalition.[1] Though these strong supporters were not threatening a withdrawal of their support, he found: "As a congressman, it simply wasn't possible to maintain it any more, the intimacy." And, he added, "I think that kind of contact and intimacy has to exist to continue . . . [to be reelected]." Efforts to pursue energetically both a Washington and a constituency career, no doubt, produced for Nolan a physically taxing experience. It was not, however, the absence of stamina that by

---

[1]There is another tension as well, the conflict between politics and familial responsibilities. Spouses and children, however patient and understanding they may be, can rightfully claim attention from the member, claims that can prove to be even more compelling than those that emanate from any member's strongest supporter. Shortly after they returned to Minnesota, Nolan and his wife divorced.

itself led him to retire. It was, instead, his own mental outlook, the absence of a "right frame of mind," and his own feeling that "I just got burned out."

Nolan's experience in Congress also contributed to his own lack of proper attitude. It was, in general, an experience of fighting many battles but winning few concrete victories. Looking back over his congressional career, he found his greatest satisfaction "from sponsoring the resolution ending America's involvement in the Vietnam war." His success on the floor with the amendment to the 1977 Farm Bill, though this victory added significantly to the economic well-being of his family farmers, was dismissed as insignificant. "Even those levels were inadequate in my judgment," he explained, "but much better than the committee ever would have passed based on their logic." For a member who believed that "basic policy change" was essential to the nation's well-being, functioning within an institution that primarily produces incremental changes was a considerable source of frustration.

Nolan might have tolerated these frustrations had the future seemed more promising. He saw instead "that the country and Congress were moving from a politically stagnant position of paralysis . . . to a period of reaction and regression personified by the popular support of conservatives, such as Ronald Reagan." If the past had seemed unproductive from a policy standpoint, the future seemed even more bleak. Of his own feelings, he observed:

> I just began to feel futile about it all. Burned out, worn out, frustrated. Finally, I found myself starting to get rather angry and bitter, resentful, excessively self-righteous and in that frame of mind, I concluded that I wasn't going to be of much use to anybody.

Lacking much concrete success in achieving his own policy goals and unable to anticipate much success in the near future, he rejected a career in Congress and turned his attention to other endeavors.

Nolan's inability to help produce the kind of policy changes that he found desirable, though it added much to his frustration in Congress, did little to dim his enthusiasm for change. "I've always believed myself to be a positive-orientated person," he noted, "and some very exciting and positive things were happening outside the government, oftentimes inspired by the government." He returned to Minnesota, intending to develop a small specialty crop farm and to establish his own export trading company. That Richard Nolan would choose to be a small businessman, given his unflattering view of business interests in his district, represented a major irony. Besides supporting himself, however, he also viewed his firm as an opportunity to "persuade American companies to go to developing countries to help them with the technology needed to improve the living conditions in Third World countries." That orientation, much as it made Richard Nolan a very unusual member of the Agriculture Committee, may also make him a businessman different from those he represented in Congress for six years.

◆ Conclusion

Does an understanding of Richard Nolan's home style help us to understand his Washington behavior? The answer to that question, I think, is yes. That such a high degree of correspondence between his home style and his committee behavior should be found is primarily due to the large measure of discretion involved in Nolan's choices at both ends of the representational relationship. From his willingness to engage in a kind of exclusive coalition building to his emphasis upon the "right" groups and the "right" philosophy, the parallels between his actions at home and his behavior in Washington were both significant and substantial. Even the intensity of his own personal commitments that fueled him at the beginning of his constituency career and helped to terminate his Washington career served as an important link between his life in the district and his life in Washington. He was the kind of member that he wanted to be, and his constituents found this behavior sufficiently attractive so that many wanted him to continue to represent them even after he had lost his heart to do battle on their behalf.

On the basis of a single case study one cannot, of course, legitimately claim that other members will display similar degrees of correspondence between their home styles and their Washington behavior or that personal factors will prove to be equally important. It is, however, tempting to speculate that where members of Congress enjoy the greatest latitude in the choice of home styles will also be found the best fit between their district and Washington behavior. Such speculation, of course, must be weighed against the possibility that Richard Nolan was a very unique congressman. We cannot, however, know how unique until we try to match the home styles of other members with their Washington behavior.

REFERENCES

Fenno, Richard F., Jr. 1978. *Home Style*. Boston: Little, Brown.

TOWARD CRITICAL THINKING

1. When home in his district, what were Rep. Nolan's primary goals? How were they inconsistent or incompatible with what he would have liked to do as a legislator?

2. British political philosopher Edmund Burke noted that legislators have different orientations. Some view themselves as "trustees," voting for what they think is best. In contrast, what he terms "delegates" vote the way they expect those they represent would like them to vote. What role did Nolan adopt? Did role conflict, at least in part, contribute to Nolan's decision to leave Congress?

· 32 ·

Congress Debates the Economic Program

RICHARD E. COHEN

Although as many of the readings in the chapter indicate, many members of Congress spend much of their time on activities geared toward their reelection, most members of Congress are very hardworking. Their chief job ultimately is *law making*. During the Reagan and Bush administrations (1981–1993), many academics and political commentators criticized the gridlock that occurred in Washington as the Democratic Congress and Republican presidents could agree on little. Bill Clinton ran on a campaign platform pledged to end this gridlock caused by what political observers have called "divided government."[*] The first year of the Clinton presidency produced many major pieces of legislation in Congress; one of the toughest to pass was the president's economic program, as explained by Richard E. Cohen.

. . .

◆ Accommodating Many Viewpoints

Before his administration could move ahead at full speed to other issues, especially health-care reform, President Clinton had to secure final congressional approval of his economic program. Because that plan's defeat would have been politically devastating, top Democrats did not want to contemplate the consequences of such a setback. Ultimately, they would achieve their goal, by the absolute barest of margins, in both the House and Senate. But the tortuous final road to enactment of the bill underlined Clinton's shaky grasp of the power levers. The debate also starkly revealed the Democrats' internal differences, which they had worked for months to paper over. Those varied difficulties were an apt metaphor for the growing problems that the Clinton administration faced in Congress as the two branches settled down to the daily routine of trying to steer the federal government. As the initial bloom of election victory and the early weeks in office faded, Clinton and his party began to pay the price for several shortcomings of the previous months: their often

---

SOURCE: From Richard E. Cohen, *Changing Course in Washington.* Copyright 1994 by Allyn and Bacon. Reprinted/Adapted by permission.

---

[*]Morris P. Fiorina, *Divided Government.* New York: Macmillan, 1992.

ambiguous campaign agenda, the 43 percent election victory, the administration's awkward start and the continued infighting among Democratic factions in Congress. Because governing is such a difficult process, even under the best of circumstances, these various political and legislative constraints became heavy burdens to carry. Still, a win is a win. And Clinton and his partners had every right to glory in the passage of their economic plan—and to breathe deep sighs of relief.

As its months in office passed, the Clinton administration also began to learn what each new team must face: Congress will grant a fresh start to a president, but most lawmakers—even supposed allies—will not wait long before they assert their own prerogatives. The House and Senate decisions in March to defer to the basic outlines of Clinton's budget plan would soon become a quaint and forgotten token of respect. When Congress reached the point of writing the final details of the new budget, hand-to-hand legislative combat was required to resolve many issues. Clinton's once-robust new energy tax was whittled to a far more modest increase in the gasoline tax, and even that plan endured harsh attacks. A similar congressional response also asserted itself on other issues, as vague campaign pledges met the realities of stark policy choices. Abortion-rights supporters, for example, were startled by a House vote that imposed continued restrictions on federal funding of abortions for low-income women. "I was shocked to learn that this is not a pro-choice Congress," said first-term Rep. Lynn Schenk, a California Democrat. "With all the hype of 'the year of the woman,' I was lulled into a false sense of change." And Clinton's promise of campaign-finance reform bogged down in the House, a victim of internal disagreements among Democrats and of the party's focus on the budget. On a few issues, however, the president was more successful. In addition to the easy Senate confirmation of Ruth Bader Ginsburg to the Supreme Court, he won final congressional approval in September of the first genuine "Clinton" proposal—a national service program to encourage volunteers to participate in community activities.

Several significant patterns began to emerge in how Clinton and Congress handled these and other issues. Prominent among them was his reliance on the Democrats' congressional leaders and key committee chairmen. Mostly, these lawmakers strongly supported his plans, and their efforts were essential to his legislative accomplishments. Although most White House officials believe that such backing ought to be unequivocal, the vital cooperation provided by Speaker Foley and Majority Leader Mitchell and their lieutenants exceeded the liaisons with several recent presidents and rescued Clinton on several occasions. By summer, however, some warning signals appeared on this horizon. When House Majority Whip David Bonior of Michigan and, later, Majority Leader

Gephardt voiced strong opposition to Clinton's bid to win approval of the proposed North American Free Trade Agreement, they showed that the party leaders would not always act as a monolith. . . . Even stalwart partners like Foley and Mitchell made pointed remarks about the White House's mishandling of congressional business.

The growing willingness of many rank-and-file congressional Democrats to criticize and vote against Clinton's program was in stark contrast to the early weeks of his administration. At that time, such opposition came chiefly from a few senior Senate Democrats, especially the independent-minded committee chairmen. With Clinton's continued decline in public-opinion polls and the need for many senators and all House members to focus on their own re-election in November 1994, however, their respect for presidential loyalty diminished. On issues ranging from the gasoline tax and the North American trade deal to gays in the military, many congressional Democrats began to define their distance from Clinton. In doing so, they hoped to show that their chief allegiance was to local constituents. One example was Democratic Rep. Collin Peterson of Minnesota. In strongly opposing the proposed trade agreement because he feared that it would cost thousands of local farming jobs, he warned that if the president tried to twist arms to secure its passage, "he won't get a lot of support from me on anything." Peterson was true to his word: After having voted for the initial House passage of the deficit-reduction plan, he was one of the eleven Democrats who switched to oppose the final House-Senate agreement.

That Clinton and the House and Senate leaders were forced to focus virtually all their attention on the deficit-reduction plan until Congress began its month-long August recess also showed the difficulties facing a president who had campaigned on the need for extensive changes in Washington. When Congress returned after Labor Day, the political cycle had moved inexorably to the point where it was almost halfway to the next set of House and Senate elections. Those campaign results and the prospect of significant Republican gains, of course, could have a major bearing on the remainder of Clinton's term. The calendar was growing short for action not only for Clinton's plan for health-care reform but also on a variety of other campaign pledges, such as "reinventing" government to make it work more efficiently and strengthening the nation's industrial sector at the same time that the military was being significantly downsized. . . .

◆ Wrapping Up the Economic Package

When the House and Senate have passed contrasting versions of the same bill, the task of resolving those differences often falls to a House-

Senate conference committee. Such a committee usually is a straightforward affair and often can complete its work in a few meetings among the senior members of the House and Senate committees that initially drafted the bill. But the budget reconciliation bill was a more complicated matter for several reasons, and it would severely test the legislative skills of congressional leaders and White House officials. During a three-week period in July, they would be forced to resolve thousands of details on hundreds of issues in a way that would gain the votes of a majority of both the House and Senate for the final bill. There would be little margin to spare.

The sheer size of the conference committee required daunting logistics. Because sixteen committees from the House and twelve more from the Senate drafted at least a small part of the conference report on the massive bill, party leaders and the White House had to closely monitor and spur completion of the conference committee deliberations, which actually took place in dozens of subconferences. . . . The House and Senate Budget Committees had the formal responsibility of coordinating the conference. But most of the key decisions rested with the House Ways and Means Committee and the Senate Finance Committee, which had jurisdiction over more than $335 billion of deficit reduction plus another $56 billion in tax cuts and new spending. . . .

Conference committees, in theory, are supposed to meet in public and exchange compromise proposals between their House and Senate members. But the reality often has been that most of the key discussions are held in private among the House and Senate committee and subcommittee chairmen. They, in turn, keep in close contact with other conferees from their committee, a majority of whom must ratify the deal before it is officially sealed. Sens. Mitchell and Moynihan carefully appointed Finance Committee conferees whom they believed that they could rely on as loyalists. As a result, they pointedly excluded Sen. Boren of Oklahoma, whose outspoken opposition to the proposed energy tax had created so many difficulties for them during the initial bill-drafting; though he was third in seniority on the Finance Committee, he was not among the seven Democratic conferees. That decision eased the leaders' task in managing the conference committee. But the one-vote margin by which the Senate initially passed the bill plus its highly controversial circumstances meant that this would be no ordinary conference committee. In effect, Boren and every other Democratic senator who had voted for the measure would hold a veto power over the bill if they objected so strongly to a particular provision that they would vote against the final deal. Similar dynamics prevailed in the larger House, although there was less public focus on specific individuals than in the Senate. In short, the Democratic managers of the bill in both chambers would be forced to constantly monitor the views of their party comrades on potential compromises. . . .

On the other side of the conference-committee table from Rostenkowski sat Daniel Patrick Moynihan, the new chairman of the Senate Finance Committee. As the negotiations convened, several news stories focused on this political odd couple—the rough-hewn ethnic politician from Chicago and the erudite former Harvard University professor from New York—and their ability to work together. "Mr. Moynihan, it is said on Capitol Hill, has written more books (sixteen at last count) than Mr. Rostenkowski has read," *The New York Times* noted. "Mr. Rostenkowski, it is said, is so savvy that he can pick the eccentric Senator's pockets." But the two principals downplayed these stereotypes as well as their stylistic differences. They aptly pointed out that they shared the goal of reaching agreement on a compromise as close as possible to Clinton's original plan. They also recognized that they had little room for ego clashes. . . .

From the start, both realized that the most difficult issue would be resolving the differences on a so-called energy tax: The House had passed the broad-based tax designed to raise $72 billion over five years, while the Senate had approved a far more limited increase of 4.3 cents per gallon on gasoline, which would raise about $23 billion during the same period. Because Clinton and congressional leaders continued to insist on a total deficit reduction of about $500 billion, the fate of several other tax provisions and proposed spending cuts would be influenced by the handling of that nearly $50 billion disparity. The higher the energy tax, the less pressure there would be on other provisions. "We have only one difficult problem: what form of energy tax we can agree to," Moynihan said. "And that problem is not determining what is a good energy tax, but what can pass the House and the Senate."

To determine what would work politically, Rostenkowski and Moynihan kept in regular contact with Foley, Mitchell and the other party leaders to review possible changes. Their private discussions typically focused more on whether an alternative could gain the needed support than on whether it made good policy sense. Much of the work was driven by symbolism. For example, when Sen. John Breaux, the Louisiana Democrat, publicly questioned the need to attain the roughly $500 billion in deficit reduction that Clinton had originally sought, he elicited a quick response from Treasury Secretary Bentsen, Speaker Foley and others about the sanctity of that goal. Likewise, a key demand on which many conservative Democrats insisted was that the final package—unlike the House-passed version—embrace a higher total in spending cuts than in new taxes. Most of all, the Democratic legislative chiefs kept in mind the overriding need to give Clinton the victory that would be crucial to establishing momentum for his presidency, which had encountered a shaky start. . . .

◆ The Bottom-Up Conference

As the conference committee on the deficit-reduction bill moved into high gear, the various factions began to flex their muscles to seek their share of the legislative pie. Their demands for fine tuning the product highlighted the conflicting pressures that Democratic leaders were forced to resolve. Although such pressure tactics are a ritualistic part of the legislative bargaining process, the many advocates posed a greater threat than usual because of the slim margins by which the House and Senate had initially passed the measure. And it often was difficult for the decision-makers to predict how much change they would have to make to win the votes of the Democrats who remained undecided. Most of the wayward lawmakers who caused the greatest consternation among the chief conferees did not even serve on the conference committee reconciling the tax provisions.

The chief source of Democratic nervousness came from members in conservative Deep South states. Not coincidentally, that was the area where Clinton's popularity had dipped to particularly weak levels, as the Democrats' devastating loss in the special election for the Texas Senate seat in early June had revealed. Although many of these conservative Democrats privately worried about the impact to the oil industry of the House-passed energy tax, they publicly focused their unhappiness on what they said was the unsatisfactory response to their demands for more spending cuts. . . . Moreover, the pressures in the conference committee were to increase spending above the Senate-passed levels. To pass the bill, as a result, Democrats apparently would need to switch a senator who had voted against it.

In the House, Rep. Charles Stenholm of Texas, who had originally voted for the much larger energy tax, said a few days later that he would oppose the bill because of its gasoline-tax increase. In a statement, he called it "unwise for substantive as well as political reasons for us to raise taxes on middle-class working men and women in order to pay for increased spending as this conference report does." Other Democrats reported that Stenholm's switch was based, in part, on the growing political opposition to the measure in his conservative district. His decision was important, at least symbolically, because he had influenced Gephardt's earlier House efforts to craft a spending-limits agreement between party conservatives and liberals. His defection was a warning to Clinton that conservative Democrats were restless.

Meanwhile, members of the Congressional Black Caucus pressed their case for fewer spending cuts, especially in programs that benefitted low-income groups. "If we're going to find a way to cushion the effect on the middle class and the working poor, if we are honest about clear deficit reduction, then we have got to be very honest about raising the revenues to do that," Rep. Kweisi Mfume of Maryland, the Caucus chairman, told reporters at the White House after a July 21 meeting with Clinton. The Black Caucus members also fought for Clinton's proposed expansion of the earned income tax credit. Designed to raise working families out of poverty, this tax-code tool was consuming a rapidly growing share of the federal budget; it also had gained support in recent years from many Republicans, who viewed it as a work incentive. The conference commit- tee's agreement to add several billion dollars a year to its annual benefits, in effect, amounted to a significant welfare expansion and showed that a "deficit-reduction" bill can also include new federal costs and policy initiatives. The credit "has won praise from liberals and conservatives alike as an effective tool for combating poverty and rewarding work," according to an analysis of its new terms. "The $20.8 billion to be spent expanding the program over the next five years is a sizable down payment on Clinton's vow to reform conventional welfare policy." The expanded credit and other smaller spending increases for the poor also proved to be an important political inducement. In the end, all 37 House Democrats in the Black Caucus voted for the plan. (The only black Republican—Gary Franks of Connecticut—voted "no," while he and several black Demo- crats feuded publicly about whether he should continue his membership in the Caucus.)

In these and other cases, the conflict among Democrats often ap- peared to be a collision of the irresistible force and the immovable object. In seeking to reconcile these forces, Rostenkowski and his House Ways and Means Committee colleagues hoped to salvage as much as possible of the increased revenues from Clinton's original energy tax. But other lawmakers—especially those from large states where more people drove long distances to work—wanted to limit the Senate-passed gasoline-tax increase. Once again, a striking feature was the control that junior law- makers exercised over the outcome. Consensus on the deficit-reduction bill required a "bottom-up" agreement, said a Rostenkowski aide. He meant that, in contrast to the typical deal that was imposed from atop the legislative hierarchy, the rank-and-file members, in effect, dictated the results on this bill because the narrow margin forced the leaders to solicit their views.

Resolving the details of the energy tax provided a striking reversal of the customary legislative pattern. Rostenkowski recognized a few days after the start of the negotiations that the broad-based "BTU" tax was a dead letter in the Senate. So, he then pressed for a nine-cent increase in the tax on a gallon of gasoline, perhaps in combination with a nationwide tax on consumers' home-utility bills. His hope was to raise from energy taxes an amount at least halfway between the House- and Senate-passed bills. After several Senate Democrats said that such a total was too high to approve and that they were increasingly skittish about any consumer-based tax, however, the House and Senate leaders tentatively reached a consensus for a gasoline-tax increase of 6.5 cents. Finally, they thought that they had a deal, which *The Washington* Post and other newspapers predicted on July 29 was close to approval. At that point, Rostenkowski said that the leaders were checking to see "if we can get the votes at 6 [cents per gallon], but I'd like to get 7."

Unfortunately for Rostenkowski and the senior Democrats, they did not account for the stubbornness of several Democratic senators, chiefly Herbert Kohl of Wisconsin. When Kohl, a multimillionaire businessman whose impact during his first five years in the Senate had been negligible, stated that he would vote against anything higher than the increase of 4.3 cents in the Senate-passed bill, he killed efforts to raise added revenues. "I don't think we should tax the middle class," Kohl told reporters. He did not offer specific alternatives. That the increase was modest had become less important than the symbolism of the issue. For the average American driver, the annual cost of the 6.5 cent increase would have been about $42 annually, or 80 cents a week. That was about 25 cents per week more than the Senate version. Yes, it was a tax increase. But was it worth one senator's stout resistance? Kohl's objection to the small sum fit the portrayal by the disgruntled freshman Sen. Patty Murray, the Democrat from Washington. "Individual senators assert their power to show their influence back home," she said. "Too many senators don't understand what compromise is all about."

. . . After all, this small gasoline-tax increase was the only defined new burden on most of the middle class. Rostenkowski summarized his unhappiness with the result: "The closer the vote, the more members become prima donnas," he said. Legislatively, the outcome also further eroded the admittedly outdated image of a legislative system in which powerful chairmen cracked the whip to get their way. "It is not unusual for a floor majority to drive" how Congress handles a tax bill, said Steven Smith, a political science professor at the University of Minnesota. "The main thing that has been different with this year's bill has been that all of this has been in the open and that the flexing of muscle has seemed more conspicuous than in the past."

TOWARD CRITICAL THINKING

1. Given the tenor of the 1992 presidential campaign and its focus on the budget deficit, why was it so difficult for Congress to pass a budget deficit reduction plan?

2. What role do conference committees play in the process of how a bill becomes a law? Who are generally key players at this stage of the process?

THINKING ABOUT CONGRESS

1. Why has it become so difficult for Congress to pass laws? How have its large size and its members' focus on reelection contributed to its difficulties?

2. How are members of Congress different today from those discussed by James Sterling Young? How are they the same? How would the Federalists view these differences?

3. Of late, Congress has been rocked by a series of scandals. What kinds of changes are necessary to redeem Congress in the eyes of the American public? Is it only scandals that make the public distrustful of Congress?

CHAPTER 7

◆ ◆ ◆

The Presidency

As the demands of the nation have increased, focus on the U.S. president has increased accordingly. The too-powerful executive feared by the Framers has not necessarily come into being, yet presidents today have so many duties that more than one political scientist and political commentator has suggested exactly what Alexander Hamilton rejected in *Federalist No. 70* (Reading 33)—more than one chief executive so that the duties of the job could be better distributed.

Most of the readings in this chapter deal with a U.S. president's ability to get things done. James David Barber (Reading 34) argues that we can predict how presidents will act (and thus how successful they will be) by looking to their character, a trait formed in childhood. According to Barber, to know how a president grew up is to understand his world view and how he will approach the job.

Also concerned with character, but more with its effect on a president's ability to wield the tremendous informal powers that come with the job, is Richard E. Neustadt (Reading 35). In recent years, according to political scientist Sam Kernell, presidents have "gone public" to bring their domestic and foreign policy agendas directly to the people.* Thus, in an age when presidents increasingly go directly to the people to sell their programs or policies, an additional layer of responsibility has been laid on presidents. Not only must they be able to persuade or bargain with lawmakers, as noted by Neustadt, but they must also carefully cultivate the public in an effort to build support for their policy objectives. When support for the North American Free Trade Agreement (NAFTA) in Congress appeared weak in 1993, for example, Vice President Al Gore Jr. appeared on *Larry King Live* to debate outspoken NAFTA opponent, Ross Perot. Public support for NAFTA rose dramatically, affecting the vote of key members of Congress. Another legislative victory was scored for the Clinton administration.

Success, however, is often dependent on presidential personality. A president's popularity usually is at an all-time high right after his election. It thus falls to an astute president to try to capitalize on this and push his

---

* *Going Public* 2nd ed. (Washington, D.C.: Congressional Quarterly Press, 1992).

programs on Capital Hill during this "honeymoon" period. Moreover, as Richard E. Cohen notes (Reading 36), successes breed success; but a president with few victories to show at the end of his first year in office is unlikely to have many more.

But in spite of successes at the polls and in Congress, character flaws have a way of coming back to haunt some presidents. As illustrated in *United States* v. *Nixon* (Reading 37), presidents are not above the law, and ultimately the system of separation of powers created by the Framers worked, letting power check power and forcing the resignation of a president who had recently been elected in a landslide victory.

· 33 ·

Federalist No. 70

ALEXANDER HAMILTON

From the beginning of the new nation, Alexander Hamilton believed that a single, vigorous executive was critical to its survival. Without a strong president, a nation, particularly a new one, would be more at risk from foreign attack and from internal dissention.

To the People of the State of New York:

There is an idea, which is not without its advocates, that a vigorous Executive is inconsistent with the genius of republican government. . . . Energy in the Executive is a leading character in the definition of good government. It is essential to the protection of the community against foreign attacks; it is not less essential to the steady administration of the laws; to the protection of property against those irregular and high-handed combinations which sometimes interrupt the ordinary course of justice; to the security of liberty against the enterprises and assaults of ambition, of faction, and of anarchy. . . .

. . . A feeble Executive implies a feeble execution of the government. . . .

Taking it for granted, therefore, that all men of sense will agree in the necessity of an energetic Executive . . . the ingredients which constitute energy in the Executive are, first, unity; secondly, duration; thirdly, an adequate provision for its support; fourthly, competent powers.

The ingredients which constitute safety in the republican sense are, first, a due dependence on the people; secondly, a due responsibility.

Those politicians and statesmen who have been the most celebrated for the soundness of their principles and for the justice of their views have declared in favor of a single Executive and a numerous legislature. . . .

That unity is conducive to energy will not be disputed. Decision, activity, secrecy, and despatch will generally characterize the proceedings of one man in a much more eminent degree than the proceedings of any greater number; and in proportion as the number is increased, these qualities will be diminished.

This unity may be destroyed in two ways: either by vesting the power in two or more magistrates of equal dignity and authority; or by vesting it ostensibly in one man, subject, in whole or in part, to the control and co-operation of others, in the capacity of counsellors to him.

TOWARD CRITICAL THINKING

1. What were the essential ingredients that Hamilton believed were critical for any president to have? Have recent presidents displayed those qualities?

2. Some people suggested that a way to guard against tyranny in the chief executive was to divide the executive powers between two or more individuals. How could such a proposal work? Has the work of chief executive today become too complex for a single individual?

· *34* ·

Presidential Character

JAMES DAVID BARBER

Political scientist James David Barber believes that presidential character comes in four varieties. According to Barber, among the most important things voters should know before they cast their ballots for president is how active the candidate is and whether he or she truly seems to enjoy political life. The answers to these two questions, says Barber, allow us to predict how a president will govern.

How can ordinary voters make these assessments? Barber urges journalists to concentrate on these questions on the numerous instances they have to observe the candidates closely. He posits that journalism can "greatly advance the public reasoning needed to get Presidents who will do the right things."[*]

The Presidency is a peculiar office. The Founding Fathers left it extraordinarily loose in definition, partly because they trusted George Washington to invent a tradition as he went along. It is an institution made a piece at a time by successive men (so far) in the White House. Jefferson reached out to Congress to put together the beginnings of political parties; Jackson's dramatic force extended electoral partisanship to its mass base; Lincoln vastly expanded the administrative reach of the office; Wilson and the Roosevelts showed its rhetorical possibilities—in fact every President's mind and demeanor has left its mark on a heritage still in lively development.

But the Presidency is much more than an institution. It is a focus of feelings. In general, popular feelings about politics are low-key, shallow, casual. For example, the vast majority of Americans knows virtually nothing of what Congress is doing and cares less. The Presidency is different. The Presidency is the focus for the most intense and persistent emotions in the American polity. The President is a symbolic leader, the one figure who draws together the people's hopes and fears for the political future. On top of all his routine duties, he has to carry that off—or fail.

SOURCE: James David Barber, *The Presidential Character: Predicting Performance in the White House,* 4th ed. (Englewood Cliffs, NJ: Prentice Hall, 1992), pp. 1–12, 484–492. Reprinted by permission of the author.

[*] James David Barber, *The Presidential Character: Predicting Performance in the White House,* 4th ed. Englewood Clifs, NJ: Prentice Hall, 1992, p. 191.

Our emotional attachment to Presidents shows up when one dies in office. People were not just disappointed or worried when President Kennedy was killed; people wept at the loss of a man most had never even met. . . . On the other hand, the death of an ex-President brings forth no such intense emotional reaction.

The President is the first political figure children are aware of (later they add Congress, the Court, and others, as "helpers" of the President). With some exceptions among children in deprived circumstances, the President is seen as a "benevolent leader," one who nurtures, sustains, and inspires the citizenry. Presidents regularly show up among "most admired" contemporaries and forebears, and the President is the "best known" (in the sense of sheer name recognition) person in the country. At inauguration time, even Presidents elected by close margins are supported by much larger majorities than the election returns show, for people rally round as he actually assumes office. There is a similar reaction when the people see their President threatened by crisis: if he takes action, there is a favorable spurt in the Gallup poll whether he succeeds or fails.

Obviously the President gets more attention in schoolbooks, press, and television than any other politician. He is one of very few who can make news by doing good things. *His* emotional state is a matter of continual public commentary, as is the manner in which his personal and official families conduct themselves. The media portray the President not as some neutral administrator or corporate executive to be assessed by his production, but as a special being with mysterious dimensions. . . .

. . . Crucial differences can be anticipated by an understanding of a potential President's character, his world view, and his style. This kind of prediction is not easy; well-informed observers often have guessed wrong as they watched a man step toward the White House. . . . Predicting with even approximate accuracy is going to require some sharp tools and close attention in their use. But the experiment is worth it because the question is critical and because it lends itself to correction by evidence.

My argument comes in layers.

First, a President's personality is an important shaper of his Presidential behavior on nontrivial matters.

Second, Presidential personality is patterned. His character, world view, and style fit together in a dynamic package understandable in psychological terms.

Third, a President's personality interacts with the power situation he faces and the national "climate of expectations" dominant at the time he serves. The tuning, the resonance—or lack of it—between these external factors and his personality sets in motion the dynamic of his Presidency.

Fourth, the best way to predict a President's character, world view, and style is to see how they were put together in the first place. That happened in his early life, culminating in his first independent political success.

But the core of the argument . . . is that Presidential character—the basic stance a man takes toward his Presidential experience—comes in four varieties. The most important thing to know about a President or candidate is where he fits among these types, defined according to (a) how active he is and (b) whether or not he gives the impression he enjoys his political life.

Let me spell out these concepts briefly before getting down to cases.

◆ Personality Shapes Performance

I am not about to argue that once you know a President's personality you know everything. But, as the cases will demonstrate, the degree and quality of a President's emotional involvement in an issue are powerful influences on how he defines the issue itself, how much attention he pays to it, which facts and persons he sees as relevant to its resolution, and, finally, what principles and purposes he associates with the issue. Every story of Presidential decision-making is really two stories: an outer one in which a rational man calculates and an inner one in which an emotional man feels. The two are forever connected. Any real President is one whole man and his deeds reflect his wholeness.

As for personality, it is a matter of tendencies. It is not that one President "has" some basic characteristics that another President does not "have." That old way of treating a trait as a possession, like a rock in a basket, ignores the universality of aggressiveness, compliancy, detachment, and other human drives. We all have all of them, but in different amounts and in different combinations.

◆ The Pattern of Character, World View, and Style

The most visible part of the pattern is style. *Style is the President's habitual way of performing his three political roles: rhetoric, personal relations, and homework.* Not to be confused with "stylishness," charisma, or appearance, style is how the President goes about doing what the office requires him to do—to speak, directly or through media, to large audiences; to deal face to face with other politicians, individually and in small, relatively private groups; and to read, write, and calculate by himself in order to manage the endless flow of details that stream onto his desk. No President can escape doing at least some of each. But there are marked differences in stylistic emphasis from President to President. . . .

A President's *world view consists of his primary, politically relevant beliefs, particularly his conceptions of social causality, human nature, and the central moral conflicts of the time.* This is how he sees the world, and what his lasting opinions are about what he sees. Style is his way of acting; world view is his way of seeing. . . .

"Character" comes from the Greek word for engraving; in one sense it is what life has marked into a man's being. As used here, *character is the way the President orients himself toward life*—not for the moment, but enduringly. Character is the person's stance as he confronts experience. . . . The President's fundamental self-esteem is his prime personal resource; to defend and advance that, he will sacrifice much else he values. Down there in the privacy of his heart, does he find himself superb, or ordinary, or debased, or in some intermediate range? . . .

Character, world view, and style are abstractions from the reality of the whole individual. In every case they form an integrated pattern: the man develops a combination which makes psychological sense for him, a dynamic arrangement of motives, beliefs, and habits in the services of his need for self-esteem.

◆ The Power Situation and "Climate of Expectations"

Presidential character resonates with the political situation the President faces. It adapts him as he tries to adapt it. The support he has from the public and interest groups, the party balance in Congress, the thrust of Supreme Court opinion, together set the basic power situation he must deal with. An activist President may run smack into a brick wall of resistance, then pull back and wait for a better moment. On the other hand, a President who sees himself as a quiet caretaker may not try to exploit even the most favorable power situation. So it is the relationship between President and the political configuration that makes the system tick.

Even before public opinion polls, the President's real or supposed popularity is a large factor in his performance. Besides the power mix in Washington, the President has to deal with a national climate of expectations, the predominant needs thrust up to him by the people. There are at least three recurrent themes around which these needs are focused.

People look to the President for *reassurance,* a feeling that things will be all right, that the President will take care of his people. . . .

Another theme is the demand for *a sense of progress and action.* The President ought to do something to direct the nation's course—or at least be in there pitching for the people. . . .

A third type of climate of expectations is the public need for a sense of *legitimacy* from, and in, the Presidency. The President should be a master politician who is above politics. He should have a right to his place and a rightful way of acting in it. The respectability—even religiosity—of the office has to be protected by a man who presents himself as defender of the faith. There is more to this than dignity, more than propriety. . . .

Over time, the climate of expectations shifts and changes. Wars, depressions, and other national events contribute to that change, but there also is a rough cycle, from an emphasis on action (which begins to look too "political") to an emphasis on legitimacy (the moral uplift of which creates its own strains) to an emphasis on reassurance and rest (which comes to seem like drift) and back to action again. . . . The point is that the climate of expectations at any given time is the political air the President has to breathe. Relating to this climate is a large part of his task.

◆ Predicting Presidents

The best way to predict a President's character, world view, and style is to see how he constructed them in the first place. Especially in the early stages, life is experimental; consciously or not, a person tries out various ways of defining and maintaining and raising self-esteem. He looks to his environment for clues as to who he is and how well he is doing. These lessons of life slowly sink in: certain self-images and evaluations, certain ways of looking at the world, certain styles of action get confirmed by his experience and he gradually adopts them as his own. If we can see that process of development, we can understand the product. The features to note are those bearing on Presidential performance. . . .

In general, character has its *main* development in childhood, world view in adolescence, style in early adulthood. The stance toward life I call character grows out of the child's experiments in relating to parents, brothers and sisters, and peers at play and in school, as well as to his own body and the objects around it. . . .

These themes come together strongly in early adulthood, when the person moves from contemplation to responsible action and adopts a style. In most biographical accounts, this period stands out in stark clarity—the time of emergence, the time the young man found himself. I call it his first independent political success. It was then he moved beyond the detailed guidance of his family; then his self-esteem was dramatically boosted; then he came forth as a person to be reckoned with by other people. The *way* he did that is profoundly important to him. Typically he grasps that style and hangs onto it. Much later, coming into the Presidency, something in him remembers this earlier victory and re-emphasizes the style that made it happen.

Character provides the main thrust and broad direction—but it does not *determine,* in any fixed sense, world view and style. The story of development does not end with the end of childhood. Thereafter, the culture one grows in and the ways that culture is translated by parents and peers shapes the meanings one makes of his character. The current world view gets learned and that learning helps channel character forces. Thus it will not necessarily be true that compulsive characters have reactionary beliefs, or that compliant characters believe in compromise. This is also true of style: historical accidents play a large part in furnishing special opportunities for action—and in blocking off alternatives. For example, however much anger a young man may feel, that anger will not be expressed in rhetoric unless and until his life situation provides a platform and an audience. Style thus has a stature and independence of its own. Those who would reduce all explanation to character neglect these highly significant later channelings. For beyond the root is the branch, above the foundation the superstructure, and starts do not prescribe finishes.

◆ Four Types of Presidential Character

The five concepts—character, world view, style, power situation, and climate of expectations—run through the accounts of Presidents . . . which cluster the Presidents since Theodore Roosevelt into four types. This is the fundamental scheme of the study. It offers a way to move past the complexities to the main contrasts and comparisons.

The first baseline in defining Presidential types is *activity-passivity*. How much energy does the man invest in his Presidency? Lyndon Johnson went at his day like a human cyclone, coming to rest long after the sun went down. Calvin Coolidge often slept eleven hours a night and still needed a nap in the middle of the day. In between, the Presidents array themselves on the high or low side of the activity line.

The second baseline is *positive-negative affect* toward one's activity—that is, how he feels about what he does. Relatively speaking, does he seem to experience his political life as happy or sad, enjoyable or discouraging, positive or negative in its main effect? The feeling I am after here is not grim satisfaction in a job well done, not some philosophical conclusion. The idea is this: is he someone who, on the surfaces we can see, gives forth the feeling that he has *fun* in political life? . . .

The positive-negative baseline, then, is a general symptom of the fit between the man and his experience, a kind of register of *felt* satisfaction.

Why might we expect these two simple dimensions to outline the main character types? Because they stand for two central features of anyone's orientation toward life. In nearly every study of personality, some form of the active-passive contrast is critical; the general tendency to act or be acted upon is evident in such concepts as dominance-submission, extraversion-introversion, aggression-timidity, attack-defense, fight-flight, engagement-withdrawal, approach-avoidance. In everyday life we sense quickly the general energy output of the people we deal with. Similarly, we catch on fairly quickly to the affect dimension—whether the person seems to be optimistic or pessimistic, hopeful or skeptical, happy or sad. The two baselines are clear and they are also independent of one another: all of us know people who are very active but seem discouraged, others who are quite passive but seem happy, and so forth. The activity baseline refers to what one does, the affect baseline to how one feels about what he does.

Both are crude clues to character. They are leads into four basic character patterns long familiar in psychological research. In summary form, these are the main configurations:

Active-Positive

There is a congruence, a consistency, between being very active and the enjoyment of it, indicating relatively high self-esteem and relative success in relating to the environment. The man shows an orientation toward productiveness as a value, and an ability to use his styles flexibly, adoptively, suiting the dance to the music. He sees himself as developing over time toward relatively well defined personal goals—growing toward his image of himself as he might yet be. There is an emphasis on rational mastery, and on using the brain to move the feet. This may get him into trouble; he may fail to take account of the irrational in politics. Not everyone he deals with sees things his way and he may find it hard to understand why.

Active-Negative

The contradiction here is between relatively intense effort and relatively low emotional reward for that effort. The activity has a compulsive quality, as if the man were trying to make up for something or to escape from anxiety into hard work. He seems ambitious, striving upward and seeking power. His stance toward the environment is aggressive and he has a persistent problem in managing his aggressive feelings. His self-image is vague and discontinuous. Life is a hard struggle to achieve and hold power, hampered by the condemnations of a perfectionistic conscience. Active-negative types pour energy into the political system, but it is an energy distorted from within.

Passive-Positive

This is the receptive, compliant, other-directed character whose life is a search for affection as a reward for being agreeable and cooperative rather than personally assertive. The contradiction is between low self-esteem (on grounds of being unlovable, unattractive) and a superficial optimism. A hopeful attitude helps dispel doubt and elicits encouragement from others. Passive-positive types help soften the harsh edges of politics. But their dependence and the fragility of their hopes and enjoyments make disappointment in politics likely.

Passive-Negative

The factors are consistent—but how are we to account for the man's *political* role-taking? Why is someone who does little in politics and enjoys it less there at all? The answer lies in the passive-negative's character-rooted orientation toward doing dutiful service; this compensates for low self-esteem based on a sense of uselessness. Passive-negative types are in politics because they think they ought to be. They may be well adapted to certain nonpolitical roles, but they lack the experience and flexibility to perform effectively as political leaders. Their tendency is to withdraw, to escape from the conflict and uncertainty of politics by emphasizing vague principles (especially prohibitions) and procedural arrangements. They become guardians of the right and proper way, above the sordid politicking of lesser men. . . .

But journalism today is in need of political improvement. Candidates' characters can best be ascertained from their biographies rather than from their stagey, momentary appearances. And biography is one of the nation's most interesting forms of learning, as is evident in the sales of books of biography, and the public's interest in such television programs as "60 Minutes." World view can be elicited by real debates in a Presidential campaign—not the "debates" in recent years, which are nothing but mini-press conferences on television. Instead, a debate should be concentrated on one question for a significant period of time, so that logic and evidence may be brought forth for citizens to evaluate the thinking of a candidate regarding one major challenge. Investigative reporting can dig out how a candidate has actually operated in the past, especially at the beginning of his or her independent political endeavor. Odd as it seems, that is a better predicter of style than what the candidate had just been doing in politics. Planning coverage, journalists should take special notice of the current climate of expectations in order to avoid the recurrent temptation to oversimplify judgment about the candidates, such as how purely moral they are, how conciliatory, how much ahead and behind in the polls, etc. And the power situation needs reporting; a potential President is too often thought of as an infinitely potent power, but that is never true. As in any sport or war or dating, the situation makes a difference. Journalism can—and it may yet—greatly advance the public reasoning needed to get Presidents who will do the right things.

FIGURE 1
Barber's Presidential Personalities

	ACTIVE	PASSIVE
POSITIVE	F. D. Roosevelt	Taft
	Truman	Harding
	Kennedy	Reagan
	Ford	
	Carter*	
	Bush	
NEGATIVE	Wilson	Coolidge
	Hoover	Eisenhower
	L. B. Johnson	
	Nixon	

*Some scholars think that Carter better fits the active-negative typology.

TOWARD CRITICAL THINKING

1. Many political scientists have criticized the Barber typology presented in Figure 7.1. What are the strengths of Barber's arguments? What are their weaknesses? In which quadrant would you place President Clinton?

2. Do Americans look for too much from their presidents? And in looking for so much, have the American public and journalists crossed the line between personal privacy and the public's right to know?

Presidential Power and the Power to Persuade

RICHARD E. NEUSTADT

As Barber notes, each man comes to the presidency with different personalities, world views, and approaches to the job of chief executive. But all men who have held the office are immediately confronted with the problem of how to govern. Harry S Truman once said of incoming president (and former general) Dwight D. Eisenhower, "He'll sit here and he'll say, 'Do this! Do that!' And nothing will happen. Poor Ike—it won't be a bit like the army. He'll find it very frustrating.' "[*] Political scientist Neustadt, a former aide to President John F. Kennedy, posits that a president governs best when he persuades. The ability to persuade, says Neustadt, turns on a president's ability to bargain while using the resources of the office effectively to maximum advantage.

. . .

The separateness of institutions and the sharing of authority prescribe the terms on which a President persuades. When one man shares authority with another, but does not gain or lose his job upon the other's whim, his willingness to act upon the urging of the other turns on whether he conceives the action right for him. The essence of a President's persuasive task is to convince such men that what the White House wants of them is what they ought to do for their sake and on their authority.

Persuasive power, thus defined, amounts to more than charm or reasoned argument. These have their uses for a President, but these are not the whole of his resources. For the men he would induce to do what he wants done on their own responsibility will need or fear some acts by him on his responsibility. If they share his authority, he has some share in theirs. Presidential "powers" may be inconclusive when a President commands, but always remain relevant as he persuades. The status and authority inherent in his office reinforce his logic and his charm.

SOURCE: Reprinted with the permission of The Free Press, an imprint of Simon & Schuster from *Presidential Power and Modern Presidents: The Politics of Leadership from Roosevelt to Reagan* by Richard E. Neustadt. Copyright © 1990 by Richard E. Neustadt.

[*] Quoted in Richard E. Neustadt, *Presidential Power: The Politics of Power from FDR to Carter* (New York: Wiley, 1980), p. 9.

Status adds something to persuasiveness; authority adds still more. When Truman urged wage changes on his Secretary of Commerce while the latter was administering the steel mills, he and Secretary [Charles] Sawyer were not just two men reasoning with one another. Had they been so, Sawyer probably would never have agreed to act. Truman's status gave him special claims to Sawyer's loyalty, or at least attention. In Walter Bagehot's charming phrase "no man can *argue* on his knees." Although there is no kneeling in this country, few men—and exceedingly few Cabinet officers—are immune to the impulse to say "yes" to the President of the United States. It grows harder to say "no" when they are seated in his oval office at the White House, or in his study on the second floor, where almost tangibly he partakes of the aura of his physical surroundings. In Sawyer's case, moreover, the President possessed formal authority to intervene in many matters of concern to the Secretary of Commerce. These matters ranged from jurisdictional disputes among the defense agencies to legislation pending before Congress and, ultimately, to the tenure of the Secretary, himself. There is nothing in the record to suggest that Truman voiced specific threats when they negotiated over wage increases. But given his *formal* powers and their relevance to Sawyer's other interests, it is safe to assume that Truman's very advocacy of wage action conveyed an implicit threat.

A President's authority and status give him great advantages in dealing with the men he would persuade. Each "power" is a vantage point for him in the degree that other men have use for his authority. From the veto to appointments, from publicity to budgeting, and so down a long list, the White House now controls the most encompassing array of vantage points in the American political system. With hardly an exception, the men who share in governing this country are aware that at some time, in some degree, the doing of *their* jobs, the furthering of *their* ambitions, may depend upon the President of the United States. Their need for presidential action, or their fear of it, is bound to be recurrent if not actually continuous. Their need or fear is his advantage.

A President's advantages are greater than mere listing of his "powers" might suggest. The men with whom he deals must deal with him until the last day of his term. Because they have continuing relationships with him, his future, while it lasts, supports his present influence. Even though there is no need or fear of him today, what he could do tomorrow may supply today's advantage. Continuing relationships may convert any "power," any aspect of his status, into vantage points in almost any case. When he induces other men to do what he wants done, a President can trade on their dependence now *and* later.

The President's advantages are checked by the advantages of others. Continuing relationships will pull in both directions. These are relationships of mutual dependence. A President depends upon the men he would persuade; he has to reckon with his need or fear of them. They too will possess status, or authority, or both, else they would be of little use to him. Their vantage points confront his own; their power tempers his.

. . .

The power to persuade is the power to bargain. Status and authority yield bargaining advantages. But in a government of "separated institutions sharing powers," they yield them to all sides. With the array of vantage points at his disposal, a President may be far more persuasive than his logic or his charm could make him. But outcomes are not guaranteed by his advantages. There remain the counter pressures those whom he would influence can bring to bear on him from vantage points at their disposal. Command has limited utility; persuasion becomes give-and-take. It is well that the White House holds the vantage points it does. In such a business any President may need them all—and more. . . .

Granting that persuasion has no guarantee attached, how can a President reduce the risks of failing to persuade? How can he maximize his prospects for effectiveness by minimizing chances that his power will elude him? . . . He guards his power prospects in the course of making choices. . . .

By "choice" I mean no more than what is commonly referred to as "decision": a President's own act of doing or not doing. Decision is so often indecisive, and indecision is so frequently conclusive, that *choice* becomes the preferable term. "Choice" has its share of undesired connotations. In common usage it implies a black-and-white alternative. Presidential choices are rarely of that character. It also may imply that the alternatives are set before the choice maker by someone else. A President is often left to figure out his options for himself. Neither implication holds in any of the references to choice throughout this [reading].

If Presidents could count upon past choices to enhance their current influence, . . . persuasion would pose fewer difficulties than it does. But Presidents can count on no such thing. Depending on the circumstances, prior choices can be as embarrassing as they were helpful. . . .

Assuming that past choices have protected influence, not harmed it, present choices still may be inadequate. If Presidents could count on their own conduct to provide them enough bargaining advantages, . . . effective bargaining might be much easier to manage than it often is. In the steel crisis, for instance, Truman's own persuasiveness with companies and union, both, was burdened by the conduct of an independent wage board and of government attorneys in the courts, to say nothing of [his aides]. Yet in practice, if not theory, many of *their* crucial choices never were the

President's to make. Decisions that are legally in others' hands, or delegated past recall, have an unhappy way of proving just the trading stock most needed when the White House wants to trade. . . .

But adequate or not, a President's own choices are the only means in his own hands of guarding his own prospects for effective influence. He can draw power from continuing relationships in the degree that he can capitalize upon the needs of others for the Presidency's status and authority. He helps himself to do so, though, by nothing save ability to recognize the preconditions and the chance advantages and to proceed accordingly in the course of the choice making that comes his way.

TOWARD CRITICAL THINKING

1. How does Neustadt define "persuasive power"? What resources can help a president "persuade" those around him or the Congress to do what he wants?

2. How does a president reduce the risks of failing to persuade? Can you think of any recent examples of presidential actions that underscore points made by Neustadt concerning presidential successes or failures to persuade?

· *36* ·

Clinton Sets the Agenda
The First 100 Days

RICHARD E. COHEN

Most presidents enjoy a so-called honeymoon period immediately after taking office when their popularity is high. That political capital can then be used to push for key legislative programs. Often, how a president fares in his first 100 days sets the tone for the rest of his administration or, at least, for his relations with Congress.

Richard E. Cohen chronicles President Clinton's efforts to pass a budget bill to reduce the federal deficit. In spite of polls that showed that the public was very concerned with the federal deficit and its consequences, ultimate passage of the bill in Congress required the president to use up a significant amount of good will, both with legislators and the general public, which ultimately probably contributed to the defeat of his health care proposals.

◆ The Brief Honeymoon

Presidents typically have their most power to influence national policy on the day that they are sworn into office. Then, they must decide how to spend their limited political capital to accomplish their own goals and to address the nation's problems. Bill Clinton decided to focus his attention initially on strengthening the economy and reducing the federal deficit. With the agreement of Democratic congressional leaders, his first legislative priority would be a plan to redirect federal spending and tax priorities while also cutting the deficit. Enacting the proposal would be a major achievement, given Washington's constant budget wars of the Reagan-Bush years. But the Democrats, now that they controlled both the White House and Congress, were confident that they could succeed. And they believed that they could not afford to fail—politically or financially—if they hoped to find the money to address other national problems later during Clinton's presidency. Getting a quick start was also important because the skeptical and impatient public was expecting change and an end to stalemate, as Clinton had often promised during the campaign. Like any new president, he entered office with a reservoir of public good will

---

SOURCE: From Richard E. Cohen, *Changing Course in Washington.* Copyright 1994 by Allyn and Bacon. Reprinted/adapted by permission.

and a widespread national hope that he would help to correct the nation's problems. A January 1993 poll conducted jointly by Democratic and Republican pollsters found that 71 percent of the respondents had a favorable impression of Clinton and 84 percent believed that he was off to a good start. But he knew that the positive feelings could dissipate quickly as the Democrats forced the nation to swallow bitter medicine. And other domestic and international events could intervene at any moment, forcing him to move in new directions. He would have little time to spare. "The early actions of a new administration are crucial to its legislative success," said presidential scholar James P. Pfiffner. "This is so both because the main legislative accomplishments of an administration are often achieved early in its first year, and also because early success or failures can set the tone for the rest of the administration in its relations with Congress."[1]

Reducing the federal deficit and stimulating the economy would require Clinton to educate the public so his goals and programs would gain broad national support. That, in turn, would force him to abandon some of his prominent campaign promises, such as a tax cut for the middle class, and to develop and sell painful medicine—tax increases and cuts in federal spending—that he had barely discussed before the election. Even after he selected his Cabinet officials and White House staff, it would take several more weeks for him to review his economic options, organize a legislative strategy and prepare the proper political climate. As the Washington community awaited his proposals, he had the time and discretion that are provided by what is sometimes called the new leader's honeymoon period. Clinton would discover, however, the vast differences between campaigning and governing. Some of the same skills are required, including the ability to communicate a compelling message to the public and the need to act as the party leader. But presidents quickly learn that they often cannot control the actions of other political players, not even their supposed allies. "Early successes will not be handed to a new president on a silver platter," Pfiffner wrote. "The idea that a 'honeymoon' with Congress naturally follows the election of a new President is greatly exaggerated."[2] And the unyielding public spotlight on the White House allows little room for hesitation or error.

Most congressional Democrats would give him the time and an extended leash to maneuver once he took office. They recognized, as Senate Majority Leader Mitchell often repeated, that they needed to stop acting as the "guardians of gridlock," who had brought so much public scorn on

---

[1] James P. Pfiffner, *The Strategic Presidency* (Chicago: The Dorsey Press, 1988), 137.
[2] Ibid.

government. Clinton also encouraged their cooperation by holding many private meetings where Democrats offered their views on what actions he should take. The president, in turn, sought to develop a team spirit in support of their common agenda. For some Democrats on Capitol Hill, however, the start of the Clinton presidency also would be a learning period of a different type. Especially in the Senate, senior Democrats chafed at their new subservient role. Even Clinton's supposed allies could not resist the temptation to lecture their new president—at the risk of publicly embarrassing him—on subjects where they believed that they were more expert and where they were unaccustomed to a challenge from within their own party. At a time when Clinton was trying to establish his credentials some of his worst enemies were Democratic committee chairmen from the Senate who dispensed advice as though Bush were still president. "All Democrats face a deep psychological adjustment from being in the opposition, where you can take shots at the president," said a senior House aide after a few embarrassing incidents. "For some, it will take time to recognize that it is in their interest to support a Democratic president." At least initially, most House Democrats gave Clinton a more friendly reception than did their Senate colleagues, and they encouraged him to show leadership on both the economy and health care.

Clinton needed their morale boost. . . . In what may have been a case of early-season nervousness, his initial days in office were marked by errors, misjudgments and lapses that placed him on the defensive. Although the incidents would soon fade in public importance, their memory would leave questions on Capitol Hill about the competence of Clinton and the advisers surrounding him. Instead of developing teamwork and a positive spirit, the new president found himself clashing publicly with Democratic senators on three separate issues during his first two weeks in office. After complaining that they had not been adequately consulted, the senators forced a retreat in each case from a position that Clinton or one of his top officials had publicly advocated. At the time, the events distracted the White House from its efforts to focus the nation's attention chiefly on addressing the economic problems. In doing so, the conflicts also short-circuited Clinton's effort to gain public attention for efforts to show that he would be the instrument of change on other issues, such as his Jan. 22 announcement of executive actions to reverse Reagan-Bush era restrictions on federal support for abortions.

First, he was forced to withdraw his support for his nominee for Attorney General, Zoe Baird, after she told the Senate Judiciary Committee that she had hired a "nanny" who was an illegal alien and had failed to make proper payment of federal taxes for child-care services. Although Clinton aides had been aware of Baird's plight, they did not believe that she should be disqualified. But after hostile reactions by radio talk-show callers and some Democratic senators' unhappiness with her explanation, the Senate Judiciary Committee, led by its chairman Joseph Biden, second-guessed the White House's handling of the nomination; in effect, the senators left Clinton with little choice but to abandon her. She announced her withdrawal on Jan. 22, two days after his inauguration. Biden complained to reporters after the incident about Clinton's failure to consult him on the Baird nomination, noting that the new team was "behind the curve in getting started." The next mini-crisis came the following week, when Senate Armed Services chairman Sam Nunn had a protracted and public conflict over Clinton's campaign promise to order the Pentagon to drop its policy of prohibiting gays to serve in the military. "If there's a strategy here, it hasn't been explained to me," said Nunn, with an air of condescension. Clinton agreed to delay the implementation of his pledge pending six months of study by the Pentagon and Congress and a political "cooling-off" period and eventually agreed to a less sweeping change in Pentagon policy toward gays, known as, "Don't ask, don't tell." Hardly had that problem been muffled when the new Senate Finance chairman Daniel Patrick Moynihan voiced his unhappiness over White House suggestions to limit the annual cost-of-living increase for Social Security beneficiaries and over Clinton's failure to consult him on other revenue-raising options. The proposal, which Office of Management and Budget director Leon Panetta had advocated, was "a death wish," Moynihan told reporters, and he vowed to block it. Senate Budget Committee chairman Jim Sasser quickly echoed Moynihan's view. On yet another conflict—his campaign advocacy of a line-item veto designed to cut "pork" from congressional spending bills—Clinton demurred from promoting the issue and seeking congressional action, rather than stir the ire of Senate Appropriations Committee chairman Robert Byrd, an avowed opponent of the line-item veto.

Clinton and his staff were taken aback by the zest with which the Senate barons moved to protect their turf and to warn the new team in town that it should tread carefully. Although they had a logical explanation that sought to downplay each conflict, top White House aides acknowledged that they had received a political warning shot and that they faced a test of power. The mutual pledges of cooperation, which top Democrats made during the transition period, were abandoned once Clinton decided to act. "It's possible to make too much of early stumbles, but it is also true that the early weeks of a presidency are important in defining what it hoped to accomplish and what it represents," *The Wall Street Journal* editorialized.[3] It was no wonder that, by early February, Clinton,

---

[3] "Bring Back Ham Jordan," *The Wall Street Journal,* Jan. 27, 1993: A16.

and congressional Democratic leaders sought to emphasize their areas of cooperation. Both the House and Senate, for example, passed a Bush-vetoed bill to allow employees in the private sector to take unpaid leave in the event of a family or medical emergency. Clinton spent even more time consulting with members of Congress on his economic program. And, as if to distance himself from his Washington problems, he went back on the road with a town-hall meeting from a Detroit television studio to exchange thoughts with citizens in four cities about his plans.

◆ Confronting the Deficit

The focus on Clinton's early mishaps was soon overtaken by the Democrats' decision to repair the nation's economy. That effort, which would dominate the national debate during the next several months, would be central to their party's attempt to reshape federal priorities and to recast how government operates. Because of the pervasive impact that the huge budget deficit had assumed over federal policy during the past decade, the White House and Congress had become preoccupied by their annual budget fights. Those exercises, which rarely produced credible results, had come to symbolize what ailed Washington to an unhappy public. . . .

The conflict over the causes and impact of the deficits during the 1980s and early 1990s would continue and remain unresolved. But the end of divided government in 1993 would banish questions of political accountability for federal actions. Now that Democrats controlled the White House and had majorities in both the House and Senate, they could not escape responsibility for future deficits. That shift had an immediate sobering impact on their party and its leaders. . . . Clinton also made a middle-class tax cut a major tenet of his campaign, both in the Democratic primaries and in the general election. And, in a more modest version, it was promised in the party's national platform. Leading Democrats repeatedly lambasted Bush and the Republicans for allegedly seeking to tilt the tax code to favor the wealthy. But once Clinton was elected, it did not take long for Democrats to throw overboard the vaunted middle-class tax cut—one of his first campaign promises. In early January, Speaker Foley said that earlier support for the tax cut should be "rethought" and that Democrats "have to be realistic about the problems that are facing the country." Sen. Mitchell, for his part, acknowledged that "because of the [budget] deficit" in 1993, it might not be possible to pass the tax cut, of which he had been a prime supporter. Both leaders cited the outgoing Bush administration's forecast that the projected fiscal year 1997 deficit would be about $300 billion, not the $237 billion that it had predicted six months earlier. But critics of the Democrats' change in plans noted that the widely reported congressional study in August 1992 had provided gloomy estimates that were similar to the January 1993 Bush numbers. Although incoming budget director Panetta had certainly been aware for many months of the more negative numbers, Clinton advisers in Little Rock claimed in early January that they were surprised. Despite their insistence that the comments from Capitol Hill had not been coordinated with the new president, they did not reject the leaders' assessment of the dim prospects for a tax cut.

They did not stop there. Soon after they ditched the tax cut, Democrats began to talk up a new tax on all forms of energy, which would unavoidably trigger a tax *increase* for the middle class. . . . "It took less than one week in office for the Democrats to abandon a middle-class tax cut and replace their campaign pledge with a tax increase on everyone, from poor to middle class to wealthy," Minority Whip Newt Gingrich told the House. . . .

In these cases and others, Clinton and his congressional allies were willing to go out on a political limb. They believed that the nation was ready for Washington to make tough choices and to stop pandering to the public. . . . The Democrats also believed that they faced significant pressure and a narrow time period in which to act on a legislative package that would address the nation's economic problems. Speaker Foley described "a sense of great enthusiasm" in Congress after Clinton took office. But he warned at the time that the euphoria must be tempered by the reality of the problems and that "there is a great likelihood that, if we don't succeed, there will be harsh criticism" by the public.

For the Democrats to succeed with their economic programs would be a difficult challenge. As the budget debates of recent years had shown, the "easy" political steps had been taken. And certain basic realities had to be faced. For example, most Democrats said that they supported cuts in defense spending. But the fact was that national spending for the military already had been on a steady downward slope. . . . On the domestic side of the budget, the biggest costs, by far, were for two "entitlement" programs—Social Security and Medicare. Together, they would account for an estimated $439 billion of federal spending in fiscal 1993—nearly one-third of all federal expenditures. But because of the proven political clout of senior citizens, the beneficiaries of most of this money, members of Congress from both parties feared making any changes. Another major share of the federal budget that was truly untouchable was the estimated $210 billion in 1994 interest payments that were due to bondholders who were financing the federal debt. Altogether, these three large components—defense, Social Security and Medicare, and interest payments—accounted for about 64 percent of all federal spending in the projected fiscal 1994 "baseline," which referred to the total of federal spending if no changes were made. The remainder of the federal budget comprised chiefly aid to low-income groups and "discretionary" domestic spending. But these areas already had suffered sizable reductions in recent years at the behest of Presidents Reagan and Bush. And the Democrats were not inclined to take new whacks at these program, many of which were vital to their party's political constituencies.

The outlook was hardly any brighter for cutting the federal deficit by raising revenues. Increasing taxes is never an easy political matter. Now that they controlled Washington's policy-making machine, Democrats were especially wary of fueling the Republicans' repeated charge that they are the "tax and spend" party. . . .

◆ Clinton's Package

Like a splash of icy water, the preparation and unveiling of Clinton's economic package to reduce the deficit and recharge the economy marked the end of the Democrats' post-election celebration and the start of their painful decision-making. The president extensively consulted both his own advisers and congressional Democrats to craft the plan. In addition to reviewing specific items, they made calculated economic and political assessments of the overall prospects. Although many lawmakers focused on the parochial local impact of the specific changes, the participants also recognized that they had to consider the effect on the larger national picture. . . .

Clinton was the central player in preparing his new administration's program. Shortly after the inauguration, the president and his economic advisers convened meetings nearly every day; during these sessions, which often extended for many hours, they conducted detailed reviews of budget options. With the plan scheduled to be unveiled in a speech to Congress on Feb. 17, he had less than four weeks to prepare the outlines of a budget, which normally requires several months of White House planning. That accelerated schedule had been prompted, in part, by the promise Clinton had made for one of the most "productive" early starts of any president. . . .

In extensive consultations with congressional Democrats about his budget package, Clinton sought to promote the members' comfort level with his plan by focusing on its broad features, but he steered clear of many details. At the suggestion of House leaders Foley and Gephardt, Clinton met with groups of about 30 House Democrats in the several days before he unveiled his plan. At those White House sessions, Clinton typically gave lawmakers a minute or two each to comment on budget issues that were especially important to them. But the members of Congress hardly had a chance for a dialogue on the vitally important details of Clinton's program. In fact, some of those specifics would not be resolved until months after Clinton unveiled his budget plan in February. . . .

◆ Selling the Plan to the Public

But gaining sufficient political support would require Clinton to do more than convince the legislators. To sell the package to the public, the White House launched an election-style promotional campaign across the nation, both before and after his Feb. 17 speech to Congress. "Like the marketing division of a corporation launching a product whose success is crucial to the company's future, the group had mapped out a political and communications strategy long before the final shape of the product itself was known," according to one news report after the plan was unveiled.[4] With the help of advisers from his political campaign, Clinton and top administration officials returned to the grass roots to convince the public that the nation faced serious problems and that bolstering the economy would require "shared sacrifice," a politically hazardous term that he had not invoked before Nov. 3. In his Feb. 10 town-hall meeting in the suburban Detroit television studio, for example, he listened to the views of Americans worried about their nation's future as well as their own. He referred euphemistically to the likely new taxes as the public's "contribution to the changes we have to make." Then, he traveled to Missouri, Ohio, New York, California and Washington state in the five days after his speech. As when he met earlier with members of Congress, he focused more on the general goals than on the specifics of his economic package. His constant refrain was an appeal to patriotism: "You can't just say what's in it for me. You have to ask what's in it for us."

The most important speech of Clinton's early months in the White House was the formal presentation of his domestic program. When he entered the House chamber on Feb. 17 shortly after 9 P.M. (a few minutes late for the nationally broadcast address), the new president was greeted by the most enthusiastic Democratic welcome since the heyday of President Lyndon Johnson's Great Society. . . . But the most remarkable aspect of the evening's performance was that it soon became apparent that Clinton was reading perhaps only one sentence in three from his prepared text and that he was ad libbing a large and fact-filled share of his speech. For both lawmakers and spectators in the gallery, who were accustomed to presidents who read their addresses to Congress with few diversions that appeared spontaneous, Clinton's performance had the aura of a sin-

---

[4]Dan Balz and Ruth Marcus, "The Windup for the Pitch," *The Washington Post*, March 7, 1993: A1.

cere and personal pleading to both Congress and the nation. Although the speech was not filled with memorable lines, it allowed the new president to show his well-informed efforts to change the direction of the ship of state. On issues from health care to early childhood education to his national service program, his easy grasp of detail allowed him to speak directly to his audience. But in the end, the new president focused on his opportunity to show leadership. "After so many years of gridlock and indecision, after so many hopeful beginnings and so few promising results, the American people are going to be harsh in their judgments of all of us if we fail to seize this moment."

In their post-mortem assessments of how Clinton assembled the economic package, administration officials emphasized his intense personal involvement. "Participants in the long, grueling sessions say there was scarcely a detail of the plan that wasn't reviewed and questioned by the president himself," concluded one news report.[5] Unlike Reagan and Bush, Clinton was a policy "wonk" who knew how domestic programs operated; as a former governor, he also had seen their strengths and weaknesses. But his commitment to an activist role for government in domestic affairs became something of a political down side when it came time to add up the bottom line. The "deficit-reduction" exercise had gained a sizable chunk of new spending. Included was his call for a $100 billion spending increase in the next four years to promote some of his favored domestic programs, including health services, job training and highway building plus a major expansion of the earned income tax credit, an income supplement for low-income working families. And, partly to appeal to liberals worried about spending cuts elsewhere in the budget, he proposed a separate package of economic "stimulus" proposals ($19 billion in spending and loans, $6 billion in tax incentives), which he wanted Congress to approve mostly for 1993. One major consequence of these additions was that Clinton was forced to abandon yet another campaign pledge: a 50 percent cut in the federal deficit during his first term. Making things worse, a top White House aide later conceded, was that the details of the stimulus plan were prepared "hurriedly" and late and without much consultation with potential Democratic allies in Congress. . . .

During the subsequent days and weeks, Congress and the public would gradually learn more details, and their reaction was not always positive. Often, opposition to the proposals was slow to form, if only because lobbying groups often spent many weeks scurrying to find the details or waiting for Cabinet agencies to provide the specifics. On the tax

---

[5] Alan Murray and Gerald F. Seib, "Clinton's Attention to Even Tiny Details Shaped His Budget," *The Wall Street Journal,* Feb. 19, 1993: A1.

program, for example, few public tears were shed for the increased taxes on the wealthy. But quite another matter politically was the proposed new tax on all forms of energy use, which was the plan's second biggest revenue raiser. Because of the wide discrepancies in energy use and cost across the nation, this proposal would have varied regional effects. . . .

Another big political problem in Clinton's package was its reliance on tax increases ($337 billion over the next five years, according to CBO, the non-partisan Congressional Budget Office) over domestic spending cuts. Because of his proposals for additional spending in selected programs, net domestic discretionary spending would increase from $209 billion to $262 billion annually by 1998, a projected increase of 7 percent over inflation; meanwhile, so-called "mandatory" spending such as Medicare, student loans and retirement benefits would decrease only slightly less than budget expectations. Most spending cuts came from defense programs, where the after-inflation reduction would total 21 percent in 1997. The net effect for the federal deficit was less dramatic than budget "hawks" like Panetta had initially hoped. Clinton's proposals "would make a substantial contribution to reducing the deficit, but they are not sufficient to solving the long-run problem," concluded the CBO. "The deficit would decline only through 1997 and then resume its rise.". . .

◆ Drawing the Lines

Despite some of these ominous factors, Democrats were not inclined to focus on the details in the immediate aftermath of Clinton's unveiling of the plan. Instead, most of them closed ranks and said that it was important to rally behind Clinton. "We should recognize that it is in our self-interest to support the president," Senate Majority Leader Mitchell often said. He and other congressional leaders constantly urged colleagues to show discipline and to "keep our disagreements internal," a House leadership aide said. Heeding the White House's message of previous weeks, most Democratic lawmakers already were inclined to be good soldiers, in any case. They helped to spread the message that they would sink or swim as a party. "The public wants us to get moving again and not be distracted," said Rep. Slaughter of New York. Rep. Reynolds, the Illinois Democrat and the only freshman named to the House Ways and Means Committee, said, "Let's give the president and his people an opportunity to try to change America."

But it would not be that easy. In the days immediately following Clinton's speech to Congress, some veteran Democrats said, with only a trace of humor, that they wished that they could vote without delay on Clinton's program. On one hand, with the public's initial support, they knew that they were on a political roll and they wanted to exploit the opportunity this presented. On the other hand, with their political experience, they knew that the good times could not last for long and that legislative problems inevitably would arise. . . .

Success required a delicate balance. So long as Clinton remained popular, most Democrats kept their disagreements private and closed ranks publicly. But the sense of unease was palpable. "The public needs to see decisive action," said Rep. Timothy Penny of Minnesota, who worried about a tendency to return to business as usual.

Congressional Republicans, of course, were the most obvious stumbling block for the Democrats. As the so-called loyal opposition, Republicans had several options, each of which they would use at various points. They could offer alternatives, where feasible, to present their own viewpoint. They could try to force votes on politically risky pieces of Clinton's program, to make the Democrats squirm over the partisan consequences; after all, there would be an election in November 1994 that might serve as a referendum on the Democrats' economic plan, especially if it was not working well. Or they could make use of parliamentary barriers such as the filibuster in an attempt to force delay, especially in the Senate, and to increase the public's focus on the weaknesses in Clinton's program. But whether they could effectively use the limited time to prepare a strategy highlighting problems with Clinton's program was uncertain. And Republicans conceded that, after twelve years during which they could look to the White House to take the initiative, they lacked confidence in their own ability to unify their often-disparate forces around a common set of principles and to challenge the new president. . . .

The business and economic communities also were filled with doubters. Although Clinton successfully sought support from the computer and high-tech industries, some of whose leaders had backed his election, the corporate sector generally was Republican and wary of the new president. Journalists reporting on economics soon wrote articles lamenting that the package was too limited. "We in the press helped foster a massive public deception," wrote columnist Robert J. Samuelson. "President Clinton calls his program for tax and spending changes an 'economic plan,' and we duly adopt his phrase. Yet, it isn't an economic plan—at least not as it's advertised. The immediate effect on the economy would be, at most, modest."[6] . . .

Finally, the legislative process itself was another potential bottleneck facing the Democrats. . . . Supporters hoped that they could turn the complex process to their favor. But they agreed that they faced an ambi-

---

[6]Robert J. Samuelson, "Plan? What Plan?" *The Washington Post,* April 14, 1993: A17.

tious schedule that allowed little room for slippage or error in any one area, which could result in an unraveling elsewhere.

Clinton and his Democratic allies dismissed critics who said that his program was not bold enough. They already faced a perilous few months as they worked to enact the new policies. Given the frustrations of the prior twelve years, however, it was a challenge that most of them welcomed. The election of a Democratic president creates some problems, Speaker Foley observed. "But they are different problems and they are welcome problems."

TOWARD CRITICAL THINKING

1. As Bill Clinton ran for president, he pledged to end gridlock. Yet as president he immediately ran into problems with Democratic leaders in the Senate according to Cohen. Why? Could these problems have been anticipated?

2. Bill Clinton has been likened to Ronald Reagan in that both men have been able to use the media effectively to sell their programs to the public. Yet the first few months of the Clinton administration were rife with media gaffes—ultimately causing Clinton to turn to former Ford White House operative David Gergen for help. Would better relations with the media have allowed Clinton to expend less political capital and good will as his administration tried to win passage of its economic plan?

• *37* •

United States *v.* Nixon
418 U.S. 683 (1974)

On June 17, 1972, five men broke into Democratic National
Committee headquarters in the Watergate complex in Washington, D.C.
With the help of investigative reporting from *The Washington Post* and
a no-nonsense federal district court judge, John J. Sirica, the burglars
were revealed to be associated with the Committee to Re-Elect the
President.

As the saga unfolded daily in news reports and in congressional hearings, responsibility for the break-in was being assigned to the highest officials in President Richard M. Nixon's campaign committee, including the
former attorney general of the United States, John N. Mitchell. John
Dean III, former special counsel to the president testified before Congress implicating many higher ups under a grant of immunity. While
Dean's testimony held the nation mesmerized, another White House aide
dropped another bombshell. President Nixon had installed a secret taping
system that recorded all conversations that took place in the Oval Office.
When the Special Prosecutor, who was investigating whether illegal acts
had occurred in the White House, subpoenaed the tapes, the president refused to surrender them. The Special Prosecutor then went to court to get
the tapes, which could resolve the dispute between witnesses about
whether the White House was actually involved in the burglary or the
cover up that followed.

Simultaneously with the litigation seeking the tapes, the House Judiciary Committee initiated impeachment proceedings against President
Nixon. Richard M. Nixon continued to refuse to turn over the tapes in
spite of a direct order from a federal district court. Nixon claimed that
it was his right under the doctrine of executive privilege to decide what
tapes could remain secret. A major constitutional crisis was in the offing
as President Nixon refused to comply with an order from a federal
court and a request from Congress as it considered several articles of
impeachment.

Sensing the potential crisis, the U.S. Supreme Court agreed to hear
the case on an expedited basis in July 1974, bypassing the federal Court
of Appeals. *United States* v. *Nixon* produced a unanimous 8–0 decision
from the Court; Justice William Rehnquist did not participate because he
had formerly worked in the Justice Department with some of the lawyers
involved in what ultimately became known as the Watergate scandal.

Opinion: Chief Justice Warren Burger
Vote: 8–0

. . .

[W]e turn to the claim that the subpoena should be quashed because it demands "confidential conversations between a President and his close advisors that it would be inconsistent with the public interest to produce." [The] first contention is a broad claim that the separation of powers doctrine precludes judicial review of a President's claim of privilege. The second contention is that, if he does not prevail on the claim of absolute privilege, the court should hold as a matter of constitutional law that the privilege prevails over the subpoena duces tecum.

In the performance of assigned constitutional duties each branch of the Government must initially interpret the Constitution, and the interpretation of its powers by any branch is due great respect from the others. The President's counsel [reads] the Constitution as providing an absolute privilege of confidentiality for all Presidential communications. Many decisions of this Court, however, have unequivocally reaffirmed the holding of [*Marbury,* that] "[i]t is emphatically the province and duty of the judicial department to say what the law is.". . .

No holding of the Court had defined the scope of judicial power specifically relating to the enforcement of a subpeona for confidential Presidential communications for use in a criminal prosecution, but other exercises of power by the Executive Branch and the Legislative Branch have been found invalid as in conflict with the Constitution. . . .

. . . [Notwithstanding] the deference each branch must accord the others, the "judicial Power of the United States" vested in the federal courts [can] no more be shared with the Executive Branch than the Chief Executive, for example, can share with the Judiciary the veto power. [Any] other conclusion would be contrary to the basic concept to separation of powers and the checks and balances that flow from the scheme of a tripartite government. [We] therefore reaffirm that it is the province and duty of this Court "to say what the law is" with respect to the claim of privilege presented in this case.

In support of his claim of absolute privilege, the President's counsel urges two grounds, one of which is common to all governments and one of which is peculiar to our system of separation of powers. The first ground is the valid need for protection of communications between high Government officials and those who advise and assist them in the performance of their manifold duties; the importance of this confidentiality is too plain to require further discussion. Human experience teaches that those who expect public dissemination of their remarks may well temper candor with a concern for appearances and for their own interests to the detriment of the decisionmaking process. Whatever the nature of the privilege of confidentiality of Presidential communications in the exercise of Art. II powers, the privilege can be said to derive from the supremacy of each branch within its own assigned area of constitutional duties. Certain powers, and privileges flow from the nature of enumerated powers; the protection of the confidentiality of Presidential communications has similar constitutional underpinnings.

The second ground asserted by the President's counsel in support of the claim of absolute privilege rests on the doctrine of separation of powers. Here it is argued that the independence of the Executive Branch within its own sphere [insulates] a President from a judicial subpoena in an ongoing criminal prosecution, and thereby protects confidential Presidential communications.

However, neither the doctrine of separation of powers, nor the need for confidentiality of high-level communications, without more, can sustain an absolute, unqualified Presidential privilege of immunity from judicial process under all circumstances. The President's need for complete candor and objectivity from advisers call for great deference from the courts. However, when the privilege depends solely on the broad, undifferentiated claim of public interest in the confidentiality of such conversations, a confrontation with other values arises. Absent a claim of need to protect military, diplomatic or sensitive national security secrets, we find it difficult to accept the argument that even the very important interest in confidentiality of Presidential communications is significantly diminished by production of such material for *in camera* inspection with all the protection that a district court will be obliged to provide.

The impediment that an absolute, unqualified privilege would place in the way of the primary constitutional duty of the Judicial Branch to do justice in criminal prosecutions would plainly conflict with the function of the courts under Art. III. In designing the structure of our Government and dividing and allocating the sovereign power among three co-equal branches, the Framers of the Constitution sought to provide a comprehensive system, but the separate powers were not intended to operate with absolute independence.

[To] read the Art. II powers of the President as providing an absolute privilege as against a subpoena essential to enforcement of criminal statutes on no more than a generalized claim of the public interest in confidentiality of nonmilitary and nondiplomatic discussions would upset the constitutional balance of "a workable government" and gravely impair the role of the courts under Art. III.

Since we conclude that the legitimate needs of the judicial process may outweigh Presidential privilege, it is necessary to resolve those competing interests in a manner that preserves the essential functions of each branch. The right and indeed the duty to resolve that question does not free the Judiciary from according high respect to the representations made on behalf of the President.

The expectation of a President to the confidentiality of his conversations and correspondence, like the claim of confidentiality of judicial deliberations, for example, has all the values to which we accord deference for the privacy of all citizens and, added to those values, is the necessity for protection of the public interest in candid, objective, and even blunt or harsh opinions in Presidential decisionmaking. A President and those who assist him must be free to explore alternatives in the process of shaping policies and making decisions and to do so in a way many would be unwilling to express except privately. These are the considerations justifying a presumptive privilege for Presidential communications. The privilege is fundamental to the operation of Government and inextricably rooted in the separation of powers under the Constitution. . . .

But this presumptive privilege must be considered in light of our historic commitment to the rule of law. This is nowhere more profoundly manifest than in our view that "the twofold aim [of criminal justice] is that guilt shall not escape or innocence suffer." We have elected to employ an adversary system of criminal justice in which the parties contest all issues before a court of law. The need to develop all relevant facts in the adversary system is both fundamental and comprehensive. The ends of criminal justice would be defeated if judgments were to be founded on a partial or speculative presentation of the facts. The very integrity of the judicial system and public confidence in the system depend on full disclosure of all the facts, within the framework of the rules of evidence. To ensure that justice is done, it is imperative to the function of courts that compulsory process be available for the production of evidence needed either by the prosecution or by the defense. . . .

In this case the President challenges a subpoena served on him as a third party requiring the production of materials for use in a criminal prosecution; he does so on the claim that he has a privilege against disclosure of confidential communications. He does not place his claim of privilege on the ground they are military or diplomatic secrets. As to these areas of Art. II duties the courts have traditionally shown the utmost deference to Presidential responsibilities.

[No] case of the Court, however, has extended this high degree of deference to a President's generalized interest in confidentiality. Nowhere in the Constitution [is] there any explicit reference to a privilege of confidentiality, yet to the extent this interest relates to the effective discharge of a President's powers, it is constitutionally based.

The right to the production of all evidence at a criminal trial similarly has constitutional dimensions. The Sixth Amendment explicitly confers upon every defendant in a criminal trial the right "to be confronted with the witnesses against him" and "to have compulsory process for obtaining witnesses in his favor." Moreover, the Fifth Amendment also guarantees that no person shall be deprived of liberty without due process of law....

In this case we must weigh the importance of the general privilege of confidentiality of Presidential communications in performance of the President's responsibilities against the inroads of such a privilege on the fair administration of criminal justice. The interest in preserving confidentiality is weighty indeed and entitled to great respect. However, we cannot conclude that advisers will be moved to temper the candor of their remarks by the infrequent occasions of disclosure because of the possibility that such conversations will be called for in the context of a criminal prosecution.

On the other hand, the allowance of the privilege to withhold evidence that is demonstrably relevant in a criminal trial would cut deeply into the guarantee of due process of law and gravely impair the basic function of the courts. A President's acknowledged need for confidentiality in the communications of his office is general in nature, whereas the constitutional need for production of relevant evidence in a criminal proceeding is specific and central to the fair adjudication of a particular criminal case in the administration of justice. Without access to specific facts a criminal prosecution may be totally frustrated. The President's broad interest in confidentiality of communications will not be vitiated by disclosure of a limited number of conversations preliminarily shown to have some bearing on the pending criminal cases.

We conclude that when the ground for asserting privilege as to subpoenaed materials sought for use in a criminal trial is based only on the generalized interest in confidentiality, it cannot prevail over the fundamental demands of due process of law in the fair administration of criminal justice. The generalized assertion of privilege must yield to the demonstrated, specific need for evidence in a pending criminal trial....

... [I]t is obvious that the District Court has a very heavy responsibility to see to it that Presidential conversations, which are either not relevant or not admissible, are accorded that high degree of respect due the President of the United States.

... It is therefore necessary in the public interest to afford Presidential confidentiality the greatest protection consistent with the fair administration of justice. The need for confidentiality even as to idle conversations with associates in which casual reference might be made concerning political leaders within the country or foreign statesmen is too obvious to call for further treatment. We have no doubt that the District Judge will at all times accord to Presidential records [a] high degree of deference and will discharge his responsibility to see to it that until released to the Special Prosecutor no *in camera* material is revealed to anyone....

Affirmed.

TOWARD CRITICAL THINKING

1. President Nixon complied with the subpoena and soon thereafter resigned from office. Although the full impeachment mechanisms were never put into use in this case, the separation of powers principle incorporated in the Constitution by the Framers worked. What might have happened if the president had refused to comply with the Supreme Court's affirmance of the lower court's order?

2. President Nixon argued in Court that all conversations in his office were privileged; without a guarantee of secrecy, aides and the president would be unlikely to speak with candor. Is this a valid assessment? Did the Supreme Court's direction to the trial judge to listen to the tapes carefully and release only those pertaining to the Watergate affair undercut Nixon's claims?

THINKING ABOUT THE PRESIDENCY

1. Can character attributes actually be used to predict how a person will perform as president? What other factors might be important?

2. Is the increasing media focus on the president's personal successes and failures likely to produce a series of one-term presidents?

3. What are the optimum personal and political conditions for a successful presidency?

CHAPTER 8

• • •

The Bureaucracy

The bureaucracy occupies a unique place in the American political system. Most bureaucrats work in the executive branch; others work in independent agencies, which were created to remove politics from policy making, a process described by James Q. Wilson in "The Rise of the Bureaucratic State" (Reading 40).

When Thomas Jefferson first gathered his Cabinet together, as described by James Sterling Young (Reading 39), he wasn't thinking about "big government"; rather, he was bringing together a group of advisors to advise him on policy. And not only was government smaller in Jefferson's day, but there also were far fewer departments of government.

The growth of the U.S. bureaucracy has made it appear—at least to some citizens and commentators—to be too removed from the people, a fear often voiced by Anti-Federalists. Even Federalist Alexander Hamilton probably failed to envision how large the national government and its bureaucracy would become. Its very size and apparent remoteness has led some citizens to distrust public officials and bureaucrats. This feeling about government, especially in the post-Watergate era, led to a series of ethics laws. Those laws affecting the day-to-day activities of many members of the bureaucracy are discussed in Reading 41, "No Free Lunch?"

· *38* ·

Federalist No. 72

ALEXANDER HAMILTON

The size of government discussed by Morris P. Fiorina in Reading 29 is a relatively new phenomenon. Yet the Framers realized from the start that actually running the national government—or executing the laws as written by Congress or interpreted by the Supreme Court—would require the work of more than one individual. As Hamilton, who went on to become a member of George Washington's Cabinet as Secretary of the Treasury, notes in *Federalist No. 72,* the proper administration of government requires the assistance of deputies chosen by the president who hold ideas consistent with his.

The administration of government, in its largest sense, comprehends all the operations of the body politic, whether legislative, executive, or judiciary; but in its most usual and perhaps in its most precise signification, it is limited to executive details, and falls peculiarly within the province of the executive department. The actual conduct of foreign negotiations, the preparatory plans of finance, the application and disbursement of the public moneys in conformity to the general appropriations of the legislature, the arrangement of the army and navy, the direction of the operations of war—these, and other matters of a like nature, constitute what seems to be most properly understood by the administration of government. The persons, therefore, to whose immediate management these different matters are committed ought to be considered as the assistants or deputies of the Chief Magistrate, and on this account they ought to derive their offices from his appointment, at least from his nomination, and ought to be subject to his superintendence. This view of the subject will at once suggest to us the intimate connection between the duration of the executive magistrate in office and the stability of the system of administration. To reverse and undo what has been done by a predecessor is very often considered by a successor as the best proof he can give of his own capacity and desert; and in addition to this propensity, where the alteration has been the result of public choice, the person substituted is warranted in supposing that the dismission of his predecessor has proceeded from a dislike to his measures; and that the less he resembles him, the more he will recommend himself to the favor of his constituents. These considerations, and the influence of personal confidences and attachments, would be likely to induce every new President to promote a change of men to fill the subordinate stations; and these causes together could not fail to occasion a disgraceful and ruinous mutability in the administration of the government.

TOWARD CRITICAL THINKING

1. Cabinet secretaries and other high governmental officials are appointed by the president but must be confirmed by the U.S. Senate before taking office. Most appointments are *pro forma;* but not all presidential appointments are confirmed. Keeping Hamilton's thoughts in mind, do you think that Senate confirmation lessens a president's ability to govern with full confidence in his subordinates?

2. Are there any duties or tasks mentioned by Hamilton that are particularly well suited to be delegated to subordinates? Conversely, are there any responsibilities for which the president should be solely responsible?

Presidential Cabinets in the Jeffersonian Era

JAMES STERLING YOUNG

As historian James Sterling Young notes, an examination of a president's cabinets is key "to any exploration of presidential leadership." Some presidents have chosen to lead through their cabinets; others have not. Jefferson, in particular, made effective use of his cabinet as a policy forum to deal with problems his administration encountered in Congress and in setting foreign policy. Jefferson also recognized the importance of having consensus among his department secretaries so that a joint front could be presented to Congress. Other early presidents were not so lucky; they found their cabinet secretaries allied with congressional leaders against them.

The cabinet [is] a key institution for any exploration of presidential leadership in the Jeffersonian era. A committee of department heads and the Attorney General, convened and chaired by the Chief Executive, it was the only institution in the executive community which brought spokesmen for different sections, political factions, and bureaucratic interests together in a work group affording the President a leadership role.

The cabinet was not new to the Jeffersonian period, having already become established in practice during the administrations of Washington and Adams. Without constitutional status, it had originally been devised to serve as a policy-making organ which would substitute for the Chief Executive when he was absent from the seat of government. By 1793, however, department heads were being convened in the presence of the President to deliberate crisis questions, particularly those relating to foreign policy. It is apparently under precedent of this usage that the committee acquired the designation of "cabinet," and that the device originally intended as a substitute for an absent President became a regularly employed device of the President for discussing a wide range of policy issues with his subordinate officers.

Such use of the cabinet was continued throughout the Jeffersonian era, Monroe most frequently convening the group with roughly ten meet-

SOURCE: *The Washington Community 1800–1828,* James Sterling Young, 1966.
© Columbia University Press, New York. Reprinted with permission of the publisher.

ings monthly. Meetings were . . . used as policy forums, to discuss matters on which presidential action was contemplated or required and which would involve the President in a political commitment. . . . Foreign policy questions were perhaps the most frequent subject of cabinet business. Presidential nominations were occasionally discussed. White House communications to Congress were a major item on the cabinet agenda throughout the Jeffersonian era, and the most important of these was the President's annual State of the Union message. What the President said in these messages, including recommendations for legislation, was, in every administration, largely the product of joint effort by the cabinet. . . .

In the Jeffersonian era it seems clear, therefore, that the cabinet was a political device "in both the partisan and policy meanings of the term." No other rationale for continued use of this Federalist device is discernible. Given the small number of departments and the diminutive size of the Washington bureaucracy, the need for administrative coordination was clearly not such as to necessitate group consultations with the President. . . .

. . . Jeffersonian Presidents must have recognized the importance of consensus among Secretaries whose support they needed to carry their programs both on the Hill and into the lower levels of the administrative structure. Having no personal staff and depending largely upon their cabinet members for political liaison with Congress, they must have been aware that their chances for rallying congressional support depended largely on their ability to rally their department heads in support of their policy objectives. . . .

The Jeffersonian cabinet thus appears to have been a device employed by Chief Executives in recognition of the independent political power wielded by their Secretaries; in recognition of the political risks to themselves of failing to achieve a working consensus among them; and in recognition of forces always working to destroy a sense of common purpose among executives with widely divergent interests. The cabinet, in other words, was the executive equivalent of a legislative caucus, intended to preconcert the policy views of party members representing different political interests. . . .

Madison's accession to the Presidency brought a dramatic and disastrous change. "Our Cabinet presents a novel spectacle in the political world," wrote a congressman in 1811; "divided against itself, and the most deadly animosity raging between its principal members, what can come of it but confusion, mischief, and ruin?" Personal vendettas between department heads, their active involvement in legislative intrigues, and insubordination to the President which not even a grave national emergency served to suspend became the order of the day. . . .

Presidential efforts to enlist the aid of cabinet members in rallying Congress were evaded or rebuffed. Mending their own fences on the Hill took priority over helping the President, and Madison was obliged to ferret out legislators individually and to ask them secretly to introduce bills that his Secretaries would not press on his behalf. Department heads sent facts and reports to Congress of which they did not apprise the President, with the result of undercutting presidential policy requests already submitted to the legislature. His administration "aground at the pitch of high tide," nothing remained to Madison "but to lighten the ship," and he resorted to removals from the cabinet. . . . But resignations and dismissals were a poor substitute for consensus; on the contrary, they merely made it more difficult to achieve. Madison simply could not hold a cabinet together.

So it went, too, with Monroe's cabinet. Animosities of the sort that generated resignations and dismissals in Madison's cabinet led to intensified infighting among Monroe's department heads, most of whom remained in office from beginning to end of the Monroe administration. . . .

Cabinet unity could not possibly be maintained against the doubly divisive impact of different congressional committees "now set as watch over the heads of departments" and of competition for the Presidency among the Secretaries, whose "partisans in Congress are making a handle of [policy issues] to help or hurt those for or against whom they are." . . .

By contrast with the regimes of Madison and Monroe, the single term of John Quincy Adams' administration witnessed a period of relative calm within the executive establishment. Because detailed reports of all but a few cabinet meetings are lacking for this period, and because Adams apparently convened the cabinet rather less regularly and less frequently than his predecessor, harmony among the department heads may have been more apparent than real. Nevertheless, the final four years of the Jeffersonian era did not exhibit the intense internal warfare within the executive establishment that had raged for sixteen years prior to Adams' election.

TOWARD CRITICAL THINKING

1. What are the hallmarks of a good cabinet? A bad one? Is there any way a president can avoid problems with his cabinet before they arise?

2. The divided cabinet presided over by James Madison marked the beginning of presidential conflicts with their cabinets. During Jimmy Carter's presidency, for example, he requested letters of resignation from all of his cabinet secretaries before they assumed their positions and used those letters to remove several department heads who he believed were disloyal to him. Young notes that, as Congress developed, department heads were called on more and more to answer to committee chairs about their activities, thus really serving two masters. Is this an unsolvable problem in an era of complex government?

· 40 ·

The Rise of the Bureaucratic State

JAMES Q. WILSON

As demands for new services grew—from farmers in the 1850s and 1860s to the poor in the Great Depression—the national government responded by creating new agencies and departments to address the needs of particular clienteles. According to Wilson, these clientele agencies are virtually self-perpetuating and nearly impossible to eliminate.

The tremendous growth of the executive branch of the national government and the resultant bureaucracy that has been created to administer new programs have transferred a considerable amount of political power to unelected officials, posing important questions about the nature of American democracy. Almost every new presidential administration has pledged to cut costs and bureaucracy, but few have made any meaningful change. Wilson explains why change is so difficult.

During its first 150 years, the American republic was not thought to have a "bureaucracy," and thus it would have been meaningless to refer to the "problems" of a "bureaucratic state." There were, of course, appointed civilian officials: Though only about 3,000 at the end of the Federalist period, there were about 95,000 by the time Grover Cleveland assumed office in 1881, and nearly half a million by 1925. Some aspects of these numerous officials were regarded as problems—notably, the standards by which they were appointed and the political loyalties to which they were held—but these were thought to be matters of proper character and good management. The great political and constitutional struggles were not over the power of the administrative apparatus, but over the power of the President, of Congress, and of the states.

The Founding Fathers had little to say about the nature or function of the executive branch of the new government. The Constitution is virtually silent on the subject and the debates in the Constitutional Convention are almost devoid of reference to an administrative apparatus. This reflected no lack of concern about the matter, however. Indeed, it was in part

SOURCE: James Q. Wilson, "The Rise of the Bureaucratic State," *The Public Interest,* 41 (Fall 1975): 77–103. Reprinted with permission.

because of the Founders' depressing experience with chaotic and inefficient management under the Continental Congress and the Articles of Confederation that they had assembled in Philadelphia. Management by committees composed of part-time amateurs had cost the colonies dearly in the War of Independence and few, if any, of the Founders wished to return to that system. The argument was only over how the heads of the necessary departments of government were to be selected, and whether these heads should be wholly subordinate to the President or whether instead they should form some sort of council that would advise the President and perhaps share in his authority. In the end, the Founders left it up to Congress to decide the matter.

There was no dispute in Congress that there should be executive departments, headed by single appointed officials, and, of course, the Constitution specified that these would be appointed by the President with the advice and consent of the Senate. . . .

◆ The "Bureaucracy Problem"

The original departments were small and had limited duties. The State Department, the first to be created, had but nine employees in addition to the Secretary. The War Department did not reach 80 civilian employees until 1801; it commanded only a few thousand soldiers. Only the Treasury Department had substantial powers—it collected taxes, managed the public debt, ran the national bank, conducted land surveys, and purchased military supplies. Because of this, Congress gave the closest scrutiny to its structure and its activities.

The number of administrative agencies and employees grew slowly but steadily during the 19th and early 20th centuries and then increased explosively on the occasion of World War I, the Depression, and World War II. It is difficult to say at what point in this process the administrative system became a distinct locus of power or an independent source of political initiatives and problems. What is clear is that the emphasis on the sheer *size* of the administrative establishment—conventional in many treatments of the subject—is misleading.

The government can spend vast sums of money—wisely or unwisely—without creating that set of conditions we ordinarily associate with the bureaucratic state. For example, there could be massive transfer payments made under government auspices from person to person or from state to state, all managed by a comparatively small staff of officials and a few large computers. . . .

. . . Max Weber, after all, warned us that in capitalist and socialist societies alike, bureaucracy was likely to acquire an "overtowering" power position. Conservatives have always feared bureaucracy, save perhaps the police. Humane socialists have frequently been embarrassed by their inability to reconcile a desire for public control of the economy with the suspicion that a public bureaucracy may be as immune to democratic control as a private one. Liberals have equivocated, either dismissing any concern for bureaucracy as reactionary quibbling about social progress, or embracing that concern when obviously nonreactionary persons (welfare recipients, for example) express a view toward the Department of Health, Education, and Welfare indistinguishable from the view businessmen take of the Internal Revenue Service.

◆ Political Authority

There are at least three ways in which political power may be gathered undesirably into bureaucratic hands: by the growth of an administrative apparatus so large as to be immune from popular control, by placing power over a governmental bureaucracy of any size in private rather than public hands, or by vesting discretionary authority in the hands of a public agency so that the exercise of that power is not responsive to the public good. These are not the only problems that arise because of bureaucratic organization. From the point of view of their members, bureaucracies are sometimes uncaring, ponderous, or unfair; from the point of view of their political superiors, they are sometimes unimaginative or inefficient; from the point of view of their clients, they are sometimes slow or unjust. No single account can possibly treat of all that is problematic in bureaucracy; even the part I discuss here—the extent to which political authority has been transferred undesirably to an unaccountable administrative realm—is itself too large for a single essay. But it is, if not the most important problem, then surely the one that would most have troubled our Revolutionary leaders, especially those that went on to produce the Constitution. It was, after all, the question of power that chiefly concerned them, both in redefining our relationship with England and in finding a new basis for political authority in the Colonies. . . .

◆ Bureaucracy and Size

During the first half of the 19th century, the growth in the size of the federal bureaucracy can be explained, not by the assumption of new tasks by the government or by the imperialistic designs of the managers of existing tasks, but by the addition to existing bureaus of personnel performing essentially routine, repetitive tasks for which the public demand was great and unavoidable. The principal problem facing a bureaucracy thus enlarged was how best to coordinate its activities toward given and noncontroversial ends.

The increase in the size of the executive branch of the federal government at this time was almost entirely the result of the increase in the size of the Post Office. . . .

The problem with the Post Office, however, was not omnipotence but impotence. It was a government monopoly. Being a monopoly, it had little incentive to find the most efficient means to manage its services; being a government monopoly, it was not free to adopt such means even when found—communities, Congressmen, and special-interest groups saw to that.

✦ The Military Establishment

Not all large bureaucracies grow in response to demands for service. The Department of Defense, since 1941 the largest employer of federal civilian officials, has become, as the governmental keystone of the "military-industrial complex," the very archetype of an administrative entity that is thought to be so vast and so well-entrenched that it can virtually ignore the political branches of government, growing and even acting on the basis of its own inner imperatives. In fact, until recently the military services were a major economic and political force only during wartime. . . .

In sum, from the Revolutionary War to 1950, a period of over 170 years, the size and deployment of the military establishment in this country was governed entirely by decisions made by political leaders on political grounds. The military did not expand autonomously, a large standing army did not find wars to fight, and its officers did not play a significant potential role except in wartime and occasionally as Presidential candidates. No bureaucracy proved easier to control, at least insofar as its size and purposes were concerned.

✦ A "Military-Industrial Complex"?

The argument for the existence of an autonomous, bureaucratically-led military-industrial complex is supported primarily by events since 1950. Not only has the United States assumed during this period worldwide commitments that necessitate a larger military establishment, but the advent of new, high-technology weapons has created a vast industrial machine with an interest in sustaining a high level of military expenditures, especially on weapons research, development, and acquisition. This machine, so the argument goes, is allied with the Pentagon in ways that dominate the political officials nominally in charge of the armed forces. . . .

But despite all this, the military has not been able to sustain itself at its preferred size, to keep its strength constant or growing, or to retain for its use a fixed or growing portion of the Gross National Product. . . .

The bureaucratic problems associated with the military establishment arise mostly from its internal management and are functions of its complexity, the uncertainty surrounding its future deployment, conflicts among its constituent services over mission and role, and the need to purchase expensive equipment without the benefit of a market economy that can control costs. Complexity, uncertainty, rivalry, and monopsony are inherent (and frustrating) aspects of the military as a bureaucracy, but they are very different problems from those typically associated with the phrase, "the military-industrial complex." The size and budget of the military are matters wholly within the power of civilian authorities to decide—indeed, the military budget contains the largest discretionary items in the entire federal budget. . . .

◆ Bureaucracy and Clientelism

After 1861, the growth in the federal administrative system could no longer be explained primarily by an expansion of the postal service and other traditional bureaus. Though these continued to expand, new departments were added that reflected a new (or at least greater) emphasis on the enlargement of the scope of government. . . .

What was striking about the period after 1861 was that the government began to give formal, bureaucratic recognition to the emergence of distinctive interests in a diversifying economy. As Richard L. Schott has written, "whereas earlier federal departments had been formed around specialized governmental functions (foreign affairs, war, finance, and the like), the new departments of this period—Agriculture, Labor, and Commerce—were devoted to the interests and aspirations of particular economic groups."

The original purpose behind these clientele-oriented departments was neither to subsidize nor to regulate, but to promote, chiefly by gathering and publishing statistics and (especially in the case of agriculture) by research. . . .

. . . The pattern of bureaucratic clientelism was set in a way later to begin a familiar feature of the governmental landscape—a subsidy was initially provided, because it was either popular or unnoticed, to a group that was powerfully benefited and had few or disorganized opponents; the beneficiaries were organized to supervise the administration and ensure the funding of the program; the law authorizing the program, first passed because it seemed the right thing to do, was left intact or even expanded because politically it became the only thing to do. A benefit once bestowed cannot easily be withdrawn.

◆ Public Power and Private Interests

. . . The New Deal was perhaps the high water mark of at least the theory of bureaucratic clientelism. Not only did various sectors of society, notably agriculture, begin receiving massive subsidies, but the government proposed, through the National Industrial Recovery Act (NRA), to cloak with public power a vast number of industrial groupings and trade associations so that they might control production and prices in ways that would end the depression. The NRA's Blue Eagle fell before the Supreme Court—the wholesale delegation of public power to private interests was declared unconstitutional. But the piecemeal delegation was not, as the continued growth of specialized promotional agencies attests. . . .

◆ "Cooperative Federalism"

The growing edge of client-oriented bureaucracy can be found, however, not in government relations with private groups, but in the relations among governmental units. In dollar volume, the chief clients of federal domestic expenditures are state and local government agencies. To some degree, federal involvement in local affairs by the cooperative funding or management of local enterprises has always existed. The Northwest Ordinance of 1784 made public land available to finance local schools and the Morrill Act of 1862 gave land to support state colleges, but what Morton Grodzins and Daniel Elazar have called "cooperative federalism," though it always existed, did not begin in earnest until the passage in 1913 of the 16th Amendment to the Constitution allowed the federal government to levy an income tax on citizens and thereby to acquire access to vast sources of revenue. Between 1914 and 1917, federal aid to states and localities increased a thousandfold. By 1948 it amounted to over one-tenth of all state and local spending; by 1970, to over one-sixth. . . .

. . . What David Stockman has called the "social pork barrel" grows more or less steadily. Between 1950 and 1970, the number of farms declined from about 5.6 million to fewer than three million, but government payments to farmers rose from $283 million to $3.2 billion. . . .

◆ Self-perpetuating Agencies

If the Founding Fathers were to return to examine bureaucratic clientelism, they would, I suspect, be deeply discouraged. James Madison clearly foresaw that American society would be "broken into many parts, interests and classes of citizens" and that this "multiplicity of interests" would help ensure against "the tyranny of the majority," especially in a federal regime with separate branches of government. Positive action would require a "coalition of a majority"; in the process of forming this coalition, the rights of all would be protected, not merely by self-interested bargains, but because in a free society such a coalition "could seldom take place on any other principles than those of justice and the general good." To those who wrongly believed that Madison thought of men as acting only out of base motives, the phrase is instructive: Persuading men who disagree to compromise their differences can rarely be achieved solely by the parceling out of relative advantage; the belief is also required that what is being agreed to is right, proper, and defensible before public opinion.

Most of the major new social programs of the United States, whether for the good of the few or the many, were initially adopted by broad coalitions appealing to general standards of justice or to conceptions of the public weal. This is certainly the case with most of the New Deal legislation—notably such programs as Social Security—and with most Great Society legislation—notably Medicare and aid to education; it was also conspicuously the case with respect to post-Great Society legislation pertaining to consumer and environmental concerns. . . .

But when a program supplies particular benefits to an existing or newly-created interest, public or private, it creates a set of political relationships that make exceptionally difficult further alteration of that program by coalitions of the majority. What was created in the name of the common good is sustained in the name of the particular interest. Bureaucratic clientelism becomes self-perpetuating, in the absence of some crisis or scandal, because a single interest group to which the program matters greatly is highly motivated and well-situated to ward off the criticisms of other groups that have a broad but weak interest in the policy.

In short, a regime of separated powers makes it difficult to overcome objections and contrary interests sufficiently to permit the enactment of a new program or the creation of a new agency. Unless the legislation can be made to pass either with little notice or at a time of crisis or extraordinary majorities—and sometimes even then—the initiation of new programs requires public interest arguments. But the same regime works to protect agencies, once created, from unwelcome change because a major change is, in effect, new legislation that must overcome the same hurdles as the original law, but this time with one of the hurdles—the wishes of the agency and its client—raised much higher. As a result, the Madisonian system makes it relatively easy for the delegation of public power to private groups to go unchallenged and, therefore, for factional interests that have acquired a supportive public bureaucracy to rule without submitting their interests to the effective scrutiny and modification of other interests.

◆ Bureaucracy and Discretion

For many decades, the Supreme Court denied to the federal government any general "police power" over occupations and businesses, and thus most such regulation occurred at the state level and even there under the constraint that it must not violate the notion of "substantive due process"—that is, the view that there were sharp limits to the power of any government to take (and therefore to regulate) property. What clearly was within the regulatory province of the federal government was interstate commerce, and thus it is not surprising that the first major federal regulatory body should be the Interstate Commerce Commission (ICC), created in 1887.

What does cause, if not surprise, then at least dispute, is the view that the Commerce Act actually was intended to regulate railroads in the public interest. It has become fashionable of late to see this law as a device sought by the railroads to protect themselves from competition. The argument has been given its best-known formulation by Gabriel Kolko. Long-haul railroads, facing ruinous price wars and powerless to resist the demands of big shippers for rebates, tried to create voluntary cartels or "pools" that would keep rates high. These pools always collapsed, however, when one railroad or another would cut rates in order to get more business. To prevent this, the railroads turned to the federal government seeking a law to compel what persuasion could not induce. But the genesis of the act was in fact more complex: Shippers wanted protection from high prices charged by railroads that operated monopolistic services in certain communities; many other shippers served by competing lines wanted no legal barriers to prevent competition from driving prices down as far as possible; some railroads wanted regulation to ease competition, while others feared regulation. And the law as finally passed in fact made "pooling" (or cartels to keep prices up) illegal.

The true significance of the Commerce Act is not that it allowed public power to be used to make secure private wealth but that it created a federal commission with broadly delegated powers that would have to reconcile conflicting goals (the desire for higher or lower prices) in a political environment characterized by a struggle among organized interests and rapidly changing technology. In short, the Commerce Act brought forth a new dimension to the problem of bureaucracy: not those problems, as with the Post Office, that resulted from size and political constraints, but those that were caused by the need to make binding choices without any clear standards for choice.

The ICC was not, of course, the first federal agency with substantial discretionary powers over important matters. The Office of Indian Affairs, for a while in the War Department but after 1849 in the Interior Department, coped for the better part of a century with the Indian problem equipped with no clear policy, beset on all sides by passionate and opposing arguments, and infected with a level of fraud and corruption that seemed impossible to eliminate. There were many causes of the problem, but at root was the fact that the government was determined to control the Indians but could not decide toward what end that control should be exercised (extermination, relocation, and assimilation all had their advocates) and, to the extent the goal was assimilation, could find no method by which to achieve it. By the end of the century, a policy of relocation had been adopted *de facto* and the worst abuses of the Indian service had been eliminated—if not by administrative skill, then by the exhaustion of things in Indian possession worth stealing. By the turn of the century, the management of the Indian question had become the more or less routine administration of Indian schools and the allocation of reservation land among Indian claimants. . . .

◆ Majoritarian Politics

The creation of regulatory bureaucracies has occurred, as is often remarked, in waves. The first was the period between 1887 and 1890 (the Commerce Act and the Antitrust Act), the second between 1906 and 1915 (the Pure Food and Drug Act, the Meat Inspection Act, the Federal Trade Commission Act, the Clayton Act), the third during the 1930's (the Food, Drug, and Cosmetic Act, the Public Utility Holding Company Act, the Securities Exchange Act, the Natural Gas Act, the National Labor Relations Act), and the fourth during the latter part of the 1960's (the Water Quality Act, the Truth in Lending Act, the National Traffic and Motor Vehicle Safety Act, various amendments to the drug laws, the Motor Vehicle Pollution Control Act, and many others).

Each of these periods was characterized by progressive or liberal Presidents in office (Cleveland, T. R. Roosevelt, Wilson, F. D. Roosevelt, Johnson); one was a period of national crisis (the 1930's); three were periods when the President enjoyed extraordinary majorities of his own party in both houses of Congress (1914–1916, 1932–1940, and 1964–1968); and only the first period preceded the emergence of the national mass media of communication. These facts are important because of the special difficulty of passing any genuinely regulatory legislation: A single interest, the regulated party, sees itself seriously threatened by a law proposed by a policy entrepreneur who must appeal to an unorganized majority, the members of which may not expect to be substantially or directly benefitted by the law. Without special political circumstances—a crisis, a scandal, extraordinary majorities, an especially vigorous President, the support of media—the normal barriers to legislative innovation (i.e., to the formation of a "coalition of the majority") may prove insuperable.

Stated another way, the initiation of regulatory programs tends to take the form of majoritarian rather than coalitional politics. The Madisonian system is placed in temporary suspense: Exceptional majorities propelled by a public mood and led by a skillful policy entrepreneur take action that might not be possible under ordinary circumstances (closely divided parties, legislative-executive checks and balances, popular indifference). The consequence of majoritarian politics for the administration of regulatory bureaucracies is great. To initiate and sustain the necessary legislative mood, strong, moralistic, and sometimes ideological appeals are necessary—leading, in turn, to the granting of broad mandates of power to the new agency (a modest delegation of authority would obviously be inadequate if the problem to be resolved is of crisis proportions), or to the specifying of exacting standards to be enforced (e.g., *no* carcinogenic products may be sold, 95 per cent of the pollutants must be eliminated), or to both.

Either in applying a vague but broad rule ("the public interest, convenience, and necessity") or in enforcing a clear and strict standard, the regulatory agency will tend to broaden the range and domain of its authority, to lag behind technological and economic change, to resist deregulation, to stimulate corruption, and to contribute to the bureaucratization of private institutions.

It will broaden its regulatory reach out of a variety of motives: to satisfy the demand of the regulated enterprise that it be protected from competition, to make effective the initial regulatory action by attending to the unanticipated side effects of that action, to discover or stretch the meaning of vague statutory language, or to respond to new constituencies induced by the existence of the agency to convert what were once private demands into public pressures. For example, the Civil Aeronautics Board, out of a desire both to promote aviation and to protect the regulated price structure of the industry, will resist the entry into the industry of new carriers. If a Public Utilities Commission sets rates too low for a certain class of customers, the utility will allow service to those customers to decline in quality, leading in turn to a demand that the Commission also regulate the quality of service. If the Federal Communications Commission cannot decide who should receive a broadcast license by applying the "public interest" standard, it will be powerfully tempted to invest that phrase with whatever preferences the majority of the Commission then entertains, leading in turn to the exercise of control over many more aspects of broadcasting than merely signal interference—all in the name of deciding what the standard for entry shall be. If the Antitrust Division can prosecute conspiracies in restraint of trade, it will attract to itself the complaints of various firms about business practices that are neither conspiratorial nor restraining but merely competitive, and a "vigorous" antitrust lawyer may conclude that these practices warrant prosecution.

✦ Bureaucratic Inertia

Regulatory agencies are slow to respond to change for the same reason all organizations with an assured existence are slow: There is no incentive to respond. Furthermore, the requirements of due process and of political conciliation will make any response time consuming. For example, owing to the complexity of the matter and the money at stake, any comprehensive review of the long-distance rates of the telephone company will take years, and possibly may take decades. . . .

Finally, regulatory agencies that control entry, fix prices, or substantially affect the profitability of an industry create a powerful stimulus for direct or indirect forms of corruption. The revelations about campaign finance in the 1972 presidential election show dramatically that there will be a response to that stimulus. Many corporations, disproportionately those in regulated industries (airlines, milk producers, oil companies), made illegal or hard to justify campaign contributions involving very large sums.

✦ The Era of Contract

It is far from clear what the Founding Fathers would have thought of all this. They were not doctrinaire exponents of laissez faire, nor were 18th-century governments timid about asserting their powers over the economy. Every imaginable device of fiscal policy was employed by the states after the Revolutionary War. Mother England had, during the mercantilist era, fixed prices and wages, licensed merchants, and granted monopolies and subsidies. (What were the royal grants of American land to immigrant settlers but the greatest of subsidies, sometimes—as in Pennsylvania—almost monopolistically given?) European nations regularly operated state enterprises, controlled trade, and protected industry. But as William D. Grampp has noted, at the Constitutional Convention the Founders considered authorizing only four kinds of economic controls, and they rejected two of them. They agreed to allow the Congress to regulate international and interstate commerce and to give monopoly protection in the form of copyrights and patents. Even Madison's proposal to allow the federal government to charter corporations was rejected. Not one of the 85 *Federalist* papers dealt with economic regulation; indeed, the only reference to commerce was the value to it of a unified nation and a strong navy. . . .

. . . With the growth of client-serving and regulatory agencies, grave questions began to be raised—usually implicitly—about that theory. A client-serving bureau, because of its relations with some source of private power, could become partially independent of both the executive and legislative branches—or in the case of the latter, dependent upon certain committees and independent of others and of the views of the Congress as a whole. A regulatory agency (that is to say, a truly regulatory one and not a clientelist or promotional agency hiding behind a regulatory fig leaf) was, in the typical case, placed formally outside the existing branches of government. Indeed, they were called "independent" or "quasi-judicial" agencies (they might as well have been called "quasi-executive" or "quasi-legislative") and thus the special status that clientelist bureaus achieved *de facto,* the regulatory ones achieved *de jure.*

It is, of course, inadequate and misleading to criticize these agencies, as has often been done, merely because they raise questions about the problem of sovereignty. The crucial test of their value is their behavior, and that can be judged only by applying economic and welfare criteria to the policies they produce. But if such judgments should prove damning, as increasingly has been the case, then the problem of finding the authority with which to alter or abolish such organizations becomes acute. In this regard the theory of the separation of powers has proved unhelpful.

The separation of powers makes difficult, in ordinary times, the extension of public power over private conduct—as a nation, we came more slowly to the welfare state than almost any European nation, and we still engage in less central planning and operate fewer nationalized industries than other democratic regimes. But we have extended the regulatory sway of our national government as far or farther than that of most other liberal regimes (our environmental and safety codes are now models for much of Europe), and the bureaus wielding these discretionary powers are, once created, harder to change or redirect than would be the case if authority were more centralized.

The shift of power toward the bureaucracy was not inevitable. It did not result simply from increased specialization, the growth of industry, or the imperialistic designs of the bureaus themselves. Before the second decade of this century, there was no federal bureaucracy wielding substantial discretionary powers. That we have one now is the result of political decisions made by elected representatives. Fifty years ago, the people often wanted more of government than it was willing to provide—it was, in that sense, a republican government in which representatives moderated popular demands. Today, not only does political action follow quickly upon the stimulus of public interest, but government itself creates that stimulus and sometimes acts in advance of it.

All democratic regimes tend to shift resources from the private to the public sector and to enlarge the size of the administrative component of government. The particularistic and localistic nature of American democracy has created a particularistic and client-serving administration. If our bureaucracy often serves special interests and is subject to no central direction, it is because our legislature often serves special interests and is subject to no central leadership. For Congress to complain of what it has created and it maintains is, to be charitable, misleading. Congress could change what it has devised, but there is little reason to suppose it will.

TOWARD CRITICAL THINKING

1. What are three ways in which political power may be gathered undesirably into the hands of the bureaucracy? Can you think of others?

2. How does bureaucratic clientelism work? Name some groups that have been beneficiaries of this system. Which groups or interests are most likely to gain from the system?

· *41* ·

No Free Lunch?

A Comprehensive Code of Conduct for Federal Employees

G. JERRY SHAW, WILLIAM L. BRANSFORD, and RICHARD A. MOORE

Much has been written about the revolving door that appears to operate after every election and even in between; members of the outgoing presidential administration (or continuing one) often secure very high paying jobs in Washington, D.C. Companies, law firms, and other types of employers are happy to pay top dollar for the governmental access and expertise these men and women bring. While attention usually focuses at top-level, high-paying jobs, all federal bureaucrats are bound by a fairly strict code of ethics as Shaw et al. discuss.

On Feb. 3, [1993,] after years of pains-taking development by the Office of Government Ethics [OGE], the first comprehensive federal ethics regulations will go into effect.

The new rules cover seven areas of federal-employee behavior that carry the potential for ethical conflict: accepting gifts from sources outside the government; gift-giving between government employees; conflicting financial interests; impartiality in performing official duties; seeking other employment; misuse of a government position; and outside activities.

The regulations are a result of the Ethics Reform Act of 1989 and the ensuing President's Commission on Federal Ethics Law Reform. In the fall of 1990, President Bush signed an executive order requiring the ethics office to implement the commission's recommendations for standardized government-wide ethics rules.

More comprehensive and detailed than any previous federal ethical guidelines, the new regulations will apply uniformly to all employees. They will replace the more than 100 existing sets of ethical standards that various agencies have developed.

SOURCE: G. Jerry Shaw, William L. Bransford, and Richard A. Moore, "No Free Lunch?" *Government Executive* (January 1993). Reprinted with permission.

Critics, though, have said OGE has gone too far in its attempt to fore-stall every possible ethical dilemma, no matter how trivial or unlikely....

The OGE regulations include numerous hypothetical examples. We will use some of those examples to help clarify the intricate ethical puzzles addressed in the rules.

◆ Gifts from Outsiders

Alfred, a purchasing agent for a Department of Veterans Affairs hos-pital, routinely deals with representatives of pharmaceutical manufactur-ers who provide information about new company products. Because of his crowded calendar, Alfred has offered to meet with manufacturer repre-sentatives during his lunch hours Tuesdays through Thursdays. The rep-resentatives routinely arrive at Alfred's office bringing a sandwich and a soft drink for him. The value of such a lunch is about $6.

The purpose of the outside-gift rules is to prevent not only outright favoritism but also the appearance of bias toward certain members of the public. Only very modest, customary, personal or infrequent gifts are excluded from a general prohibition against accepting gifts. . . .

In general, employees may accept gifts having a market value of $20 or less per occasion, as long as the yearly sum of these gifts does not exceed $50.

Even if Alfred's lunches would not violate either cost limit, though, he cannot accept them. The pharmaceutical representatives who provide the food are what OGE calls "prohibited sources." They regularly seek official action by Alfred's agency, they do business with the agency, and their field is regulated and affected by agency action. It appears Alfred did not solicit or coerce the gifts, but he does receive them on a regular basis. This presents at least the appearance of impropriety. . . .

◆ Gifts between Employees

Brenda, a supervisory employee at the Agency for International De-velopment, has just been reassigned from Washington to Kabul, Afghani-stan. To say farewell, twelve of Brenda's employees have decided to take her out to lunch at the Khyber Repast. The employees will each pay for their own lunches and will split the cost of Brenda's meal; the exact amount each will contribute won't be known until Brenda orders. . . .

Brenda's case clearly involves a supervisory-subordinate relationship. In addition, the amount of the gift appears involuntary, since the subordi-nates are not free to choose exactly how much they will contribute. There is no personal relationship involved that might automatically render the gift appropriate.

At the same time, the occasion of Brenda's departure is infrequent (probably, in fact, unique), so that the difficulty encountered by Alfred in the above example is avoided here. (In fact, the new rules specifically exempt gifts given on occasions that terminate supervisory-subordinate relationships, such as retirements, resignations or transfers.) Also, the exact amount of each employee's contribution, although unknown until after Brenda orders, can be estimated. Besides, the decision to attend and contribute to the luncheon is voluntary. So Brenda and her subordinates may go out to lunch without violating the new rules. . . .

◆ Impartiality

Debra, an employee of the Department of Labor, is providing technical assistance in drafting occupational safety and health legislation that will affect all employers of five or more persons in the United States. Within the past year, just before her arrival at Labor, Debra stepped down as consultant to Mammoth Company, a large corporation that will incur additional costs if the proposed legislation is enacted.

The purpose of the impartiality rules is to prevent the appearance of impropriety in a federal employee's personal and business relationships outside the government, which might lead to bias or favoritism in the performance of official duties. . . .

Debra's consulting work for Mammoth within the past year is a "covered relationship" under the new regulation, since the fact that she has worked as a consultant for the company within the last year raises questions as to her impartiality.

However, although the legislation on which Debra is working will have an impact on Mammoth, it is not a specific matter affecting a specific company; it will have a general effect on many companies. Consequently, she need not be concerned that it will raise a question in the mind of a reasonable person concerning her impartiality. . . .

◆ Misuse of Position

Rhonda, a supervisor at the Department of the Treasury, is asked to provide a letter of recommendation for a personal friend who is seeking federal employment. Rhonda agrees to write the letter on office stationery, signed with her official title. Rhonda's secretary, also a friend of the prospective employee, offers to type the letter at home during non-duty hours.

The misuse rules deal with highly specific circumstances involving official titles, government property, nonpublic information and official time. Their purpose is to prevent unauthorized personal or private gain from government service or position. . . .

Under the new rules, Rhonda may use office stationery and sign with her title when drafting a letter of recommendation, as long as the person being recommended either has worked for the federal government or is seeking a federal job.

The rules do not allow a superior to direct a secretary to type personal correspondence on official time. However, the letter of recommendation in this case is not strictly personal, since what Rhonda, a federal supervisor, has to say about a prospective federal employee is of genuine interest to the government.

Even if the correspondence had been personal, Rhonda could accept her secretary's offer to type it at home if the offer was entirely voluntary. However, an appropriate level of compensation must be offered. Here, no compensation was offered. Rhonda probably should simply tell her secretary to type the letter at work on official time.

◆ Outside Activities

George, a career attorney with the Environmental Protection Agency, is paid to teach a course at a state college on the subject of environmental law. In addition, George decides to write a book on the history of the environmental movement in the United States, which includes references to the creation of EPA and its responsibilities. He receives royalties and other compensation for his book. . . .

Because George is a career employee teaching a general course at an accredited school, he may be paid for his services and will not be in violation of the congressionally imposed ban on the receipt of honoraria by government lecturers or authors. Similarly, George will not run into trouble with his book, as long as he avoids addressing specific programs or issues from his work.

For career employees, the new rules prohibit the following: being paid for speeches related to one's work other than those made for an accredited educational institution; writing articles or books for pay that address the specifics of an employee's work; revealing non-public information; misusing an official title as an advertisement or false endorsement by the government; and reproducing knowledge gleaned from government service for a profit. . . .

At first, some federal employees will no doubt be confused by the new rules and will keep agency ethics officials busy answering questions. Eventually, however, a working knowledge of the regulations will likely spread throughout the federal workforce. Only then will it become clear whether the level of detail they contain solves more problems than it creates.

TOWARD CRITICAL THINKING

1. Will the kinds of situational ethics rules discussed in Reading 41 improve the public's perceptions of the bureaucracy?

2. Is there really a need for a strict code of ethics for federal employees at the level discussed here?

THINKING ABOUT THE BUREAUCRACY

1. Does the very nature of the bureaucracy make it an unlikely target of successful reform? Can the American bureaucracy, in Vice President Al Gore Jr.'s term, be "reinvented?"

2. Anti-Federalists feared that the new national government would remove it from control of and accountability to the people. What kinds of solutions would Anti-Federalists offer to make the bureaucracy more responsive to the people?

3. What place does a bureaucracy have in a democratic political system?

CHAPTER 9

◆ ◆ ◆

The Judiciary

Contrary to Alexander Hamilton's original belief that the judiciary would be "the least dangerous" branch of government (Reading 42), in a little more than 200 years, the federal judiciary has gone from the least to the most dangerous branch of government, at least some critics would say. Since Chief Justice John Marshall claimed for the Court the right to review the constitutionality of the first acts of Congress and soon thereafter the laws of the states, the power and influence of the Supreme Court and other lower federal courts have grown (Reading 43).

Recognition of that influence has been an important reason for the tremendous increase in the number of cases appealed each year to the high court. As Karen O'Connor and John R. Hermann note in Reading 44, to help the Justices winnow down those appeals, clerks have become an important yet largely unrecognized part of the decision-making process of the Court.

Once the 7,000 or so petitions for review are screened by Supreme Court clerks, the Justices decide which cases to hear. As Ted Gest notes (Reading 46), although the Court is deciding fewer cases each year, decisions ultimately have important policy consequences. The Justices appeared mindful of this responsibility as they deliberate the issues that come before them, as Chief Justice William Rehnquist notes in his insider's account of "How the Supreme Court Arrives at Decisions" (Reading 45).

· *42* ·

Federalist No. 78

ALEXANDER HAMILTON

In defending the Framers' creation of an independent, unelected federal judiciary, Alexander Hamilton expressed his belief that the judiciary would be "the least dangerous" branch of government, having no control over the "sword" or the "purse"—sources of potential power for the other two branches of government. He also touches on the principle of judicial review, the authority of the judiciary to review the constitutionality of acts of the other two branches of government, since that principle was never explicitly included in the Constitution.

Whoever attentively considers the different departments of power must perceive, that, in a government in which they are separated from each other, the judiciary, from the nature of its functions, will always be the least dangerous to the political rights of the Constitution; because it will be least in a capacity to annoy or injure them. The Executive not only dispenses the honors, but holds the sword of the community. The legislature not only commands the purse, but prescribes the rules by which the duties and rights of every citizen are to be regulated. The judiciary, on the contrary, has no influence over either the sword or the purse; no direction either of the strength or of the wealth of the society; and can take no active resolution whatever. It may truly be said to have neither FORCE nor WILL, but merely judgment; and must ultimately depend upon the aid of the executive arm even for the efficacy of its judgments.

This simple view of the matter suggests several important consequences. It proves incontestably that the judiciary is beyond comparison the weakest of the three departments of power; that it can never attack with success either of the other two; and that all possible care is requisite to enable it to defend itself against their attacks. It equally proves that though individual oppression may now and then proceed from the courts of justice, the general liberty of the people can never be endangered from that quarter; I mean so long as the judiciary remains truly distinct from both the legislature and the Executive. For I agree, that "there is no liberty, if the power of judging be not separated from the legislative and executive powers." And it proves, in the last place, that as liberty can have nothing to fear from the judiciary alone, but would have every thing to fear from its union with either of the other departments; that as all the effects of such a union must ensue from a dependence of the former on the latter, notwithstanding a nominal and apparent separation; that as, from the natural feebleness of the judiciary it is in continual jeopardy of being overpowered, awed, or influenced by its coördinate branches; and that as nothing can contribute so much to its firmness and independence as permanency in office, this quality may therefore be justly regarded as an indispensable ingredient in its constitution, and, in a great measure, as the citadel of the public justice and the public security. . . .

Some perplexity respecting the rights of the courts to pronounce legislative acts void, because contrary to the constitution, has arisen from an imagination that the doctrine would imply a superiority of the judiciary to the legislative power. It is urged that the authority which can declare the acts of another void must necessarily be superior to the one whose acts may be declared void. As this doctrine is of great importance in all the American constitutions, a brief discussion of the ground on which it rests cannot be unacceptable.

There is no position which depends on clearer principles than that every act of a delegated authority, contrary to the tenor of the commission under which it is exercised, is void. No legislative act, therefore, contrary to the Constitution, can be valid. To deny this would be to affirm that the deputy is greater than his principal; that the servant is above his master; that the representatives of the people are superior to the people themselves; that men acting by virtue of powers may do not only what their powers authorize, but what they forbid.

BOX 9.1

The Early Supreme Court

JAMES STERLING YOUNG

. . .

The place intended for the Supreme Court on the north shore of the Tiber swamp remained unoccupied and undeveloped. Probably the expense of clearing the area, covered with brambles where it was not sunk in bogs, was considered unwarranted by the small size of the court establishment and the small volume of business handled by the judges during their brief stay in Washington each year. The Court made itself inconspicuous and served justice in the basement of the Capitol. "It is by no means a large or handsome apartment; and the lowness of the ceiling, and the circumstance of its being under ground, give a certain cellar-like aspect, which . . . tends to create . . . the impression of justice being done in a corner . . . while the business of legislation is carried on with . . . pride, pomp, and circumstance." The proceedings of the Court attracted, on the whole, only slight attention in the capital except when lawyers of wide repute were arguing cases, and "the moment they sat down, the whole audience arose, and broke up, as if the court had adjourn'd."

BOX 9.1   *(Continued)*

As to residential arrangements, the justices lived in the style of the broth-erhood they felt themselves to be, all rooming and taking meals at a common table in the same lodginghouse on Capitol Hill. "The Judges here live with perfect harmony . . . in the most frank and unaffected intimacy," wrote Justice Story. "We are all united as one. . . . We moot every question as we proceed, and . . . conferences at our lodgings often come to a very quick, and, I trust, a very accurate opinion, in a few hours." Not until 1845, apparently, did the judicial fraternity break up, with four justices going to live in one house and three in another.

The justices of the Supreme Court can have only a minor place in a study of the governmental community during the Jeffersonian era, despite the impor-tant legal precedents established by the Marshall court and despite their dra-matic but brief clashes with Congress and the President in the Chase impeachment and the Burr trial. In the sociological sense the justices were barely members of the Washington community, spending only two months of the year, usually, at the capital. The unanimity of their case decisions provides little food for political analysis, beyond the observation that their singlemind-edness on policy questions conformed to the fraternal character of their life style; and the justices were too secretive about their activities in their board-inghouse to afford insights about the group *in camera*. Moreover, they lived such a reclusive existence that the community record does little more than note their presence in the capital. They rarely received guests and they rarely ventured out of their lodgings after hours except to make obligatory appear-ances at official functions and to pay an annual courtesy call, en bloc, at the executive mansion. Just how reclusive their existence was is suggested by the fact that Justice Paterson traveled a full day in a stagecoach with Thomas Jefferson, neither man aware of the other's identity. Only after the journey's end did the Justice learn that his fellow traveler was the Secretary of State during his first term on the Court and the man who may even have been Vice President or President at the time of their encounter. Justice Story perhaps spoke for the group when he wrote: "I scarcely go to any places of pleasure or fashion . . . [and] have separated myself from all political meetings and asso-ciations. . . . since I am no longer a political man."

SOURCE: The Washington Community 1800–1828, James Sterling Young, 1966. © Columbia University Press, New York. Reprinted with permission of the publisher.

TOWARD CRITICAL THINKING

1. Was Hamilton correct in his assessment that the judiciary was the "least danger-ous" branch of government? (See also Box 9.1.) Thinking back to *Webster* v. *Reproductive Health Services* (Reading 13) or *Brown* v. *Board of Education of Topeka* (Reading 21), has Hamilton's assessment withstood the test of time?

2. Why did Hamilton believe that the people's liberty could never be endangered by the federal courts?

· 43 ·

Marbury v. Madison

5 U.S. 137 (1803)

At the close of his administration, recently defeated Federalist President John Adams appointed William Marbury to be a justice of the peace for the District of Columbia. The Federalist-controlled Senate confirmed Marbury and a host of other judicial appointments on March 3, 1801. But in the confusion over the change of administrations, several of the formal commissions were never delivered to the confirmed judges by the next day, when Thomas Jefferson, the new Democratic-Republican president, took office. Jefferson, infuriated by Adams's and the Federalist Senate's efforts to pack the national judiciary with Federalist judges, ordered his Secretary of State, James Madison, not to transmit the commissions. (Ironically, Adams's Secretary of State was John Marshall, who had been sworn in as Chief Justice of the Supreme Court in February but continued to serve as Secretary of State until the end of the Adams administration.) William Marbury and four others went to court to compel Madison to give them their commissions. One section of the Judiciary Act of 1789, which created the structure of the federal judicial system, authorized that actions compelling federal officials to do their job (called *writs of mandamus*) were to be filed with the U.S. Supreme Court. That's what Marbury did.

Before the Supreme Court could hear Marbury's challenge, the Democratic-Republican Congress abolished the 1802 term of the Court. It also threatened to impeach several Federalist judges, and Thomas Jefferson declared that he would not comply with any order from the Court directing him to give Marbury his commission.

Chief Justice John Marshall thus faced a terrible political dilemma: The Court, as clearly indicated in Reading 42 and Box 9.1, was viewed as a poor relation of the other two branches of government. If the Marshall Court issued an order that was not heeded, the Court's prestige would be further reduced. Marshall came up with a brilliant solution.[*] The actual holding or decision, of *Marbury* v. *Madison* was that the Supreme Court lacked the authority to render a decision in the case because it lacked jurisdiction. Writing for the Court, Marshall found that the section of the Judiciary Act of 1789 authorizing the Court to hear writs of mandamus was unconstitutional because the Court's original jurisdiction is specified in the U.S. Constitution. Thus, the Court's jurisdiction could be altered only by a constitutional amendment. In heading off a direct

---

[*] But see Robert Lowery Clinton, "Game Theory, Legal History, and the Origins of Judicial Review: A Revisionist Analysis of *Marbury* v. *Madison*," 38 *American Journal of Political Science* (May 1994): 285–302, in which he argues that both Marshall and Jefferson were rational actors in this political game.

conflict with Jefferson, however, Marshall used the case to offer a stern lecture to the president about the nature of the Court's authority and its right to review acts of Congress in order to determine their constitutionality. Alexander Hamilton addressed this issue in *Federalist No. 78*, but this was the first time that the Court actually reviewed an act of Congress and found it to be unconstitutional. The right of judicial review—the justification of which is set out by Marshall in *Marbury*—was eventually to be the basis of expanded judicial power in the federal system.

Opinion: Chief Justice John Marshall

Vote: 6–0 (only six justices sat on the Court at that time)

. . .

This original and supreme will organizes the government, and assigns to different departments their respective powers. It may either stop here, or establish certain limits not to be transcended by those departments.

The government of the United States is of the latter description. The powers of the legislature are defined and limited; and that those limits may not be mistaken, or forgotten, the constitution is written. To what purpose are powers limited, and to what purpose is that limitation committed to writing, if these limits may, at any time, be passed by those intended to be restrained? The distinction between a government with limited and unlimited powers is abolished, if those limits do not confine the persons on whom they are imposed, and if acts prohibited and acts allowed, are of equal obligation. It is a proposition too plain to be contested, that the constitution controls any legislative act repugnant to it; or, that the legislature may alter the constitution by an ordinary act.

Between these alternatives there is no middle ground. The constitution is either a superior paramount law, unchangeable by ordinary means, or it is on a level with ordinary legislative acts, and, like other acts, is alterable when the legislature shall please to alter it.

If the former part of the alternative be true, than a legislative act contrary to the constitution is not law: if the latter part be true, then written constitutions are absurd attempts, on the part of the people, to limit a power in its own nature illimitable.

Certainly all those who have framed written constitutions contemplate them as forming the fundamental and paramount law of the nation, and, consequently, the theory of every such government must be, that an act of the legislature, repugnant to the constitution, is void.

This theory is essentially attached to a written constitution, and, is consequently, to be considered, by this court, as one of the fundamental principles of our society. It is not therefore to be lost sight of in the further consideration of this subject.

If an act of the legislature, repugnant to the constitution, is void, does it, notwithstanding its invalidity, bind the courts, and oblige them to give it effect? Or, in other words, though it be not law, does it constitute a rule as operative as if it was a law? This would be to overthrow in fact what was established in theory; and would seem, at first view, an absurdity too gross to be insisted on. It shall, however, receive a more attentive consideration.

It is emphatically the province and duty of the judicial department to say what the law is. Those who apply the rule to particular cases, must of necessity expound and interpret that rule. If two laws conflict with each other, the courts must decide on the operation of each.

So if a law be in opposition to the constitution; if both the law and the constitution apply to a particular case, so that the court must either decide that case conformably to the law, disregarding the constitution; or conformably to the constitution, disregarding the law; the court must determine which of these conflicting rules governs the case. This is of the very essence of judicial duty.

If, then, the courts are to regard the constitution, and the constitution is superior to any ordinary act of the legislature, the constitution, and not such ordinary act, must govern the case to which they both apply.

Those, then, who controvert the principle that the constitution is to be considered, in court, as a paramount law, are reduced to the necessity of maintaining that courts must close their eyes on the constitution, and see only the law.

This doctrine would subvert the very foundation of all written constitutions. It would declare that an act which, according to the principles and theory of our government, is entirely void, is yet, in practice, completely obligatory. It would declare that if the legislature shall do what is expressly forbidden, such act, notwithstanding the express prohibition, is in reality effectual. It would be giving to the legislature a practical and real omnipotence, with the same breath which professes to restrict their powers within narrow limits. It is prescribing limits, and declaring that those limits may be passed at pleasure.

That it thus reduces to nothing what we have deemed the greatest improvement on political institutions, a written constitution, would of itself be sufficient, in America, where written constitutions have been viewed with so much reverence, for rejecting the construction. But the peculiar expressions of the constitution of the United States furnish additional arguments in favour of its rejection.

The judicial power of the United States is extended to all cases arising under the constitution.

Could it be the intention of those who gave this power, to say that in using it the constitution should not be looked into? That a case arising under the constitution should be decided without examining the instrument under which it arises?

This is too extravagant to be maintained. . . .

Why otherwise does it direct the judges to take an oath to support it? This oath certainly applies in an especial manner, to their conduct in their official character. How immoral to impose it on them, if they were to be used as the instruments, and the knowing instruments, for violating what they swear to support!

The oath of office, too, imposed by the legislature, is completely demonstrative of the legislative opinion on this subject. It is in these words: "I do solemnly swear that I will administer justice without respect to persons, and do equal right to the poor and to the rich; and that I will faithfully and impartially discharge all the duties incumbent on me as, according to the best of my abilities and understanding, agreeably to *the constitution* and laws of the United States."

Why does a judge swear to discharge his duties agreeably to the constitution of the United States, if that constitution forms no rule for his government? If it is closed upon him, and cannot be inspected by him? If such be the real state of things, this is worse than solemn mockery. To prescribe, or to take this oath, becomes equally a crime.

It is also not entirely unworthy of observation, that in declaring what shall be the *supreme* law of the land, the *constitution* itself is first mentioned; and not the laws of the United States generally, but those only which shall be made in *pursuance* of the constitution, have that rank.

Thus, the particular phraseology of the constitution of the United States confirms and strengthens the principle, supposed to be essential to all written constitutions, that a law repugnant to the constitution is void; and that courts, as well as other departments, are bound by that instrument.

TOWARD CRITICAL THINKING

1. Given Justice Marshall's role in failing to deliver the commissions, should he have excused himself from participating in the decision? Would his nonparticipation in this case have made any difference?

2. *Marbury* v. *Madison* and Marshall's articulation of justification for judicial review are considered by many commentators to be the most important decision ever rendered by the Court. Why? What reasons does Marshall offer for judicial review?

The Role of Clerks in the Work of the U.S. Supreme Court

KAREN O'CONNOR and JOHN R. HERMANN

To the general public, law clerks are a fairly invisible part of the Supreme Court, already the most mysterious branch of government. Not many Americans can name the Chief Justice of the United States Supreme Court let alone describe what goes on in the highest court in the land. As the number of appeals that reach the Supreme Court continues to increase—in 1994 more than 7,000 petitions were filed there for review—it often falls to the clerks, young men and women not long out of law school, to winnow down the cases for the Court's deliberations. In essence, clerks help the Court decide what to decide.

◆ Introduction

Law clerks are an important part of the United States Supreme Court's support staff. Since the first clerk was hired in the late nineteenth century, law clerks have provided invaluable assistance to the justices. While there continues to be much debate regarding the extent of the influence that clerks wield in the Court's decision-making, the clerks undeniably play a significant role in screening the more than 7,000 petitions for review filed each term.

◆ History

In 1882, Justice Horace Gray became the first justice to hire a law clerk, carrying over a practice he began while serving as Chief Justice of the Massachusetts Supreme Court. Gray's clerk's duties included cutting his hair as well as running personal errands, responsibilities quite different from those of today's clerks. In 1886, Congress specifically authorized each justice to hire a "stenographic clerk" and, following the lead of Justice Gray, four justices hired their own personal clerks, who often combined legal research with more "domestic" chores including paying their respective justices' bills.[1]

---

[1] Newland 1961, p. 311.

Gradually, other justices hired an additional personal assistant. For some, it was secretarial help; for others, legal assistance. In 1941, Justice John Marshall Harlan II became the first justice to have four assistants— two legal and two secretarial.[2]

While most clerks today serve one justice for one term, there have been some notable exceptions. Several clerks served for more than one justice and some clerks practically made a career of clerking. One clerk for Justice Pierce Butler, for example, served sixteen years and Justice Joseph McKenna's first clerk stayed with him for twelve years.[3] Today, these kinds of carry overs are rare. It is common, however, for clerks to stay on for a few extra weeks to help out their novice replacements.

Through the 1946 to 1969 terms, it became the norm for all of the associate justices to employ two clerks. By 1970, most began to hire three; by 1980, all but Justices Rehnquist, Stevens, and Stewart had four. This growth in clerks had many interesting ramifications on the Court. First, as noted by Richard A. Posner, "between 1969 and 1972—the period in which the justices each became entitled to a third law clerk— . . . the number of [Supreme Court] opinions increased by 50 percent and the number of words [in each decision] tripled."[4] After the justices were authorized to hire a fourth clerk in 1980, a mushrooming in the number of citations [to other cases] and footnotes in each case also occurred.[5] And, until recently, the number of cases decided annually by the Court in-creased as more help was available to the justices.

◆ Criteria for Clerk Selection

The historical increase in the number of clerks had a profound impact on the clerk selection process. Selection of clerks is solely left to the discretion of the individual justices. While it is an exceptionally important duty of any justice, no hard and fast guidelines for selection exist as they sift through the 250 to 300 applications that come to each chamber annually. But, according to David M. O'Brien, four basic considerations appear to be key factors in the selection process: the justices' preferences for (1) particular law schools; (2) particular geographic regions; (3) prior clerking experience on particular courts or for certain justices; and, (4) personal compatibility.[6]

---

[2] Ibid.

[3] O'Brien, 1990, p. 159.

[4] Posner, 1985, p. 114.

[5] Ibid.

[6] O'Brien 1990, pp. 159–160.

While the justices are more inclined to choose clerks from Ivy League law schools, there is now greater diversity in the clerk selection process. Many justices also tend to choose clerks from their alma maters [although all but Justice Stevens attended Ivy League law schools or Stanford]. Geography, too, has long figured in the clerk selection process, especially once the justices were entitled to more than one clerk. In Justice Hugo Black's case, for example, one former clerk noted that, "The perfect clerk for Justice Black was an Alabama boy who went to Alabama law school. If that wasn't possible, then someone from the South who went to a leading law school."[7]

While several clerks from the earlier period had not graduated from law school, clerks now are not only law school graduates but increasingly have been selected from the chambers of lower federal court judges. Certain justices appear to favor clerks who have served with certain lower federal court judges. The chambers of Judge Skelly Wright of the D.C. Circuit Court of Appeals, for example, have often served as a training ground for future Supreme Court clerks. For six years, beginning in 1979, all of his clerks "graduated" to United States Supreme Court clerkships.[8]

Personal compatibility is also highly valued. Justice James McReynolds often insisted that his clerks be single and not smoke or chew tobacco. His own personal behaviors often made it difficult for him to secure clerks.[9] Given the close working relationships between the justices and the clerks, personal compatibility is essential.

◆ Functions of Supreme Court Clerks

Considerable debate exists over the role that clerks play in the Court's decision-making and opinion writing process. More often than not, however, the clerks' responsibilities vary with the justice. Dean Acheson, a former clerk of Justice Louis Brandeis, for example, remarked that, "He wrote the opinion; I wrote the footnotes.[10] On the other end of the spectrum, Justice Frank Murphy's clerks were known to draft virtually all of the justice's written decisions.[11] Most of the clerk's responsibilities fall somewhere in between these two extremes.

---

[7] McGurn 1980, p. 100.

[8] Brigham 1987, p. 123.

[9] Newland 1961, p. 306.

[10] O'Brien 1990, p. 161

[11] O'Brien 1990, p. 160

There is no dispute, however, concerning the clerks' role in screening the more than 7,000 petitions that come before the Court each year for review. From that batch, it is the clerks who play a key role in winnowing those petitions to the approximately 80–100 cases that the justices ultimately decide to hear.

The practice of clerks reviewing petitions started during Chief Justice Charles Evan Hughes' tenure when he used his clerks to review *in forma pauperis* (*ifp*) petitions.[12] From Hughes to Warren, the chief justices' clerks were responsible for reviewing these petitions and preparing short memos about each case. These memos were then distributed to the chambers of the associate justices. Eventually, the growing number of *ifp* petitions became too burdensome for the chief justice's clerks and the petitions were divided among the chambers of the other justices for the clerks' review.[13]

In addition, prior to 1972, each justice relied on his clerks to prepare a memorandum about each petition for *certiorari*. In 1972, a "cert pool" was created whereby one clerk writes a single memorandum condensing the facts and arguments of the petitions (often referred to as a "pool memo") that is forwarded to all of the justices participating in the pool. The format for these memos is well established. Each case is identified along with information about the lower courts' decisions. A brief summary of the case is provided along with the germane facts. The contentions of each party are also presented and Section 5 of the memo includes a recommendation on the disposition of the case. These memos vary significantly in length, ranging from two to thirty pages.

◆ The Clerk Advantage

This experience with cert petitions is invaluable to clerks. It gives them the opportunity to see first hand what issues, facts, arguments, or forms of presentation styles appeal to their justices as well as the other eight. One former Rehnquist clerk, Robert Guiffra Jr., has gone so far as to author an article entitled "Teachings of the Rehnquist Court: The Chief's Former Clerk Offers a Dozen Tips for Presenting Cases to the Nine" (1991). While this article is undoubtedly helpful to practitioners, it cannot replace the first-hand experience gleaned from serving on the Court.

---

[12] *In forma pauperis* petitions are appeals that come before the Supreme Court from litigants who cannot afford to pay the Court costs.

[13] O'Brien 1990, pp. 164–165

This insider knowledge probably endows clerks with the kind of "repeat player" status that only long years of participation and practice afford to others. Law clerks clearly attempt to exploit this advantage. Karen O'Connor and John R. Hermann, for example, find that more than half of the clerks serving during the 1958–1985 terms have later appeared as a party or filed an *amicus curiae* (friend of the Court) brief at least one time before the Court.[14]

Clerks may be well suited to file briefs at the Court because they enjoy unique knowledge of the internal dynamics of the justices' and Court's decision-making. The Court, itself, appears well aware of this clerk advantage. Court rules dictate that former clerks cannot appear before the Court for two years after they leave.

Law firms also recognize and exploit the clerk connection. They offer clerks generous bonuses for their experience—as much as $35,000 on top of an $80,000 salary.[15] High-powered firms perceive—whether correctly or not—that the clerk experience can give their clients a distinct advantage before the nation's highest Court. And, having former clerks on their staff increases law firms' prestige as evidenced by the yearly competition to sign clerks that rivals the NBA draft.

◆ Conclusion

When Justice Horace Gray hired the Court's first law clerk in 1882, he probably did not realize that he was beginning a rich clerk tradition. Law clerks today are a major part of the Court's support staff. In selecting their clerks, the justices usually base their decisions on four central criteria: the justices' preferences for particular law schools, particular geographic regions, prior clerking experience on particular courts or with certain justices, and personal compatibility.

While speculation abounds about how much the justices rely on their clerks or whether clerks exercise too much power in the decision-making process, there is little controversy regarding the clerks' important role in screening the more than 7,000 *certiorari* petitions that are filed each term. From their unique experiences as clerks, they later attempt to exploit this advantage by filing briefs before the Court. The clerks understand the internal decision-making processes of the justices as well as the Court. With this in mind, both government and private law firms actively recruit clerks to act later as "players" before the Court. Clerks become part of an elite Supreme Court community.

---

[14] O'Connor and Hermann 1993, p. 11.
[15] Conlin 1990.

◆ Sources

Brigham, John. 1987. *The Cult of the Court.* Philadelphia: Temple University Press.

Conlin, Jennifer. 1990. "Decisions, Decisions." *The Washingtonian,* June, pp. 65–73.

Guiffra, Robert Jr. 1991. "Teachings of the Rehnquist Court." *The Recorder,* October 17, LEXIS.

McGurn, Barrett. 1980. "Law Clerks—A Professional Elite." *1980 Yearbook of the Supreme Court Historical Society.*

Newland, Chester A. 1961. "Personal Assistants to Supreme Court Justices: The Law Clerks." 40 *Oregon Law Review:* 299–317.

O'Brien, David M. 1990. *Storm Center.* New York: W.W. Norton.

O'Connor, Karen and John R. Hermann. 1993. "The Clerk Connection: A History and Analysis of Clerk Participation Before the U.S. Supreme Court." Paper delivered at the 1993 annual meeting of the Midwest Political Science Association.

Posner, Richard A. 1985. *The Federal Courts: Crisis and Reform.* Cambridge, MA: Harvard University Press.

TOWARD CRITICAL THINKING

1. What are the four basic considerations that most justices seem to use when selecting clerks? Do you think the close ties that most clerks develop with their respective justices give them an advantage if they later appear before the Court to argue cases?

2. Some scholars and politicians argue that the Supreme Court—unelected by the people—has too much power. Can the same criticism be levied at clerks?

· 45 ·

How the Supreme Court Arrives at Decisions

WILLIAM H. REHNQUIST

Once cases are accepted for review, they are argued orally before the full Court. The Justices then meet in secret to discuss their views on the case and the issues it presents. Few minds are changed at this stage. Thus, according to Chief Justice Rehnquist, the conference stage is perhaps the most important stage because initial votes are taken there. Based on that vote, either the Chief Justice (if he is in the majority) or, if he is in the minority, the most senior justice in the majority is determined so that the writing of the opinion can be assigned.

Potter Stewart, with whom it was my privilege to sit as a member of the Court for nearly ten years, passed on to me more than one bit of sound advice in the years when I was the junior member of the Court. I remember his saying that he thought he would never know more about a case than when he left the bench after hearing it orally argued, and I have found that his statement also holds true for me. When one thinks of the important ramifications that some of the constitutional decisions of the Supreme Court have, it seems that one could never know as much as he ought to know about how to cast his vote in a case. But true as this is, each member of the Court must cast votes in about one hundred and fifty cases decided on the merits each year, and there must come a time when pondering one's own views must cease, and deliberation with one's colleagues and voting must begin.

That time is each Wednesday afternoon after we get off the bench for those cases argued on Monday, and Friday for those cases argued on Tuesday and Wednesday. During most of the year the Friday conferences begin at 9:30 A.M., but after the conclusion of oral arguments they begin at 10:00 A.M. because there are no longer argued cases as well as petitions for certiorari to be discussed. A buzzer sounds—or, to put it more accurately, is supposed to sound—in each of the nine chambers five minutes before the time for conference, and the nine members of the Court then

SOURCE: William H. Rehnquist, *The Supreme Court at Work: Deciding the Cases* (New York: William Morrow and Co., 1987), pp. 287–303. Reprinted by permission.

congregate in the Court's conference room next to the chambers of the Chief Justice. We all shake hands with one another when we come in, and our vote sheets and whatever other material we wish to have are at our places at the conference table. Seating at this long, rectangular table is strictly by seniority. . . .

To one and all familiar with the decision-making process in other governmental institutions, the most striking thing about our Court's conference is that only the nine justices are present. There are no law clerks, no secretaries, no staff assistants, no outside personnel of any kind. If one of the messengers from the Marshal's Office who guard the door of the conference knocks on the door to indicate that there is a message for one of the justices, the junior justice opens the door and delivers the message. The junior justice is also responsible for dictating to the staff of the clerk's office at the close of the conference the text of the orders that will appear on the Court's order list issued on the Monday following the conference. . . .

In discussing cases that have been argued, the Chief Justice begins by reviewing the facts and the decision of the lower court, outlining his understanding of the applicable case law, and indicating either that he votes to affirm the decision of the lower court or to reverse it. The discussion then proceeds to Justice Brennan and in turn down the line to Justice Scalia. For many years there has circulated a tale that although the discussion in conference proceeds in order from the Chief Justice to the junior justice, the voting actually begins with the junior justice and proceeds back to the Chief Justice in order of seniority. I can testify that, at least during my fifteen years on the Court, this tale is very much of a myth; I don't believe I have ever seen it happen at any of the conferences that I have attended.

The time taken in discussion of a particular case by each justice will naturally vary with the complexity of the case and the nature of the discussion which has preceded his. The Chief Justice, going first as he does, takes more time than any one associate in a typical case, because he feels called upon to go into greater detail as to the facts and the lower-court holding than do those who come after him. Justice Brennan, who frequently disagrees with me (and also disagreed with Chief Justice Burger) in important constitutional cases, and is therefore the first to state the view of the law with which he agrees, also frequently takes more time than the other associates. The truth is that there simply are not nine different points of view in even the most complex and difficult case, and all of us feel impelled to a greater or lesser degree to try to reach some consensus that can be embodied in a written opinion that will command the support of at least a majority of the members of the Court. The lack of anything that is both previously unsaid, relevant, and sensible is apt to be frustrating to those far down the line of discussion, but this is one of the prices exacted by the seniority system. With occasional exceptions, each justice begins and ends his part of the discussion without interruption from his colleagues, and in the great majority of cases by the time Justice Scalia is finished with his discussion, it will be evident that a majority of the Court has agreed upon a basis for either affirming or reversing the decision of the lower court in the case under discussion. . . .

Each member of the Court has done such work as he deems necessary to arrive at his own views before coming into conference; it is not a bull session in which off-the-cuff reactions are traded, but instead a discussion in which very considered views are stated. We are all working with the same materials, dealing with the same briefs, the same cases, and have heard the same oral argument; unlikely as it may seem to the brand-new justice, the point that he seizes upon has probably been considered by some of the others and they have not found it persuasive. It is not as if we were trying to find a formula for squaring the circle, and all of those preceding the junior justice had bumblingly admitted their inability to find the formula; then suddenly the latter solves the riddle, and the others cry "Eureka! He has found it." The law is at best an inexact science, and the cases our Court takes to decide are frequently ones upon which able judges in lower courts have disagreed. There simply is no demonstrably "right" answer to the question involved in many of our difficult cases. . . .

The upshot of the conference discussion of a case will, of course, vary in its precision and detail. If a case is a relatively simple one, with only one real legal issue in it, it will generally be very clear where each member of the Court stands on that issue. But many of the cases that we decide are complex ones, with several interrelated issues, and it is simply not possible in the format of the conference to have nine people answering either yes or no to a series of difficult questions about constitutional law. One justice may quite logically believe that a negative answer to the very first of several questions makes it unnecessary to decide the subsequent ones, and having answered the first one in the negative will say no more. But if a majority answers the first question in the affirmative, then the Court's opinion will have to go on and discuss the other questions. Whether or not the first justice agrees with the majority on these other issues may not be clear from the conference discussion. The comment is frequently heard during the course of a discussion that "some things will have to be worked out in the writing" and this is very true in a number of cases. Oral discussion of a complex case will usually give the broad outlines of each justice's position, but it is simply not adequate to fine-tune the various positions in the way that the written opinion for the majority of the Court, and the dissenting opinions, eventually will. The broad outlines emerge from the conference discussion, but often not the refinements. . . .

. . . My sixteen years on the Court have convinced me that the true purpose of the conference discussion of argued cases is not to persuade one's colleagues through impassioned advocacy to alter their views, but instead by hearing each justice express his own views to determine therefrom the view of the majority of the Court. This is not to say that minds are never changed in conference; they certainly are. But it is very much the exception, and not the rule, and if one gives some thought to the matter this should come as no surprise. . . .

During a given two-week session of oral argument, we will have heard twenty-four cases. By the Friday of the second week we will have conferred about all of them. Now the time comes for assignment to the various members of the Court of the task of preparing written opinions to support the result reached by the majority.

In every case in which the Chief Justice votes with the majority, he assigns the case; where the Chief Justice has been in the minority at conference, the senior associate justice in the majority assigns the case. Although one would not know it from reading the press coverage of the Court's work, the Court is unanimous in a good number of its opinions, and these of course are assigned by the Chief Justice. Since the odds of his being in a minority of one or two are mathematically small, he assigns the great majority of cases in which there is disagreement within the Court but which are not decided by a close vote. When the conference vote produces three or even four dissents from the majority view, the odds of course increase that the Chief Justice will be one of the dissenters; I have during my tenure received assignments not only from the Chief Justice, but from Justice Douglas, Justice Brennan, Justice White, and Justice Marshall. Sometimes the assignments come around during the weekend after the second week of oral argument, but sometimes they are delayed until early the following week. Since there are nine candidates to write twenty-four opinions, the law of averages again suggests that each chambers will ordinarily receive three assignments.

I know from the time during which I was an associate justice how important the assignment of the cases is to each member of the Court. The signed opinions produced by each justice are to a very large extent the only visible record of his work on the Court, and the office offers no greater reward than the opportunity to author an opinion on an important point of constitutional law. When I was an associate justice I eagerly awaited the assignments, and I think that my law clerks awaited them more eagerly than I did. Law clerks serve for only one year, and if I was assigned seventeen or eighteen opinions during the course of the year, each of the law clerks would have an opportunity to work on five or six opinions. My law clerks were always in high hopes that one of the cases on which they had worked or in which they were really interested and regarded as very important would be assigned to me. Unfortunately, they were frequently disappointed in this respect, because not every one of the twenty-four cases argued during a two-week term is both interesting and important.

Now that I am Chief Justice, of course, I have the responsibility for assigning the writing of opinions for the Court in cases where I have voted with the majority. . . .

. . . The Chief Justice is expected to retain for himself some opinions that he regards as of great significance, but he is also expected to pass around to his colleagues some of this kind of opinion. . . .

[After I assign opinions,] I sit down with the law clerk who is now responsible for the case, and go over my conference notes with him. My conference notes are unfortunately not as good as they should be because my handwriting, always poor, has with advancing age become almost indecipherable to almost anyone but me. But the combination of the notes and my recollection of what was said at conference generally proves an adequate basis for discussion between me and the law clerk of the views expressed by the majority at conference, and of the way in which an opinion supporting the result reached by the majority can be drafted. After this discussion, I ask the law clerk to prepare a first draft of a Court opinion, and to have it for me in ten days or two weeks. . . .

When I receive a rough draft of a Court opinion from a law clerk, I read it over, and to the extent necessary go back and again read the opinion of the lower court and selected parts of the parties' briefs. The drafts I get during the first part of the term from the law clerks require more revision and editing than the ones later in the term, after the law clerks are more used to my views and my approach to writing. I go through the draft with a view to shortening it, simplifying it, and clarifying it. A good law clerk will include in the draft things that he might feel could be left out, simply to give me the option of making that decision. Law clerks also have been exposed to so much "legal writing" on law reviews and elsewhere that their prose tends to stress accuracy at the expense of brevity and clarity. . . .

. . . Occasionally, but not often, a draft submitted by a law clerk will seem to me to have simply missed a major point I think necessary to support the conclusion reached by the majority at conference; I will of course rewrite the draft to include that point.

The practice of assigning the task of preparing first drafts of Court opinions to law clerks who are usually just one or two years out of law school may undoubtedly and with some reason cause raised eyebrows in the legal profession and outside of it. Here is the Supreme Court of the United States, picking and choosing with great care one hundred and fifty of the most significant cases out of the four or five thousand presented to it each year, and the opinion in the case is drafted by a law clerk!* I think the practice is entirely proper: The justice must retain for himself control not merely of the outcome of the case, but of the explanation for the outcome, and I do not believe this practice sacrifices either.

I hope it is clear from my explanation of the way that opinions are drafted in my chambers that the law clerk is not simply turned loose on an important legal question to draft an opinion embodying the reasoning and the result favored by the law clerk. Quite the contrary is the case. The law clerk is given, as best I can, a summary of the conference discussion, a description of the result reached by the majority in that discussion, and my views as to how a written opinion can best be prepared embodying that reasoning. The law clerk is not off on a frolic of his own, but is instead engaged in a highly structured task which has been largely mapped out for him by the conference discussion and my suggestions to him.

This is not to say that the clerk who prepares a first draft does not have a very considerable responsibility in the matter. The discussion in conference has been entirely oral, and as I have previously indicated, nine oral statements of position suffice to convey the broad outlines of the views of the justices but do not invariably settle exactly how the opinion will be reasoned through. . . .

When I have finished my revisions of the draft opinion, I return it to the law clerk, and the law clerk then refines and on occasion may suggest additional revisions. We then send the finished product to the printer, and in short order get back printed copies with the correct formal heading for the opinion.

When the Supreme Court first began to hand down written opinions in the last decade of the eighteenth century, the author of the opinion was designated, for example, "Cushing, Justice." This style was followed until the February 1820 term of the Court when it was replaced by the form, for example, "Mr. Justice Johnson" as the author of the opinion. This style endured for more than one hundred and fifty years, indeed until a year or two before Justice O'Connor was appointed to the Court in 1981. In 1980 Justice White with great prescience suggested to the conference that since in the very near future a woman justice was bound to be appointed, we ought to avoid the embarrassment of having to change the style of desig-

---

* The Court now receives more petitions but hears fewer cases than the numbers indicated by the Chief Justice.—Author.

nating the author of the opinion at that time by doing it before the event. The conference was in entire agreement, and very shortly thereafter, without any explanation, the manner of designating the author of the opinion became simply, for example, "Justice Brennan." . . .

At any rate, [after we] circulate [drafts] to the other chambers, . . . we wait anxiously to see what the reaction of the other justices will be, especially those justices who voted with the majority at conference. If a justice agrees with the draft and has no criticisms or suggestions, he will simply send a letter saying something such as "Please join me in your opinion in this case." If a justice agrees with the general import of the draft, but wishes changes to be made in it before joining, a letter to that effect will be sent, and the writer of the opinion will, if possible, accommodate the suggestions. The willingness to accommodate on the part of the author of the opinion is often directly proportional to the number of votes supporting the majority result at conference; if there were only five justices at conference voting to affirm the decision of the lower court, and one of those five wishes significant changes to be made in the draft, the opinion writer is under considerable pressure to work out something that will satisfy the critic, in order to obtain five votes for the opinion. . . .

But if the result at conference was reached by a unanimous or a lopsided vote, a critic who wishes substantial changes in the opinion has less leverage. I willingly accept relatively minor suggestions for change in emphasis or deletion of language that I do not regard as critical, but resist where possible substantial changes with which I do not agree. Often much effort is expended in negotiating these changes, and it is usually effort well spent in a desire to agree upon a single opinion that will command the assent of a majority of the justices.

The senior justice among those who disagreed with the result reached by the majority at conference usually undertakes to assign the preparation of the dissenting opinion in the case if there is to be one. In the past it was a common practice for justices who disagreed with the opinion of the Court simply to note their dissent from the opinion without more ado, but this practice is very rare today. The justice who will write the dissent notifies the author of the opinion and the other justices of his intention to prepare a dissent, and will circulate that opinion in due course. Perhaps it would be a more rational system if, in a case where a dissent is being prepared, all of those, except the opinion writer, who voted with the majority at conference, as well as those who dissented, would await the circulation of the dissent, but in most cases this practice is not followed. One reason for the current practice is probably that for one reason or another dissents are usually circulated weeks, and often months, after the majority opinion is circulated. A justice who was doubtful as to his vote at conference, or who has reservations about the draft of the Court opinion, may tell the author that he intends to await the dissent before deciding which opinion to join. But this is the exception, not the rule; ordinarily those justices who voted with the majority at conference, if they are satisfied with the proposed Court opinion, will join it without waiting for the circulation of the dissent.

At our Friday conferences the first order of business is the decision as to what opinions are ready to be handed down. The Chief Justice goes in order, beginning with Justice Scalia, and will ask him if any of his opinions are ready to be handed down. If all of the votes are in in a case where he has authored the draft of the Court's opinion, he will so advise the conference, and unless there is some objection, his opinion for the Court will be handed down at one of the sittings of the Court the following week. On that day, the Clerk's Office will have available at 10:00 A.M. for anyone who wishes it copies of Justice Scalia's opinion in that particular case. Meanwhile, the first order of business after the Court goes on the bench will be the announcement by Justice Scalia of his opinion from the bench. He will describe the case, summarize the reasoning of the Court, announce the result, and announce whatever separate or dissenting opinions have been filed. The decision-making process has now run full circle: A case in which certiorari was granted somewhere from six months to a year ago has been briefed, orally argued, and now finally decided by the Supreme Court of the United States.

TOWARD CRITICAL THINKING

1. Why is the assignment of opinion writing such an important part of the Court's decision-making processes?

2. Do you think that unanimous decisions should have greater weight of law than decisions that produce sharp divisions on the Court, such as the *Bakke* case? (See Reading 25.)

· 46 ·

The Court
Deciding Less, Writing More

TED GEST

Over the years the U.S. Supreme Court has played a crucial role in deciding major social and political dilemmas of our time. But in the last few terms, the Court—often badly divided when it does decide cases—is taking fewer and fewer cases to review in spite of the fact that the number of petitions filed with it each year continues to grow. According to many legal scholars, this has left major legal issues unsettled and has created confusion among both lower courts and lawyers. Some blame this on the quality of the jurists themselves. Has the political hoopla that has surrounded the confirmation process of several recent nominees to the Court produced lessor justices than have sat on the high court in the past?

To most Americans, the Supreme Court is a revered institution that "decides the most significant questions of our times." . . . Indeed, in earlier years the court played a pre-eminent role in resolving delicate issues of privacy, race and crime. Yet, a close look at its recent work shows disturbing and puzzling trends: Not only are the justices writing many fewer opinions—a projected 108 in the term ending this month compared with 151 a decade ago—but, in the view of those who follow the court closely, the quality of its work is mediocre. A *U.S. News & World Report* survey completed by 60 academic experts, regular practitioners before the court and federal judges rated the court under William Rehnquist, chief justice since 1986, average or below in key measures of quality.

As the term winds down, the court's agenda seems small compared with the era between 1953 and 1986, when Earl Warren and Warren Burger presided. "It is striking that there are so few cases of great public importance," says Lloyd Cutler, a prominent Washington lawyer. The court's unwillingness to settle many disputes leaves much legal doctrine unsettled and creates inequities based on geography. And many litigants

---

SOURCE: "The Court: Deciding Less, Writing More," *U.S. News and World Report,* 114:25 (June 28, 1993):24–28. Copyright, June 28,1993, U.S. News and World Report.

who might have expected a generation ago that the court would resolve issues involving their basic rights can no longer be so sure the nation's highest tribunal will hear them. The justices behave as if they are "punching a time clock," says law Prof. Thomas Merrill of Northwestern University, a former law clerk there. "They are disinclined to hear cases and many they do decide are handled in a perfunctory manner."

That view was echoed in the *U.S. News* survey, which solicited a wide range of conservative and liberal views. Experts were asked to compare the Rehnquist, Burger and Warren courts and to assess the quality of the current justices' work. Asked to rate courts of different eras in deciding the "most significant legal issues in a timely fashion," respondents ranked Rehnquist's court far below the Warren tribunal.

This is a sharp contrast from a decade ago, when justices and scholars were bemoaning how the court was drowning in cases. With the problem seemingly destined to worsen, critics suggested a new national court to decide important issues the justices were unable to hear. The idea faded as the court started cutting down on its own. The docket may shrink further after Byron White retires from the court. He was often the lone voice beseeching his colleagues to expand the docket. Usually, his pleas came to no avail.

The justices offer no public explanations of why their output has plummeted, but several factors are at work. Philosophically, the conservatives who have dominated the court in recent years want to limit its role in American life. With two-thirds of the lower-court judges named by conservative presidents, the justices see fewer cases they want to overturn. In fact, lower-court rulings that favor persons charging civil-rights violations make up the largest single category of cases that has disappeared from the high court's docket, says a study by law Prof. Arthur Hellman of the University of Pittsburgh.

◆ Real losers

But the main losers as the docket shrivels are those disputing vital, if less visible, issues like taxes, pensions, federal benefits and maritime law. Such cases end up being decided by the eleven federal appeals courts, whose views on identical issues often conflict. . . .

◆ Unfairness

In criminal cases, courts often issue conflicting interpretations of sentencing guidelines. Different results on issues like whether possessing a gun amounts to a violent crime can vary a term by ten years. Criminal-law expert Fred Bennett of Catholic University says the Supreme Court "should be more vigilant when years of people's liberty are at stake." In general, experts say it is unfair when chances of winning depend on litigants' locations. "In a well-run system, these cases would not be left unresolved," says Pittsburgh's Hellman, who is conducting a federal study of the problem.

Paradoxically, as its caseload has dropped, the court's verbosity has multiplied. It is deciding half as many cases each year as in 1940 with twice as many pages of opinions. John Frank, a Phoenix constitutional-law expert who calculates that the current page count of all court rulings runs to 3,000 annually, contends that the outpouring of verbiage lowers the overall quality of the court's work product. Experts surveyed by *U.S. News* agreed, rating Rehnquist's tribunal below its immediate predecessors in such qualities as the analysis of legal issues and the accurate expression of legal doctrine.

When the justices disagree among themselves, it is typical for them to issue separate opinions noting dissent from sections, paragraphs and even sentences of their colleagues' work. Last week, David Souter issued a ruling in a pension case in which Antonin Scalia refused to join "Part III–B–1–b," and Sandra Day O'Connor did not "join the sentence to which [footnote] 29 is attached." A handful of observers praise the court for stating precisely where each member stands rather than papering over differences. But most analysts agree with Prof. Eugene Gressman of Seton Hall University, co-author of a widely used text on the court, who calls the "ungodly fractured opinions" a "terrible way of making decisions that makes it very difficult to figure out the result."

The justices are bound to disagree on controversial questions of abortion, church-state separation and affirmative action. However, they also do a poor job of resolving less visible issues that affect large numbers of citizens. A few recent examples:

> **Federal programs.** Last year, the court threw out an appeal charging that Illinois was mishandling a federal effort to place children in foster care. A footnote by Rehnquist cast doubt on a wide range of challenges to programs involving children, the elderly and disabled, setting off a flurry of expensive litigation nationwide over which cases could be pursued. Because the court had not heard arguments on that issue in the Illinois case, says Dean John Kramer of Tulane School of Law, even some of the justices "did not understand what was at stake." Now, both social-reform advocates and state officials are lobbying Congress to negate the effects of the ruling. . . .

> **Taxes.** Critics cite murky opinions on tax issues as another court shortcoming. In one infamous example last January, the court denied a Virginia anesthesiologist's claim for a deduction for expenses of business done at his home. Some experts gripe that the justices are

oblivious to the way small businesses operate; others say the fault lies with tax-law writers. In any case, it was impossible to draw firm conclusions from the case about who is eligible for the deduction. "The ruling muddied the waters so much that it is difficult to advise clients," says David Sokolow, the doctor's attorney.

In another tax issue bedeviling the court, the justices ruled last week that Virginia must refund improper taxes on federal workers' retirement benefits. But dissenter O'Connor complained that the court's "hopelessly muddled" doctrines will introduce "uncertainty and disorder into this already chaotic area."

◆ Consensus: Mediocre

Why does the court so often fall short? Few say it aloud for fear of alienating powerful jurists, but the consensus is that they are a mediocre bunch. Many think only Justice Antonin Scalia, an ex-professor known for clear writing and bold opinions, ranks close to previous court giants. The increasing reliance by justices on young law clerks is blamed for much of the problem. In simpler times, justices did most of their own work. But as more petitions have poured into the court for review, clerks have done most screening of incoming cases and writing of first-opinion drafts. Although typically the top graduates of elite law schools, they are inexperienced in the real world of litigation. And with only one year to make a mark, many would rather spend time on high-profile issues than slog through nuances of tax law. "They want to be able to say they wrote critical memos in exciting cases," says court expert Karen O'Connor of Emory University. Given the shorter docket, she says, clerks write longer drafts and justices say, "If they went to all that trouble, I'll leave in their material." ...

The splintering of opinions may be reduced by the likely ascendancy of Ginsburg. Last year, she declared that "overindulgence in individualistic judging is counterproductive" and called for courts to function more as collegial bodies that stress "retreat, accommodation and compromise." Yet she would be only one member of an institution that operates as nine fiercely independent law offices. Change will come only slowly to a court that lacks coherence on pressing legal issues.

TOWARD CRITICAL THINKING

1. What are some reasons to explain the decline in the number of cases decided by the Court?

2. Should the Court have an obligation to accept cases that have produced different results in various lower courts or should major policy disputes involving statutory interpretation be a job for the Congress?

THINKING ABOUT THE JUDICIARY

1. Much has been written about whether judges should interpret the Constitution as it was meant in 1789. Do you agree or disagree?

2. What kind of checks exist on a too-powerful or too-activist judiciary? Should there be more?

3. Much of what the president does in public sessions of Congress are televised, and most committee meetings are open. Why does the Supreme Court shroud its activities in secrecy?

❖ PART THREE ❖

Political Behavior and the Political Processes of Government

In the Constitution, the Framers set out the basic shape and form of the new government, but they could not foresee how government would actually work and how the U.S. system of democracy would function. The framework of government was there, but how would "the people" act and react? These concerns are the focus of Part III.

The topics covered in the four chapters in Part III, "Public Opinion," "Political Parties and Interest Groups," "Campaigns, Elections, and Voting," and "The Media," although not formal institutions of government, play important roles in the governmental system. They also are as interrelated to each other as are Congress, the president, and the judiciary, and they frequently even function as unofficial checks on each other. Public opinion, for example, not only acts as a check on legislators and other government officials, but it also affects elections and how people vote. Similarly, parties and interest groups have been greatly affected by the emerging technologies—especially in the media—that have changed the way they work to attract supporters. And as Chapter 13 reveals, the media are playing an increasingly important and controversial role in the governmental process. The growth in talk radio and talk TV has allowed presidents, other elected officials, and candidates to take their cases directly to the people, bypassing more traditional forms of politicking.

These changes have resulted in profound changes in political life never confronted by the Framers. As you read the chapters in Part III, consider whether you think these changes are for the good or bad.

"Public Opinion" is the focus of Chapter 10. What is public opinion? How does the public come to express its views on the workings of government? What effect does polling have on public opinion? These are just some of the questions posed in this chapter.

"Political Parties and Interest Groups" are the focus of Chapter 11. In spite of James Madison's warnings about "factions" contained in *Federalist No. 10* (Reading 52), political cleavages and ideological differences within the populace soon led to the creation of political parties. Over the years, the names and basic themes of the dominant political parties in our two-party system have changed. Thus, why parties and interest groups form and what they do are key issues addressed in this chapter.

"Campaigns, Elections, and Voting" are explored in Chapter 12. As Alexander Hamilton noted in *Federalist No. 22,* elections are the linchpin of any democracy. The nature of campaigns and elections has changed dramatically since the early days of the republic, as has the nature of the electorate, campaigns, and elections.

"The Media," Chapter 13, concludes Part III. The press and, later, other forms of media have played major roles in the political process. *The Federalist Papers* were published in newspapers throughout the United States to garner support for the new Constitution and its federal form of government. Years later, Abraham Lincoln, who presided over the Union during the Civil War, was to refer to Harriet Beecher Stowe, the author of *Uncle Tom's Cabin,* as the "little woman who started the big war." The power of the pen, and later of the airwaves, to sway public opinion, to organize people into political parties and interest groups, and to affect campaigns, elections, and voting continues to grow.

As you read the chapters in Part III, keep in mind these questions:

1. How pertinent do the concerns of the authors of *The Federalist Papers* continue to be?

2. How do each of the topics covered in these chapters ("Public Opinion"; "Political Parties and Interest Groups"; "Campaigns, Elections, and Voting"; and "The Media") relate to and influence each other?

3. What changes, if any, do you think are needed in the political processes of government?

CHAPTER 10

◆ ◆ ◆

Public Opinion

Public opinion, at first blush, appears to be fairly straightforward. What does the public think about X, Y, or Z? Or, in the context of American politics, what does the public, or some subset of the public (such as registered voters, likely voters, actual voters, women, African Americans, the young, the retired) feel or think about a candidate, issue, or set of issues? But defining and then measuring public opinion can be very tricky.

As James Madison pointed out in *Federalist No. 49* (Reading 47), "public passions" can be moved and motivated with important (and not always good) consequences for elected leaders and governmental actions. Thus, what Robert Nisbet defines as "popular opinion"—the widely fluctuating changes in public support for governmental policies that occur on account of the "transitory thoughts that citizens have about topical events,"* are quite different from more enduring, long lasting, deeply held political beliefs. And as distinguished political scientist V. O. Key Jr. notes in Reading 48, "[T]o speak with precision of public opinion is a task not unlike coming to grips with the Holy Ghost."

But as the volatile public opinion polls taken in the 1992 presidential election indicate (or in the aftermath of the hearings on the nomination of Clarence Thomas to the Supreme Court indicate) (see Box 10.2), public opinion can shift quickly. After all, if public opinion was not subject to change, and quick change at that, presidential elections would be much easier to predict for both professional pollsters and political scientists.

The study of public opinion has important consequences in our democratic system. Says political scientist Benjamin Ginsburg, polls not only make pollsters more important in the democratic process, but they also decrease the influence of traditional pressure groups. In Reading 49 he notes that, in spite of the problems inherent in defining public opinion underscored by Key, in any democracy, elected officials, in particular, must listen to public opinion. And today, says Ginsburg, pollsters can provide. a scientific "read" of the pulse of the public other than the rantings of group leaders.

---

*Robert Nisbet, "Popular Opinion versus Public Opinion," *Public Interest,* 1975, p. 167.

The meaning of polls, however, isn't always clear to policy makers or the public. In Box 10.1, journalist Paula Wade provides a concise introduction to polls and how to read them. Pollsters themselves don't always get it right, as Michael W. Traugott highlights in Reading 50, where he discusses the pitfalls of polling that occurred during the 1992 elections. From exit to tracking polls, he questions not only the accuracy of these devices, but also the reporting of those polls *and* their possible effects on the presidential election. In essence, he presents the classic chicken-and-egg problem: do polls drive public opinion, or does public opinion drive the polls?

Not only, then, is the question of how accurate is our knowledge and assessment of public opinion important, but we also need to be mindful of an equally serious question: To what degree should public officials be moved by public opinion? As James Madison warned in *Federalist No. 10* (Reading 52), a government that follows public opinion too slavishly creates its own set of dangers. The purpose of the Republic, wrote Madison, was to "refine and enlarge the public views, by passing them through the medium of a chosen body of citizens, whose wisdom may best discern the true interest of their country, and whose patriotism and love of justice, will be least likely to sacrifice it to temporary or partial considerations." Kathleen Frankovic and Joyce Gelb (Reading 51) note that some senators seemed to ground their vote on the Clarence Thomas nomination to the U.S. Supreme Court on polling information. As the polls taken a year after the Thomas nomination reveal (Box 10.2), public opinion about Clarence Thomas and Anita Hill had shifted considerably in only one year's time.

· 47 ·

Federalist No. 49

JAMES MADISON

In *Federalist No. 49,* James Madison argues strongly against proposals to allow constitutional conventions to be called at regular intervals. As he carefully sets out grounds against periodic conventions, he details Federalist arguments against direct democracy, and also repeatedly expresses his concern about the possible sway of public opinion and the disastrous consequences it could have on the stability of government.

. . .

If it be true that all governments rest on opinion, it is no less true that the strength of opinion in each individual, and its practical influence on his conduct, depend much on the number which he supposes to have entertained the same opinion. The reason of man, like man himself, is timid and cautious when left alone, and acquires firmness and confidence in proportion to the number with which it is associated. When the examples which fortify opinion are *ancient* as well as *numerous,* they are known to have a double effect. . . .

The danger of disturbing the public tranquillity by interesting too strongly the public passions, is a still more serious objection against a frequent reference of constitutional questions to the decision of the whole society. Notwithstanding the success which has attended the revisions of our established forms of government, and which does so much honor to the virtue and intelligence of the people of America, it must be confessed that the experiments are of too ticklish a nature to be unnecessarily multiplied. We are to recollect that all the existing constitutions were formed in the midst of a danger which repressed the passions most unfriendly to order and concord; of an enthusiastic confidence of the people in their patriotic leaders, which stifled the ordinary diversity of opinions on great national questions; of a universal ardor for new and opposite forms, produced by a universal resentment and indignation against the ancient government; and whilst no spirit of party connected with the changes to be made, or the abuses to be reformed, could mingle its leaven in the operation. The future situations in which we must expect to be usually placed, do not present any equivalent security against the danger which is apprehended.

But the greatest objection of all is, that the decisions which would probably result from such appeals would not answer the purpose of maintaining the constitutional equilibrium of the government. We have seen that the tendency of republican governments is to an aggrandizement of the legislative at the expense of the other departments. The appeals to the people, therefore, would usually be made by the executive and judiciary departments. But whether made by one side or the other, would each side enjoy equal advantages on the trial? Let us view their different situations. The members of the executive and judiciary departments are few in number, and can be personally known to a small part only of the people. The latter, by the mode of their appointment, as well as by the nature and permanency of it, are too far removed from the people to share much in their prepossessions. The former are generally the objects of jealousy, and their administration is always liable to be discolored and rendered unpopular. The members of the legislative department, on the other hand, are numerous. They are distributed and dwell among the people at large. Their connections of blood, of friendship, and of acquaintance embrace a great proportion of the most influential part of the society. The nature of their public trust implies a personal influence among the people, and that they are more immediately the confidential guardians of the rights and liberties of the people. With these advantages it can hardly be supposed that the adverse party would have an equal chance for a favorable issue.

But the legislative party would not only be able to plead their cause most successfully with the people. They would probably be constituted themselves the judges. The same influence which had gained them an election into the legislature, would gain them a seat in the convention. If this should not be the case with all, it would probably be the case with many, and pretty certainly with those leading characters on whom every thing depends in such bodies. The convention, in short, would be composed chiefly of men who had been, who actually were, or who expected to be, members of the department whose conduct was arraigned. They would consequently be parties to the very question to be decided by them.

It might, however, sometimes happen that appeals would be made under circumstances less adverse to the executive and judiciary departments. The usurpations of the legislature might be so flagrant and so sudden as to admit of no specious coloring. A strong party among themselves might take side with the other branches. The executive power might be in the hands of a peculiar favorite of the people. In such a posture of things, the public decision might be less swayed by prepossessions in favor of the legislative party. But still it could never be expected to turn on the true merits of the question. It would inevitably be connected with the spirit of preëxisting parties, or of parties springing out of the question itself. It would be connected with persons of distinguished character and extensive influence in the community. It would be pronounced by the very men who had been agents in, or opponents of the measures to which the decision would relate. The *passions,* therefore, not the *reason* of the public would sit in judgment. But it is the reason, alone, of the public, that ought to control and regulate the government. The passions ought to be controlled and regulated by the government.

TOWARD CRITICAL THINKING

1. Madison sets out a series of arguments *against* periodic conventions that would give the people greater opportunity to amend the U.S. Constitution. What arguments can you think of *for* giving the public greater opportunity to change their Constitution?

2. Throughout *Federalist No. 49* Madison appears very uncomfortable with direct democracy, that is, with allowing the people a greater say in their own governance. What were some of his fears? Were they reasonable?

• *48* •

The Meaning of Public Opinion

V. O. KEY JR.

V. O. Key Jr., one of the most eminent political scientists of his day, was an astute observer of politics who also recognized how difficult it was to understand all facets of the political system. Public opinion, notes Key, is a particularly thorny area because even the term itself is so difficult to define. Not only are there "special publics," he says, there is also private-versus-public opinion with which to contend.

During the 1993 confirmation hearings on Ruth Bader Ginsburg's nomination to the U.S. Supreme Court, she repeatedly declined to give her opinion on the death penalty. Noting that she had never written or taught about the Eighth Amendment and its ban on "cruel and unusual punishments," she claimed it would be inappropriate for her to give "an opinion" on an issue that would likely come before the Court.[*] Key recognizes that there are situations in which personal opinions thus become public opinions. Do you think the Ginsburg hearings are a good example of the private-versus-public opinion distinction he draws?

Key also notes the scholarly effort that has been put into ascertaining what he calls the "characteristics" of public opinion. Direction of opinion and its intensity are also important facets of public opinion and a reminder of Madison's cautions contained in *Federalist No. 49*.

. . .

✦ New Situational Limits to Public Opinion

Without doubt the conditions affecting the relations between government and public opinion have been radically altered during the past half-century. The means for informing and influencing the public have undergone a transformation. With the concentration in large corporations, in labor unions, and in other organizations of the powers of private decision formerly widely dispersed has come a parallel concentration of the power of autonomous political decision into relatively fewer hands. . . .

. . . Despite all these developments, it is too early to conclude that governments can ignore public opinion or that democratic government amounts only to a hoax, a ritual whose performance serves only to delude

SOURCE: V. O. Key Jr., *Public Opinion and American Democracy* (New York: Alfred A. Knopf, Inc., 1961), pp. 6–14. Reprinted by permission.

[*] In the first death penalty case in which she participated, *Tuilqepa* v. *California,* 114 S. Ct. 2630 (1994), Ginsburg voted with the majority to uphold the constitutionality of the death sentence at issue.

the people and thereby to convert them into willing subjects of the powers that be. The most superficial comparison of American public policy in 1900 and in 1960 indicates that there have been changes of no little consequence for the average man. Not all these policy innovations have been willed by a power elite of 100 or 200 persons; nor have they been entirely unconnected with mass sentiment. Unless mass views have some place in the shaping of policy, all the talk about democracy is nonsense. As Lasswell has said, the "open interplay of opinion and policy is the distinguishing mark of popular rule."[1] Yet the sharp definition of the role of public opinion as it affects different kinds of policies under different types of situations presents an analytical problem of extraordinary difficulty. . . . Among philosophers, publicists, and spare-time commentators on public affairs, the discussion of public opinion is conducted with style. Aphorisms, epigrams, axioms, and figures embellish the verbal display.

. . . One can observe, with the authors of *The Federalist,* that "all government rests on opinion." . . . One can assert that governments derive their powers from the "consent of the governed" or can picture public opinion as "a giant who is fickle and ignorant yet still has a giant's strength, and may use it with frightful effect."[2]

Such metaphors serve principally to ornament prose rather than to enlighten the reader about the nature of public opinion. Yet the discussion of public opinion becomes murky when meticulous scholars try to define their conceptions and to form distinctions that enable them to make statements that seem to fit the observable realities of the interaction of public opinion and government. This murkiness by no means flows solely from the incomprehensibility of men of learning. To speak with precision of public opinion is a task not unlike coming to grips with the Holy Ghost. . . .

. . . Nevertheless, a brief review of some of the conceptions and distinctions that have been developed by scholars in their discussions of the topic should be of value as an aid in orientation.

◆ Public As Organic Entity

Some speculators on public opinion have imagined the public to be a semiorganized entity that in some way or another could move through stages of initiation and debate and reach a recognizable collective decision on an issue. The images of the city-state and of the New England town meeting often color such attempts to form a conception of the reality of

---

[1] Harold D. Lasswell: *Democracy Through Public Opinion* (Menasha, Wis.: Banta; 1941), p. 15.
[2] Thomas A. Bailey: *The Man in the Street* (New York: Macmillan; 1948), p. 1.

public opinion in the modern state. The intricate structure of the nation-state cannot easily be grasped, and some students seek in the processes of opinion formation the equivalent of the citizenry gathered in the town hall or in the market place to discuss, debate, and settle public issues. In its simplest form this analogous thinking personifies the public: "The public expects"; "The public demands"; "Public opinion swept away all opposition."[3]. . .

More is lost than is gained in understanding by the organismic view of the public. Occasionally, in relatively small communities, citizen concern and involvement over an issue may be widespread and community consideration may move in close articulation with the mechanisms of authority to a decision that can realistically be said to be a decision by public opinion. At far rarer intervals great national populations may be swept by a common concern about a momentous issue with a similar result. Yet ordinarily a decision is made not by the public but by officials after greater or a lesser consideration of the opinion of the public or of parts of the public.

♦ Special Publics and the General Public

While the organismic conceptions of the public and of the opinion process may be of more poetic than practical utility, other distinctions developed by students of public opinion serve as handy aids to thought on the subject. There is, for example, the distinction between special publics and the general public. At one time it was the custom to speak of "the public." In due course it became evident that on only a few questions did the entire citizenry have an opinion. The notion of special publics was contrived to describe those segments of the public with views about particular issues, problems, or other questions of public concern. In actual politics one issue engages the attention of one subdivision of the population, while another arouses the interest of another group, and a third question involves still another special public. This distinction between general and special publics does, of course, do violence to the basic idea that "the" public shall prevail; it also warps the meaning of the term "public." Yet the usage mirrors the facts of political life and, incidentally, creates a problem for the public opinion theorist. He sometimes copes with the difficulty by the assertion that when the concern of a small special public prevails, it does so with the tacit consent of the general public.

. . . Whether this notion has validity, the question of who has what kind of opinion is of basic significance in a consideration of interactions between public and government.

---

[3]For a discussion of such fictions and fallacies, see F. H. Allport: "Toward a Science of Public Opinion," *Public Opinion Quarterly,* 1 (January, 1937), 7–23.

◆ Public and Private Opinion

. . . On what range of topics may opinion be considered public? Not all opinions of the public, even when widely held within the population, are to be properly regarded as public opinion. It may be assumed that opinion about the desirability of tailfins on Chevrolets are not public opinions, or that preferences for striped or solid white toothpaste fall outside the concern of the student of public opinion. On the other hand, opinion about the length of automobile tailfins may become public opinion if the question becomes one of whether the length of nonfunctional automobile ornamentation has become a public nuisance by its pressure on the available parking acreage. Goldhamer suggests that an opinion is public "if it attaches to an object of public concern," [4] The content of the phrase, "object of public concern," may vary from time to time with the changing scope of governmental action, or it may differ from society to society.

Many American students of public opinion have limited themselves to a narrow range of public opinion; they have tended to regard public opinion as concerned with substantive issues of public policy. That focus results from the basic tenet that public opinion should determine public policy, but it excludes a range of opinions of undoubted political relevance. Opinions about candidates, views about political parties, attitudes about the performance of governments, basic assumptions about what is right and proper in public affairs, and general beliefs and expectations about the place of government in society are also opinions of political relevance, as would be such opinions or states of mind as are embraced by the term "national morale."

◆ Characteristics of Public Opinion

The differentiation between opinions about public objects and about private objects crudely defines the outer limits of the opinion sphere that may be regarded as public. It leaves untouched the question of the characteristics of public opinion. In recent decades considerable scholarly effort has been devoted, principally by social psychologists, to ascertaining the characteristics of public opinion. In an earlier day the practice was to treat the direction of opinion in simple pro and con categories. The majority could be described as for or against, as voting yes or no. The psychometricians have made it clear that a pro-and-con categorization of opinion often conceals wide gradations in opinion. They have contrived scales to measure opinion in its dimension of direction. For example, a

---

[4] Herbert Goldhamer: "Public Opinion and Personality," *American Journal of Sociology,* LV (1949–50), 346.

division of people who support and oppose government ownership of industry does not provide a useful indication of the nature of public opinion on the question of government policy toward economic activity. Views on economic policy may be arranged along a scale from the extreme left to the extreme right. The opinion of an individual may be located at any one of many points along such a scale. One person may favor governmental ownership of all the means of production; another may be satisfied with a large dose of governmental regulation; still another may prefer only the most limited control of the economy; and others may wish to abolish whatever controls exist. The determination of the distribution of the population along such scales measuring the direction of opinion makes possible a more informed estimate of the nature of public opinion, in its dimension of direction, than did earlier and cruder conceptions.

Closely related to the conception of direction of opinion are ideas about the qualities or properties of opinion. Intensity of opinion is one of these qualities. A person may be an extreme conservative or radical on the scale of direction of opinion, but he may care a great deal, a little, or scarcely at all about that opinion; that is, opinions may vary in the intensity with which they are held. Obviously the incidence of opinion intensity within the electorate about an issue or problem is of basic importance for politics. An issue that arouses only opinion of low intensity may receive only the slightest attention, while one that stirs opinions of high intensity among even relatively small numbers of people may be placed high on the governmental agenda. Another quality of opinion of some importance is its stability. An individual, for example, may have a view, expressed on the basis of little or no information, which may readily be changed. On the other hand, an opinion may be so firmly held that it is not easily altered. Issues that relate to opinions of high stability widely held within the population present radically different problems for government than do those matters on which opinion is unstable. . . .

◆ Prerequisites for the Existence of Public Opinion

Students of public opinion have also sought to identify those broad conditions under which public opinion could sensibly be said to exist as a force in government. Democratic theorists that they were, they specified democratic conditions as a prerequisite for even the existence of public opinion. Freedom of speech and discussion, for example, are said to be prerequisites, since it is by public discussion that opinion is formed. Closely associated with this condition is that of the free availability of information about public issues and public questions; those problems handled by government in secrecy can scarcely be a subject of informed public debate. . . .

In keeping with this general vein of thought, Lowell sharply restricted the content of the term "public opinion." In his system the views of people generally on public questions of all sorts did not constitute public opinion. For a "real" public opinion to exist, it had to be a community opinion. Thus, when two highwaymen meet a traveler on a dark road and propose to relieve him of his wallet, it would be incorrect to say that a public opinion existed favorable to a redistribution of property. Public opinion, Lowell thought, need not be a unanimous opinion, but it should create an "obligation moral or political on the part of the minority," an obligation, at least under certain conditions, to submit. He laid great stress on the grounds of consensus as a basis for public opinion. "A body of men are politically capable of a public opinion only so far as they are agreed upon the ends and aims of government and upon the principles by which those ends shall be attained." No public opinion could exist in nations with large minorities unwilling to abide by majority decision. Moreover, public opinion could exist only when "the bulk of the people are in a position to determine of their own knowledge or by weighing a substantial part of the facts required for a rational decision," or when the question involves an issue of "apparent harmony or contradiction with settled convictions."[5]

It seems clear that consensus does not have to prevail for opinions to exist to which governments must accord weight. Yet the emphasis on consensus identifies special problems in governments that accord deference to public opinion. If the public is to project its opinions into public policy, some sectors of the public must be prepared to accept actions distasteful to them. The limits of the general consensus may fix the limits within which widespread participation in public affairs may lead to decisions distasteful yet acceptable to those whose opinions do not prevail.

TOWARD CRITICAL THINKING

1. Think about items in the news the last few months. What item or issue has drawn a lot of attention nationally or in your community? In Key's terminology, what publics have been affected? Have different publics held different opinions about these issues? How has that difference affected the direction of public opinion?

2. Key notes that freedom of speech is a prerequisite in a democracy "since it is by public discussion that opinion is formed." Do you agree?

---

[5] A. Lawrence Lowell: *Public Opinion and Popular Government* (New York: Longmans, Green; 1913), chs. 1, 2.

· *49* ·

How Polling Transforms Public Opinion

BENJAMIN GINSBURG

In "How Polling Transforms Public Opinion," Ginsburg takes a position very different from the one posited by James Madison. Madison feared that the public could sway legislators; Ginsburg instead bemoans the fact that the polls have transformed public opinion from a potentially powerful force for change to a more diffuse phenomenon. Polling actually "domesticates" public opinion by allowing pollsters to set the agenda. Thus, public dissatisfaction with government in general and with Congress in particular only rarely prompts massive demonstrations.

Not only are these massive uprisings or demonstrations by groups infrequent, says Ginsburg, but public opinion polls also further weaken the political forces of organized groups by providing a counterforce to their demands. Thus, while gay activists, for example, may march on Washington, D.C., in record numbers, legislators and policy makers can point to public opinion polls to justify their votes against gay rights legislation. Moreover, polls often serve to minimize even the statements of interest group leaders. After all, if a *scientific* poll indicates something different from what a group or group leader claims, the poll will be considered to be a more accurate reflection of the wishes of the public.

... Much of the prominence of opinion polling as a civic institution derives from the significance that present-day political ideologies ascribe to the will of the people. Polls purport to provide reliable, scientifically derived information about the public's desires, fears and beliefs, and so to give concrete expression to the conception of a popular will. The availability of accurate information certainly is no guarantee that governments will actually pay heed to popular opinions. Yet, it has always been the belief of many students and practitioners of survey research that an accurate picture of the public's views might at least increase the chance that governments' actions would be informed by and responsive to popular sentiment.

Unfortunately, however, polls do more than simply measure and re-cord the natural or spontaneous manifestation of popular belief. The data reported by opinion polls are actually the product of an interplay between opinion and the survey instrument. As they measure, the polls interact with opinion, producing changes in the character and identity of the views receiving public expression. The changes induced by polling, in turn, have the most profound implications for the relationship between public opin-ion and government. In essence, polling has contributed to the domestica-tion of opinion by helping to transform opinion from a politically potent, often disruptive, force into a more docile, plebiscitary phenomenon.

◆ Publicizing Opinion

Over the past several decades, polling has generally come to be seen as the most accurate and reliable means of gauging the public's senti-ments. Indeed, poll results and public opinion are terms that are used almost synonymously.

. . . Means of ascertaining public opinion certainly existed prior to the development of modern survey techniques. Statements from local notables and interest-group spokespersons, letters to the press and to public officials, and sometimes demonstrations, protests and riots provided indications of the populace's views long before the invention of the sample survey. Governments certainly took note of all these symptoms of the public's mood. As Chester Barnard once noted, prior to the availability of polling, legislators "read the local newspapers, toured their districts and talked with voters, received letters from the home state, and entertained delega-tions which claimed to speak for large and important blocks of voters".

Obviously, these alternative modes of assessing public sentiment con-tinue to be available. Polling has not become the only possible source of information about popular opinion. But it is significant that whenever poll results differ from the interpretation of public opinion offered by some other source, it is almost invariably the polls that are presumed to be correct. The labor leader whose account of the views of the rank and file differs from the findings of a poll is automatically assumed to have misrepresented or misperceived membership opinion. Politicians who dare to quarrel with the polls' negative assessments of the popularity of their programs are immediately derided by the press.

This presumption in favor of the polls stems from both the scientific and representative character of opinion polling. Survey research is mod-eled after the methodology of the natural sciences and at least conveys an impression of technical sophistication and scientific objectivity. Occa-sional press accounts of deliberate bias and distortion of survey findings only partially undermine this impression.

At the same time, the polls can claim to offer a more representative view of popular sentiment than any alternative source of information is likely to provide. Group spokespersons sometimes speak only for themselves. The distribution of opinion reflected by letters to newspapers and public officials is notoriously biased. Demonstrators and rioters, however sincere, are seldom more than a tiny and unrepresentative segment of the populace. The polls, by contrast, at least attempt to take equal account of all relevant individuals. And indeed, by offering a representative view of public opinion the polls have often served as antidotes for false spokespersons, correctives for mistaken politicians, and guides to popular concerns that might never have been mentioned by the individuals writing letters to legislators and newspaper editors.

Nevertheless, polling does more than offer a scientifically derived and representative account of popular sentiment. The substitution of polling for other means of gauging the public's views also has the effect of changing several of the key characteristics of public opinion. Critics of survey research have often noted that polling can affect both the beliefs of individuals asked to respond to survey questions and the attitudes of those who subsequently read a survey's results. However, the most important effect of the polls is not a result of their capacity to change individuals' beliefs. The major impact of polling is, rather, on the cumulation and translation of individuals' private beliefs into collective public opinion. Four fundamental changes in the character of public opinion can be traced to the introduction of survey research.

Changing the Character of Public Opinion

First, polling alters both what is expressed and what is perceived as the opinion of the mass public by transforming public opinion from a voluntary to an externally subsidized matter. Second, polling modifies the manner in which opinion is publicly presented by transforming public opinion from a behavioral to an attitudinal phenomenon. Third, polling changes the origin of information about public beliefs by transforming public opinion from a property of groups to an attribute of individuals. Finally, polling partially removes individuals' control over the subject matter of their own public expressions of opinion by transforming public opinion from a spontaneous assertion to a constrained response.

Individually and collectively, these transformations have profound consequences for the character of public opinion and, more important, for the relationship of opinion to government and policy. To the extent that polling displaces alternative modes of gauging popular sentiment, these four transformations contribute markedly to the domestication or pacification of public opinion. Polling renders public opinion less dangerous,

hostile action in the voting booth. Polling has certainly become one of the chief means employed by democratic political elites to attempt to anticipate and avert the electorate's displeasure. But, in both the democratic and dictatorial contexts, governments have also employed polling extensively to help forestall the possibility of popular disobedience and unrest. . . .

◆ From Group to Individual

Mass behavior was not the sole source of information about popular opinion prior to the advent of polling. Reports on the public's mood could usually also be obtained from the activists, leaders, or notables of the nation's organized and communal groups. Public officials or others interested in the views of working people, for example, would typically consult trade union officers. Similarly, anyone concerned with the attitudes of, say, farmers would turn to the heads of farm organizations. . . .

The advent of polling transformed public opinion from a property of groups to an attribute of individuals. Opinion surveys can elicit the views of individual citizens directly, allowing governments or other interested observers to bypass group leaders, social notables, party bosses, or any other putative spokespersons for public opinion. The polls have never fully supplanted communal and interest-group leaders as sources of information about popular attitudes. Yet, the polls do lessen the need for such intermediaries by permitting whatever agencies or organizations are interested in learning the public's views to establish their own links with opinion-holders. . . .

This conversion of public opinion from a property of groups and their leaders to a more direct presentation of popular preferences has several consequences. On the one hand, the polls undoubtedly provide a somewhat more representative picture of the public's views than would usually be obtained from group leaders and notables. Leaders and group representatives sometimes carelessly or deliberately misrepresent their adherents' opinions. But, even with the best of intentions, the leaders of a group may be insufficiently sensitive to the inevitable disparity of viewpoints between activists and ordinary citizens. Polling can be a useful antidote to inaccuracy as well as to mendacity. . . .

At the same time, however, by undermining the capacity of groups, interests, parties, and the like to speak for public opinion, polling can also diminish the effectiveness of public opinion as a force in political affairs. In essence, polling intervenes between opinion and its organized or collective expression. Though they may sometimes distort member opinion, organized groups, interests and parties remain the most effective mechanisms through which opinion can be made to have an impact on government and politics. The polls' transformation of public opinion into an attribute of individuals increases the accuracy but very likely reduces the general efficacy with which mass opinion is publicly asserted. . . .

◆ From Assertion to Response

In the absence of polling, individuals typically choose for themselves the subjects of any public assertions they might care to make. Those persons or groups willing to expend the funds, effort, or time needed to acquire a public platform, normally also select the agenda or topics on which their views will be aired. The individual writing an angry letter to a newspaper or legislator generally singles out the object of his or her scorn. The organizers of a protest march typically define the aim of their own wrath. . . .

The most obvious problem stemming from this change is that polling can create a misleading picture of the agenda of public concerns. The matters which appear significant to the agencies sponsoring polls may be quite different from the concerns of the general public. Discrepancies between the polls' agenda and the general public's interests were especially acute during the political and social turmoil of the late 1960s and early 1970s. Though . . . polling was used by the government during this period to help curb disorder, the major commercial polls took little interest in the issues which aroused so much public concern. The year 1970, for example, was marked by racial strife and antiwar protest in the United States. Yet, the 1970 national Gallup Poll devoted only 5 percent of its questions to American policy in Vietnam and only 2 of 162 questions to domestic race relations. . . .

In essence, rather than offer governments the opinions that citizens want them to learn, the polls tell governments—or other sponsors—what they would like to learn about citizens' opinions. The end result is to change the public expression of opinion from an assertion of demand to a step in the process of persuasion.

◆ Making Opinion Safer for Government

Taken together, the changes produced by polling contribute to the transformation of public opinion from an unpredictable, extreme, and often dangerous force into a more docile expression of public sentiment. Opinion stated through the polls imposes less pressure and makes fewer demands upon government than would more spontaneous or natural assertions of popular sentiment. Though opinion may be expressed more democratically via the polls than through alternative means, polling can give public opinion a plebiscitary character—robbing opinion of precisely those features that might maximize its impact upon government and policy. . . .

◆ Government: From Adversary to Manager of Opinion

Because it domesticates public opinion, polling has contributed to one of the twentieth century's major political transformations—the shift from an adversarial to a managerial relationship between government and popular opinion. . . .

. . . As a result of governments' fear of popular sentiment, before the 20th century the two basic policies of most regimes toward public opinion were secrecy and censorship. Incumbent elites might occasionally attempt to sway popular feelings. But, on a routine basis, the central thrust of official action was to block access to information about governmental plans and operations and to seek, through secrecy, to inhibit the development of potentially hostile opinion on as many matters as possible. . . .

Polling is the spearhead of this vast opinion-management apparatus. Opinion surveys provide governments with more or less reliable information about current popular sentiment, offer a guide to the character of the public relations efforts that might usefully be made, and serve as means of measuring the effect of "information programs" upon a target population. Though it cannot guarantee success, polling allows governments a better opportunity to anticipate, regulate, and manipulate popular attitudes. Ironically, some of its early students believed that polling would open the way for "government by opinion". Instead, polling has mainly helped to promote the governance of opinion.

TOWARD CRITICAL THINKING

1. Do you agree with Ginsburg's assessment of the role of public opinion polls? Do polls really dissipate public sentiments?

2. What kinds of evidence of public opinion should legislators and other policy makers take into account? Which are the best indicators of public opinion? The worst?

BOX 10.1

A Short Course in How to Read Opinion Polls

PAULA WADE

As the presidential race tightened this week, a CNN-*USA Today* poll gave Democrat Bill Clinton a razor-thin lead of 2 percentage points over President Bush. But a *Washington Post* poll put Mr. Clinton's lead at 10 percent, and ABC and NBC-*Wall Street Journal* said it was 7 percent.

Polls released by three television networks Thursday showed Mr. Clinton leading Mr. Bush by 3, 5 and 9 percentage points.

Which one do you believe? How reliable are they?

An opinion poll is supposed to reflect the opinions of a certain group at a certain time by asking neutral questions of a representative sample of the group. And the rule for trying to interpret a poll is the same as trying to decide between candidates: Voter beware.

"The media are treating the polls as more significant, more real, and more telling than they really are," said John Barry, director of the Roper Center for Public Opinion Research at the University of Connecticut. "All the polls can do at this point is give very broad generalizations about where people seem to be leaning right now."

Here's a reader's guide of what to look for in interpreting polls:

THE SAMPLE: First, figure out who has been polled, when, and by what method. Some polls try to include only registered voters; others say their results reflect the views of "likely voters." In truth, all pollsters can do is ask the respondent whether he or she is registered, and then whether he or she is planning to vote.

The Census Bureau regularly asks people whether they're registered and whether they voted in the last election. Statistics show that about 10 percent will say they voted when they really didn't.

THE TIMING: A poll is a "snapshot" of what respondents are saying at a certain time. A poll taken over several days generally will even out what pollsters call "spikes"—momentary opinion shifts due to some particularly good or bad event.

THE NUMBERS: The number of people in the sample must be large enough and diverse enough to accurately reflect the population the pollster is trying to study. The larger the sample, the more likely the results are to be accurate.

The method of contacting respondents is important as well. Generally, national polls use the random dialing of telephone numbers in various areas of the country. The drawback of that method is that it excludes people without phones, people who screen their calls through answering devices, and people who work during the polling hours.

To correct for those deficiencies and others, some pollsters will "weight" their samples so that the polls reflect the population. In other words, if the poll respondents happen to be 59 percent women and 41 percent men, the pollster

BOX 10.1   *(Continued)*

might adjust the data by counting the responses of men more heavily than women to reflect the actual breakdown of women and men in the population.

THE QUESTIONS: The biggest variant is the wording of poll questions.

For the presidential race, the question asked by most national surveys is, "If the election were held today, would you vote for George Bush, Bill Clinton or Ross Perot?" But Pollster Berje Yacoubian of Memphis, Tenn., argues that such questions generally force voters to name a choice even if they haven't truly decided yet—giving an untrue picture of candidates' true levels of support.

THE ERROR FACTOR: A national poll should have between 1,000 and 1,500 respondents from different areas of the country to have a margin of error of about 3.5 percentage points. That means the poll results are within plus or minus 3.5 percentage points of reflecting the feelings of the population of the survey.

For example, if a survey shows that 55 percent of likely voters polled plan to vote for Mr. Clinton, the real intentions of all likely voters in the country would be anywhere between 51.5 percent and 58.5 percent.

SOURCE: Paula Wade, "Election '92: A Short Course in How to Read Opinion Polls," *Atlanta Journal-Constitution,* (October 30, 1992): B–1. Reprinted by permission of the author.

· *50* ·

The Polls in 1992

It Was the Best of Times;
It Was the Worst of Times

MICHAEL W. TRAUGOTT

Political scientist Michael W. Traugott points out many of the problems in polling that took place during the 1992 presidential election season. Beginning with the way exit poll questionnaires were constructed and finishing with the tracking polls that flourished during the summer of 1992 up to the November election, Traugott finds fault with the way polls were taken and perhaps, most important, reported to the public.

It was the best of times and—on occasion—the worst of times for pollsters and journalists who reported on polls in the 1992 presidential campaign. Most pollsters are justly satisfied with their work. But there were some ominous signs that some pollsters need to be more vigilant about how they do their work, and reporters more careful about how they write about the findings.

Around the time of the New Hampshire primary, there were two signs of trouble. One involved the first exit poll of the year, and the other initial reporting of the "character" issue. Later, the rise of "tracking polls" fed the seemingly insatiable appetite of the media for "horse race" coverage. But possibly shoddy methods and careless reporting misrepresented the dynamics of the end game of the campaign. The few problematic incidents reconfirm the need for full disclosure of survey methods and analysis techniques, as well as the need to make data available for secondary analysis by a wide range of survey methodologists in order to understand what happened and how to improve future work.

◆ The New Hampshire Exit Poll

Exit polls have a special place in the coverage of American elections because they provide, in principle, for an independent assessment of why

---

SOURCE: Michael W. Traugott, "The Polls in 1992: It Was the Best of Times, It Was the Worst of Times," *The Public Perspective,* 4:1 (November/December 1992): 14. Reprinted by permission.

voters supported particular candidates—free from the spin that managers and candidates alike place on the "meaning" of an election.

When the networks consolidated their operations for 1990 under the umbrella of Voter Research and Surveys (VRS), there were immediate and significant cost savings for all of them. But the construction of a single questionnaire with the results combined into a single dataset meant that all analysis would flow from a single source. If the resulting data were valid, that presented no problem of interpretation. But a significant difference between the exit poll estimate of the outcome and the actual vote totals could produce problems of either estimation or analysis, without—for most analysts on election night—an independent data source for verification.

In the 1992 New Hampshire primary, first in line with particular significance in our "front loaded" nomination system, the VRS data greatly overestimated the support for Patrick Buchanan. The consequence was to color the editorial content of the early evening coverage and to suggest that President Bush was in much more trouble than expected (or than in fact he turned out to be). The exit poll data suggested a narrow Bush victory, while the vote total eventually showed him getting a substantial sixteen point margin.

The problem was not the projected winner, but the newsworthiness of the (slight) margin. Given the methodology of exit polls and the early availability of the data, the editorial commentary began with the evening news broadcasts and continued on into the segments when the race was called just after the polls closed. Many Americans went to bed that night thinking the president had been badly damaged. And for most reporters and editors there was no second source of information, until all of the votes were counted, to counteract this editorial tone.

Warren J. Mitofsky, director of VRS, has described what happened with the VRS data on that day, and speculated on the source of the estimation error.[1] There has been no public review of the exit poll methodology in New Hampshire or elsewhere, and such a review is badly needed. The problem may have been as simple as a bad sample, but the fact the same error was shared by three other exit polls suggests it may have been more methodologically complicated. In any case there is a public as well as corporate interest in understanding and explaining what went wrong.

◆ Reporting on the Character Issue

The tendency of media pollsters to report the marginals for individual questions and rarely cross-tabulate results beyond demographic charac-

---

[1]Warren J. Mitofsky, "What Went Wrong with Exit Polling in New Hampshire?" *The Public Perspective,* March/April 1992, p. 17.

teristics of respondents is well known. There are other ways that election survey data can and should be reported more meaningfully. A potent example occurred in the surveys conducted after the allegations by Gennifer Flowers that she had had an affair with Bill Clinton. The basic reporting suggested that relatively large segments of the electorate had concerns about a candidate's marital fidelity and the Clinton-Flowers case in particular.

But extended analysis of one survey conducted by ABC News and the *Washington Post* suggested that respondents' predispositions toward the candidates affected their attitudes on the importance of the fidelity issue.[2] Those who supported Bush over Clinton at that time, irrespective of party, were more likely to be concerned about the issue than those who had already decided to support Clinton. This analysis suggested an alternative, equally important story that could have been developed from the survey data. By reporting a relationship rather than the marginal distributions of single questions, readers and viewers would have been better informed as to the political significance of the event.

✦ The Tracking Polls

The most disconcerting element of polling in the 1992 campaign was the advent of "tracking" polls by several news organizations. This insidious development played upon all of the worst tendencies of journalists to focus almost entirely upon who is ahead and by how much. The coverage at the end of the campaign was complicated by faulty polling and faulty reporting. Both of these developments should be nipped in the bud. It's not sufficient to evaluate pre-election polls on the basis of their "average" estimate of the outcome, as was commonly done in the last few days before the election. Each poll must be evaluated on its own methodological merits, errors identified, and corrective measures taken the next time.

Tracking polls were introduced as a device through which candidates could assess campaign strategy and developments on a very short-term horizon. They involve relatively small samples of interviews conducted every twenty-four hours, that are usually combined in some kind of moving average to boost sample size and hence statistical reliability. One-day surveys present substantial problems of nonsampling error. In order to complete enough interviews, sampling is conducted with limited or no call backs. Such samples may be highly skewed because certain

---

[2]Michael Traugott and Jennifer Means, "Problems of Character: Was It the Candidate or the Press?" *The Polling Report,* September 7, 1992.

groups may be away from home at the time the calls are made much more than are other groups.[3]

At the end of the campaign, ABC News, the Tarrance organization in an enterprise known as Battleground '92, and the Gallup Organization separately conducted tracking polls. The Gallup effort for CNN/*USA Today* was reported as showing a more substantial tightening of the race in the last two weeks and received considerably more coverage. There were two problems with this conclusion: the survey data were most likely faulty, and the reporting was certainly faulty. The problem with the survey data was that two different interviewing periods were used—during the week (from 5 to 9 P.M.), and on the weekend (all day long).[4] Generally, one call was made to a house per day, unless there was a busy signal. Numbers where there was no contact were moved to the next day's sample. Gallup selected respondents using a "youngest male/oldest female at home" criterion. This produces something akin to an availability sample of people at home during those hours. One consequence of this methodology was to increase the likelihood that midweek interviews would produce candidate preference distributions that would favor Bush more than would weekend interviews. This raises the prospect that a methodological artifact would suggest that the presidential race was tightening and then opening up again just before election day.

This problem was complicated by two important shifts in analysis. The first involved a move from "registered" to "likely" voters as the base, and the second was a change in the way that Gallup allocated the "undecided" voters in its final estimate. The shift in the analytical base is common to most surveys as election day nears. In national elections it always produces a more Republican estimate of the outcome because of the greater propensity of Republicans to vote and hence to appear as "likely voters."[5] But these findings this year were not consistently reported as "what would have been expected" by the shift in reference numbers. One problem was that CNN and *USA Today* persisted in displaying the surveytime series continuously, instead of separating the data from "registered" and "likely" voters into the two time series. As a result, the

---

3 Michael W. Traugott "The Importance of Persistence in Respondent Selection for Preelection Surveys," *Public Opinion Quarterly,* Spring 1987, pp. 48–57.

4 "Polls Apart," *Newsweek,* November 9, 1992, p. 6.

5 Michael W. Traugott and Clyde Tucker, "Strategies for Predicting Whether a Citizen Will Vote and Estimation of Electoral Outcomes," *Public Opinion Quarterly,* Spring 1984, pp. 330–343. Although the delineation of "likely voters" is an area where the art of polling comes into play, research shows that there is little difference in the estimate produced by two commonly used methods to define the likely electorate—partitioning the data and discarding information from those deemed unlikely to vote, and using probability weighting for all respondents.

"narrowing" of the race, an inherently more newsworthy story, was exaggerated.

Since 1988, Gallup has based its final pre-election estimate of the outcome of the election on telephone interviews, rather than face-to-face interviews employing a secret ballot. In 1992, Gallup also revised its method for allocating the "undecided" respondents in its final estimate of the election outcome. Their review of past results suggested that the survey estimated the incumbent's proportion of the actual vote quite well, but underestimated the challenger's. So they allocated virtually all of the "undecided" respondents in their final survey to the Clinton total, producing an estimate of a 12 percentage point margin for Clinton over Bush. Clinton was in fact to win by 5.5 points.

Why are these matters important? Because they contribute to a developing folklore about the 1992 campaign. Was George Bush catching up, with momentum on his side, only to be derailed by the release of material from a new indictment of Casper Weinberger, just four days before the election? Or was the Clinton margin steady throughout the last ten days of the campaign, with no effect from the indictment? Such a post-hoc search for meaning is inherently difficult and unsatisfactory because only certain plausible alternative methodological hypotheses can be tested. Nevertheless, it should be attempted in this instance.

The dangers of tracking polls and their misinterpretation need to be highlighted before their use becomes more widespread. It is crucial that an open inquiry be conducted. It could be mounted under the auspices of either the National Council of Public Polls or the American Association for Public Opinion Research.

It should address a number of questions. Was there a shift in candidate support at the end of the campaign independent of survey timing and methodology? Information on date and circumstances of interviews could be used to address these questions. Was there a shift in candidate support independent of the reference sample analyzed—registered or likely voters? Does a content analysis indicate that the survey results could have been reported with greater care to minimize confusion in their interpretation? The important issue is maintaining public confidence in survey research.

TOWARD CRITICAL THINKING

1. Recall V. O. Key's discussion of the direction and intensity of public opinion (Reading 48). How do you think polls affected the 1992 presidential vote? In which direction?

2. Do polling organizations or the news networks have a responsibility to explain their poll results better to the American public? If they do not, do you think the government should (or could) take steps to regulate them?

· *51* ·

Public Opinion and the Thomas Nomination

KATHLEEN FRANKOVIC and JOYCE GELB

The Supreme Court historically has been considered removed from the pressures of public opinion. Still, many believe that the Court can be moved by the election returns. Although appointed for life, the justices read newspapers and probably follow public opinion polls, too. As Frankovic and Gelb note, until the 1980s there was generally little interest in Supreme Court appointees or in polling the public about nominees (or about the Court, for that matter). The failed nomination of Robert Bork in 1987, however, changed much of that. And the unique Clarence Thomas hearings, which presented issues of race, political ideology, and sexual harassment, garnered more public attention than any previous nomination. Not surprisingly, then, numerous public opinion polls were taken at various points in the Thomas nomination process. Frankovic and Gelb conclude that many senators used those polls to help them make up their minds on how to vote on the Thomas confirmation.

Until recently, the nomination of a justice to the U.S. Supreme Court had little public opinion relevance. Questions might be raised about the nominee's qualifications, perhaps including his or her liberalism or conservatism, but the American people tended to acquiesce in Court appointments. That changed during the Reagan administration, when opponents of the president's choice of Robert Bork decided that public opinion did matter and effectively campaigned to turn the public against Bork.

The Thomas nomination, however, raised even more questions about public opinion. Race and the role it should play in Court nominations was as important as Clarence Thomas's legal opinions. And, as soon as Anita Hill's charges of sexual harassment became public, other aspects of public opinion came into prominence.

♦ Court Nominations and Public Approval

Until recently, there has been little interest in polling the public for its reactions to Supreme Court nominees. The constitutional process of presi-

SOURCE: Kathleen Frankovic and Joyce Gelb, "Public Opinion and the Thomas Nomination," *PS: Political Science & Politics,* XXV:3 (September 1992):481–484. Reprinted by permission.

dential appointment and Senate confirmation put the Court several stages away from public involvement. The few times the public was polled, before the 1980s, it was more to affirm decisions already made than to provide input into the decision-making process.

. . . In the 1980s, the nomination of Sandra Day O'Connor allowed pollsters to discover whether the American people thought a woman should be on the Court (they did). It was, however, the failed nomination of Robert Bork that changed the role of public opinion and the Court.

In the course of the Senate hearings on the Bork nomination, the American people *were* asked their opinions. Pollsters learned that the American people wanted a justice on the Court who agreed with them on the issues, that they trusted the Senate more than the president and expected the confirmation process to be fair. In addition, Bork, like Frankfurter and Black, began with the public on his side, or at least willing to suspend judgment. While the Senate rejected the Bork nomination, many Americans never made up their minds to oppose Bork, although it was clear that the hearings hurt the federal judge.

Clarence Thomas faced the same situation. Americans wanted a justice they could agree with, and as at the start of the Bork proceedings, gave Thomas the benefit of the doubt. A majority of Americans agreed with some of Thomas's opinions, especially with his concerns about welfare abuses, but disagreed with others.

Thomas's personal opinions appeared to generate mixed emotions, especially when they seemed to be in conflict with his own background. Most Americans, black and white, agreed that anyone who had benefitted from affirmative action programs should support them for others.

But the racial issues were much more basic. The resignation of Justice Thurgood Marshall made the issue one of race *on* the Court. Was it important that there always be at least one black justice? Overall, Americans split on that question. Polls suggest that Americans would like things to be determined on a race-blind basis. With regard to the significance of race in court nominations, 51 percent of whites say it is not important; three-quarters of blacks say it is (CBS News/*New York Times* Poll, September 9, 1991). Blacks in particular appear to strongly support remedial action related *both* to racial and gender based discrimination.

Self-interest and group interest obviously play a role in determining what matters in the character and background of a justice. On the role of gender as a relevant factor in court nominations, 60 percent of men say it is not important; 60 percent of women say it is.

While most Americans oppose additional legislation to protect blacks and women from job discrimination, the response to this issue again varies by gender, race and partisanship. An overwhelming percentage of blacks support anti-discrimination legislation for blacks (77 percent) and women (58 percent), while working women are more likely to support such legislation for women (52 percent). Democrats (50 percent) are more in favor of additional laws to protect against discrimination than Republicans (CBS/*NYT* Poll, May 7–8, 1991).

Survey data from 1985 to 1992 have shown a near split among the Americans surveyed on questions asking whether job preference should be given to women discriminated against in the past. A majority of women respondents support preference for women who have been victimized. Polls reveal less support for such preference for blacks during the same era. Again, blacks are most likely to support affirmative action for both blacks (from three-fifths to four-fifths of respondents) and women (generally three-quarters of respondents).

At the beginning, Clarence Thomas was unknown to most of the public, but he was given the benefit of the doubt. Blacks supported the nomination; so did women. There was no gender gap.

Once the charges of sexual harassment became public, several things happened almost immediately. First, Americans began to pay more attention to the nomination. An ABC News/*Washington Post* poll conducted the evening after Anita Hill's first press conference found that over 80 percent of the public were aware of her charges.

Americans said that if Hill's charges were true, Thomas should not be confirmed, but by better than two to one, they said that the charges were probably *not* true, and by a similar two-to-one margin, they said Thomas *should* be confirmed. Hill lost some potential support because she had not made her charges public at the time the incidents occurred but, by and large, Americans felt that her charges needed to be taken seriously by the Senate.

The hearings themselves, well-watched media events, served only to make the charges and the opinions about them even more murky, with few clear on where the truth lay. But the hearings turned into a quasi-judicial event, with the burden of proof place on the "prosecution," Anita Hill, while the "accused," Clarence Thomas, was given the benefit of the doubt.

Many things did not change. Before the hearings began, twice as many people thought the charges were not true than thought they were. After the hearings were over, the distribution of opinion was generally the same. By two to one, Americans thought Clarence Thomas should be confirmed before the hearings. After they were over, they still favored confirmation.

The murkiness came in the search for truth. When it was all over, 28 percent thought Thomas was telling the entire truth; 11 percent thought

Hill was. But most Americans thought *both* Hill and Thomas were hiding something about their relationship. With no obvious truth, Thomas retained the benefit of the doubt.

Many of the Senators decided to vote to confirm in the last hours before the vote. Multiple public opinion polls, done by media organizations, were available to Senators. Many surely used those polls to help make up their minds, or to justify minds they had already made up. The Senate was confused about who was telling the truth. Given the sensitivity of male Senators to a sexually charged confrontation, they sought to validate their position by recourse to the public's judgment. . . .

Anita Hill's charges extended public awareness of an issue that had already appeared as a public policy concern. While the Thomas nomination highlighted the issue of sexual harassment in a graphic fashion, even prior to the controversy over the nomination it had become an issue with considerable salience for the American public. . . .

It is noteworthy that awareness of the issue of harassment has greatly increased. Seventy-eight percent of men and women (NCRW 1992) describe harassment as not just physical contact but other unwanted attentions, though women are more likely to describe a given situation as more threatening than men.

◆ Conclusions

Support for the Thomas nomination does not imply a change in attitudes on other issues, merely a continuation of previous opinion. His nomination highlighted these issues. Endorsement of Thomas as a Supreme Court nominee does not imply endorsement of his political stands, nor does his confirmation mean that the public is opposed to affirmative action or has experienced a change in support for feminist issues.

Although at the time of the hearings more women sided with Thomas than with Anita Hill, the 1992 primary races indicate the continuing relevance of the Thomas nomination to women voters. This is illustrated by the Democratic primaries in Illinois and Pennsylvania. Senator Alan Dixon lost his party's nomination to the Cook County Recorder of Deeds, Carol Moseley Braun, a black woman who cobbled together a coalition of urban blacks and white suburban women who opposed the confirmation of Justice Thomas, as a result of Anita Hill's charges. Lynn Yeakel came from behind to defeat two male candidates in Pennsylvania and will run against Senator Arlen Specter who grilled Hill during the hearings. Braun and Yeakel declared their candidacies immediately after the Senate voted to confirm Thomas. Their primary victories demonstrate that, six months after the Thomas confirmation hearings, the issues of fairness and harassment continue to play a strong political role.

TOWARD CRITICAL THINKING

1. What gender differences appeared concerning the issues involved in the Thomas nomination? How do these differences illustrate the special publics discussed by Benjamin Ginsburg (Reading 49)?

2. Given the problems with polling discussed by Michael Traugott (Reading 50), what indicators of public opinion (if any) do you believe senators should consider in weighing how to vote on confirmation of Supreme Court nominees? Do the polling results reported in Box 10.2 below affect or change your answer?

BOX 10.2

Year Later, Hill Has Edge in 'He Said, She Said' Saga

MARIA PUENTE

In the believability stakes, Anita Hill has edged out Clarence Thomas—a big change from a year ago, when more people believed his denials than her accusations.

A new *USA Today*/CNN/Gallup Poll of 1,015 people, conducted Oct. 1–3, [1992] found that 43 percent of those questioned now believe Hill's accusation that Thomas sexually harassed her; 39 percent believe Thomas' categorical denial.

Last October, shortly after Hill made her charge, polls showed that 54 percent of those questioned believed Thomas and just 27 percent believed Hill.

What happened? A greater understanding of the nature and pervasiveness of sexual harassment, says Helen Neuborne, head of NOW Legal Defense and Education Fund.

"For a year, women have been talking to each other about what is sexual harassment, and they began to believe her," Neuborne says.

Nonsense, says conservative leader and Thomas defender Phyllis Schlafly. Hill, she says, made the whole thing up.

If there's a change in public opinion, it's only because of a year of "favorable media publicity" for Hill, she says. "The only polls that matter are the ones at the time that showed most . . . believed Thomas."

The *USA Today*/CNN/Gallup Poll has a margin of error of plus or minus 3 points. The Thomas-Hill question was added to a poll tracking the presidential race.

SOURCE: Maria Puente, "Year Later, Hill Has Edge in 'He Said, She Said' Saga," *USA Today*, (October 5, 1992):10A. Copyright 1992, *USA Today.* Reprinted with permission.

(Continued)

BOX 10.2 *(Continued)*

Hill's Credibility Grows

Here is the percentage[1] of people believing Anita Hill's charges of sexual harassment by Clarence Thomas compared with a year ago after Senate hearings on the claims:

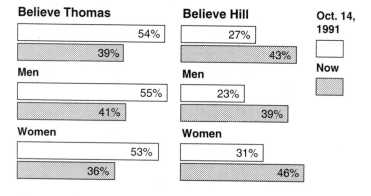

[1]Other responses not shown.

SOURCE: A USA TODAY/CNN/Gallup nationwide telephone poll of 1,015 registered voters conducted Oct. 1–3 by the Gallup Organization. Margin of error: 3 percentage points.

THINKING ABOUT PUBLIC OPINION

1. Several of the readings point to the fact that legislators can be influenced by polls. Given the weaknesses in some polling methods and their subsequent reporting pointed out by Michael Traugott (Reading 50), what are the pitfalls inherent in the tendency of public officials to rely on public opinion polls?

2. What role does public opinion play in a democracy (other than its effect on voting)? What gauges of public opinion should policy makers consider?

3. What role did public opinion about the president and Congress play in the last national elections?

CHAPTER 11

◆ ◆ ◆

Political Parties and Interest Groups

Although James Madison warned of the evils of faction and argued for the need for national government to control it, factions, or organized interests, have become a way of life in the United States. One form of faction—political parties—has actually become the organizing force behind elections as well as the organization of the U.S. Congress and all fifty state legislatures.

Unlike other democracies, in the United States two political parties quickly came to dominate the system. In fact, so deeply ingrained is the two-party system that it is nearly impossible for third-party or independent candidates to seek national or state office. *Williams* v. *Rhodes* (1968) (Reading 55) was an effort by the Supreme Court to stop some forms of discrimination against third parties. But as the well-funded presidential candidacy of Ross Perot in 1992 proved, without the backing of one of the two major political parties, election to office is difficult, if not nearly impossible.

In spite of the importance of political parties, some political scientists, including Alan Ware (Reading 54), argue that the strength of political parties is on the decline. Cash-rich or highly popular independent and third-party candidates can go directly to the voters through mass mailings, the media, and even Internet (see Reading 59).

Other political scientists attribute the decline in the importance of political parties to the rise of interest groups. The number of interest groups has increased significantly since the 1970s, says Philip A. Mundo (Reading 57), and they also lead more people to become involved in politics, even if that involvement is only on an issue-by-issue basis.

Noted interest-group theorist David B. Truman has advanced the argument that the government acts to keep special interests in check, or what he calls "equilibrium," much in the way that James Madison understood the need to control factions.* Common Cause's Deborah Baldwin

---

The Governmental Process: Political Interests and Public Opinion (New York: Alfred A. Knopf, 1951).

illustrates this point in her discussion of the Information Superhighway (Reading 59). Before some Americans could adjust to cable TV, says Baldwin, old interest groups saw the need to make their views on various aspects and possible consequences of the superhighway known. Similarly, other new groups were formed to pressure the government for policies they wanted. Within a few years, large and small interest groups emerged in this new policy arena to lobby for interests.

Both interest groups and political parties try to influence the results of elections but in at least one way different from the kinds of influence they exerted during earlier times. The development of political action committees (PACs), discussed here by journalist Hedrick Smith (Reading 58) and by Alan I. Abramowitz and Jeffrey A. Segal in Chapter 12 (Reading 61), has added a new twist to campaigns and elections. Interest groups and political parties use PACs to reward their friends in Congress. They also use sizable PAC contributions to help the election efforts of those candidates who, if elected, will advance PAC positions in Congress.

· 52 ·

Federalist No. 10

JAMES MADISON

In one of the most famous *Federalist Papers, Federalist No. 10,*
Madison makes a strong case for the new national government. With its
built-in system of checks and balances, he argues that the new government can control what he terms "factions"—citizens united and activated
by common impulses or passions. Madison sees the proposed new national government as able to control these factions. Yet it is clear that although he foresaw factions as inevitable, he never envisioned how
quickly political parties and interest groups would come to play a major
role in the functioning and even organization of the new government.

. . .

Among the numerous advantages promised by a well-constructed
Union, none deserves to be more accurately developed than its tendency
to break and control the violence of faction. . . .

. . . The instability, injustice, and confusion introduced into the public
councils, have, in truth, been the mortal diseases under which popular
governments have everywhere perished. . . .

. . . These must be chiefly, if not wholly, effects of the unsteadiness
and injustice with which a factious spirit has tainted our public administration.

By a faction, I understand a number of citizens, whether amounting to
a majority or minority of the whole, who are united and actuated by some
common impulse of passion, or of interest, adverse to the rights of other
citizens, or to the permanent and aggregate interests of the community.

There are two methods of curing the mischiefs of faction: the one, by
removing its causes; the other, by controlling its effects.

There are again two methods of removing the causes of faction: the
one, by destroying the liberty which is essential to its existence; the other,
by giving to every citizen the same opinions, the same passions, and the
same interests.

It could never be more truly said than of the first remedy, that it is
worse than the disease. Liberty is to faction what air is to fire, an aliment
without which it instantly expires. But it could not be less folly to abolish
liberty, which is essential to political life, because it nourishes faction,
than it would be to wish the annihilation of air, which is essential to
animal life, because it imparts to fire its destructive energy.

The second expedient is as impracticable as the first would be unwise. As long as the reason of man continues fallible, and he is at liberty to exercise it, different opinions will be formed. . . .

The inference to which we are brought is, that the *causes* of faction cannot be removed, and that relief is only to be sought in the means of controlling its *effects*.

If a faction consists of less than a majority, relief is supplied by the republican principle, which enables the majority to defeat its sinister views by regular vote. It may clog the administration, it may convulse the society; but it will be unable to execute and mask its violence under the forms of the Constitution. When a majority is included in a faction, the form of popular government, on the other hand, enables it to sacrifice to its ruling passion or interest both the public good and the rights of other citizens.

TOWARD CRITICAL THINKING

1. What methods did Madison see as ways to end the causes of faction? Is it feasible or even desirable to end factions in a democratic society?

2. Given that strong Anti-Federalist sentiment had already emerged to challenge ratification of the Constitution, why doesn't Madison appear to address this type of "faction"?

· *53* ·

Party Government

E. E. SCHATTSCHNEIDER

Although Madison apparently failed to predict the importance of
political parties in the political system, political scientist E. E. Schattschneider posits that political parties are the "most important institutions
of democratic government." In this excerpt from his classic book, *Party
Government,* Schattschneider defines political parties as power seekers.
He also cautions that parties are not voters; they are associations formed
to seek power.

Broadly, there are two fundamental types of political organizations,
political parties and pressure groups. In the United States it is necessary
to distinguish a third type, the minor party, which differs from the major
party or the real party more fundamentally than in size, merely. That is,
the minor party is not a smaller edition of the real party; it is not a party
at all. . . .

What is a political party? A party may be defined in terms of its
purpose and in terms of the *methods* used to attain its purpose. A political
party is first of all an organized attempt to get power. Power is here
defined as control of the government. That is the objective of party
organization. The fact that the party aims at control of the government as
a whole distinguishes it from pressure groups. The fact that the major
party bids for power at all distinguishes it from minor parties whose
interest in power is too remote to have a determinative effect on their
behavior. . . .

Whether or not a given political organization is a real party is a
question of fact. Does it in fact have control of the government or has it
in fact been able to create a general belief that it will take control of the
government at a date early enough to be so exciting and serious as to
determine the behavior of the people who are participating in the adven-
ture? Since control of a government is one of the most important things
imaginable, it follows that a real party is one of the most significant
organizations in society.

Parties are defined in terms of the bid for power because it is impossible to define them in terms of any other objective. . . . [Noted English political philosopher Edmund] Burke obscured the issue first by defining a party as an association of men who have agreed on some principle of public policy, but it is equally just to say that parties are held together by the "cohesive power of public plunder." It is obvious that men will not get power unless they want it. . . .

In the second place, the bid for power must be made by way of certain special and characteristic means. What is the party method? First, it is a peaceable method. The parties do not seize power by a *coup d'etat.* They act within the framework of the regime. This presupposes also that the parties are free to use peaceful methods. The precondition of party government is that the parties and the government tolerate each other, in other words, that there is a certain comity between the party in power and the opposition party. . . .

Whatever else the parties may be, they are not associations of the voters who support the party candidates. That is to say, the Democratic party is not an association of the twenty-seven million people who voted for Mr. Roosevelt in November, 1940. . . .

The Republican party professes to be an association of all Republicans, i.e., of all partisans who vote for Republican candidates. It follows that these partisans are "members" of the Republican party. The parties have drawn this portrait of themselves so successfully that assumptions concerning the nature of the parties, wholly unjustified by the facts, have gained general acceptance. One of the incidental consequences of the common notion that the parties are associations of large masses of partisans is that the states have enacted a large body of legislation regulating the internal processes of the parties in the interests of their "members." . . . .

It is, however, one thing to be a partisan and another thing to be a member of an association. Let us suppose that the owner of a professional baseball club issued a membership certificate with each ticket sold and that these certificates entitled each "member" of an imaginary association of patrons to buy tickets to all future games and to cheer lustily for the home team. How would the purely promotional "association" so created differ from the Republican and Democratic parties, conceived of as associations of partisans?

. . . As a matter of fact, membership in a political party has none of the usual characteristics of membership in an association. In most states the party has no control over its own membership. Any legal voter may on his own initiative and by his own declaration execute legal formalities before a duly designated *public* official making himself a registered member of the party.

. . . Moreover, the member assumes no obligations to the party. He takes no oath prescribed by the party. He does not subscribe to a declaration of party principles and does not sign articles of incorporation. He does not pay membership dues, is not liable for the debts of the party, and has no equity in its property. He has no duties whatever to perform as a condition of membership. He is not required to solicit votes, is not required to participate in the campaign, need not attend party rallies, and need not vote for the party candidates. In fact, he need not vote at all. . . . Membership in a political party is therefore highly unreal because the party has no control over its own membership and the member has no obligations to the party.

. . . Thus we arrive at the "iron law of oligarchy" formulated by Robert Michels, who, however, wrote primarily about the parties in European multiparty systems. The party is divided into two entities: (1) an organized group of insiders who have effective control of the party and (2) a mass of passive "members" who seem to have little to say about it.

. . . The unfortunate result of the confusion created by the concept of the party as a large association of partisans is that it blackens the name of the parties. The parties are the most important instrumentalities of democratic government.

TOWARD CRITICAL THINKING

1. According to Schattschneider, what distinguishes a political party from a pressure group? A major from a minor political party? How does Robert Michels "iron law of oligarchy" help to explain political parties?

2. How do political parties gain power? Does a landslide Republican presidential victory mean that the Republican Party is the choice of a majority of Americans?

· 54 ·

Disappearing Parties?

ALAN WARE

Since shortly after its Founding period, the United States, unlike
most nations, has had a two-party political system. The decentralized nature of both parties today—Republican and Democrat—is a key feature
of their organizational structure and is reflective of the federal system.
But changes that occurred in the late 1950s through the mid-1970s, have
substantially altered the nature of political parties in the United States.

Like gridiron football, American political parties are a peculiarly
American version of a more general phenomenon. . . . Now there are,
perhaps, four features of these parties which would immediately strike
any observer as being unusual. First, no other large country in the western
world has such an unqualified two-party system; at neither the federal nor
the state levels of government are parties other than the Democrats and
Republicans represented. Secondly, the two parties are very old; not since
the Republicans replaced the Whigs in the 1850s, when America was a
predominantly agricultural nation with a mere thirty-two states in the
Union, has a new party displaced an old one. Thirdly, these parties have
retained in modified form a caucus form of organization and a cadre style
of membership which they developed in the first half of the nineteenth
century. Finally, in the twentieth century American parties became public
rather than private institutions—at least at the state level; their organizational structures are controlled by state laws, as are their procedures for
nominating candidates.

Yet, if in one respect parties in the United States have been very stable
institutions, they did undergo a major transformation between the early
1960s and the mid-1970s. From one perspective, this transformation can
be described as party collapse, but from another the essential character of
the American parties remained unaltered.

◆ The Party Structure

. . . The key feature of the organizational structures which the American parties established was decentralization. Parties were groups of local
political 'influentials' who came together to put up candidates to contest

SOURCE: Alan Ware, *Political Parties: Electoral Change and Structural Response*
(Oxford, England: Blackwell Publishers, 1987), pp. 117–136. Reprinted by permission.

elections, so that, looked at from the national perspective, parties were nothing more than coalitions of local party elites. . . . Indeed, by the 1830s the very decentralization of government at all levels—through the federal system, the separation of powers, and the Jacksonian attempts to make most public offices elective—worked against the emergence of centralized parties. This institutional framework restricted subsequent party development. On the other hand, American parties did find a solution to the problem of how to recruit a party workforce to perform electoral tasks. The spirit of voluntarism in American communities, noted by de Tocqueville in the 1830s, could be utilized in political mobilization, though, in the second half of the nineteenth century, even this would have produced relatively ineffective parties in the rapidly expanding cities. But, by then, a new form of political organization had developed in the cities, first in the immigrant Irish communities and later among other immigrant groups. This was the hierarchically organized, patronage-based, political machine.

. . . In the first twenty years of the twentieth century there were two developments which further bolstered the decentralized nature of America's parties. Both resulted from attempts by progressive reformers to check the corruption and abuses of power associated with party machines. Most states enacted laws defining the organizational form which a major party must have. Thus, in many places the basic unit of the party became the precinct committeeman who was elected in a primary election. . . . Again, in most states, the direct primary was adopted as a nominating device for public office. In the context of an already decentralized party structure, this helped to strengthen one element of this decentralization— the individual candidate.

By the mid twentieth century American party organizations appeared to have reached a position of stability, after the initial impact of the progressive reforms had been absorbed. To understand the later changes, it is worth describing the position at that time. The most important point to note is that, although all state parties exhibited decentralization, there were considerable variations in the relationships between party organizations, candidates and other elements in the parties. This ranged from party powerlessness in western states like California, where the party organizations had few resources of their own, to dominance by the organizations in the nomination of candidates and in election campaigns. . . .

. . . From about the end of the 1950s, the American parties were affected by three developments, the interaction of which was to profoundly change their nature by the mid-1970s. . . . In the first place, there were a number of changes in state laws relating to elections and parties, and these weakened the position of some party organizations. One of the most important was the 'one-man one-vote' requirement which, in the early 1960s, the U.S. Supreme Court included in its decisions on the reapportionment of electoral districts; this led to an increase in the use of single-member districts in state legislature elections, which was a device less conducive to party control than multi-member districts. Again, new campaign techniques became increasingly available to candidates, and they could now more easily acquire campaign resources which were independent of those controlled by the party organizations. Television advertising, opinion polls, computerized direct mail solicitations and the like were devices candidates could buy directly, and thereby bypass the parties. . . .

. . . Moreover, the political upheavals of the 1960s had a major impact on the Democratic party. In the 1950s 'issue-oriented' liberals had become a new force in the Democratic party organizations of a number of cities, and at that time they had generally been loyal to their party. The effects of the Vietnam War, civil rights and other controversies weakened the party orientation of newer liberal activists, and this further strengthened the position of Democratic candidates *vis-à-vis* their party organizations. However, an indirect consequence of these upheavals was a radical change in the system of presidential nomination. At the bitterly divisive National Convention in 1968 the Democrats agreed to examine the process by which delegates would be selected for future conventions. At the time this seemed a small victory for the minority group of anti-war liberals. In the event, the party accepted the report of the commission which the convention had set up, the McGovern–Fraser Commission, and this transformed the nomination process. In one respect the process was centralized, in that the national party was to set criteria which state parties would have to meet when selecting delegates. For the first time in American party history, a national party was claiming authority over the affairs of the state parties. More importantly, though, the reforms decentralized presidential selection, by making voters in presidential primary elections a far more important element in the process. This had not been the intention of most of those responsible for the reforms. Their aim had been to give greater weight to party activists in delegate selection but, for many parties in states which used caucuses and conventions for this purpose, compliance with the new regulations was seen as being too complex. They opted for the administratively easier solution of switching to the use of a primary election. Because a primary attracts more publicity than a convention, Republican parties generally followed the Democrats' lead in abandoning the use of conventions. The result was that during the 1970s the number of states using primaries more than doubled, to over 30, as did the proportion of delegates selected in primaries. By 1980 about three-quarters of all delegates were chosen through primary elections. This greatly diminished the role of party organizations in presidential nominations and increased that of the candidates themselves. The central actor in the process was now the candidate appealing directly to party voters.

By the end of the 1970s the importance of party organizations in helping to nominate candidates, and in election campaigns, had been greatly reduced. American parties remained decentralized, but it was the organizations of individual public officials and challenging candidates, rather than party organizations, which were at the center of this system. However, this transformation did not lead to the complete collapse of party in America. . . . On the contrary, if anything, both in Congress and in state legislatures, the parties were becoming more distinct ideologically; excluding the special case of the South, the Democrats were becoming a more pronounced centre–liberal party while the Republicans were losing this element and becoming a genuinely conservative party. . . .

So far we have described developments in American party organizations up to about 1980, and we must now consider the potential for further changes. The most likely prospect is for a continuing shift towards candidate-centred parties, but perhaps more slowly than in the period from the late 1950s to the mid-1970s. There are four points which can be made about this. First, there are still some states where traditional party organizations have influence in the nomination process. Small patronage 'operations' still survive—some in economically declining, industrial cities, some because of a stable system of patronage income from the courts, and some for other reasons. They may well endure for decades. Although we would expect further weakening of party structures, as these 'operations' come to be controlled by individual public officials rather than the more cohesive party organizations, the remnants of the old machines will be more difficult to displace than the parties which collapsed in the 1960s. Secondly, successful fund raising by the national Republican Party has already spurred the Democrats to develop this function themselves, so that we might expect a deceleration in the declining importance of national parties as fund raisers. However, it is less likely that state and local parties would be able to revive their status as major financial contributors. Thirdly, the application of new campaign techniques to lower levels of public office will continue but it may slow down. . . .

. . . This will tend to reduce further the importance of party organization workers in campaigns. Finally, there would seem to be little momentum for significant changes in the new presidential nomination system. While it is widely criticized as being too long and expensive, there are no groups within the parties which have the power to effect a return to the more 'balanced' system of the pre-1968 era or a shift to a single, nationwide primary election. Yet dissatisfaction with the expensive and highly fragmented procedures which emerged after 1968 may pre-empt some changes to the system. For example, in 1985 the governors of southern states agreed to try to hold their primaries on the same day in 1988, in a bid to increase southern influence in the process. In other words, in general, we may see further modifications rather than a continuing revolution in party organization.

♦ Intra-party Relations

There are three kinds of significant power relations within political parties: those between party activists and organization leaders, those between organization leaders and the party's representatives in public office, and those between the activists and the public officials. Up to the early 1950s the most usual arrangement in America was that the public officials had little to fear from the activists. In states with weak party organizations, neither the activists nor the organization leaders had the resources to be more than one element among many on which the public official could draw when mounting a reelection campaign. In strong party states the organizations would have considerable leverage over public officials, but neither group would face much opposition from grass-roots activists. . . .

♦ Concluding Remarks

It should now be clear why outside observers have so much difficulty in understanding American parties. Just as the smile of the Cheshire cat remained after the cat's disappearance, so American parties have survived the decline of the party organizations. . . . However, the main reason why the growing importance of the *individual* public official has not led to the collapse of party politics is that the nominating power of the ideological activist base of the Republican Party has reduced the range of political views which Republican public officials represent. In the 1980s the Republican Party is a conservative party. There is no reason for believing that this trend towards conservative dominance of the party will not continue into the 1990s; even in Massachusetts, a state where Republicans traditionally nominated moderates for major offices, a conservative won the nomination for the U.S. Senate in 1984. Yet, just as the parties become more ideologically distinct, so their structures are likely to become even weaker. In the 1990s the parties may well have declined further yet be as much in evidence as they were a hundred years ago.

TOWARD CRITICAL THINKING

1. What were the three developments that affected the nature of the political parties from the 1950s to the 1970s? Do these kinds of developments continue to affect one or both parties today?

2. What differences do you see in the two parties? Box 11.1 summarizes some key differences in the platforms, or statements of beliefs, of the two major political parties. Can you think of other differences? Is Ware correct in characterizing its conservative base as a major reason for the continued successes of the Republican Party? Could this ideological core ever be more of a hindrance than a help?

BOX 11.1

The 1992 Republican and Democratic Party Platforms Compared

	Domestic Policy	
	REPUBLICANS	DEMOCRATS
Abortion	"Support human life amendment to the Constitution . . . oppose the use of public revenues for abortion"	"Stand behind the right of every woman to choose . . . regardless of ability to pay"
Gay rights	"Oppose efforts . . . to include sexual preference as a protected minority"	"Provide civil rights protection for gay men and lesbians"
Taxes	"Oppose any attempt to increase taxes"	"Forc[e] the rich to pay their fair share"
Campaign reform	"Oppose arbitrary spending limits for congressional candidates"	"We must limit overall campaign spending [for congressional candidates]"
	Foreign Policy	
South Africa	"Condemn all violence . . . and applaud those who seek reconciliation"	"Consider reimposing [U.S. government] sanctions against South Africa"
China	"Maintain the relationship with China so that we can effectively encourage [democratic] reform"	"Condition . . . favorable trade terms for China on respect for human rights"

Sources: 1992 Democratic and Republican Party Platforms.

· 55 ·

Williams v. Rhodes
393 U.S. 23 (1968)

Both E. E. Schattschneider and Alan Ware note that the United
States is unique in the dominance of a two-party system. Congress, for example, uses political party affiliation to organize itself, and minority
party members or independents must ally themselves with one of the two
major parties in order to get committee assignments.

Minority parties are also handicapped by the decentralized nature of
the party system discussed by Ware. All states, for example, allow the Republican and Democratic parties to receive relatively low percentages of
the popular vote in the preceding election to maintain their places on the
next year's ballot. (Ohio required them each to attract 10 percent of the
votes cast.) In contrast, most states make it much more difficult for third
or minority parties to get their candidates on the ballot and to keep the
party's spot on the ballot in subsequent elections.

At issue in *Williams* was an Ohio statute that required a new political
party seeking a spot on the ballot for its presidential candidate to collect
signatures from registered voters totaling 15 percent of the total population
that voted in the last gubernatorial election. Moreover, these signatures had
to be secured by the February before the November presidential election.
This was a nearly impossible task for third parties or independent candidates.

The facts of the case are contained in Justice Black's opinion below.
Williams was actually two cases that the Supreme Court joined; only portions of the opinion dealing with the new American Independent Party
are included.

Opinion: Justice Black
Vote: 8 to 1

. . .

The State of Ohio claims the power to keep minority parties and
independent candidates off the ballot under Art. II, Sec. 1, of the Constitution, which provides that:

"Each State shall appoint, in such Manner as the Legislature thereof may direct, a Number of Electors, equal to the whole Number of Senators and Representatives to which the State may be entitled in the
Congress. . . ."

The Ohio American Independent Party . . . brought suit to challenge
the validity of these Ohio laws as applied to them, on the ground that they
deny the Party and the voters who might wish to vote for the equal
protection of the laws, guaranteed against state abridgement by the Equal
Protection Clause of the Fourteenth Amendment. . . .

The cases arose in this way:

The Ohio American Independent Party was formed in January 1968 by Ohio partisans of former Governor George C. Wallace of Alabama. During the following six months a campaign was conducted for obtaining signatures on petitions to give the Party a place on the ballot and over 450,000 signatures were eventually obtained, more than the 433,100 required. The State contends and the Independent Party agrees that due to the interaction of several provisions of the Ohio laws, such petitions were required to be filed by February 7, 1968, and so the Secretary of the State of Ohio informed the Party that it would not be given a place on the ballot. Neither in the pleadings, the affidavits before the District Court, the arguments there, nor in our Court has the State denied that the petitions were signed by enough qualified electors of Ohio to meet the 15 percent requirement under Ohio law. Having demonstrated its numerical strength, the Independent Party argued that this and the other burdens, including the early deadline for filing petitions and the requirement of a primary election conforming to detailed and rigorous standards, denied the Party and certain Ohio voters equal protection of the laws. The three-judge District Court unanimously agreed with this contention and ruled that the State must be required to provide a space for write-in votes. A majority of the District Court refused to hold, however, that the Party's name must be printed on the ballot, on the ground that Wallace and his adherents had been guilty of "laches" by filing their suit too late to allow the Ohio Legislature an opportunity to remedy, in time for the presidential balloting, the defects which the District Court held the law possessed. The appellants in No. 543 then moved before Mr. Justice Stewart, Circuit Justice for the Sixth Circuit, for an injunction which would order the Party's candidates to be put on the ballot pending appeal. After consulting with the other members of the Court who were available, and after the State represented that the grant of interlocutory relief would be in the interests of the efficient operation of the electoral machinery if this Court considered the chances of successful challenge to the Ohio statutes good, Mr. Justice Stewart granted the injunction. . . .

We turn . . . to the question whether the court below properly held that the Ohio laws before us result in a denial of equal protection of the laws.

. . . In the present situation the state laws place burdens on two different, although overlapping, kinds of rights—the right of individuals to associate for the advancement of political beliefs, and the right of qualified voters, regardless of their political persuasion, to cast their votes effectively. Both of these rights, of course, rank among our most precious freedoms. We have repeatedly held that freedom of association is protected by the First Amendment. And of course this freedom protected against federal encroachment by the First Amendment is entitled under the Fourteenth Amendment to the same protection from infringement by the States. Similarly we have said with reference to the right to vote: "No right is more precious in a free country than that of having a voice in the election of those who make the laws under which, as good citizens, we must live. Other rights, even the most basic, are illusory if the right to vote is undermined."

. . . No extended discussion is required to establish that the Ohio laws before us give the two old, established parties a decided advantage over any new parties struggling for existence and thus place substantially unequal burdens on both the right to vote and the right to associate. The right to form a party for the advancement of political goals means little if a party can be kept off the election ballot and thus denied an equal opportunity to win votes. So also, the right to vote is heavily burdened if that vote may be cast only for one of two parties at a time when other parties are clamoring for a place on the ballot. In determining whether the State has power to place such unequal burdens on minority groups where rights of this kind are at stake, the decisions of this Court have consistently held that "only a compelling state interest in the regulation of a subject within the State's constitutional power to regulate can justify limiting First Amendment freedoms." *NAACP* v. *Button,* 371 U.S. 415, 438 (1963).

The State has here failed to show any "compelling interest" which justifies imposing such heavy burdens on the right to vote and to associate.

The State asserts that the following interests are served by the restrictions it imposes. It claims that the State may validly promote a two-party system in order to encourage compromise and political stability. The fact is, however, that the Ohio system does not merely favor a "two-party system"; it favors two particular parties—the Republicans and the Democrats—and in effect tends to give them a complete monopoly. There is, of course, no reason why two parties should retain a permanent monopoly on the right to have people vote for or against them. . . . New parties struggling for their place must have the time and opportunity to organize in order to meet reasonable requirements for ballot position, just as the old parties have had in the past. . . .

. . . Under the circumstances we require Ohio to permit the Independent Party to remain on the ballot, along with its candidates for President and Vice President, subject, of course, to compliance with valid regulatory laws of Ohio, including the law relating to the qualification and functions of electors.

TOWARD CRITICAL THINKING

1. Why do states make it so much easier for the two major parties to put their candidates on the ballot?

2. How does the Court rationalize its finding that Ohio's requirements discriminate against third parties? Are laws such as Ohio's the only reason so few new political parties arise? What do the major parties do to discourage the formation of third parties?

· 56 ·

The Logic of Collective Action

MANCUR OLSON JR.

Economists, political scientists, and other social scientists have long been concerned not only with the development of political parties, but also with interest groups. Defining interest groups, as well as speculating on why individuals join them, are issues that have attracted considerable scholarly attention. Economist Mancur Olson Jr. argues that at least when economic or pocketbook issues are involved, it is incorrect to assume that large groups of individuals with common interests will act together to pursue a common goal. Thus, for example, although large numbers of people may see the need for a system of better health care, Olson posits that it would not be rational for all of them to work for change in the system because if change is obtained through the efforts of others, all who favored change will profit, regardless of whether they worked for it.

It is often taken for granted, at least where economic objectives are involved, that groups of individuals with common interests usually attempt to further those common interests. Groups of individuals with common interests are expected to act on behalf of their personal interests. This opinion . . . has, in addition, occupied a prominent place in political science, at least in the United States, where the study of pressure groups has been dominated by a celebrated "group theory" based on the idea that groups will act when necessary to further their common or group goals. . . .

. . . The view that groups act to serve their interests presumably is based upon the assumption that the individuals in groups act out of self-interest. If the individuals in a group altruistically disregarded their personal welfare, it would not be very likely that collectively they would seek some selfish common or group objective. Such altruism, is, however, considered exceptional, and self-interested behavior is usually thought to be the rule, at least when economic issues are at stake; no one is surprised when individual businessmen seek higher profits, when individual workers seek higher wages, or when individual consumers seek lower prices. The idea that groups tend to act in support of their group interests is

SOURCE: Reprinted by permission of the publishers of *The Logic of Collective Action: Public Goods and the Theory of Groups* by Mancur Olson, Cambridge, Mass.: Harvard University Press. Copyright © 1965, 1971 by the President and Fellows of Harvard College.

supposed to follow logically from this widely accepted premise of rational, self-interested behavior. In other words, if the members of some group have a common interest or objective, and if they would all be better off if that objective were achieved, it has been thought to follow logically that the individuals in that group would, if they were rational and self-interested, act to achieve that objective.

But it is *not* in fact true that the idea that groups will act in their self-interest follows logically from the premise of rational and self-interested behavior. It does *not* follow, because all of the individuals in a group would gain if they achieved their group objective, that they would act to achieve that objective, even if they were all rational and self-interested. Indeed, unless the number of individuals in a group is quite small, or unless there is coercion or some other special device to make individuals act in their common interest, *rational, self-interested individuals will not act to achieve their common or group interests.* In other words, even if all of the individuals in a large group are rational and self-interested, and would gain if, as a group, they acted to achieve their common interest or objective, they will still not voluntarily act to achieve that common or group interest. The notion that groups of individuals will act to achieve their common or group interests, far from being a logical implication of the assumption that the individuals in a group will rationally further their individual interests, is in fact inconsistent with that assumption.

. . . If the members of a large group rationally seek to maximize their personal welfare, they will *not* act to advance their common or group objectives unless there is coercion to force them to do so, or unless some separate incentive, distinct from the achievement of the common or group interest, is offered to the members of the group individually on the condition that they help bear the costs or burdens involved in the achievement of the group objectives. Nor will such large groups form organizations to further their common goals in the absence of the coercion or the separate incentives just mentioned. These points hold true even when there is unanimous agreement in a group about the common good and the methods of achieving it.

The widespread view, common throughout the social sciences, that groups tend to further their interests, is accordingly unjustified, at least when it is based, as it usually is, on the (sometimes implicit) assumption that groups act in their self-interest because individuals do. There is paradoxically the logical possibility that groups composed of either altruistic individuals or irrational individuals may sometimes act in their common or group interests. . . . Thus the customary view that groups of individuals with common interests tend to further those common interests appears to have little if any merit.

TOWARD CRITICAL THINKING

1. Olson is famous for his enunciation of what is called the "free rider problem." What is a free rider? Can you think of examples in which free riders have profited from the work of organized interests?

2. Why does Olson draw a distinction between large and small groups? Which type of group is likely to be more effective in the legislative arena, or does size really not matter?

· 57 ·

A Sympathetic View of the Role of Interest Groups

PHILIP A. MUNDO

> As Mundo notes, despite Madison's warnings about the evils of fac-
> tions, diverse interest groups today play an important role in the political
> process. As the number of interest groups in the United States has in-
> creased, so has their tendency to foster political participation, which
> Mundo views as a benefit not anticipated by Madison. Moreover, interest
> groups use a variety of strategies and tactics to advance their goals in the
> public arena.

✦ A Sympathetic View of the Role of Interest Groups

Despite Madison's early warning of the mischiefs of factions, interest groups do convey the concerns of their members to government officials, and thus they are one means by which citizens can influence government. The link between government and interest-group members is typically more specialized than the one provided by political parties.

Interest groups are also a major source of political information for their members. Through regular publications—newsweeklies, news-letters, magazines—interest-group officials inform and educate members about politics. In some interest groups, personal contact through business meetings and social gatherings further helps to disseminate information.

Interest groups also foster political participation, with the minimal act of joining an interest group counting as participation in itself. Through membership, citizens indicate a political preference or perhaps tacit ap-proval of a set of political positions, or less demanding still, acquiescence with respect to the political positions taken by their group.

Finally, to the extent that interest groups influence government offi-cials, they make those officials more responsive to the groups' members. Relatedly, interest groups monitor government officials, making them accountable for their actions. For example, environmental groups follow the enforcement activities of the Environmental Protection Agency (EPA),

SOURCE: Philip A. Mundo, *Interest Groups* (Chicago, Ill.: Nelson-Hall Publishers, 1992), pp. 6–13. Reprinted by permission.

and the American Pharmaceuticals Association keeps a close eye on the studies conducted by the Food and Drug Administration.

◆ Trends in Political Intermediation

Changes in interest groups in the United States roughly parallel those in American politics. In sweeping terms, American government is more open now than ever before, in the sense that there are more access points to decisions and they are increasingly dispersed throughout government. Thus, interest groups as well as individual citizens may try to influence government by going directly to Congress, the bureaucracy, and increasingly, the courts.

As decision making has become scattered throughout the national government, Congress and the bureaucracy have opened their decision processes. The number of congressional subcommittees has increased, creating more access to congressional decision making. Similarly, administrative proceedings have been opened to the public, once again allowing increased access to government decision making for anyone who can and wants to take advantage of it.

As government decision making opens up, the connection between government and citizen becomes more direct. The decline of American political parties has added overwhelmingly to this development. As the significance of party declines in the eye of the citizen, parties' functions of organizing politics, defining issues, and shaping participation decline with it. Parties no longer connect citizens to government in the way they used to. Something else must; the mass media and interest groups have emerged to fill the gap left by parties, but the way they link citizens to government is different from the way political parties once did.

Mass Media

As a main link between citizens and government, the mass media have to some extent supplanted the roles traditionally played by parties and interest groups. The news media, especially television and radio, play critical roles in coverage of election campaigns. The thirty-second sound bite and the photo opportunity have become commonplace in modern presidential and congressional campaigns. And candidates spend millions of dollars every election in television campaign advertising.

Similarly, members of Congress and the president use television to communicate directly with the people. Both the House and the Senate have elaborate television studios that allow members to broadcast messages directly to their constituents. And presidents shepherd their use of television to give their policies and popularity maximum benefit. Thus, the mass media have allowed contact between elected officials and citizens that is direct in many ways.

As this has occurred, there has been a vague trend toward centralizing political conflict at the national level. The major decisions, even those affecting what state and local governments do, are increasingly made in Washington. Congress and the federal bureaucracy hand out the money that is often crucial to state and local programs. And national regulations—say, with respect to environmental issues—are frequently the guidelines used by the states. The lesson has not been lost on the news media. The convenience of satellite hookups has enabled local television stations from around the country to establish bureaus in the capital, from which they broadcast reports on national politics and developments in Washington that are relevant to their regions.

◆ Interest Groups: More of Them and More Active

The most dramatic development in interest groups in recent years is the explosion in the number of interest groups engaged in politics at the national level. John T. Tierney and Kay Lehman Schlozman found that "of the 2,800 organizations that had lobbying offices in the capital as of 1982, 40 percent have been founded since 1960, and 25 percent since 1970." And interest groups have been busier than they had been in the past. They engage more frequently in the whole range of interest-group activity in Washington—"direct lobbying of officials, testifying at hearings, helping to plan legislative strategy, making financial contributions to electoral campaigns, mounting grassroots lobbying efforts, filing lawsuits."

In addition to dramatic growth in the number of interest groups operating at the national level, the kinds of concerns represented by interest groups in the United States have changed, though perhaps less dramatically than conventional wisdom might lead one to believe. Business groups still dominate organized interests in American politics. According to Tierney and Schlozman, "A full 70 percent of all the interests that have some form of Washington representation are business, especially trade associations and corporations." People with lesser resources, while finding some representation in Washington in recent years, are still vastly underrepresented compared with business interests. "Of the nearly 7,000 organizations that have their own lobbying operation or representation by lobbyists-for-hire, less than 5 percent represent those in society with few resources." Such groups pursue issues associated with civil rights, minority rights, social welfare, poverty, the elderly, the handicapped, and women's rights. The "public" interest is represented by only 4 percent of the universe of interest groups in Washington.

However, the dominance of business organizations is less overwhelming if only organized interest groups are counted and not every organization with some presence in Washington—either from within the organization or from a hired lobbyist. In this case, 25 percent of interest groups represent business interests, social welfare interests are represented by 11 percent of groups, and roughly 14 percent pursue "public affairs" interests. . . .

The discrepancy in the two distributions is attributable to the definition of represented interest. In the Tierney and Schlozman view, any organization with some presence in Washington, including a hired lobbyist, counts as representing an interest. Defining 'represented interest' to include only formal interest groups produces a more balanced distribution of interest groups in national politics. . . . The difference in the results produced by these two counting techniques highlights a stubborn measurement problem for those who analyze interest groups. Should one count hired lobbyists? How does one count an organization—say, a business firm—that is represented in several ways: by its own lobbyist, by a hired lobbyist, by membership in several trade associations, and by membership in two of the major business all-purpose associations? Given these questions, absolute judgments on the data must be made with caution. Nevertheless, the essential point that business interests comprise the largest set of represented interests remains clear.

Organized labor in the United States makes up another critical aspect of the interest-group universe. Union membership peaked as a percentage of the work force in 1970 when 25.4 percent of workers belonged to labor unions. By 1988, only 17 percent of workers were union members. While organized labor in general was shrinking, the distribution of membership among unions changed. Large industrial unions like the United Automobile Workers (UAW), the United Steel Workers, and the International Association of Machinists (IAM) lost sizeable portions of their memberships. At the same time, upstart unions whose members come from service industries (including government) faired better. Thus, the Service Employee International Union and the American Federation of State, County, and Municipal Employees have grown in recent years. The place of organized labor as an important part of interest-group representation in the United States has been significantly affected by the overall shrinkage in union membership and the redistribution of members among unions.

Recently, single-issue groups, ideological groups, public interest groups, religious groups, and environmental groups, though not entirely new, have gained prominence in Washington and reflect some of the changes in political currents in American politics. Although single-issue groups have been active in politics throughout the twentieth century (note, for example, the activities of the Anti-Saloon League), in recent years the sharpness of their goals and volume of their voices have attracted the attention of the news media and scholars alike. Such groups as the National Right-to-Life Committee, the National Abortion Rights Action League, the National Rifle Association (NRA), and Handgun Control, Inc. specialize in trying to place their special concerns at the top of the national political agenda. Similarly, environmental groups, although present on the American political scene for many years, have gained notoriety in their efforts to initiate and influence environmental policy, and they have enjoyed healthy expansion in the 1980s, owing in part to the anti-environmental policies of the Reagan administration. The activities of religious groups reflect a social and religious conservatism that gained renewed strength in the 1980s. Beginning around the late 1960s and early 1970s, public interest groups sought to represent unrepresented concerns, and the strident efforts of such groups as Common Cause and Public Citizen (one of the groups spawned by Ralph Nader) have had a marked effect on national policy.

There is little that is absolutely new about what interest groups do to achieve their goals. Lobbying, grassroots activity, public relations, litigation, and contributing to political campaigns still constitute the core of interest-group strategies. But interest groups are using the full range of strategies to a greater extent than they have in the past.

Interest-group representatives try to affect public policy through direct contact with members of Congress and bureaucrats, and such direct lobbying remains the centerpiece of the interest groups' arsenal of influence. Familiar activities include one-to-one meetings with key officials or their staffs, testifying at congressional and administrative hearings, providing technical and political information on issues, drafting legislation and administrative rules, and maintaining social ties to government officials. There is nothing novel about these activities; lobbyists have used these techniques for years.

Grassroots lobbying—efforts to influence government officials by organizing and channeling public opinion to support or oppose a policy—has become more prevalent among interest groups' strategies. Such activities include public rallies, attendance at meetings with public officials, and mass communications with public officials through letter writing, telegram, and telephone campaigns. Interest groups frequently use these strategies in tandem with more traditional lobbying. This "inside-outside" strategy allows a group to enhance its effectiveness by giving the lobbyist extra clout in the form of public pressure. A U.S. representative, for example, is more likely to be sympathetic to a lobbyist's argument if she or he is getting strong support for it from her or his constituents.

Grassroots strategy is frequently associated with single-issue, ideological, and public interest groups. The NRA, for example, relies on its huge membership to pressure members of Congress to oppose gun control. Similarly, the Sierra Club calls upon its members to become involved in its political activities by writing letters, making telephone calls, and occasionally visiting Washington to apply direct pressure on public officials.

More traditional interest groups use grassroots strategies as well. For example, rank-and-file labor union members mail postcards to their elected representatives expressing a position on an issue with which the union is concerned. Business groups have also used grassroots strategies; the United States Chamber of Commerce has one of the most developed grassroots networks in the United States. Relying on local and state chambers of commerce, the national organization is able to exert influence on members of Congress from all around the country.

Another strategy that is increasingly being used is for interest groups to go to court to achieve their goals. Indeed, filing lawsuits has become an effective way to influence public policy. This is especially true with respect to environmental policy, where so much activity is governed by administrative and regulatory agencies such as the EPA and the Occupational Safety and Health Administration (OSHA). Even when they are not actually litigants, interest groups frequently file *amicus curiae* briefs in court cases.

Although interest groups cannot legally make campaign contributions in federal elections, they can do so through a PAC, which formally funnels money to candidates. A lot of ink has been spilled over the activities of PACs. Scholars have documented the number of PACs involved in congressional and presidential elections and statistics are readily available describing the size of PACs, to whom they contribute, and how much they spend. Equally available is information about sources of a particular candidate's money. The controversy over the effect of PACs on elections and public policy rages on. The debate centers on two issues: (1) Does the price of getting elected prevent qualified candidates from running for office? (2) Does money buy influence, thus favoring special interests at the expense of the public interest?

Regardless of the actual relationship between campaign money and influence, interest groups consider campaign contributions an important element of their overall strategies. Lobbyists may find access to members of Congress eased by contributions to their campaigns by the PAC affiliated with the organization the lobbyist represents. This does not mean that the legislators will do as the lobbyist instructs. But it does mean that they will listen to the lobbyist, whereas without the campaign contributions, they may not.

Recent trends in American politics have not diminished the importance of political intermediation in the United States, but they have changed its nature. Parties are less important—certainly they are not the same institutions they were once thought to be—and the news media do not compare favorably with parties as political intermediaries. The recent developments among interest groups in American politics call for a closer examination of their character. What do interest groups look like as political organizations? What are their main features? How do they differ from one category to the next? In what ways do new interest groups differ from old ones? These questions grow out of a concern for interest groups as political institutions and organizations. The concern is for their structure and internal processes. Since interest groups are key elements of the American political system, what does it mean for a citizen to be a member of one? The organizational properties of an interest group determine the group's quality as a link between citizens and government.

TOWARD CRITICAL THINKING

1. How have changes in interest groups paralleled changes in other parts of the political system?

2. What are the different types of interest groups? Are certain types of groups more likely to be more successful in some forums of government than others?

· 58 ·

PAC Power

HEDRICK SMITH

One of the most potent tactics of interest groups is the development of political action committees (PACs). Money is the mother's milk of politics. As PACs have grown, so has their influence in Congress, a body some pundits have alleged is the best legislature "that money can buy." Interest groups spend millions of dollars each year on lobbyists; and through their PACs they also contribute enormous sums to the campaigns of candidates for public office, especially incumbents. In 1992, for example, PACs contributed nearly 180 million dollars to congressional candidates, with the lion's share going to incumbents. And although calls for reforms in the way campaigns are financed are as common as ants at a picnic, little substantive change has actually occurred.

◆ PAC-Man: Raising Big Money

The big gun of lobbying, the political weapon of choice, is money. It looms over the political landscape like the Matterhorn. It is the principal common denominator between the old lobbying game and the new lobbying game, except that the dimensions of the game—the staggering sums involved, and the sheer constant crazy circus of fund-raising—have made money a more visible force than ever before. Legislators are not so readily bought nowadays as during the Yazoo land frauds of the 1790s; nor are they owned outright by a single patron, as in the time of Ulysses S. Grant. Nor does any legislator act quite so openly as agent for a company, as Senator Lyndon Johnson did, for Brown & Root. But organized money oils the machinery of many a congressional subcommittee.

Our political system is literally awash with money, rising to new levels every presidential election. In 1984, a total of $595 million was spent on the presidential race and congressional races. In 1986, even without a presidential race, $450 million was spent on congressional elections. The Republicans have steadily been outstripping the Democrats. In 1986, for example, the Republican National Committee and its two congressional arms spent $254.2 million, compared to $62.7 million for the Democratic National Committee and its congressional arms.

SOURCE: From *The Power Game: How Washington Works* by Hedrick Smith. Copyright © 1988 by Hedrick Smith. Reprinted by permission of Random House, Inc.

Paradoxically, the campaign finance reforms of 1974 granted legitimacy to organized fund-raising and gave a rocket thrust to the new giant of American politics—PAC-Man, the inside-the-beltway nickname of the ubiquitous political action committees. Nowadays, it is routine for a corporation, union, trade association, or interest group to have a PAC to raise funds from its members and then funnel cash to political candidates, in order to push the political agenda of its parent organization.

The reforms of 1974 were aimed at stopping individual fat cats and secret corporate slush funds from bankrolling pet legislators and covertly buying influence. To reduce risk of corruption, the reformers established contribution limits for individuals ($1,000), for political action committees ($5,000 per candidate per election), and for political parties (varied limits and formulas based on the office and the size of the electorate). All candidates were forced to report funding sources. But that reform, like many others, had unintended consequences. Court decisions, interpreting the law, legalized PACs formed by government contractors; that opened the floodgates and made PACs more attractive to business. Suddenly, PACs became the major new money channel. In 1985–86, for example, the top political spenders were the National Congressional Club (Jesse Helm's PAC): $15.8 million; the National Conservative PAC: $9.3 million; the National Committee to Preserve Social Security PAC: $6.2 million; the Realtors PAC: $6 million; the American Medical Association PAC: $5.4 million; and the National Rifle Association Political Victory Fund: $4.7 million.

PACs had their origin in the 1940s with the CIO, but really sprang to life in the 1970s. Their number shot up from 608 in 1974 to 4,157 in 1986; their contributions to congressional campaigns skyrocketed even more sharply, from $8.5 million in 1974 to $132.2 million in 1986. By far the steepest growth came among corporate PACs: eighty-nine in 1974 up to 1,902 in 1986 (compared to 418 for organized labor). More important, the legal limits on PAC giving are full of loopholes. PACs have learned how to "bundle" and "target" their bankrolls to gain a tremendous wallop, making a mockery of the ceilings.

"PAC money is destroying the electoral process," Barry Goldwater protested in a public hearing. "It feeds the growth of special interest groups created solely to channel money into political campaigns. It creates an impression that every candidate is bought and owned by the biggest givers." . . .

"The change has been monumental," fumed Fred Wertheimer, the head of Common Cause. "You look at the amount of money spent to hire lobbyists, the amount of money spent on campaign contributions, the amount of money spent on speaking fees to members of Congress, the amount of money spent to stimulate direct mail and grass-roots lobbying campaigns, the amount of money spent on institutional advertising, the amount of money spent to influence the process here on television—no one has any idea what that adds up to. It's a very subtle system. There are no smoking guns. It's designed so there are no smoking guns. There's a $5,000 limit on PAC campaign donations, but the players in the game do not see that as a limit. They see that as a license."

Lloyd Cutler, former white House counsel for President Carter, was more direct. "It's one step away from bribery. PACs contribute because they count on you to vote with them. . . .

Many lobbyists who decry the current system take part in it. Anne Wexler, a former Carter White House official turned lobbyist, feels the spiraling money game has gotten out of control. "But you have to give," she told me. "It's part of how you do business here. And you want to help out the people you like and respect in Congress." In 1986, Wexler gave about $25,000 of her personal money to candidates, a tiny fraction of what she was asked for. Invitations to political fund-raisers come to her by the bushel—probably two thousand in one campaign year, seeking a total of several hundred thousand dollars. "Our firm gets as many as ten a day," Wexler said. "We could go to literally two or three every night."

Actually, the way political poker is now played, having a PAC or buying a ticket to a $250 or $1,000-a-head fund-raiser, is just the price of admission for a lobbyist—the ante for the first deal. A hustling lobbyist must sweeten the kitty by joining the "steering committee" for a candidate, which means sponsoring and pushing that candidate, selling tickets to his fund-raisers to others. Veteran lobbyists help each other out by trading tickets to fund-raisers. Tommy Boggs, the well-known lawyer, holds something of a record—serving on more than fifty steering committees. But for big stakes, a lobbyist must play host to fund-raising dinners at home, personally raising cash donations.

"The small dinner is a big deal now—thirty to forty people, mostly Washington types," explained a lobbyist with long congressional experience. "Some people call it 'face time' because they get to meet face to face with political big names. You see, it's not just our PACs that the senators and congressmen want; we are expected to go out and raise money ourselves."

Then he paused and burst out: "I *hate* fund-raising. I do not go to dinners or cocktail parties. But our trade association will probably do $400,000 in contributions this election cycle, through our PAC and through other activities. I will raise probably ten to fifteen thousand dollars personally for people who don't take PAC contributions. It's like a stoop labor. It's arduous and unpleasant."

. . . The incumbents tell you, 'If you don't do this, you'd better look out.' It's particularly bad in the Senate. They are strongarming contributors. 'You'd better cough up or the next time your item comes up before our committee, we won't be for it.' . . .

Other lobbyists complain of virtual shakedowns by politicians. One lobbyist told me that a business partner telephoned for an appointment with a Republican congressman, but the congressman's administrative assistant replied: "We're sorry, we're not going to have a meeting with you. We looked at our contribution list and you haven't given to any of our campaigns." And a Democratic staffer told me of a close and heated debate in the Defense Appropriations Subcommittee in 1985 over whether to shift some funding from F-16 fighters made by General Dynamics to F-20 fighters made by Northrop. The shift of one vote would tip the balance. According to this staff aide, one committee Democrat proposed: "Let's set this aside for a day. I'm going to take bids from both contractors tonight."

◆ What Does PAC Money Buy?

Most lobbyists and legislators are smart enough to use language vague enough to deny illegal vote buying. "There are still conventions observed," I was told by an experienced lobbyist. "You never talk about political money in the same conversation as you discuss a legislative issue. I will not do that, because I remember Senator Brewster. Remember the case?* There was nothing explicit," my lobbyist friend went on. "It was implicit. But the legal point was that the nature of the exchange was such that there was a relationship between the campaign contribution and Brewster's actions."

Bob Strauss, Tommy Boggs, Charles Walker, Anne Wexler, and other lobbyists contend that political donations merely get access: the return phone call, an office drop-in, or a quiet dinner with a client, the chance to make your case. That can be crucial, especially if the other side lacks equal access. "Access is important precisely because *there is no equal access*," emphasized David Cohen, former head of Common Cause. "It's unequal access because there's a limited amount of time for members to consider anything. Access is important because it's what comes up on a legislator's screen that influences him." . . .

Most politicians handle the entire question with kid gloves. Very few will discuss it candidly for direct quotation, unless they are retired or about to retire. . . . Senator Tom Eagleton . . . was more honest, talking shortly before his retirement in 1987. With the very process of cultivating

---

*Former Senator Daniel Brewster of Maryland, a member of the Post Office and Civil Service Committee, was convicted in 1971 of accepting an unlawful gratuity—$24,500—to influence his action on postal-rate legislation.

special interest lobbies, he said "you begin to lose your sense of independence." When I suggested that officeholders probably felt psychologically beholden, he replied: "The nicest word is *predisposed.*" The money clearly works on a politician's innards. It creates a sense of obligation that canny lobbyists know how to activate. . . .

◆ Special Interest PACs Work Incumbents

. . . PACs look for winners. They want entrée after election day. That means that their donations go first to incumbents. PAC money does not yet equal individual contributions in volume, but it is getting close. In 1986 House incumbents got 45 percent of their campaign money from PACs, well up from 21 percent in 1974. Second priority are "open seats," those up for grabs because some incumbent has retired. Last come challengers, and only those given a strong chance of upset victory.

As Senator Joseph Biden said, PAC money underwrites the "tyranny of the incumbency." Early funding—well before the election—goes heavily to incumbents. For example, in 1985, PACs gave $10.5 million to 27 senators seeking reelection and only $1.1 million to their challengers. The safe money sticks with sure winners who will be on important committees when the real business gets going. . . .

In 1985, Common Cause released studies showing how the Finance Committee and its House counterpart, the Ways and Means Committee, were plastered by donations from groups with major interest in tax legislation. In 1985, for example, the 20 senators and 36 House members collected $6.7 million in PAC money, nearly two and a half times what they got in 1983, when they had no major tax bill to work on—indicating clear efforts to buy influence. Another Common Cause report in February 1986 showed the 1985 PAC contributions of the most generous lobbies: labor PACs, $1,153,857; insurance industry PACs, $969,213; and energy PACs, $956,742—and that excludes bundling. Those are all powerful constituencies with strong influence among Finance Committee members in any circumstance. PAC contributions reinforce existing political linkage. . . .

. . . But as Barry Goldwater asserted, the sheer volume of PAC money has made the appearance of venality seem pervasive. Without some reforms, many politicians and lobbyists are fearful that some scandal of blatant vote buying will bring a voter backlash and blow the lid off the PAC-man game and big-bucks lobbying. For the most astute Washington players clearly fear that deep-pockets, me-first politics has gotten out of hand.

Certainly, there have been other periods of American history when graft and corruption were more rampant than today. A mental flashback to the Nixon campaign and its sordid record of under-the-table cash payoffs and millions of dollars in illegal slush funds is a reminder that, fifteen years ago, things were much worse.

TOWARD CRITICAL THINKING

1. Why are calls for campaign finance reform so common, yet yield so few results?

2. Do PACs give certain interest groups too much political clout in Washington, D.C.? Should interest groups be limited in the amounts of money they can give to candidates? In *Federal Election Commission* v. *National Conservative Political Action Committee* (1985), the U.S. Supreme Court ruled that expenditure ceilings cannot be applied to groups or PACs that spend money independently in support of publicly funded candidates.

· *59* ·

Interest Groups and the Information Superhighway

DEBORAH BALDWIN

Political scientist David B. Truman advanced what is often called the stability, disruption, protest model of interest-group formation. Viewing society as a system in balance, Truman observed that from time to time, disequilibrium occurs as changes negatively effect some segments (or interests) in society. At these points, people mobilize into interest groups to protest change and to pressure the government to accommodate their interests. Thus, government serves to balance the interests of competing groups. In describing the astoundingly quick rise of the information superhighway and the disequilibrium it created, Deborah Baldwin, the editor of *Common Cause Magazine,* provides some important insights about the nature of interest groups and their activities in a new policy area. The information superhighway spawned interest groups on all sides of several issues that its development presented. It also created a new way to lobby. And, the information superhighway provided another reason for political action committees (PACs) to be created that will contribute money to certain legislators to advance the PACs' positions on a variety of issues involving the information superhighway.

It's hard to say when it happened exactly, but at some point around Halloween things started moving very quickly on the telecommunications front.

Suddenly, what was once a fanciful vision of the distant future—when Americans would be able to communicate with their appliances via cell phone and carry on conversations with their loved ones via computer—became as immediate as next season's sitcoms. . . .

As if all this weren't bad enough, computer hackers—known in some circles as mouse potatoes—got sex appeal. It was hard to keep dismissing people who whiled away their time at the keyboard (what—didn't they have jobs? couldn't they get dates?) when their hero Bill Gates was the richest man in America. . . .

Maybe most Americans would rather have lower monthly utility rates, safer schools and a new washing machine than a connection to global

SOURCE: Deborah Baldwin, "If This Is the Information Superhighway, Where Are the Rest Stops?" *Common Cause Magazine,* (January/February/March 1994). Reprinted by permission.

E-mail, but the Information Age had arrived, and the media brought the message forth in a tsunami of articles about the Internet, a loose network of computers that until recently was of concern only to science nerds, academics and computer junkies. Today, according to countless breathless accounts commissioned by editors clearly concerned about how all this may affect their profession, the number of Americans with access to the Internet is fifteen million—and climbing.

. . .

◆ Virtual Government

"When I started in 1990, there were damn few people working on this," says Jamie Love, who in three short years has established himself as Ralph Nader's telecommunications policy guru and Internet gadfly. Nowadays, when Love drops by meetings of public interest types who want to join in the telecommunications fun, there are so many Johnny Come Latelys he can barely find a chair.

Part of the attraction is the prospect of participating in a bleeding-edge campaign that has none of the baggage of such aging issues as saving the spotted owl, reforming federal prisons and making automobiles more energy efficient. The revolution in telecommunications is all new and it's all up for grabs.

And before long, a growing chorus of advocates says, it will be too late for the public interest community to try to influence telecommunications policy—to make interactive TV channels available, for example, for democratic discourse and the like. Already, money from cable, broadcast, telephone, home shopping and Hollywood is pouring through Congress like Mississippi River floodwaters—at the rate of about $10 million in 1991–92, according to one analysis. And the raw economic power of media chieftains like John Malone, the zillionaire co-founder of TCI, coupled with their dazzling appeal in a city better known for pushing paper than global vision, is threatening to turn policy makers into whimpering schoolchildren.

Still, if Wall Street barons are on the edges of their seats awaiting some signal from the marketplace about what Americans really want (video-porn delivered by phone? a hair-care channel?), Washington's public interest community is at a similar turning point. Many groups have heard the call. But it's one thing to have a passionate interest in telecommunications policy. It's another to develop a grassroots Information Superhighway lobbying group—and raise enough money to keep it going.

◆ There's No Escaping Now

In case you're still at the stage I was four months ago—curious about the Information Superhighway but genuinely worried about having to program anything more complicated than a VCR—here's what all the hype is about. It's been about 10 years since the PC and Mac turned typewriters into landfill; a new kind of computerized communications will similarly eclipse the telephone. It will tie our computers at home and work to the outside world, enabling us to plunder the world's entertainment and information resources at the push of a button.

In the beginning was the Internet, a network of computer networks tied together by high-speed wire. Devised by the Pentagon as a way to protect the flow of military information during a nuclear holocaust, the Internet was embraced early on by academic researchers, who soon learned to use it to open up the electronic card catalogues at other colleges, communicate with colleagues in faraway places (exchanging dissertations became popular) and bellyache about tenure. Anyone with a modem and a subscription to a local Internet exchange can also communicate by E-mail—a cheap, convenient alternative to having to rummage for a stamp and envelope or wait for discount phone rates to apply. You type your message, fire it off and wait for the inevitable snappy comeback, which will be typed at the sender's convenience and read at yours—making the notion of human beings walking from house to house to deliver mail as quaint as ice wagons. The Internet also offers the possibility of conversations with like-minded souls (there are news groups devoted to every imaginable topic, from Iran-contra to Jerry Seinfeld) and access to umpteen kinds of information that have been dumped onto the system.

No one's foolish enough, however, to assume that the John Malones of the world will go out of their way to provide services that don't automatically make money—things like the local equivalent of C-SPAN, for example. Cable TV companies didn't think up community access stations on their own, and they're not likely to sweat about electronic democracy unless someone makes them. Same applies to the phone companies that are so anxious to build Information Superhighway on-ramps everywhere: the only reason they charge relatively low rates for basic service now is because regulators set the prices. Let 'em loose so they can start delivering video by phone, and they'll charge what the market will bear.

Enter the media reform movement, which began in the early 1970s as an effort to advance such things as the Fairness Doctrine (a requirement that broadcasters give time to both sides of a political debate) and equal time (access to the airwaves for opposing candidates). The 1980s were a bad time for media reform—"from my perspective, it was devastating," says Andrew Blau, coordinator of the Benton Foundation's Communications Policy Project—because the buzzwords changed from "public" and "access" to "deregulation," the latter responsible for the untrammeled growth of cable TV—not to mention cable TV rates. . . .

Attempting to take root under the Information Superhighway's grow lights today are a handful of groups, ranging from Ralph Nader's tiny Taxpayer Assets Project to the brash Electronic Frontier Foundation, which was bankrolled by the inventor of Lotus software. There's the twenty-year-old Media Access Project—still lobbying to bring back the Fairness Doctrine—and the Consumer Federation of America, which wants to protect consumers from gouging by the regional Bell operating companies, or RBOCs (pronounced Are Box), which are anxious to get into fancy new lines of work like video. Add the fourteen-year-old Benton Foundation, the two-year-old Center for Media Education and the nascent Center for Civic Networking . . . plus the ACLU, whose former Washington director is now director of the Electronic Frontier Foundation, the Center for Policy Alternatives and Computer Professionals for Social Responsibility. Also active are the librarians—yes, the librarians—who have provided the contemporary media reform movement with some of its few female leaders. (As a showcase for brainy, techie types, telecommunications boasts a large number of fast-thinking, faster-talking men, who compete to see who gets the most invites to testify on Capitol Hill and who has greater impact at the White House.)

Galvanizing this eclectic group is the sheer size and political clout of the opposition, a composite of media-communications-entertainment interests about as consumer friendly as the Terminator. The RBOCs alone—collectively, individually—comprise a fantastic political force both in Washington and locally, where they badger regulators for rate hikes and sweet-talk about getting schools and hospitals onto the highway.

"It's just huge," says Gene Kimmelman, formerly with the Consumer Federation of America and now an aide to Sen. Howard Metzenbaum (D-Ohio). "In one year the seven [RBOCs] put together $22 million" to lobby in Washington—"and that doesn't include public relations." Kimmelman counts the number of phone company lobbyists in Washington in "the hundreds," and reminds his caller of where the money came from to pay their hourly fees: Thanks to consumers, the phone companies already have a $90-billion-a-year operating cash flow.

Some of that money helped the U.S. Telephone Association snap up top Clinton aide Roy Neel for a reported $500,000 salary and brought Peter Knight—a former top Senate aide to Vice President Albert Gore—to Bell Atlantic's account at one prestigious law firm and Clinton Campaign Adviser Thomas Casey to its account at another. Virtually every major Washington firm works in some way for the telecommunications industry, says Kimmelman, with phone company money providing a significant part of the business. .

"When you talk about the phone companies you are talking about political power unlike any other," says Nick Johnson, a consumer advocate who served on the Federal Communications Commission (FCC) in the early '70s. Pointing to the Bell Atlantic-TCI merger, Johnson anticipates "absolutely overpowering" political pressure on Washington to let the Big Guys run the Superhighway anyway they want."

What way is anybody's guess at this point, because no one knows for sure how the highway will shape up. (Well, a few things are certain: People want to be able to put their videos on hold when they go to the bathroom, and they like to order things over the phone.) So what brings the big Guys to Washington? A desire for carte blanche—for the right to compete in a new era of hands-off government as they keep splitting like amoebas, mating like rabbits and cashing in like casinos. The RBOCs, with control of local phone service, want access to money-making long-distance services now dominated by AT&T, Sprint and MCI—and vice versa; the cable companies want access to money-making phone-services—and vice versa; the entertainment giants want to cut deals with the most lucrative producers—and vice versa; and everybody wants the right to merge with everybody else without having bothersome antitrust lawyers breathing down their necks. "The thing that frightens me most is the merger mania," Rutgers University political scientist Benjamin Barber said in a November speech.

In communities where computers are old hat, citizens already are experimenting with electronic lobbying. Computer Professionals for Social Responsibility is setting up an interactive network in Seattle, home of Boeing. And Santa Monica, Calif. . . . has such advanced computer communications that the homeless recently used terminals installed at libraries and other public places to lobby for shower facilities, bathrooms, a laundromat and lockers so they could get cleaned up for job interviews. Now people who can't afford housing on their own are using the terminals to find roommates, and donated computer equipment is being used to train the unemployed for jobs, says local activist Michelle Wittig.

◆ In Government They Distrust

Santa Monica aside, right now the average electronic lobbyist is less likely to be one of the homeless than one the of the computer gentry—folks who joined the electronic revolution years ago as the first ones on their block to buy a modem, who already enjoy access to the Internet through either an academic institution or a monthly subscription to a local network, who've conveniently forgotten the tens of millions of dollars the government has invested in creating the Internet and who don't understand what all the fuss is about in Washington.

Asked how he harnesses the Internet constituency to fight for change in Congress, Danny Weitzner, who lobbies for the Electronic Frontier

Foundation, responds, "That's an interesting issue. . . . In terms of our supporters, a lot are skeptical when we talk about the need to legislate. They say, "Ah—the government is just going to screw it up again.""

At issue are two major bills, one introduced by House Judiciary Committee Chair Jack Brooks (D-Texas), and House Energy and Commerce Committee Chair John Dingell (D-Mich.), which would set the terms for RBOCs wanting entree into long-distance service, the other an ambitious rewrite of the 1934 Communications Act introduced by Rep. Edward Markey (D-Mass.), chair of the telecommunications subcommittee. In exchange for allowing phone companies to get into video delivery, and cable companies to get into phone service, the bill would encourage a system of universal (everyone can get it) access to the Information Superhighway and direct the FCC to figure out a way to bring about an "open platform"—a way for anyone to distribute information as well as receive it.

Another provision in the Markey bill would bar companies from owning both the local cable TV franchise and local phone service, a measure meant to protect the public from a media takeover by the twenty-first century equivalent of the Rockefellers. The provision lapses after five years, an arrangement Jamie Love rejects as a sellout and the Media Access Project's Andrew Jay Schwartzman compares to "coitus interruptus—just when things get going, it ends."

Because the bill contains affordable service and open platform provisions, however, it has won the endorsement of the Electronic Frontier Foundation (EFF), which takes some pride in the fact that it is a pragmatic, coalition-building group with good political connections and few delusions about who really controls the telecommunications debate. (Hint: It's not Ralph Nader.)

Co-founded by Mitchell Kapor, who bagged multimillions as a founder of the Lotus Development Corp. before dropping out and getting political, EFF has described itself as "a public interest organization dedicated to realizing the democratic potential of new computer and communications media." In political circles, EFF likes to play mainstream to Jamie Love's gadfly extremism.

Asked about the debate within the public interest Telecommunications Policy Roundtable over the Markey bill, EFF executive Director Jerry Berman says, "We believe Markey is the vehicle (for negotiating). The idea that we should go off and build a perfect bill is just wrongheaded. We've got to make common cause (with the Big Guys)."

Love, who dismisses all of Congress as a tool of special interests, naturally disagrees, and he just can't resist taking potshots at EFF, arguing that it is accommodating because it too takes money from such industry giants as AT&T, Bell Atlantic, MCI, Apple and IBM. Perched on a broken chair in a warehouse labyrinth that appears to be crammed with all the paper ever generated by Nader's Center for the Study of Responsive Law, Love takes the purist's position. He can afford to, as his two-person staff, which gets slim funding from the center and has a few foundations, is perennially broke.

EFF, in contrast, recently opened smart offices in downtown Washington, where a staff of eleven uses state-of-the-art equipment to debate the big issues and keep track of its appointments on Capitol Hill. "We do not shade our positions," says Berman, referring to the flap over EFF's funding. "We take them and try to build coalitions behind them." Groups that rely on foundation money, he suggests, aren't as credible as those that depend on support from the real world of business and commerce.

Like some members of Congress, Berman suggests that contributions from lots of sources tend to cancel themselves out, and lots of contributions represent, in classic checkbook democracy fashion, lots of constituents. Clearly annoyed by ongoing debate on the Internet about EFF's politics, he continues, "I've been in the public interest community for many years, when I could have been with (the fat cat lawyer-lobbying firm) Covington and Burling, and I resent the implication that as an individual or organization we've been paid off." When it is suggested that the problem may be one of having to mingle in the corporate world he responds, "I don't know where else to mingle!"

One alternative is to build a membership of small contributors, something EFF has toyed with doing. But that's an expensive endeavor, especially if it's done through direct mail, and EFF's efforts to advertise $40 memberships over the Internet have had only limited success. (The foundations has about 1,300 members.) One problem is that "netiquette" discourages requests for money—perhaps because of the Internet's historic ties to high-minded academia, or perhaps because the greatest fear among Internet users is that someday someone will figure out a way to make them pay.

"There's a debate going on among users of the Internet and groups like EFF about whether the Internet should be used to solicit funds: is it such sacrosanct ground that it shouldn't be sullied by commercialism?" says Roger Craver, a public-interest fundraising consultant who does most of his work through conventional snail mail. But the real problem, he believes, isn't netiquette but the nature of the system, which is so large and encompassing that it's impossible for fundraisers to target relatively narrow audiences. "There's the sheer size. . . . You hang out your message and hope someone sees it," he explains. "If you're tying to build membership you need targeting of some sort."

In other words, there is no direct mail fundraising without a List.

That phenomenon is one reason why so much of the public interest activity on the telecommunications front is funded by foundations and corporations: No one's figured out how to do it differently. And it's another reason so much of the lobbying is done by tax-exempt nonprofits like EFF: If EFF were set up only as a lobbying group, it wouldn't be able to take tax-deductible grants.

Andrew Schwartzman of the Media Access Project, which accepts small amounts of industry money, says the debate over funding is misplaced. "We all want the same thing; the question is how we get there." In the meantime, "There is a false sense of urgency: 'The train is leaving the station!' But another year isn't going to make a difference. The technology doesn't even exist yet. Wall Street is pressing this because the big companies want to take advantage before policymakers realize they are giving away the store."

No matter who ends up with the goods, says Schwartzman, "ten years from now you're still going to be looking to Dan Rather and his successors." What matters isn't the Superhighway of the year 2008 but the transition, he argues, and that means fighting for the same old reforms that put people to sleep during the '80s—things like the Fairness Doctrine and rules barring the phone company from controlling the content of the information it carries. By focusing too much on the distant future, he argues, we may end up giving everything to three or four companies. "That will transform the democratic process," he predicts, and not for the better.

TOWARD CRITICAL THINKING

1. How does the interest group activity described by Deborah Baldwin illustrate points made by Mancur Olson Jr. and David B. Truman concerning group formation?

2. Is it likely that the information superhighway will change the way interest groups act? How could it facilitate interest-group formation?

THINKING ABOUT POLITICAL PARTIES AND INTEREST GROUPS

1. Drawing on the readings by Alan Ware, Mancur Olson Jr., and Philip A. Mundo, in particular, how are political parties and interest groups similar? How are they different? How are their goals and/or strategies alike? How are their respective roles in the political process similar or even complementary?

2. Mancur Olson Jr. posits that it's not rational for large economic or business groups to organize. Do you agree or disagree? Does the flurry of interest organization around the Internet support your position?

3. How have the media diminished or enhanced the role of political parties and interest groups in the 1990s?

CHAPTER 12

◆ ◆ ◆

Campaigns, Elections, and Voting

One of the earliest political campaigns in the United States was the one to win ratification of the new Constitution. Lively debates occurred in meeting halls around the thirteen states, and numerous tracts and missives including *The Federalist Papers* were written and published on both sides of the ratification issue.

Public debates continued as one of the most common methods of campaigning, and some debates between famous orators attracted large audiences. The Lincoln/Douglas debates, for example, which occurred in the 1858 Illinois state election campaign, continue to stand as some of the clearest statements of burning issues of the day, including slavery.*

Candidate debates—particularly at the presidential level—continue to draw significant attention from the voters; but money and the media have forever changed the look of U.S. elections. While the factors that motivate voters continue to be of concern to candidates and politicians, the role and importance of the media have brought about changes in campaigning and political parties. Money—not volunteer time—has become a critical force in elections, and political action committee (PAC) dollars are important ingredients of any candidate's campaign coffers.

PACs also allow candidates to purchase more media time. And while candidates are using the media to try to get their messages across to the electorate, the media themselves also play a role in shaping how campaign strategies are written and revised. The media's widespread reporting of a gender gap in voting leads candidates scrambling to find ways to attract women voters (see Reading 63); the media also highlighted several issues such as abortion in the 1992 election and crime and health care in the 1994 national election, forcing candidates to clarify their positions on those matters.

Reading 64, "A Day in the Life of the Campaign," vividly demonstrates how candidates and their handlers pitched their messages toward the media in order to get elected. However, Seymour Martin Lipset

---

*At that time, U.S. senators were elected by state legislatures, thus Lincoln and Douglas took their respective campaigns directly to the people, hoping to get them to cast ballots for state legislative candidates who supported them.

(Reading 65) notes that once elected, President Clinton needed to start running for office again, almost as soon as he was sworn in as president. Lipset, like V. O. Key Jr. (Reading 62), underscores the actual significance of any election.

As you read the chapter that follows, consider the following questions: (1) Were the 1992 elections, with their three-way race for president and an electorate up in arms over congressional scandals particularly unusual? (2) What factors contributed to the largest number of new women in history elected to Congress? (3) How has the changing nature of the electorate changed election outcomes?

· *60* ·

Federalist No. 39

JAMES MADISON

The Framers, although they created a lower house (the House of Representatives) to be closer and more responsive to the people, did not give much thought to the actual nature of elections. In fact, most of the "elected" officials in the new national government were to be elected only indirectly by "the people." Furthermore, at the time of the Philadelphia convention, voting was fairly limited by most states, which allowed only white, male, property owners to vote. In fact, the Constitution specifies that the qualifications for voters are to be left to the states. Over the years, however, voting rights have been expanded through constitutional amendment, statute, and decisions by the U.S. Supreme Court. In the 1780s, voting *per se* was not of much concern; instead, Federalists stressed that *some* positions were elective in a republican form of government.

If we resort for a criterion to the different principles on which different forms of government are established, we may define a republic to be, or at least may bestow that name on, a government which derives all its powers directly or indirectly from the great body of the people, and is administered by persons holding their offices during pleasure for a limited period, or during good behavior. It is *essential* to such a government that it be derived from the great body of the society, not from an inconsiderable proportion or a favored class of it; otherwise a handful of tyrannical nobles, exercising their oppressions by a delegation of their powers, might aspire to the rank of republicans and claim for their government the honorable title of republic. It is *sufficient* for such a government that the persons administering it be appointed, either directly or indirectly, by the people; and that they hold their appointments by either of the tenures just specified; otherwise every government in the United States, as well as every other popular government that has been or can be well organized or well executed, would be degraded from the republican character. According to the constitution of every State in the Union, some or other of the officers of government are appointed indirectly only by the people. . . .

. . . The House of Representatives, like that of one branch at least of all the State legislatures, is elected immediately by the great body of the people. The Senate, like the present Congress and the Senate of Maryland, derives its appointment indirectly from the people. The President is indirectly derived from the choice of the people, according to the example in most of the States. Even the judges, with all other officers of the Union, will, as in the several States, be the choice, though a remote choice, of the people themselves. The duration of the appointments is equally conformable to the republican standard and to the model of State constitutions. The House of Representatives is periodically elective . . . for the period of two years. . . . The Senate is elective for the period of six years. . . . The President is . . . to continue in office for the period of four years. . . . The tenure by which the judges are to hold their places is, as it unquestionably ought to be, that of good behavior.

TOWARD CRITICAL THINKING

1. Why were the "form" of elections or qualifications for voting of little apparent concern to the Framers?

2. Does the campaign process produce a Congress in tune with the American people? Would term limits (which would limit members to a fixed number of terms) result in more meaningful elections and give voters greater opportunity to reveal their wishes?

· *61* ·

Money in Senate Elections

ALAN I. ABRAMOWITZ and JEFFREY A. SEGAL

Even though the Framers didn't give much consideration to elections, as discussed in Chapter 6, reelection is a driving force behind the actions of many elected officials. As underscored in *Federalist No. 39* (Reading 60), members of the U.S. Senate initially were selected not by the people but by their state legislatures. With ratification of the Twentieth Amendment in 1933, however, senators, like representatives, became directly accountable to the people at the ballot box, and the nature of Senate campaigns changed. Money as well as political organization became important. And since 1974, when the first data about senatorial election spending became available, total spending by senate candidates has risen astronomically.

Political scientists Abramowitz and Segal examine campaign finance law reform and suggest that Republicans, who blocked early proposals for spending caps, may not be hurt and, indeed, may profit from voluntary spending caps. Republicans, they suggest, could benefit because party expenditures are not covered under proposed laws.

Running for the U.S. Senate has become a very expensive proposition. Between 1974 and 1990, total spending by Senate candidates more than doubled after controlling for inflation, and this does not include independent expenditures by individuals and PACs or coordinated expenditures by party committees on behalf of Senate candidates, which have increased even more rapidly than spending by the candidates.[1] In the 1990 Senate elections, the sixty-seven major party candidates reported spending a total of 173 million dollars, down slightly from the record 190 million dollars spent by Senate candidates in 1988. The average Senate candidate in 1990 spent just under 2.6 million dollars.

In 1988, the most recent year for which information is available, state and national party committees spent almost 17 million dollars on behalf of Senate candidates, while independent expenditures by individuals and

SOURCE: Alan I. Abramowitz and Jeffrey A. Segal, *Senate Elections* (Ann Arbor: The University of Michigan Press, 1992), pp. 123–124, 139–143. Reprinted by permission.

[1] Under the current campaign finance laws, party committees are allowed to spend up to a fixed amount of money on behalf of a Senate candidate. The spending limit is based on the population of the state and expenditures may be coordinated with a candidate's campaign. Independent expenditures by individuals or PACs to support or oppose Senate candidates are not limited and may not be coordinated with a candidate's campaign.

PACs supporting or opposing Senate candidates totaled over 4 million dollars. Altogether, more than 200 million dollars were spent on the 1988 Senate elections—an average of close to 6 million dollars per seat.[2]

The rising cost of Senate campaigns has made fund-raising an increasingly onerous task for Senate candidates. In recent years, a number of incumbents and would-be candidates have cited the time and effort required for fund-raising as reasons for retiring or deciding not to run for the Senate in the first place. Skyrocketing campaign costs have also led to increased demands for changes in the campaign finance laws to limit spending by Senate candidates.

✦ Campaign Finance Laws and Senate Elections

The financing of Senate campaigns is governed by the Federal Election Campaign Act (FECA) of 1971. This law, for the first time, required House and Senate candidates to disclose their contributions and expenditures. In 1974, in the aftermath of the Watergate scandal, Congress enacted several major amendments strengthening the FECA, including limitations on individual contributions and total expenditures. However, the Supreme Court's 1976 decision in the case of *Buckley* v. *Valeo* overturned several provisions of the FECA and severely restricted Congress's ability to regulate campaign finance.

Under the provisions of the FECA, all House and Senate candidates who spend over $5,000 on their campaigns are required to file reports with the Federal Election Commission (FEC) detailing their expenditures and listing all individuals and groups contributing $100 or more. Individual contributions to a single candidate cannot exceed $1,000, while political action committees are limited to $5,000. Despite inflation, these ceilings have not been changed since 1974.[3]

One of the most important FECA amendments adopted by Congress in 1974 allowed corporations and trade associations to form political action committees. Since then, the number of PACs has grown from under 600 to over 4,000, and their contributions to House and Senate candidates have skyrocketed from less than $10 million in 1972 to almost $150

---

[2] Data on the 1990 election was taken from a preliminary report issued by the Federal Election Commission; no data were available on coordinated expenditures by party committees or independent spending in the 1990 Senate elections. All earlier data on campaign spending, except the expenditures by individual candidates, are taken from Norman Ornstein, Thomas Mann, and Michael Malbin, *Vital Statistics on Congress, 1989–1990* (Washington, D.C.: Congressional Quarterly Press, 1990), 67–112. Data on expenditures by individual candidates are taken from various editions of *The Almanac of American Politics.*

[3] Frank J. Sorauf, *Money in American Elections* (Glenview, Ill.: Scott, Foresman, 1988), 34–39.

million in 1990. PACs now provide about one-third of all campaign funds in House elections and one-fourth of all campaign funds in Senate elections.

In *Buckley* v. *Valeo,* the Supreme Court threw out several provisions of the Federal Election Campaign Act, including limits on candidates' total expenditures, limits on the amount of money a candidate is allowed to spend on his or her own campaign, and limits on the amount of money an individual or PAC can independently spend to support or oppose a candidate. The Court held that these limitations on campaign spending violated the First Amendment's guarantee of freedom of speech. However, the Court upheld the provision of the FECA that set spending limits in presidential campaigns, which were tied to candidates' voluntary acceptance of federal campaign funds.[4]

Since the *Buckley* decision there have been several unsuccessful attempts to legislate limits on congressional campaign expenditures. The most important of these was a bill introduced by Senator David Boren (D-Oklahoma) in 1987 that would have set voluntary spending ceilings for Senate campaigns and provided public financing for any candidate abiding by the spending ceiling whose opponent exceeded the ceiling. However, this bill was blocked by a Republican filibuster. . . .

◆ Campaign Spending and Election Outcomes: Who Benefits?

Perhaps the most important question about campaign spending is how it affects the outcomes of elections. What types of Senate candidates have been most advantaged or disadvantaged in the electoral arena by virtue of their campaign finances? At first glance, the answer to this question might appear to be fairly obvious: candidates who have more money to spend—primarily incumbents—are advantaged, while candidates who have less money to spend—primarily challengers—are disadvantaged. In reality, though, the answer is more complicated. All campaign money is equal, but, when it comes to influencing voters, some campaign funds are more equal than others.

In evaluating the effects of campaign spending on election outcomes, the most important distinction is that between incumbents and either challengers or candidates for open seats. An incumbent Senator running for reelection has already had at least six years to get his or her message across to the voters. What he or she says or does during the campaign is likely to have only a marginal impact on public attitudes toward his or her

---

[4] Sorauf, *Money,* 40.

candidacy. In contrast, a challenger or a candidate for an open Senate seat usually begins the campaign as a relatively unknown quantity to most of the electorate. Even if a candidate has held a statewide office, his or her record may provide voters with very little information about how he or she would perform in the Senate. Therefore, what a challenger or candidate for an open seat says or does during the campaign should have a much stronger influence on public attitudes toward his or her candidacy than we would expect to find in the case of an incumbent.

It follows from the preceding argument that, dollar for dollar, spending by challengers and open seat candidates should produce a greater electoral return than spending by incumbents. In fact, there is a considerable body of evidence supporting this hypothesis in the case of House elections.[5] . . . Nonincumbents' campaign spending also has a much greater impact than incumbents' campaign spending in Senate elections. In the incumbent support model, the estimated effect of challenger spending was three times as great as the estimated effect of incumbent spending and challenger spending was the most influential variable determining election outcomes, far outweighing the partisan and ideological composition of the electorate and national political conditions. In the open seat model, relative campaign spending along with relative candidate experience were by far the most influential determinants of election outcomes.

Between 1974 and 1990, the average Senate challenger increased his or her share of the vote by about 10 percentage points as a result of campaign expenditures while the average Senate incumbent increased his or her share of the vote by about 5 percentage points as a result of campaign expenditures. Combining these estimates, the net impact of campaign spending in an average Senate race was to increase the challenger's share of the vote by about 5 percentage points, even though the average incumbent outspent the average challenger by a substantial margin.

Based on the estimated effects of campaign spending by incumbents, challengers, and open seat candidates, we can measure the net impact of campaign spending on each party's share of the vote in an average Senate race. [Figure 1] shows the results for each election since 1974. Once again, there is no evidence that either party has consistently benefited as a result of campaign spending patterns. In five out of nine elections, including three of the last four, Democratic candidates had a net advantage as a result of campaign spending. Even though most Democratic candidates were outspent by their Republican opponents in 1986, they got

---

[5] See Stanton A. Glantz, Alan I. Abramowitz, and Michael P. Burkart, "Election Outcomes: Whose Money Matters?" *Journal of Politics* 38 (June, 1988): 385–403; Gary C. Jacobson, "The Effects of Campaign Spending in Congressional Elections," *American Political Science Review* 72 (June, 1978): 469–91; Jacobson, *Money*, 136–62.

FIGURE 1
Net Impact of Campaign Spending on the Average Democratic Vote, 1974–90

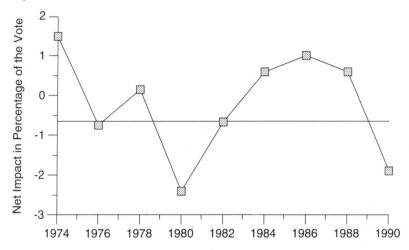

a much higher average rate of electoral return from their campaign dollars because so many of them were challengers. Only twice, in 1980 and 1990, did GOP Senate candidates enjoy a large net advantage (+2.4 percent and +1.9 percent) as a result of campaign spending. In 1980, most of the challengers were Republicans, while, in 1990, the Democrats fielded an exceptionally weak group of challengers and open seat candidates. Combining all nine elections, the net impact of campaign spending was an average Republican advantage of 0.2 percent of the vote.

◆ Evaluating the Consequences of Campaign Spending Limits

What effect would spending limits have on party fortunes in Senate elections? We addressed this question by using the estimates obtained for our incumbent support and open seat models and substituting the spending ceilings proposed in the Boren bill for the actual expenditures of all candidates who exceeded these limits in the 1986 Senate elections. [Table 1] displays the actual results of all thirty-two contested Senate races in 1986 and the estimated impact of the proposed spending ceiling on each race. These results are based on the assumption that all candidates would have adhered to the spending limit proposed in the bill in order to avoid having their opponents receive public campaign funds.

Even though challenger spending has a much stronger impact on the outcomes of Senate elections than incumbent spending, only six challengers (four Democrats and two Republicans) would have been adversely

TABLE 1
Estimated Effects of Spending Limits on the Democratic Share of the Major Party Vote in 1986 Senate Elections

State	Incumbent	Actual Vote Percentage	Estimated Effect	Predicted Vote Percentage
Alabama	R	50.2	+0.8	51.0
Arizona	None	39.5	+3.3	42.8
Arkansas	D	62.3	–0.7	61.6
California	D	50.7	+0.9	51.6
Colorado	None	50.8	–0.0	50.8
Connecticut	D	65.1	–1.0	64.1
Florida	R	54.7	–0.5	54.2
Georgia	R	50.9	+0.8	51.7
Idaho	R	48.4	–1.4	47.0
Illinois	D	65.9	NA	65.9
Indiana	R	38.9	+0.3	39.2
Iowa	R	33.7	+1.1	34.8
Kansas	R	30.0	NA	30.0
Kentucky	D	74.4	NA	74.4
Louisiana	None	52.8	+3.3	56.1
Maryland	None	60.7	NA	60.7
Missouri	None	47.4	+1.0	48.4
Nevada	None	52.8	+1.3	54.1
New Hampshire	R	33.9	NA	33.9
New York	R	42.0	+1.5	43.5
North Carolina	None	51.8	+1.0	52.8
North Dakota	R	50.3	+1.1	51.4
Ohio	D	62.4	NA	62.4
Oklahoma	R	44.8	–1.6	43.2
Oregon	R	36.4	+1.8	38.2
Pennsylvania	R	43.2	+0.3	43.5
South Carolina	D	63.4	–0.9	62.5
South Dakota	R	51.7	–3.7	<u>48.0</u>
Utah	R	26.9	NA	26.9
Vermont	D	64.6	+0.9	65.5
Washington	R	51.0	+0.5	51.5
Wisconsin	R	48.2	+1.1	49.3

SOURCE: Almanac of American Politics 1988 and analysis conducted by authors.

Notes: NA = not applicable because neither candidate exceeded proposed spending limit. The predicted result is underlined if the outome would have been altered by the spending limit.

affected by the Boren bill. This is because very few challengers exceeded the spending ceiling proposed in the bill. In only one race, in South Dakota, does it appear that the proposed spending ceiling would probably have cost a challenger (a Democrat) the election. The average Democratic or Republican challenger would have received an additional 0.1 percent of the vote if the spending ceilings had been in effect.

Democratic candidates for open seats would have been the major beneficiaries if the proposed spending ceilings had been in effect in 1986. They would have gained an average of 1.3 percent of the vote. Overall, Democratic candidates would have benefited slightly from the spending ceilings, gaining an average of 0.3 percent of the vote. However, according to this analysis, not one defeated Democratic candidate would have been elected as a result of the spending limits.

◆ Discussion and Conclusions

Republican opposition to campaign spending limits has been based on the argument that such limits would work to the disadvantage of the minority party, because its challengers would need to spend more than the allowable limit in order to overcome the electoral advantage enjoyed by Democratic incumbents. In 1986 and 1988, however, only four of twenty-four Republican Senate challengers were able to reach the proposed spending limit for their state. In general, Republican challengers have done poorly in terms of fundraising, especially in comparison with their party's incumbents and open seat candidates. Both individual Republican contributors and business PACs have tended to concentrate their contributions on Republican incumbents and open seat candidates, while largely ignoring GOP challengers even when political conditions appeared promising for the party. As long as this situation continues, spending limits such as those proposed in the Boren bill will have little impact on the campaigns of Republican challengers.

In the long run, spending limits might well work to the advantage of Republican Senate candidates. In the first place, the spending limits would not include expenditures by party committees. Since 1974, Republican Senate candidates have enjoyed a significant advantage in terms of party expenditures. Moreover, as Sorauf has argued, the figures on party contributions and coordinated expenditures undoubtedly understate the benefits that accrue to Republican candidates as a result of the GOP's enormous advantage over the Democrats in party finances—in 1988, local, state, and national Republican committees reported expenditures of $257 million compared with $122 million for Democratic committees.[6]

Independent expenditures may pose an even greater potential threat to Democratic Senate candidates than party expenditures because, unlike contributions and coordinated expenditures by party committees, they are

---

[6] Sorauf, *Money,* 153.

not limited by law. In the last three presidential elections, the Republican candidates enjoyed a huge advantage in the area of independent expenditures. In 1988, almost $13 million was spent on behalf of George Bush's candidacy, compared with less than $1 million on behalf of Michael Dukakis's candidacy. Rising independent expenditures have made the legal spending limits in presidential campaigns virtually meaningless.

If spending limits are imposed on Senate campaigns, then something very similar to what has happened in presidential elections may occur in Senate elections: a diversion of candidate spending into independent expenditures. Based on the history of recent presidential campaigns, the Republican party will probably be much more successful in this venture than the Democratic party. Before Senate Democrats enact a campaign reform law incorporating spending ceilings in Senate campaigns, they would do well to consider the consequences that spending ceilings have had in presidential campaigns.

TOWARD CRITICAL THINKING

1. What are some reasons that have contributed to congressional failure to pass meaningful campaign finance reform? Which party appears to have been helped most by PAC money in the last election?

2. Why do incumbents usually enjoy such an advantage in Senate elections?

· *62* ·

The Responsible Electorate

V. O. KEY JR.

Key notes that much can be read from the election returns—both for isolated elections and in the patterns that have emerged historically. Some elections represent a new order, such as the election of 1936. Political scientists refer to this election as a realigning election because it signalled a dramatic change in voter allegiances. Other elections, while possibly providing a mandate for a particular candidate, are not nearly so dramatic. Elections also legitimize the government says Key—a point also noted by Madison in *Federalist No. 39* (Reading 60).

◆ Elections in the Democratic Process

Presidential elections constitute decisions of fundamental significance in the American democratic process. The trooping of millions of voters to the polls symbolizes self-rule and legitimizes the authority of governments. But beyond such mystical functions of the electoral process, elections are pivotal decisions which in turn control many lesser determinations made in the name of the people. Our explorations have been in quest of some understanding of what the electorate does decide or of its role in the democratic process. Obviously the voters decide which party is to govern. That choice tends to bring in its train predictable consequences in direction if not in detail of governmental action, given the contrasting composition and policy orientations of the competing party leaderships. But what beyond the choices of governors do elections decide? Nothing, it may be said. Or a theorist with rationalistic inclinations may picture the party platform as a program of action which the winners are, by their solemn compact with the majority, bound to execute. Neither of these views satisfactorily reflects the reality. Considered in the framework of the flow of events and of the available alternatives it seems clear that elections decide more than simply who shall govern. Yet the scope and nature of the decision may not be apparent until some time after the election. Nor can it be contended that the voters in the prevailing majority invariably sense the broad meaning of their collective action.

SOURCE: V. O. Key Jr., *Politics, Parties, and Pressure Groups,* 4th ed. (New York: Thomas Y. Crowell Co., 1942), pp. 589–590. Reprinted by permission.

Some elections, it has been argued, express clearly a lack of satisfaction with the performance of the crowd that has been in charge. The possibility of so efficacious an expression of discontent underlies the discipline of a democratic people over its government. Elected officials must live under the threat of defeat or disavowal. Other elections may be plausibly interpreted as a vote of confidence. More commonly the electorate may bring in a mixed verdict; some voters are happy with the course of affairs and others are deeply dissatisfied. Even these confused elections may, in their situational context, be meaningful decisions. Thus the election of 1896 rejected the upsurge of western silver-agrarian radicalism and gave popular blessing to a coalition which governed until at least 1912. The election of 1936 ratified a sharp turn in public policy and successive Democratic victories clinched the reforms of the New Deal. The terms of the electoral decision of 1952 brought Republican acquiescence in the new order. A series of elections may fix the contours that guide the broad flow of public policy. Specific elections may give an unmistakable mandate for a change of direction. Others may approve a newly instituted order of affairs. Still others may record a majority support for the status quo but the rumblings of the minority may be a portent of a growth of discontent.

Retrospective judgments by the electorate seem far more explicit than do its instructions for future action. An approval of the continuation of the prevailing course of action may be clear enough. Or a rejection of past performance may be resounding. Yet the most acute ear attuned to the voice of the people can sense only the vaguest guidance for innovation to cope with the questions that must be met day by day as an Administration governs. The efficacy of self-government thus depends on party or governmental leadership with the initiative and imagination necessary to meet the public problems that develop and with the courage to assume the political risks involved. The vocabulary of the voice of the people consists mainly of the words yes and no; and at times one cannot be certain which word is being uttered. On occasion it seems that assiduous but myopic dedication to the doctrine of self-rule brings governmental stagnation or paralysis as timorous politicians listen vainly for positive instructions from the voice of the people. Popular government demands that politicians be accountable but it does not relieve them of the duty of initiative.[1]

These explorations provide a general conception of the limits and nature of the role of the electorate. As one attempts to see national

---

[1] The prediction of public reaction to new courses of action is so primitive an art that thoughtful politicians remark that the only course to follow is to take the action that seems right, on the assumption that it will be defensible at the next election.

elections in their place in the governing process—in their relation to the party system, in their bearing on the operations of government—it is well to ponder about the mores, the understandings, the customs, the conditions that make feasible these interpositions by the mass of the people in affairs of state. For a political order to withstand periodic electoral clashes, the electorate itself must possess appropriate expectations and inner restraints. Party leaderships in their relationships to the electorate and to each other must keep party warfare within tolerable limits. Governing officials must be bound by an intricate set of norms which, if they do not absolutely limit governmental action, fix procedures and forms of action that maximize acceptance of authority and thereby make contemplation of the consequences of elections bearable, if not invariably comforting.[2]

TOWARD CRITICAL THINKING

1. What kinds of elections can be taken as mandates for change?
2. V. O. Key Jr. posits that the "electorate itself must possess appropriate expectations and inner constraints." What does he mean by this statement?

---

[2] This chapter has been directed solely toward national elections. Elections in smaller jurisdictions reveal a far wider variety of electoral phenomena, much of it of a droll nature. The battles of the Smiths and the Jones over which clan will name the county supervisor involves matters of a different order than presidential elections. Or a competition of three Irishmen and four Italians for a nomination in a mixed district may combine civic training and a lottery.

· *63* ·

Gender and Voting in the 1992 Presidential Election

MARY E. BENDYNA and CELINDA C. LAKE

The questions of if and how men and women vote differently have received increasing attention in the past two decades. Bendyna and Lake examine the differences in men's and women's voting patterns in the context of the 1992 presidential vote. Bendyna and Lake find, like other election analysts, that a gender gap exists, with women voting for more Democrats than for Republicans. Moreover, because women now make up the majority of voters, their electoral participation and the gender gap have important implications for campaigning, representation, and policy. Bendyna and Lake note that in some elections, the gender gap, coupled with women's increased participation rates, can provide a candidate with a margin of victory.

. . .

◆ The Emergence of the Gender Gap

The voting patterns of women and men that were evident in 1992 were a continuation of trends that first emerged in 1964 and were solidified in the 1980 election. . . . In the 1952, 1956, and 1960 presidential elections, women were more likely than men to vote for the Republican candidate. In 1964, however, Goldwater's militaristic rhetoric and his attacks on the welfare state led to a gender gap in which women were more likely than men to vote for the Democratic candidate. This pattern has been repeated in every presidential election since 1964. In 1964 and 1972 the gender gap was substantial, but in 1968 and 1976 women were only slightly more likely than men to vote for Hubert Humphrey and Jimmy Carter. In most elections, a variety of polls show slightly different results. The exit poll data presented later in this chapter does not show any gender gap in the 1976 election. Yet from 1964 until 1980, women appear to have at least marginally preferred Democratic candidates.

The 1980 presidential election marked a significant turning point in the voting behavior of women and men in presidential elections in the

SOURCE: Reprinted from "Gender and Voting in the 1992 Presidential Election," Mary E. Bendyna and Celinda C. Lake, in *The Year of the Woman: Myths and Realities,* Elizabeth Cook, Sue Thomas, and Clyde Wilcox, 1994) by permission of Westview Press, Boulder, Colorado.

United States. The gender gap in the presidential vote in 1980 was larger than any presidential election before or after, and the 1980 election also marked a widening of differences in the partisanship of women and men. . . . This partisan gender gap was not produced by women moving into the Democratic party, but by men shifting to the Republican party at higher rates than women. This growing partisan gender gap solidified the gender gap in presidential voting. . . .

In addition to signifying a shift in patterns of party identification and partisan vote choice, the 1980 election also witnessed the culmination of a trend in changing participation rates of women and men in presidential elections. In the elections before 1980, women consistently turned out to vote at lower rates than men. This male participation advantage eroded with each passing election, and since 1980, women have turned out to vote at higher rates than men in each presidential election. . . .

The confluence of changing patterns or turnout, partisanship, and vote choice in 1980—and subsequent presidential elections—produced what has come to be known as the "gender gap.". . .

◆ Turnout

In one of the earliest comprehensive studies of American voters, Campbell et al. estimated that the voter participation rate of women was consistently 10 percent below that of men. . . .

Campbell et al. found that there was a great deal of variation in participation rates among social groupings and suggested that changing role definitions might lead to increased participation among women. Among other things, they found that gender differences in voter turnout were greater in the South and in non-metropolitan areas than in other sections of the country. They also found that older women and women with young children were less likely to vote than their male counterparts. Perhaps their most interesting finding was that while gender differences were large among those with lower levels of education, there was little difference in turnout between college-educated women and college-educated men. Moreover, among younger people who were single or married without children, women with a college education were actually more likely to vote than their male counterparts. Campbell et al. presciently predicted that "sex differentials" in voter turnout might diminish as women became more highly educated and as "new sex role definitions" became more widely diffused in rural areas and among those with lower levels of education. . . .

[Figure 1] shows the percentages of women and men who reported voting in presidential elections from 1964 through 1992, according to Census Bureau surveys. These data indicate that turnout rates for both

FIGURE 1
Gender Differences in Presidential Election Turnout, 1964–1992

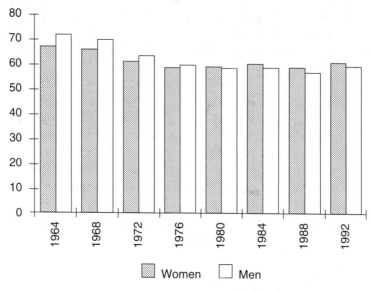

Source: U.S. Bureau of the Census

women and men have generally declined since the 1960s. However, turnout rates for women have not declined as sharply as those for men.

As a result, women have voted at higher rates than men since 1980. The [figure] also indicates that while voter turnout rates increased for both women and men in 1992, the percentage increase was slightly higher for women than for men. Because women comprise a larger proportion of the population than men, the increasingly higher turnout rates for women relative to men take on even greater significance. The combination of more women in the potential electorate and a higher rate of voting among women meant that in 1992, 53 percent of the electorate were women, and 47 percent were men. These figures indicate that there were 6.3 million more women than men in the electorate in 1992.

◆ Partisanship

[Table 1] shows the changes in partisan identification for women and men from 1952 through 1992, according to data from the American National Election Studies. As some of the early studies of voting behavior suggested, women were slightly more likely to identify as Republicans than were men in the 1950s and 1960s ... and this trend continued through 1980. However, these data also show that women have consistently been more likely than men to identify as Democrats since 1960, and

TABLE 1
Gender Differences in Party Identification, 1952–1992

		Women	Men
1952	Democrats	49	48
	Independents	20	26
	Republicans	30	26
1956	Democrats	45	46
	Independents	21	28
	Republicans	34	26
1960	Democrats	51	46
	Independents	18	26
	Republicans	31	28
1964	Democrats	54	51
	Independents	21	25
	Republicans	26	24
1968	Democrats	48	43
	Independents	28	31
	Republicans	24	26
1972	Democrats	44	38
	Independents	32	39
	Republicans	24	23
1976	Democrats	43	37
	Independents	31	42
	Republicans	26	21
1980	Democrats	45	38
	Independents	32	40
	Republicans	23	22
1984	Democrats	41	33
	Independents	32	39
	Republicans	27	28
1988	Democrats	40	30
	Independents	32	41
	Republicans	28	29
1992	Democrats	40	32
	Independents	37	40
	Republicans	23	28

SOURCE: Center for Political Studies, American National Election Studies, 1952–1992.
Independents who lean toward parties are coded as Independents.

that the gap between women and men has generally widened. This seeming inconsistency—that women in the 1970s were both more Republican and more Democratic than men—is possible because women were less likely than men to consider themselves to be Independents.

The net partisanship gender gap became much wider during the 1980s, as women became slightly less likely than men to identify as Republicans and much more likely than men to identify as Democrats.

Both women and men became more Republican (and less Democratic) in the 1980s, but men defected from the Democratic to the Republican party at higher rates than women. . . .

◆ Vote Choice

[Table 2] shows the voting patterns of selected groups of women and men in the presidential elections from 1976 through 1992 as reported in CBS News and CBS/*New York Times* exit polls. The data in this table indicate that in 1976 there were no significant differences between women and men in vote choice. Beginning in 1980, however, women consistently have been more supportive of the Democratic candidate than their male counterparts across a range of demographic categories. Women voters had far more reservations about Reagan's policy priorities and personality than men, and these different reactions to Reagan were the catalyst for the formation of the gender gap that persisted through the next twelve years. . . .

The figures in Table 2 indicate that the gender gap in the vote for the Democratic candidate was largest in 1980, when women were 9 percent more likely than men to favor incumbent Democrat Jimmy Carter over Republican challenger Ronald Reagan. The Democratic gender gap was only slightly smaller in 1984 and 1988. In these two elections, women were more supportive of Democratic challengers Walter Mondale and Michael Dukakis by margins of 7 percent and 8 percent, respectively.

It is important to note that although women were more likely than men to support the Democratic candidate, the CBS News/*New York Times* exit polls in Table 2 show at least a plurality of women voting for Republican candidates throughout the 1980s. Some other exit polls in 1988 showed that Dukakis won a narrow plurality of women's votes, and the National Election Study showed women splitting their votes evenly between Bush and Dukakis. . . . The existence of a gender gap in the 1980s did not mean that a sizable majority of women voted for Democratic candidates, but rather that women were more likely than men to cast Democratic ballots.

Nonetheless, the gender differences in the Republican margins of victory in the 1980s are striking. In the presidential elections of the 1980s, the Republican candidate defeated the Democratic candidate among men by large margins of 19, 25, and 16 percent, respectively. Although women preferred Reagan to Mondale by a fairly large margin of 12 percent in 1984, women were only 2 percent more likely to favor Reagan over Carter in 1980 and less than 1 percent more likely to favor Bush over Dukakis in 1988. This means that any imputed electoral mandate from the 1980

TABLE 2
Gender Differences in Vote Choice, 1976–1992

	1976		1980			1984		1988		1992		
	JC	GF	JC	RR	JA	WM	RR	MD	GB	BC	GB	RP
Total Vote	50	48	41	51	7	40	59	45	53	43	38	19
Gender												
Men	50	48	36	55	7	37	62	41	57	41	38	21
Women	50	48	45	47	7	44	56	49	50	46	37	17
Race												
White Men	47	51	32	59	7	32	67	36	63	37	41	22
White Women	46	52	39	52	8	38	62	43	56	41	41	18
Black Men	80	19	82	14	3	85	12	81	15	77	15	9
Black Women	86	14	88	9	3	93	7	91	9	86	9	5
Age												
Men, 18–29	50	47	39	47	11	36	63	43	55	38	36	26
Women, 18–29	51	47	49	39	10	44	55	50	49	48	33	19
Men, 30–44	49	49	31	59	8	38	61	40	58	39	38	22
Women, 30–44	49	49	41	50	8	45	54	49	50	44	38	18
Men, 45–59	48	51	34	60	5	36	62	36	62	40	40	20
Women, 45–59	46	53	44	50	5	42	57	48	52	43	40	17
Men, 60 and over	44	55	40	56	3	37	62	46	53	49	37	14
Women, 60 and over	49	50	43	52	4	42	58	52	48	51	39	10
Education												
Men, < High School			47	51	2	47	52	50	49	49	30	21
Women, < High School			56	41	2	52	46	62	38	58	27	15
Men, High School			42	53	3	37	62	49	50	43	34	23
Women, High School			44	50	5	41	58	50	50	43	38	19
Men, Some College			31	59	8	33	65	38	60	39	37	24
Women, Some College			39	52	8	41	58	45	54	43	38	18
Men, College Grad			28	59	11	36	63	36	63	40	41	19
Women, College Grad			44	42	12	47	52	51	49	49	35	16

SOURCES: 1976 CBS News Exit Poll; 1980, 1984; 1988 CBS News/*New York Times* Exit Polls; 1992 Voter Research and Surveys Exit Poll.

and 1988 elections came almost entirely from male voters. The preferences of women working outside the home and women under 50 contributed most to the pro-Democratic edge among women during this period.

The data in Table 2 also show that the gender gap after 1980 was consistently higher among blacks than among whites, and also higher among men and women with college degrees, or with less than a high school education. It is interesting that the gender gap was greatest among the most and least educated Americans. . . .

◆ Election Results

According to exit poll data collected by Voter Research and Surveys and reported in the *New York Times* and elsewhere, Bill Clinton won 43 percent of the vote, George Bush won 38 percent of the vote, and Ross Perot won 19 percent of the vote. There was a 5-point gender gap in the Clinton vote, with Clinton winning 46 percent of the votes cast by women and 41 percent of the votes cast by men. There was a gender gap in the vote for Perot as well with 4 percent more men than women voting for the independent candidate. There was virtually no gender gap in the vote for Bush, with the incumbent president winning 38 percent of men and 37 percent of women. Viewed in terms of the two-party vote, however, the gender differences in candidate choice are more striking: Clinton defeated Bush by 9 percent among women but by only 3 percent among men. These figures, along with other relevant data from the exit polls, are presented in Table 2. . . .

Although a wide range of variables contributed to Clinton's margin of victory, his success among certain groups of women may have been a decisive factor in winning the 1992 presidential election. Clinton ran particularly well among both college-educated women and women with less than a high school education, among women from the youngest and oldest age groups, and among working women, African-American women, and women with Democratic or Independent party identification.

As the data in Table 2 indicate, the differences between women and men with a college education and between women and men with less than a high school education were particularly large. In both cases, the gender gap was 9 percent. Perhaps even more notable is the fact that Clinton's margin of victory over Bush among women with less than a high school education was 21 points. These women came into the election least impressed by and interested in Bush's foreign policy victories and most worried about the U.S. economy. These women felt themselves to be marginal elements of the nation's economy, and they were greatly concerned with their children's future and their own families' economic futures. They wanted a president who represented change and someone who would get the economy moving again.

Among women with a college education, the margin was 14 points. Although this margin was smaller than that among voters with less than a high school degree, the gap is more significant because these women made up one-fifth of the electorate and are especially likely to be ticket-splitting voters. As noted earlier, Clinton ran particularly well among college-educated women throughout the general election campaign. These voters liked Clinton's economic plan, pro-choice stance, and general values.

Clinton also ran very well among women from both the youngest and the oldest age cohorts. Women aged eighteen to twenty-nine were 10 percent more likely to vote for Clinton than their male counterparts. Although a majority of women aged sixty and over voted for Clinton, the gender gap was not large because men in this age cohort also favored Clinton by a significant margin. Interestingly, women in the thirty to forty-four and forty-five to fifty-nine age categories were only 3 to 5 percent more likely to favor Clinton than their male counterparts. Clinton and Bush ran even among men in each of these age categories.

Another group among whom Clinton ran well was working women, who favored Clinton over Bush by a 10-point margin. The support of working women was particularly important to the Clinton campaign since these women comprised almost a third of the electorate. One of the few groups of women among whom Clinton did not fare well was homemakers. According to the exit polls, 45 percent of homemakers supported Bush, while only 36 percent supported Clinton. Although Clinton lost this group, the 9-point Republican edge was much smaller than the margin in favor of the Republican candidate in either 1984 or 1988, when homemakers favored Reagan over Mondale and Bush over Dukakis by 24 percent and 17 percent, respectively (see Table 2).

Although Clinton did relatively well among most groups of women, it is important to note than he did not win a plurality of white women. White women split their votes evenly between Clinton and Bush, giving each of the candidates 41 percent of their vote. Nonetheless, white women gave a higher percentage of their vote to Clinton than did white men: Clinton lost the votes of white men by 4 percent. Moreover, because white women made up a larger proportion of the electorate than did white men, they accounted for a substantial share of the Clinton vote. According to the exit polls, women accounted for 55 percent of all votes for Clinton. Finally, it should be noted that although the gender gap among African-American voters was larger than the gap among white voters, overwhelming majorities of black women and black men favored Clinton.

Although the national gender gap was relatively small, it was much more substantial within certain states. In the 1992 elections, women backed Clinton by double-digit margins in twenty states; men backed Clinton by such large margins in only six states. Moreover, women provided the winning margin for Clinton in six states. In three of these states—Nevada, New Hampshire, and Tennessee—Clinton and Bush ran even among men, but Clinton won among women. In three other states—Georgia, Iowa, and Oregon—Clinton lost among men but won among women voters. In Georgia, Clinton lost to Bush by 6 points among men, but won among women by 5 points. Because women comprise a larger proportion of the electorate, Clinton was able to narrowly win the state. In Iowa and Oregon, Clinton lost to Bush among men by 10 points and 3 points, respectively, but ran ahead among women by large margins of 16 points in Iowa and an astounding 24 points in Oregon. These 6 states accounted for 46 electoral votes. . . .

Data from the Voter Research and Surveys exit polls suggest that women voters were also motivated by somewhat different issues and other research shows that women often view the same issues through different experiences. Voters were asked what one or two issues most influenced their votes, and what one or two candidate qualities were important in helping them decide which candidate to support. Although men and women who voted for Clinton shared a common set of concerns, women were relatively more interested [in] issues such as education, health care, and abortion, and male Clinton voters were relatively more interested in the budget deficit and the general state of the economy. During the campaign, Clinton emphasized both additional spending programs to deal with the "social deficit," and cuts in spending on other programs, along with increased taxes on the wealthy to help deal with the fiscal deficit. Women were more concerned with the former, men with the latter.

Women and men who supported each candidate focused on a common set of candidate characteristics that influenced their vote, but again there were differences in emphasis. Women voters showed more interest in the candidate's character than did men. Women who voted for Clinton were more likely to indicate that they supported him because he represented change and because he cared, while men were somewhat more likely to stress his experience as governor. Women who voted for Bush were far more likely than men to say that they valued his experience, while men were more likely to indicate that Bush had the best plan for the economy. Interestingly, very few women who voted for Bush indicated that they supported him because he cared, but men were much more likely to perceive Bush as concerned about average Americans. . . .

Women who work outside the home were most concerned with two issues in 1992: how to combine work and family, and how to make enough money to help their families make ends meet. Women who were more economically secure—higher income, better educated, middle and upper class—tended to be most concerned with combining work and family, and with having enough time for their families. Women who were less economically secure were more worried about the immediate concern of having enough money to pay bills.

Women in 1992 had an agenda, and to a surprising extent they agreed—whatever their class or race—about what the agenda should be.

By far, the three policies women most wanted were health care (86 percent wanted guaranteed health insurance for everyone, 49 percent indicated that it was a top priority), flextime (58 percent of women preferred flextime to a traditional schedule), and equal pay; all items reflecting women's basic economic concerns.

These issues directly affect the daily lives of women and their families, and they are the issues of a broad-based women's movement. Women view the economy in very personal terms, and in 1992 the economy was the most important issue to women. Although some younger, college-educated women voted the abortion issue, women were less worried on a personal level about policies such as day care and abortion rights—policies that are often the focal point of activity for the women's movement. These issues mattered less in their votes. Women were primarily concerned in 1992 about the economic well-being of their families.

◆ Conclusion

The gender differences in voting that were evident in the 1992 election were generally similar to those that have existed in presidential elections since 1980. Of course, the obvious difference between the 1992 presidential election and the three presidential elections that preceded it is that the Democratic candidate won. Although the gender differences in 1992 were not very large, the votes of women were certainly significant in building the coalition that gave Clinton his margin of victory. As shown in the data presented above, women have not only continued to be more supportive of the Democratic candidate than men, they have also continued to turn out to vote at higher rates than men and thus to comprise a larger share of the electorate than men.

The 1992 presidential election thus confirmed a number of important trends in American politics. In addition to continuing trends in turnout, partisanship, and vote choice, the 1992 election also showed that even when women and men arrive at the same conclusions, they may have different perspectives and experiences that influence their judgment of candidates and their priorities on policies. The 1992 presidential election also suggests that at the margin, women and men continue to make different choices in politics that can affect the fortunes of candidates and the outcome of elections. For example, if women's support for Clinton had never exceeded that of men, Clinton would have won a far more narrow victory, which might have made governing more difficult. If women had fewer doubts about Perot, he might have surged earlier and more forcefully.

Although the 1992 election confirmed important gender differences, it also suggested that differences among groups of women can be greater than those between women and men. Large differences in preferences continue to appear between homemakers and women who work outside the home and between religious right women and more secular college-educated women. However, while women may have disagreed about the final results, the presidential elections of 1980 and through 1992 show that women bring a different perspective to politics than men. In 1992, women gave greater weight to style and character issues and had greater reservations about both Clinton and Perot than did men. Women also had economic issue perspectives and priorities that were different from those of men. This was reflected in their greater concern for the personal economics of their families than about macro-accounting issues like the deficit. Candidates who ignore these important differences risk generating even greater gender gaps in the future.

TOWARD CRITICAL THINKING

1. What factors lured male voters to the Republican party in the 1980s? Why did these same factors appeal less to women voters? Is this difference likely to continue?

2. How has the perception that women vote more as a bloc than do men influenced campaign strategies?

· *64* ·

A Day in the Life of the Campaign

THE WASHINGTON POST

U.S. presidential candidates campaign long and hard for the nation's top post—much longer than leaders of any other western democracy. Indeed, with the increasing importance of state primaries, some candidates' formal candidacies begin as much as two years before the November election.

A look at "A Day in the Life of the Campaign" illustrates the constant activity and strategy that make up the modern presidential campaign. The increasing presence of the media and public opinion polls has forced campaign managers to plan in the short term in order to best shape and respond to ever-changing news—as well as to fashion their campaigns in order to attract free positive media attention. While reading this selection, keep in mind that this summary represents only one day in the life of Bill Clinton and George Bush as they campaigned for the presidency in 1992.

Dawn, Wed., Oct. 21, Spartanburg, S.C.
The Secret Service agents are hastily checking under the griddle at the Waffle House. They're looking behind the counter, eyeballing the narrow booths, whispering up their sleeves. The president is coming! It's an unexpected campaign stop, a kind of elaborate wisecrack in which rhetoric is transformed into spontaneous theater. Waffle House. As in what Bill Clinton does. The campaign strategists had cooked up the idea the night before, brainstorming across the street at the Ramada Inn, trying to find some magic as the campaign enters the endgame.

An advance worker, John Herrick, orders the presidential breakfast: scrambled eggs, bacon, a waffle, syrup, butter, coffee and a big glass of milk. At half past 7, the Leader of the Free World strolls in with his son Marvin at his side. The men sit down at the counter between two surprised locals. The cameras roll. In the corner, Torie Clarke, the campaign press secretary, feeds quips to the quip-hungry press. "We want to keep the waffles at the Waffle House, where they belong," she says.

SOURCE: "A Day in the Life of the Campaign," *The Washington Post* (October 23, 1992):C1. © 1992 The Washington Post. Reprinted with permission.

But President Bush doesn't deliver the sound bite. Maybe he's being subtle. Maybe he just needs a few gulps of his morning coffee. Maybe he's gloomy because the Kennebunkport paper endorsed Clinton. In any case, when a reporter asks about the symbolism of Waffle House, the president says, straight-faced, "I wouldn't jump to any conclusions if I were you."

A real person approaches. Her name is Wendy Mergeenghaler. It is rare that a real person gets to speak to the president in an unscripted moment. This is what she says: "Railroad crossing, look out for the cars. How do you spell that without any R's?"

Bush draws a blank.

"You spell that "T-H-A-T'!" says the woman.

The president laughs heartily. "Funny one! Funny one!" he roars.

He has one of his own.

"Did you hear the one," Bush asks, "about the duck that went into the bar?"

Pause.

"Bartender looks at the duck and says, 'Your pants are down.'"

Silence.

"Down! Duck down! Get it?"

The crowd laughs appreciatively; it's the kind of polite laughter that is owed, regardless of circumstance, to the commander in chief....

Bush is almost speechless. What he's thinking at this moment is unknowable—though perhaps he has pondered the fact that he, The Most Powerful Man on Earth, a man who has negotiated arms treaties with Yeltsin and waged war in the Persian Gulf, is stuck in a greasy spoon ... and behind by double digits! How did it come to this?

His eggs are cold, the sun is rising. A train beckons. It is 13 days before the election that will decide his future, and for George Bush, it's going to be a long, interesting day.

A presidential campaign is like a Fellini film—lots of strange things are happening at once, and it's hard to figure out what it all means. Not even C-SPAN can capture all the raw, rushing madness: the million hours of strategizing and sign-painting, of drafting speeches and inflating balloons; the miles of motorcades following carefully planned routes; the burst faxes and pamphlet drops and mass mailings and focus groups; the crowds drummed up and the camera angles plotted; the ceaseless flood of words that pour from the candidates in speeches, conferences, powwows, summits, fund-raisers and fleeting face-to-face encounters with ordinary voters....

The campaign tale changes day by day and hour by hour; which details are kept (Bush went to the Waffle House) and which are omitted (he told a lame joke) depend on formats, time and space restrictions, and most of all [on] the motive and purpose of the storyteller.

If the story makes sense to you, then you are the smartest of citizens—
or else the professionals have done their job, and you've been had.

7 A.M. EDT, the Airwaves

Americans wake up to see the president on TV doing the Atlanta
Braves fans' "tomahawk chop." This is from Tuesday. All the networks
have pretty much the same story: Clinton is heading today into Republican turf, while Bush is backfilling, trying to shore up his Southern base,
"just trying to avoid humiliation here," in the dire words of an NBC
reporter. . . .

Clinton is seen campaigning in the Midwest. He is saying nothing new
—at this point his voice is elevator music, a raspy, harmless Muzak. . .

On the "Today" show, Tipper Gore shows Katie Couric snapshots she
has taken on the campaign trail, and says: "I have learned a lot, particularly the breadth of people that are out there. There are children. There are
older people. There are people that come on oxygen. There are people that
come in wheelchairs, on stretchers." . . .

But where's Ross? The stealth candidate, billionaire Ross Perot,
hasn't been seen since Monday. There are reports that he is in Dallas,
holding strategy sessions. There are no confirmed sightings.

8 A.M. (7 CDT), Little Rock, Ark.

Bob Boorstin, the Clinton campaign's deputy communications director, yearns for sleep. He woke up this morning at 5:40, instantly feeling
his stomach flip over. A manic-depressive, the scraggly-bearded Boorstin
takes daily medication and must take care to get proper rest, he says, lest
he have an "episode" like the two he had during the Dukakis campaign.

But there's no way anyone can rest these days in Little Rock. The
senior campaign aides say they're worried that the race may tighten up
considerably, and that Ross Perot may screw up their carefully mapped
Electoral College strategy. And so when the seventy bleary-eyed staffers—zombies on overdrive—assemble in the War Room for the regular
morning meeting, Boorstin issues a warning: Don't be overconfident.
Michael Dukakis, he says, could have won the 1988 election if he had
gotten 550,000 more votes in the right states. What he doesn't tell them
is that he's making this number up, just to scare them.

Top strategist James Carville arrives a few minutes later. The campaign's overnight polls have shown a sizable Perot blip. Very worrisome.
Carville tells the staff that there mustn't be any talk of "landslides"
or "mandates"—and he's really worried about a photo that ran in the
morning papers. It shows Clinton happily tossing a football on an airport tarmac with running mate Gore. Bad symbolism! If Clinton looks
too cocky, Carville fears, the voters will become annoyed. And punish
him.

8:50 A.M., Thomasville, N.C.

Gerald Hege, chairman of the Davidsonville County Republican Party, reaches the top of the town's 150-foot-tall water tower. He and a friend, wearing their black satin Tusk Club jackets and billed hats, unfurl a black sign that other volunteers finished painting only a few hours before. It says:

"Bush Country, USA" in white block letters, and below that, "Davidson County is G.O.P. Country—Tusk Club" in red. It is 14 feet tall and 120 feet long. Another sign, big and red and positioned right where the TV cameras will catch it, says "Thomasville Trusts George Bush." This one was supplied by the Bush campaign's advance team, which has been using the word "trust" as a not-so-subliminal message.

The campaign has another request: Thomasville Firearms, with its window display of camouflage gear, will have to stay closed today. As one of the advance people had told the city council the other night, "It's very rare to have a firearms store" so close to the site of a presidential speech. . . .

9 A.M., Jackson, Mich.

Something is mysteriously wrong with Dan Quayle's stump speech. The people in the audience here at Spring Arbor College are sitting on their hands. The vice president is delivering a depressing summary of the Jimmy Carter years—high interest rates, gas lines etc.—which he says illustrates the dangers of electing Democrats. So why aren't they clapping? What gives?

And then it hits him. When Carter was president, some of these kids still had training wheels on their bikes.

"You know, maybe the college kids don't remember what it was like under Jimmy Carter," Quayle says. "But let me just remind you, . . . it is nothing but a recipe for disaster."

After the rally, as Quayle travels by bus across southern Michigan, he decides to add an explanation of who Jimmy Carter was, exactly.

10 A.M., New York City

Subtle images are everywhere. Al Gore is at the MTV studio, which has been shrouded in red and blue papier-mache until it looks like a cave. MTV calls this the "Choose or Lose" forum.

Gore is wearing a raucous tie that resembles a shattered stained-glass window. It's the Wooden Wonder's way of showing he can be hip too. But when asked to name his favorite rap artist, all he can come up with is the lame and waning Hammer. And, before correcting himself, he bobbles the name of MTV's political effort—he calls it "Choose to Lose."

10:23 A.M., Washington

At CNN headquarters, Tom Hannon, the network's political director, walks by with a hot document: the latest CNN-*USA Today* tracking poll. "Seen the tracking? Clinton's down, Bush and Perot are up," he says.

This might be news—might be. Every four years the press vows not to follow every bleep and bloop in the polls, and every four years the temptation proves too strong.

Hannon asks CNN analyst William Schneider "to work up a how-Bush-could-win segment" for "Inside Politics," the all-important 4:30 show. Hannon dismisses talk that the race is over. "We've still got to cover this thing for the next 13 days," he says.

That seems so short a period—and yet for some countries 13 days is enough for an entire campaign. No other nation has so long, so indulgent a campaign for national leadership. Foreigners think what happens here is bizarre, but admirable—a demonstration of democracy at almost preposterous intensity.

11 A.M., Little Rock

Boorstin orders a "grainy" photo made off a video of Bush doing the "tomahawk chop," to be printed and distributed among Native Americans. . . .

11:21 A.M., Little Rock

The Clinton motorcade pulls onto the airport tarmac. This is the first of fourteen times that Bill Clinton will change vehicles today. About seventy reporters and media technicians are pressing around him, even though he's protecting his voice, speaking so softly that it's almost impossible to hear him. Every utterance from the man is noted and recorded.

"I don't feel comfortable, and I'm not relaxed," says the relaxed, comfortable-looking governor as he boards his chartered 727 campaign plane. He has Arkansas turkey sausage in his belly, his muscles pumped from a morning workout at the local YMCA.

Either Clinton is just cool or he's pyched himself into a super-efficient way of conserving energy. A campaign is an endurance test, an epic performance of strength. Clinton's smile is warm, but reserved. His wave is a royal one that flexes at the upraised elbow, ever so slightly.

Clinton has been campaigning almost nonstop since 1978, when he first sought the governorship of Arkansas. Because the state has only a two-year gubernatorial term, Clinton has rarely had much more than a year off from the hectic pace of selling himself. A Clinton aide jokes: If Clinton wins on Nov. 3, they'll have to put a straitjacket on him to make him stop shaking hands.

11:30 A.M., Thomasville

Gerald Hege changes into a white dress shirt from his jacket and T-shirt, but refuses to wear a suit and tie. "I don't like them sissy things," he says. Hege, who's to emcee the event, has recently wrested the party leadership away from the country club Republicans.

Putting on an event like this is something like juggling five circuses. You need 5,000 feet of rope, you need grommets to make holes in the bedsheet signs, you need ticket takers and metal-detector watchers, local high school bands to rev up the crowd, a gift for the president, you need forty-one telephone lines put in for the press.

At least Sue Hunter, a Republican county commissioner, has the gift for the president. She is scurrying around getting the plaque affixed to the miniature reproduction of The Chair she'll present him along with a sign, "Keep Your Seat in '92." Thomasville, population 15,915, is a furniture-making town in North Carolina's Piedmont. Known to its residents as Chair City, it contains within its otherwise not particularly photogenic boundaries The Largest Chair in The World.

1:05 P.M., Kannapolis, N.C.

Weird as it was, the nets loved Waffle House. ("Nets" as in "networks," as in Big TV, as in the only thing that matters. Reporters who write are called "pencils.") But there's a basic problem with the Waffle House theme: Bush didn't mention waffling during his first speech of the day, in Gaston County, N.C. The nets can't use the Waffle House photo op without a specific mention of waffling. Bush is blowing it!

Ann Compton of ABC News moves urgently from one staffer to another. She buttonholes Marlin Fitzwater, corners Torie Clarke, sidles up to Mary Matalin. She tells each one: If you want Waffle House, we need Bush to say something about waffling!

The message gets to Bush, and in Kannapolis the president says, "We had breakfast at the Waffle House. Little symbolism there."

Compton sees Clarke after the speech.

"It's still not quite right," she says.

2 P.M. (1 P.M. CDT), Dallas

There is still no sign of Ross Perot. But his commercials have arrived.

There are four spots, each with narration but barely a glimpse of Perot himself (even in his ads he's a phantom force). The commercials, which begin airing today, are shown to reporters by Orson Swindle, Perot's aide, a man with a name out of a Sinclair Lewis novel. Perot himself is said to be a few blocks away, working on more commercials. . . .

2:08 P.M., Thomasville

Gerald Hege, standing on the back of a flatbed truck, tells the crowd of about 10,000 that the president will be arriving in five minutes.

"Let's go, folks!" he shouts, "We're on CNN!"

The band plays "Carolina in the Morning," the cheerleaders leap up, the people wave flags. For a full five minutes, they yell and holler.

No train.

2:23 P.M., The Airwaves

CNN cuts to a Clinton stump speech in Pueblo, Colo. Clinton delivers his standard applause lines, railing against "four more years of trickle-down economics," but the speech is marred by audio difficulties. CNN bails out of live coverage.

2:30 P.M., The Airwaves

Sprinkled amid the Bush and Clinton speech segments, the new Perot ads air regularly on CNN.

2:40 P.M., Little Rock

Boorstin, already slightly irritable after his brief nap, gets bad news over the phone. A staffer tells him that the photo studio won't do the job on the tomahawk chop picture unless it has a legal release from NBC, the source of the original video. "Well," Boorstin snaps into his telephone headset, "we'll just have to go to a place that won't give us a hard time."

2:42 P.M., Thomasville

Hege cranks it up again. "Let's wave them flags!" he cries. Overhead a helicopter appears, signaling the approach of the leader.

"You are making a part of history!" Hege shouts.

Ten minutes later—right on time—the presidential train can be heard chugging around the curve, whistle blowing, flags flying. The place erupts in a deafening outburst of cheers, horn blasts, yelling and whooping.

The train arrives . . . and arrives . . . and arrives. Twenty-one very long cars . . . Finally, there he is! Wearing a light blue shirt, tieless, and waving.

He gives a speech. It's just like the speech he's been giving all day, but with a few bows to the local folks.

"You've got to make the best furniture in the world!" he says.

Fifty-two minutes after it arrived, the train pulls away. Bush's voice grows faint . . . He's smiling . . . He's saying, "Thanks for a great day . . ."

It's over.

2:45 P.M., Newark

Al Gore's motorcade is making its way though an inner city neighborhood. He's visiting the Children's Health Fund Van, which serves homeless people and poor children. Just as Gore and singer Paul Simon are about to enter the van, several local residents implore them to stop and talk.

"Talk to us. That's why we are here. Damn the press, they get theirs," one young black man says. Another shouts, "We have ideas, we know what to do." Gore turns and says, "I'm going to. . . . After I do this, I'll come right back."

Nearly an hour passes. Local officials drone on. Chatter from inside the van is piped out to the crowd on a mistakenly open mike. Simon's wife, Edie Brickell, is pregnant, he says, and they are "going to do Lamaze." The candidate approves. "We did . . . with all four." Then the sound system goes off. By the time Gore emerges, the residents with the "ideas" are gone.

3 P.M., Somewhere in North Carolina

The railroads have rigged up a second train on a parallel track so that TV crews can shoot pictures of the president waving to adoring crowds. Good gimmick. But there's a catch. The two-train feat is performed in the middle of nowhere. Although Bush had huge crowds all day, the footage that's shot shows the president waving to nobody. . . .

4:07 P.M., Washington

CNN anchorman Bernard Shaw emerges from the makeup room and slips into his chair on the set of "Inside Politics." He fiddles with his script, asks that the TelePrompTer be adjusted and muses on the seemingly routine nature of the day's news.

"You've got to be eternally vigilant in the last two weeks of a campaign," he says. "You want to report any changes in tone or message. You're watching for any indication of a change in tactics."

The script says that "George Bush still maintains he's going to win four more years." Shaw crosses out "maintains" with a felt-tip pen and writes in "claims."

"Maintains," he says, "is too mild a word."

4:30 P.M., The Airwaves

"Inside Politics" is on the air. Charles Bierbauer's piece opens with a picture of Bush eating a waffle. "Waffling is a staple of Bush's criticism," Bierbauer says. The president issues the half-baked sound bite, "We had breakfast at the Waffle House, a little symbolism. . . . " At last The Message dribbles out, but to limited effect. Bierbauer closes by saying that some analysts "suggest that short of a miracle, Bush cannot win.". . .

5 P.M., Little Rock

"I have spilkes," says Clinton campaign chief of staff Eli Segal, using the Yiddish expression for butterflies in the stomach, "only because I've been involved in a lot of losing campaigns.". . .

5:30 P.M., Little Rock

James Carville bounds into the office of George Stephanopoulos, the campaign's main spinner. "We just got the biggest crowd in the history of

Wyoming!" Carville shouts. "It was at least 5,000 people, and they only got 3,000 in 1984."

For Reagan, it needn't be said.

Stephanopoulos raises his fist in a power-to-the-people salute. (But not a confident power-to-the-people salute.)

5:42 P.M., Burlington, N.C.

Bush has another crack at the sound bite. A good-sized crowd has turned out to hear him.

"You cannot be the Waffle House if you want to be in the White House!"

Darn. Doesn't quite make sense.

But Bush is on a roll. He's been loose and almost giddy all day, and getting looser and giddier all the time.

He drew the contrast between himself and Al Gore, whom he has been calling "Ozone Man."

"I'm an environmental man," he says, "but I'm not going to throw every worker out of work because of some snail darter, or some [pause] SMELT, [pause] or some owl!"

Some smelt! You could hear people asking each other: Is the smelt endangered? Can't you buy smelt in the grocery store? (It turns out there is an endangered Delta smelt somewhere far, far from North Carolina, and its name sprang to the presidential mind just in time to keep his rhythm going.)

The press has never seen him more pure. Bush looks unfiltered, unrestrained, unconcerned. Take the waffle line, for instance. At some point in his career he might have surrendered to his handlers and let them write down a good waffle quote that he could just glance down at and read inconspicuously. Not today! No way—Bush is skylarking.

At times the president's zest borders on downright loopiness, as if the fresh air and bright sunshine on the platform at the rear of the train were making him tipsy. But for all the verbal gymnastics, Bush is, for the first time in the campaign, sticking to his message. Which is this: Introduce friends. Bash Clinton's record in Arkansas. Bash Jimmy Carter. Promise lower taxes. Demand the line-item veto and balanced budget amendment. Bash Clinton on crime. Defend vouchers for private schools. Bash Clinton for being weak on war. Mention Barbara. Bash Clinton on flip-flops. Oppose inflation. Bash Clinton on pessimism. Bash the pollsters. Endorse the American Dream. Boast about Desert Storm. Invoke God. . . .

Uh, just which message was that again?

And the train rolls onward through territory the president should have locked up months ago; the whistle moaning what may be a forlorn valediction.

6:30 P.M., The Airwaves

ABC does not use any Waffle House footage on the evening news, though Compton puts some into her piece for the next day's morning news. She pares an awkward sound bite out of the Bush gibberish. Her piece is not entirely flattering, opening with a shot of him forking a waffle into his mouth, then talking with his mouth full, and ends with a shot of him on the rear platform waving to an empty forest.

CBS just has some fleeting images of Clinton and Bush, not even a sound bite. All that work for nothing. NBC has a report on Clinton's character in which the reporter signs off asking which Clinton would serve in the White House—the committed idealist or the calculating politician?

7:45 P.M., Little Rock

In the Clinton War Room, the news is studied keenly. Of particular interest is CBS correspondent Eric Engberg's highly critical report about Bush radio ads. Engberg says a Bush spot is "festooned . . . with make-believe assumptions. There's a word for such tactics: Slick." A cheer goes up. . . .

8:55 P.M., Raleigh, N.C.

As many of 20,000 people are gathered beside the garish lights of the Ferris wheel and the Tilt-a-whirl. The crowd lets out a huge roar as Jesse Helms, looking frail in a tan raincoat, takes the stage along with "the King himself," Richard Petty, the stock car racing legend. Petty, wearing his trademark black cowboy hat, tells the story of his memorable victory in a race at Nashville in 1967. He was fourteen laps behind the leader—"but we kept on working and kept on plugging and by the end of the race we were four laps ahead! We can do that here!". . .

Bush has clearly returned to the very base of his base, riding the rails through country that he could be certain would produce adoring crowds. The cheer he receives when he takes the stage in Raleigh is perhaps the longest and lustiest he has heard all year. They keep howling even after he starts talking.

A small group near the front of the throng begins calling out: "He waffles!" and "Waffle Man!" Maybe they are loyal CNN watchers.

"Listen," Bush says. "I'm getting to the Waffle House part. I'm just getting warmed up here."

Getting hot is more like it. He rips Clinton skillfully. Then it comes: "You can't let the White House turn into the Waffle House!"

Bingo. A clear, tight, coherent sound bite.

Too late, of course, for the nets.

9:15 P.M. (7:30 MDT), Billings, Mont.

Clinton really is a night person. Inside his mobile universe time does not exist, it's as though he revolves around his own internal sun. (Central?

Mountain? Pacific? These things don't matter.) Now he's in the packed gym of Rocky Mountain College. . . .

Speech over, he plunges into the overflow crowd outside, his emotional setting switched to "on." They chant: "We love you!"

The effective candidate is a kind of seducer. He flatters and insinuates and lightly cajoles; he shows a hint of vulnerability under a sheen of virile strength. He moves carefully, cagily, always alert to that one wrong step, wrong word, wrong grin or scowl that can cool the rising ardor of the electorate. If Clinton is the new boy in the neighborhood, the handsome suitor, then Bush is the remonstrative, stern, protective father. Don't trust that young man! says Bush. Watch out!

When it works, the candidate finds himself on a day in October standing before thousands of people passionately chanting his name. The rational gives way to the emotional; what might once have been merely preferential is now the object of desire. He is touching them, and they are touching back. For a moment it's almost possible to understand why any sane person would want to endure the rigors and torments of an American presidential campaign.

But look carefully: On all sides are tense Secret Service agents, one with a hand gripping the campaigner's belt. The candidate leans into the crowd and the crowd paws and grabs and pulls at him; at the precarious moment the agent pulls him back. It is a coupling and a devouring.

Long after Dark, Washington

Most of the offices are empty on the 12th floor of the Bush-Quayle campaign headquarters, but David Tell is still working. He's a man who knows things and keeps them secret. A thin, bearded, rather intense man of thirty-two, he has the lofty title of senior policy adviser, but what he does is called "opposition research"—that is, dig up stuff about Bill Clinton. He figures he knows Clinton as well as anyone—all through public documents. . . .

The hour is getting late, but Tell has not given up. Clinton has, as Tell delicately puts it, "an unusually tenuous relationship with the truth." And yet the trust issue hasn't quite worked. Yet.

Does Tell know something? Is there another Clinton scandal out there? Some horrid fact that will derail the Clinton Express?

He is silent for a moment. Then says in an even voice, "Stay tuned."

Midnight

The major newspapers go to press with front-page stories on the Perot phenomenon. Clinton and Bush, for all their exhaustive campaigning, have failed to generate much news and are consigned to increasingly brief snippets of the TV news programs. For Clinton, not so bad—at least no one called him overconfident; for Bush, not so good—he needs a break.

On this day, when the levers have been pulled, the buttons pushed, it is clear that the story of the day, the winner of the battle for perceived dynamism, is the man who never showed his face: Ross Perot, the billionaire, whereabouts unknown.

TOWARD CRITICAL THINKING

1. Is the modern presidential campaign more a test of stamina than of ideas? Or does the minute-by-minute coverage of campaigns offer too many ideas and perhaps not enough in-depth discussion?

2. As Reading 64 illustrates, the media and public opinion polls are constantly watched by campaign strategists. What effect do they appear to have on campaign strategies? In responding to the media and polls, are candidates ignoring the voters?

· 65 ·

The Significance of the 1992 Election

SEYMOUR MARTIN LIPSET

As noted by Bendyna and Lake in Reading 63, the gender gap played a role in the 1992 presidential election. According to political scientist Seymour Martin Lipset, however, other factors were even more important, including the candidates, the kinds of campaigns they ran, and economic conditions. "A Day in the Life of the Campaign" (Reading 64) also underscores the role that campaigning and media relations played in the campaigns of the two major party candidates for president.

Issues and ideology also played an important role. Abortion, in particular, was a salient issue in the wake of Supreme Court decisions including *Webster* v. *Reproductive Health Services* (1989) (Reading 13). Many voters feared that the election of Republicans would endanger abortion rights, and some liberal Republicans ended up rejecting pro-life Republican candidates.

Bill Clinton's win in 1992 signaled the election of the first Democratic president in twelve years. Lipset ponders whether Clinton, who ran as a new "moderate" Democrat, will learn from the problems of his predecessors or be the man to begin a new series of one-term presidents. Given how elections have changed in the United States, Clinton's 1996 reelection campaign started almost as soon as he was sworn in, not unlike Marjorie Margolies-Mezvinsky's situation in Congress (Reading 30).

The 1992 election was influenced by a number of factors. The personalities, or characteristics, of the candidates clearly played a role, as did the kind of campaign they ran. Economic conditions were particularly important. However, it is interesting to note that statistical models by economists predicting election results, which emphasize economic trends, were less successful in 1992 than in previous years. Political scientists were more successful.

✦ Models and Perceptions

. . . What defeated the Republicans was perception. What is most interesting about this particular defeat is the rate of decline in Bush's

SOURCE: Seymour Martin Lipset, "The Significance of the 1992 Election," *PS: Political Science & Politics,* XXVI:1 (March 1993):7–16.

popularity and support in one year, 1991–92. It is hard to remember that after the Gulf War, in early 1991, his approval rating stood at 90 percent. By the fall, as he was beginning to plan his election strategy, he still had a 70 percent approval rating. Many Democratic politicians have been kicking themselves because they refused to run for president, thinking that no Democrat had a chance to beat the victor of the Gulf War, a man with that kind of popular endorsement. It is to Clinton's credit or rigidity that he believed that these numbers could be turned around.

Bush, of course, contributed to the negative impact of the economy by giving the impression that he was not taking the recession seriously. He seemingly was misled by the administration's economists, who believed correctly that it was not so deep, but incorrectly anticipated that it would end soon, well before the election, without much being done by the government. By the time they woke up to the fact that the economy was not improving and was having a negative impact on the electorate, it was too late for Bush to become the candidate of change, the person who was going to fix the economy.

◆ The Perot Phenomenon

This election, of course, had some very special conditions, particularly a significant third candidate in the form of Ross Perot, who must be given a lot of the credit or blame for what happened. Before he pulled out in June, his support ran between 25 percent and 30 percent in most of the polls. Some of them even placed him in the lead, others had him number two. *Clinton was third in most of them. . . .*

Perot, however, destroyed this scenario by his initial withdrawal. Two-thirds of his backing went to Clinton. Much of the original Perot support came from people who had voted in the previous three elections for Reagan and Bush, including many so-called "Reagan or Bush Democrats." Fed up with the economy and Bush's ineptness, they had shifted to Perot in the spring. Normally, those who move from one party to another first go to the undecided category; this time they could opt for a new centrist candidate.

. . . At that point, many who had already given up on Bush and the Republicans found it easier to move to the Democrats, than they would have if they had to go directly from the Republicans to the Democrats. The fact that Perot dropped out at the time of the Democratic convention, when the Democrats had total control over the media, which were providing a stream of positive information about Clinton and his policies, facilitated these changes. And from that point on, Clinton stayed ahead in all the polls. *Not a single subsequent survey showed Bush in the lead.*

Perot then came back into the race in October. . . . He received a larger percentage on Election Day than the polls had been reporting in the previous week. These results suggest that there was a high level of discontent with the political establishment, not just with Bush and the incumbent administration, but with the Democrats and Clinton as well.

For some time now, the electorate has been exhibiting discontent with the two-party system. Consider the nonpresidential-year elections of 1990. Three states elected independent candidates: Governors Walter Hickel in Alaska and Lowell Weicker in Connecticut, and Congressman Bernard Sanders in Vermont. Two-fifths of Texans opted for "none of the above" for governor in a poll taken a week before the election. . . .

Opinion surveys conducted all through the election year reported overwhelming majorities, between 75 percent and 90 percent agreeing that "the country is on the wrong track." The opposition to traditional politics was also reflected in the considerable support given in many states to term limits for Congress—on election day, they were approved in all fourteen states where they were on the ballot.

What brought about this rejection of the traditional politics of both major parties? Essentially, our two major philosophies and ideological orientations—liberalism and conservatism—failed to adapt to new circumstances. The public does not see viable answers coming from either.

The most electorally relevant development, one which accounts for much of the malaise, is the long-term slowdown of the American economy, particularly the downswing of 1991–1992. Of course, that is not the sole explanation, since the indications of popular discontent, already evident in 1990, preceded the Bush recession. Still, the electorate sensed the economy was out of control, that the United States has been unable to reduce its foreign trade and governmental deficits. Americans have heard those problems being blamed on Republican presidents and Democratic congresses alike. . . .

◆ Bases of Diversity in 1992

Basically, the social correlates of Clinton and Bush voters resembled those for [Franklin D.] Roosevelt and [Alf] Landon in 1936. The Republicans were backed by the "haves," the Democrats by the "have-nots." The traits associated with being a "have" in this society are: white, Anglo-Saxon/Germanic/north European origin, Protestant, male, well-to-do, and middle to near old age. These characteristics have traditionally been associated with voting Republican, although with much reduced strength in the Eisenhower and Reagan elections. Conversely, to be an outsider, to be a minority, to be black, to be Jewish, to be Catholic, to be poor, to be a woman, and more often than not to be young—all have correlated with

Democratic support. These were the bases of division in the Roosevelt and Truman days. They are decisive again.

The data reported by the exit polls . . . document these generalizations. Bush's strongest base was composed of white Protestant males. They were the one group, other than the most well-to-do, among whom he led Clinton by more than ten percentage points. Bush was decisively ahead of Clinton among voters earning over $75,000. His support decreased with lower income; as might be expected, moving from high to low, Clinton's vote was greatest among the most deprived. He received over two-thirds of the vote among people in the bottom quintile of the income distribution. He led Bush by over ten percentage points among Catholics, a revival of the old pattern. During the 1980s, most Catholics had voted for Reagan and Bush. Clinton received very strong support among Jews, around 80 percent, according to different polls, up from 65 percent in 1988. Among blacks, Democratic support changed little, over four-fifths in a three-candidate race. Three-fifths of the Latinos also voted Democratic. Gays, understandably, overwhelmingly opposed Bush. They divided 72 percent Clinton, and 14 percent for Bush and Perot. As indicated, gender differentiated, Clinton was somewhat stronger among women than men. In the 1980s, Reagan and Bush, dominating the times, had secured sizable majorities among the young, the 18–24 year-olds. But in 1992, new voters went predominantly for Clinton.

◆ Issues and Ideology

Issue positions, of course, affect the way people voted. Abortion has been particularly salient in recent years. Many people take the issue very seriously, as a moral and/or religious one. The Republicans, reacting to the views of the Christian Right, now strongly oppose abortion. Some, like George Bush himself, had changed their position to accomodate the social conservatives. . . .

. . . Shifting to the right may have helped him gain support among Reagan's followers, but it contributed to the loss of the election. For he and the GOP were on the losing side of the abortion issue as far as the majority of the public are concerned. The exit polls showed 64 percent for abortion being legal in all or most cases.

The opinion polls and referenda results indicate that most Americans are pro-choice. No matter how the anti-abortion groups try to interpret the data, it is clear that at most only one-third of Americans think that abortion should be illegal. . . .

Socially liberal Republicans, particularly college graduates, professionals and executives, who are more libertarian, do not like the state enforcing morality. The 1992 Republican convention emphasized social and religious conservatism, and the party antagonized women and the very well educated, as well as moderates and independents, generally. The Democrats did much better among these groups at every income level, and within every ethnic group. Vote-wise, the GOP was on the wrong side of the cultural divide.

The important values show up strongly when the married and single, including divorced and widowed, are compared. The latter supported Clinton by 20 percent more than the former. . . .

Importantly, Clinton turned out to be the first Democratic presidential candidate since the Vietnam War years to win the battle of party loyalty. That is, Clinton secured a larger percentage of his own party's voters than Bush received of Republican voters. . . .

Another aspect of this election which was quite different from recent ones is the ideological orientation of the Democratic nominee. Bill Clinton is a different kind of Democrat from his immediate, much more liberal, predecessors. He speaks of a new Democratic Party. He criticizes the old one. He is clearly more moderate or centrist. He was the chairman of the Democratic Leadership Council (DLC), the organization of the more conservative Democrats. Ben Wattenberg reports that he was surprised when going over the tapes of Clinton's speeches during the past decade, to prepare a documentary on the parties, to find that Clinton was repeatedly reiterating positions that he has taken for years; that tapes of Clinton's speeches of five or ten years ago could have been used in the 1992 campaign. The tone, the ideology, were the same. Those who accused him of pandering or shifting his position on issues in order to get votes today are wrong.

Eight years ago, at the 1984 Democratic convention, Clinton delivered a speech that was ignored by the media. It was given in the afternoon with no television coverage. He was implicitly but clearly critical of the party nominee, Walter Mondale, and of the party's ideological direction, although Mondale, of course, was not mentioned. But in effect, Clinton said that they were heading in the wrong direction. He called for a moderate party, for more market-driven economic policies, for less reliance on government, and the like. He made the same point in a 1981 speech analyzing the reasons Reagan had been elected.

TOWARD CRITICAL THINKING

1. The 1992 presidential election was unusual in its inclusion of a strong third candidate, Ross Perot. Although Perot ultimately won no electoral college votes, what was his overall impact on the election? Does President Clinton owe his success to Perot's candidacy?

2. In the recent past, new voters—those under age twenty-five—voted Republican
   in presidential elections. That was not the case in 1992. What factors contributed to this change?

THINKING ABOUT CAMPAIGNS, ELECTIONS, AND VOTING

1. Candidates are currently allowed to spend as much of their private funds as
   they wish on their election campaigns. Are elections today then "for sale" to the
   biggest spender? Are candidates such as Ross Perot, who spend their own
   money instead of taking funds from PACs or other special interests, less likely
   to be swayed by special interests or public opinion?

2. Is the two-party system really in decline, as some authors in this chapter imply?
   Has it been supplanted by the mass media?

3. What factors contributed to President Clinton's 1992 win? Are those factors
   still in place for the 1996 election?

CHAPTER 13

◆ ◆ ◆

The Media

Since the time that John Peter Zenger was sued for libel for publishing articles critical of the colonial governor of New York and then was acquitted in 1734, the right of freedom of the press has been the bedrock of all U.S. freedoms. So widely accepted was this right that Alexander Hamilton gave the need for its protection slight mention in *The Federalist Papers.*

Throughout the readings in this chapter we see how the media permeates all levels of the U.S. political system. The press and other forms of media play a valuable role in any democracy. The media can and do educate, and they also serve as watchdogs on public officials at all levels. But since the late 1980s, in particular, some members of the media have been in what political scientist Larry J. Sabato terms a "feeding frenzy," like sharks on the lookout for blood. In Reading 67 Sabato argues that since political parties have declined in importance, the media have taken up the slack, scrutinizing candidates more closely. The question, however, is should a line be drawn, and, if so, where?

Few lines are drawn on talk radio. As Howard Fineman notes in Reading 68, talk radio, long popular in some sections of the nation, exploded on the political scene in the 1992 election and now helps drive the political agenda in Washington.

The "feeding frenzy" reported by Sabato isn't new. It's just more nationalized than the one faced by Dr. Sam Sheppard when he was on trial for the murder of his wife (see Reading 69). Those people who think that the media circus surrounding the murder of Nicole Brown Simpson, former football star O. J. Simpson's ex-wife is new need only look to the atmosphere that surrounded the Sheppard trial, where the man charged with murder *wasn't* a national celebrity.

As the readings in this chapter illustrate, the press today—long considered a guardian of our freedoms—is under almost as much attack as are the institutions of government. Just as there is often a delicate balance between individual rights and the rights of the government, the media and the American people are struggling to find a proper balance between the right of the media to report what they think is news and what some people see as solely private issues.

Federalist No. 84

ALEXANDER HAMILTON

According to Hamilton, a bill of rights guaranteeing a free press was undesirable in the proposed new national constitution. He reasoned that since New York's state constitution did not protect this liberty, no reason existed for its specific inclusion in the U.S. Constitution. Indeed, he argued that any enumeration of freedom of the press was certain to be so vague as to provide no more protection than changing legislatures and publics want to give it. Hamilton contended that a bill of rights in general was an unnecessary addition to the U.S. Constitution, especially since those specific civil liberties had been guaranteed since colonial times.

. . . On the subject of the liberty of the press, as much as has been said, I cannot forbear adding a remark or two: in the first place, I observe, that there is not a syllable concerning it in the constitution of this State; in the next, I contend that whatever has been said about it in that of any other State amounts to nothing. What signifies a declaration that "the liberty of the press shall be inviolably preserved"? What is the liberty of the press? Who can give it any definition which would not leave the utmost latitude for evasion? I hold it to be impracticable; and from this I infer that its security, whatever fine declarations may be inserted in any constitution respecting it, must altogether depend on public opinion, and on the general spirit of the people and of the government. And here, after all, as is intimated upon another occasion, must we seek for the only solid basis of all our rights. . . .

TOWARD CRITICAL THINKING

1. Was Hamilton correct that the statement of the freedom of the press in the Bill of Rights is too vague? Does it leave too much leeway for judicial interpretation?

2. Would the United States have a free press without the protection of the First Amendment? If so, where would such protections be found?

Inquisition, American Style
Attack Journalism and Feeding Frenzies

LARRY J. SABATO

Even though a free press may be essential to democracy, Larry J. Sabato argues that the U.S. press often oversteps its bounds. The media's coverage of politics frequently more closely resembles sharks in a feeding frenzy than the detached and accurate provision of information. Though attack ads have long been a part of political campaigns, "attack" journalism has become commonplace today in political reporting. In explanation, Sabato contends that the media's attempt to fill the gap left by the decline of political parties has forced the media to scrutinize politicians more closely. Rather than political parties privately determining the fitness of candidates and officials, the media now publicly make these determinations.

. . .

I would never have comprehended the anguish visited by the "death watch" of the media. To have people surrounding our home with a real carnival atmosphere, shouting questions at you with a boom microphone and long-lens cameras, it makes one feel like a hunted animal driven to his lair.

Jim Wright, former Speaker of the House

This is guilt by press. We might as well have hanging by the press. We [shouldn't] have Gestapo tactics by the media in this country.

Roger Ailes, media consultant to the 1988 Bush/Quayle campaign, commenting on the coverage of Dan Quayle.

It has become a spectacle without equal in modern American politics: the news media, print and broadcast, go after a wounded politician like sharks in a feeding frenzy. The wounds may have been self-inflicted, and the politician may richly deserve his or her fate, but the journalists now take center stage in the process, creating the news as much as reporting it, changing both the shape of election-year politics and the contours of government. Having replaced the political parties as the screening committee for candidates and officeholders, the media propel some politicians toward power and unceremoniously eliminate others. Unavoidably, this enormously influential role—and the news practices employed in exercising it—has provided rich fodder for a multitude of press critics.

These critics' charges against the press cascade down with the fury of rain in a summer squall. Public officials and many other observers see journalists as rude, arrogant, and cynical, given to exaggeration, harassment, sensationalism, and gross insensitivity. From the conservative perspective, their reporting is, more often than not, viewed as evidence of blatant liberal bias, with the facts being fitted to preconceived notions. At the same time, the left indicts the media for being too hesitant to find fault with the status quo and too close to the very establishment they are supposed to check. Moreover, critics of all stripes see journalists as hypercritical of others yet vengeful when criticized themselves, quick to accuse yet slow to correct error, willing to violate the constitutional values of due process and fair trial in the Fifth and Sixth Amendments by acting as judge and jury, yet insistent on wrapping themselves in the First Amendment when challenged on virtually anything. Especially in the post-Watergate era of institutionalized investigative reporting and "star journalism," the press is perceived as being far more interested in finding sleaze and achieving fame and fortune than in serving as an honest broker of information between citizens and government. . . .

Less reassuring, however, is another chorus of critics of modern journalism. A host of the most senior, respected, and experienced news professionals are themselves becoming equivocal about, embarrassed over, even repulsed by the conduct of some of their colleagues. While disagreeing with many of the criticisms leveled at reporters from outside the profession, they are nonetheless concerned about the media's growing distortion of the political process and deeply disturbed that legitimate press inquiry sometimes gets quickly and completely out of hand. And they fear a rising tide of antipress sentiment if the excesses are left unchecked. Already, several public opinion studies . . . have revealed a dramatic decline in citizens' confidence in, and respect for, the news media: Most Americans no longer believe that the press generally "get the facts straight," and they rate journalism among the professions with the "lowest ethical standards." Fully 78 percent in one study agreed that "the media spend too much time focusing on [campaign] things that are irrelevant, like candidates' personal lives" rather than centering their coverage on "the most important issues." The evidence also suggests that recent controversies have weakened public support for First Amendment press freedoms.

These thoughtful and credible practitioners . . . are less worried about the press's obsession with scandal—a staple of news in virtually every free society and certainly for the whole of American history—than with the *kinds* of scandals now considered reportable and the *manner* in which they are investigated and reported. First of all, scandal coverage is no longer restricted to misuse of public office, incompetence in the exercise of public responsibilities, or some other inadequacy or malfeasance in a *public* role; it extends to purely *private* misbehavior, even offenses, some of them trivial, committed long before an individual's emergence into public life. No wise politician today dares utter St. Augustine's legendary prayer: "Dear God, give me chastity and continence, but not just yet." Even a college student contemplating a political career had best think twice about youthful indulgences, given degenerating press standards. When *New York Times* columnist William Safire wrote the following words in protest just after Gary Hart's 1987 presidential withdrawal, they seemed alarmist:

> If we do not turn the tables on the titillaters, we will load future news conferences with such significant policy questions as: "Sir, there are widespread reports of your impotence; when was the last time you and your wife had sexual relations?" "Madam, how do you deal with the persistent rumors that your national security adviser is a herpes victim?" "Have you or any member of your family ever taken illegal drugs?" "Some say that you once saw a psychiatrist—exactly what was your problem?"

Since Safire's predictions appeared, variations of the latter two questions have already been asked of candidates, and one wonders only half whimsically whether fellow *Times* columnist Russell Baker's vision of "adultery disclosure forms" to be filed before the New Hampshire primary will also come to pass someday. Soon no public figure may be too unimportant for close scrutiny. Editors and reporters at several major publications are seriously considering expanding their circle of legitimate targets for private life investigations to include top aides to candidates and even people uninvolved in politics who are "in the news" prominently. Similarly, no offense may be too minor to ignore in this "bare-all" age. Journalist Timothy Noah, while at *Newsweek,* was called with a scandal tip about Republican presidential candidate Alexander Haig: He was observed parking in a spot reserved for the handicapped in a supermarket parking lot. At this rate it seems almost inevitable that a candidate will be exposed for using an express checkout lane when purchasing more than the ten-item limit.

Press invasion of privacy is leading to the gradual erasure of the line protecting a public person's purely private life. This makes the price of public life enormously higher, serving as an even greater deterrent for those not absolutely obsessed with holding power—the kind of people we ought least to want in office. Rather than recognizing this unfortunate consequence, many in journalism prefer to relish their newly assumed role of "gatekeeper," which, as mentioned earlier, enables them to substitute for party leaders in deciding which characters are virtuous enough to merit consideration for high office. As ABC News correspondent Brit Hume self-critically suggests:

> We don't see ourselves institutionally, collectively anymore as a bunch of journalists out there faithfully reporting what's happening day by day. . . . We have a much grander view of ourselves: we are the Horatio at the national bridge. We are the people who want to prevent the bad characters from crossing over into public office.

Hume's veteran ABC colleague Sander Vanocur agrees, detecting "among some young reporters a quality of the avenging angel: they are going to sanitize American politics." More and more, the news media seem determined to show that would-be emperors have no clothes, and if necessary to prove the point, they personally will strip the candidates naked on the campaign trail. The sheer number of journalists participating in these public denudings guarantees riotous behavior, and the "full-court press" almost always presents itself as a snarling, unruly mob more bent on killing kings than making them. Not surprisingly potential candidates deeply fear the power an inquisitorial press, and in deciding whether to seek office, they often consult journalists as much as party leaders, even sharing private vulnerabilities with newsmen to gauge reaction. The *Los Angeles Times*'s Washington bureau chief, Jack Nelson, had such an encounter before the 1988 campaign season, when a prospective presidential candidate "literally asked me how long I thought the statute of limitations was" for marital infidelity. "I told him I didn't know, but I didn't think [the limit] had been reached in his case!" For whatever reasons, the individual chose not to run.

. . . Able members of the news corps offer impressive defenses for all the practices mentioned thus far, not the least of which is that the press has become more aggressive to combat the legions of image makers, political consultants, spin doctors, and handlers who surround modern candidates like a nearly impenetrable shield. Yet upon reflection, most news veterans recognize that press excesses are not an acceptable antidote for consultant or candidate evils. In fact, not one of the interviewed journalists even attempted to justify an increasingly frequent occurrence in new organizations: the publications of gossip and rumor *without convincing proof.* Gossip has always been the drug of choice for journalists as well as the rest of the political community, but as the threshold for publication of information about private lives has been lowered, journalists sometimes cover politics as "Entertainment Tonight" reporters cover Hollywood. . . .

The sorry standard set on the campaign trial is spilling over into coverage of government battles. Ever since Watergate, government scandals have paraded across the television set in a roll call so lengthy and numbing that they are inseparable in the public consciousness, all joined at the Achilles' heel. Some recent lynchings, such as John Tower's failure to be confirmed as secretary of defense, rival any spectacle produced by colonial Salem. At the same time more vital and revealing information is ignored or crowded off the agenda. *Real* scandals, such as the savings-and-loan heist or the influence peddling at the Department of Housing and Urban Development in the 1980s, go undetected for years. The sad conclusion is inescapable: The press has become obsessed with gossip rather than governance; it prefers to employ titillation rather than scrutiny; as a result, its political coverage produces trivialization rather than enlightenment. And the dynamic mechanism propelling and demonstrating this decline in news standards is the "feeding frenzy."

TOWARD CRITICAL THINKING

1. Has the role of the media left that of informer of the public and entered those of judge and executioner? Or are the media simply providing the public with the information necessary to make sound political choices?

2. What types of scandals are of public political significance? Would you run for public office, or encourage a close friend to do so, in light of the coverage candidates and some public servants receive in the media?

· 68 ·

The Power of Talk Radio

HOWARD FINEMAN

The popularity of television and radio call-in shows has escalated
enormously. Furthermore, their political importance, as evidenced by candidate appearances on talk radio and TV in the 1992 presidential election,
cannot be dismissed. Fineman examines the influence of talk radio and
what it portends for American democracy. Conservatives have long successfully used the media much more effectively than have liberals, says
Fineman. More recently, conservative talk radio hosts such as Rush Limbaugh have enjoyed large followings and high ratings. (In 1994 Limbaugh was married by Justice Clarence Thomas in Thomas's home, with
"Equal Time" talk-TV-host Mary Matalin in attendance.) Recognizing the
increasing impact of talk radio, however, liberals also are trying to find a
voice on the airwaves. Fineman notes, however, that the opinions to
which politicians are increasingly tuned may not reflect those of the electorate at large.

It's two days before Bill Clinton's Inauguration. On public radio in
Washington, host Diane Rehm goes to the "open phones." Much of her
audience is, literally, inside the Beltway, people who might be sympathetic to Zoë Baird's child-care problems. The lines light up. Opinion
makers and politicos are listening. The verdict: Zoë's got to go. "If that's
the feeling here," Rehm muses, "what's happening in Sioux City?" Washington begins to get the message. Three days later Baird withdraws.

On Tuesday the Joint Chiefs of Staff meet with Secretary of Defense
Les Aspin in the "Tank," their Pentagon conference room. The topic:
whether to allow avowed homosexuals in the military. The Chiefs are
against it on military grounds. But they have other arguments. Top brass
are not known for the common touch, but they tell the president: look at
the polls, listen to the radio. Three days later Clinton moves far more
cautiously than he had wanted, merely ordering the services to quit asking
new recruits if they are gay.

Talk-show democracy changed politics in the presidential race last
year, bringing candidates phone to phone with voters. With his vision of
teledemocracy and his surprisingly strong showing in November, Ross

Perot woke up the establishment to the voters' anger. Now comes the next step: call-in government. Having tasted power, voter-callers want more; having risen through talk, Clinton is being rattled by it. "People want two-way talk," says [Larry] King. "They say, 'We want to talk to our government!' " Americans can do it through the burgeoning phenomenon of call-in shows, led by King, Rush Limbaugh and Brian Lamb on C-Span, and mirrored locally by dozens of dart-tongued, influential hosts. These shows, in turn, generate tidal waves of switchboard-clogging calls and letters-to-your-congressman. Call-in government is a needed jolt to sclerotic Washington. But it also raises the specter of government by feverish plebiscite—an entertaining, manipulable and trivializing process that could eat away at the essence of representative democracy.

◆ It's Hot

It's probably inevitable. Call-in shows are a fast-growing format, accounting for nearly 1,000 of the nation's 10,000 radio stations. "Larry King Live" is the highest rated show on CNN. . . .

Technology and demographics are the agents of change. Cheap satellite time allows local hosts like Mike Siegel of Seattle to go national with ease. . . .

Politicians are getting with the program, literally. New York Gov. Mario Cuomo is a pioneer; he's hosted a regular call-in show for years. Other local politicians are doing the same. At the Democratic National Committee, new chairman David Wilhelm is laying plans for Clinton and other administration officials to make themselves available for call-ins. If he needs any advice he can ask Susan Estrich. A former Harvard law professor, she ran Michael Dukakis's famously out-of-touch campaign in 1988. She left Cambridge, Mass., for Los Angeles, where she now teaches law—and hosts a call-in show. "Anybody who ever spent five minutes in radio," she says, "could have told you that gays in the military would strike a chord."

You could have learned the same lesson by watching C-Span. Though it is available in 58 million homes, its audience is rarely more than 2 million. But a new survey shows that an astounding 98 percent of its viewers voted in 1992, and the network provides instant feedback for them. During breaks in the Baird hearings, C-Span's Lamb fielded viewer calls in his deadpan manner. The voices grew angrier with each break—and they were being heard by the same Capitol insiders who were watching the hearing. "In the old days people would have to wait for the details on Baird," says Lamb. "Now it's in real time."

The next layer of the call-in system is CNN. Increasingly the network is including viewer call-in segments in its news shows to complement

King's prime-time appearances. The network's ratings rose sharply during the election year and stayed there. CNN's newest star is White House communications director George Stephanopoulos, whose boyishly evasive briefings garner high daytime ratings. "He's getting some of our highest numbers," says a CNN official. CNN is likely to continue carrying Stephanopoulos—and wrap call-in shows around him.

Until recently, and with the important exception of Ralph Nader, Democrats and their allies largely ignored the power of talk broadcasting. Conservatives have always understood and relied on it. While Franklin Roosevelt sold his New Deal in radio "fireside chats," Father Coughlin and Gerald L. K. Smith developed their own vast audience of naysayers. Long before he became president, Ronald Reagan sharpened his antigovernment message on the radio. Pat Buchanan hones his combative style as a call-in host in Washington. "The fact is that liberals feel empowered and conservatives don't," says Limbaugh.

If conservatives feel any sense of "empowerment" these days, it's due in large part to Limbaugh. His talk show is the most listened-to in talk radio (15 million tune in each week on 560 stations). His best-selling book, *The Way Things Ought to Be,* has sold 2 million copies in hardback; his TV call-in show is fast approaching Letterman-Leno ratings, and a new newsletter has 170,000 subscribers. Only nominally a call-in affair, Limbaugh's show offers group therapy for mostly white males who feel politically challenged and who would rather hear Rush's voice than their own. . . .

As famous as King, Limbaugh and Lamb have become, the roots and power of call-in democracy are local. Call-in shows first turned political in New York and Boston, cities in which arguing in public about politics— or anything else—is a way of life. The recent history of call-in clout begins with thirty-five-year veteran Jerry Williams in Boston, who in 1989 teamed up with Ralph Nader and others to protest a congressional pay raise. They succeeded in delaying it six months. . . .

Talk-show hosts can get results—and have been doing so for years before Rush Limbaugh arrived. In Seattle, Siegel took his microphone to a crack house and got it shut down. In Boston, Williams helped derail the state's seat-belt law, the proposed location of a state prison and numerous legislative pay increases. In 1986, he got 2,000 people to show up on Beacon Hill in a snowstorm to decry a Dukakis tax increase. "It's nothing new," Williams says of the Limbaughs of the world. "It is they who have been asleep.". . .

◆ Secular Religion

This may all be great broadcasting, but is it good government? Perot, who's busy wiring his "town halls," obviously thinks so. So do many of the 19 million Americans who voted for him. Conservatives think it's grand—a more accurate reflection of grass-roots opinion than the evening news.

. . . Free expression is America's secular religion. Tuning in—and calling in—is just a high-tech way of honoring it.

But it can be honored too much. What King calls the "hum" of talk radio can be misleading. Only the most devoted and outraged of listeners call—rarely more than 2 or 3 percent of an audience. Politicians who react slavishly can be deceived. "It's a potential early-warning sign, like radar in Greenland," says democratic polltaker Harrison Hickman. "You don't launch a strike based on that evidence alone." And its effect can be oversold. "Talk shows didn't get rid of Zoë Baird," says Limbaugh. "She got rid of herself."

The more troubling question is whether America needs a government of its angriest voices. "Only the people who feel most strongly call us," says Rehm. "But they aren't the only ones who vote." Dial-in democracy is attracting the same forces of manipulation that prey on other levers of power; interest groups on the right and left have the technology and determination to patch themselves into the national conversation. The intensity, speed and entertainment value of talk radio has a downside in a society already plagued by long-lasting problems and a short attention span. Ratings count and boredom is the enemy. There's an enormous pressure to keep the "board lit" by moving to the next hot topic.

But it's obvious how this controversy will come out. On CNN last week, "Crossfire" debated the pros and cons of dial-in democracy. The weekend shows discussed it. Rehm has scheduled a call-in show about . . . call-in shows. So all you need to do now is pick up the phone and give your opinion.

TOWARD CRITICAL THINKING

1. Are the opinions expressed on talk radio and television ones that government should heed? How representative are they of the views held by the general public?

2. Are appearances on call-in shows a way for politicians to bypass the media and speak directly to the people? What is the likely impact of this increasingly common tactic?

· *69* ·

Sheppard *v.* Maxwell
384 U.S. 333 (1966)

The media not only play a pervasive role in electoral politics, but they also play an increasingly controversial role in the judicial process. Issues of prejudicial pretrial publicity and their effects on potential jurors, on the constitutional rights of criminal defendants to a "fair and impartial jury" and trial, and even on elected judges and district attorneys and how they conduct themselves have been of major concern of late. The advent of *Court TV* and other television programs such as *Hard Copy* has escalated the attention given to so-called big cases and trials. The 1994 trial of the Menendez brothers for killing their parents, for example, drew unprecedented viewership. Even more astonishing was the 95-plus million viewers who watched as former football star O. J. Simpson led police on a five-hour "chase" after he was formally charged with the murder of his ex-wife and another man. Questions, then, immediately begin to arise concerning his ability to obtain a fair trial given his fame and the tremendous media attention given to the circumstances surrounding his arrest.

Media circuses, however, are not new, as *Sheppard* v. *Maxwell* illustrates. On July 4, 1954, Marilyn Sheppard, the pregnant wife of a well-known Cleveland physician, was brutally murdered in the couple's home. According to her husband, Dr. Sam Sheppard, after he and his wife entertained friends, she went upstairs to bed and he fell asleep on the couch, waking in the early morning hours to the sounds of her screams. He ran to her aid but was met by what he called a "form," which knocked him unconscious. When he regained consciousness, he heard sounds outside his lakeside home and ran outside in pursuit of the "form." The "form" got away, and Sheppard ran back to the house. There, he found his wife dead. He immediately called his neighbor, the mayor. The rest of the events are described in the opinion below.

Opinion: Justice Thomas Clark
Vote: 8 to 1

This federal habeas corpus application involves the question whether Sheppard was deprived of a fair trial in his state conviction for the second-degree murder of his wife because of the trial judge's failure to protect Sheppard sufficiently from the massive, pervasive and prejudicial publicity that attended his prosecution. The United States District Court held that he was not afforded a fair trial and granted the writ subject to the State's right to put Sheppard to trial again. The Court of Appeals for the Sixth Circuit reversed by a divided vote. We granted certiorari. We have concluded that Sheppard did not receive a fair trial consistent with the Due Process Clause of the Fourteenth Amendment and, therefore, reverse the judgment.

Marilyn Sheppard, petitioner's pregnant wife, was bludgeoned to death in the upstairs bedroom of their lakeshore home. . . .

From the outset officials focused suspicion on Sheppard. After a search of the house and premises on the morning of the tragedy, Dr. Gerber, the Coroner, is reported—and it is undenied—to have told his men, "Well, it is evident the doctor did this, so let's go get the confession out of him." He proceeded to interrogate and examine Sheppard while the latter was under sedation in his hospital room. On the same occasion, the Coroner was given the clothes Sheppard wore at the time of the tragedy together with the personal items in them. Later that afternoon Chief Eaton and two Cleveland police officers interrogated Sheppard at some length, confronting him with evidence and demanding explanations. Asked by Officer Shotke to take a lie detector test, Sheppard said he would if it were reliable. Shotke replied that it was "infallible" and "you might as well tell us all about it now." At the end of the interrogation Shotke told Sheppard: "I think you killed your wife." Still later in the same afternoon a physician sent by the Coroner was permitted to make a detailed examination of Sheppard. Until the Coroner's inquest on July 22, at which time he was subpoenaed, Sheppard made himself available for frequent and extended questioning without the presence of an attorney.

On July 7, the day of Marilyn Sheppard's funeral, a newspaper story appeared in which Assistant County Attorney Mahon—later the chief prosecutor of Sheppard—sharply criticized the refusal of the Sheppard family to permit his immediate questioning. From there on headline stories repeatedly stressed Sheppard's lack of cooperation with the police and other officials. Under the headline "Testify Now In Death, Bay Doctor Is Ordered," one story described a visit by Coroner Gerber and four police officers to the hospital on July 8. When Sheppard insisted that his lawyer be present, the Coroner wrote out a subpoena and served it on him. Sheppard then agreed to submit to questioning without counsel and the subpoena was torn up. The officers questioned him for several hours. On July 9, Sheppard, at the request of the Coroner, re-enacted the tragedy at his home before the Coroner, police officers, and a group of newsmen, who apparently were invited by the Coroner. The home was locked so that Sheppard was obliged to wait outside until the Coroner arrived. Sheppard's performance was reported in detail by the news media along with photographs. The newspapers also played up Sheppard's refusal to take a lie detector test and "the protective ring" thrown up by his family. Front-page newspaper headlines announced on the same day that "Doctor Balks At Lie Test; Retells Story." A column opposite that story contained an "exclusive" interview with Sheppard headlined: " 'Loved My Wife, She Loved Me,' Sheppard Tells News Reporter." . . .

On the 20th, the "editorial artillery" opened fire with a front-page charge that somebody is "getting away with murder." The editorial attributed the ineptness of the investigation to "friendships, relationships, hired lawyers, a husband who ought to have been subjected instantly to the same third-degree to which any other person under similar circumstances is subjected. . . . " The following day, July 21st, another page-one editorial was headed: "Why No Inquest? Do It Now, Dr. Gerber." The Coroner called an inquest the same day and subpoenaed Sheppard. It was staged the next day in a school gymnasium; the Coroner presided with the County Prosecutor as his advisor and two detectives as bailiffs. In the front of the room was a long table occupied by reporters, television and radio personnel, and broadcasting equipment. The hearing was broadcast with live microphones placed at the Coroner's seat and the witness stand. A swarm of reporters and photographers attended. Sheppard was brought into the room by police who searched him in full view of several hundred spectators. Sheppard's counsel were present during the three-day inquest but were not permitted to participate. When Sheppard's chief counsel attempted to place some documents in the record, he was forcibly ejected from the room by the Coroner, who received cheers, hugs, and kisses from ladies in the audience. Sheppard was questioned for five and one-half hours about his actions on the night of the murder, his married life, and a love affair with Susan Hayes. At the end of the hearing the Coroner announced that he "could" order Sheppard held for the grand jury, but did not do so.

Throughout this period the newspapers emphasized evidence that tended to incriminate Sheppard and pointed out discrepancies in his statements to authorities. . . . The newspapers also delved into Sheppard's personal life. Articles stressed his extramarital love affairs as a motive for the crime. The newspapers portrayed Sheppard as a Lothario, fully explored his relationship with Susan Hayes, and named a number of other women who were allegedly involved with him. The testimony at trial never showed that Sheppard had any illicit relationships besides the one with Susan Hayes.

On July 28, an editorial entitled "Why Don't Police Quiz Top Suspect" demanded that Sheppard be taken to police headquarters. It described him in the following language:

> "Now proved under oath to be a liar, still free to go about his business, shielded by his family, protected by a smart lawyer who has made monkeys of the police and authorities, carrying a gun part of the time, left free to do whatever he pleases. . . . "

A front-page editorial on July 30 asked: "Why Isn't Sam Sheppard in Jail?" It was later titled "Quit Stalling—Bring Him In." After calling

Sheppard "the most unusual murder suspect ever seen around these parts" the article said that "[e]xcept for some superficial questioning during Coroner Sam Gerber's inquest he has been scot-free of any official grilling. . . . " It asserted that he was "surrounded by an iron curtain of protection [and] concealment."

That night at ten o'clock Sheppard was arrested at his father's home on a charge of murder. He was taken to the Bay Village City Hall where hundreds of people, newscasters, photographers and reporters were awaiting his arrival. He was immediately arraigned—having been denied a temporary delay to secure the presence of counsel—and bound over to the grand jury.

The publicity then grew in intensity until his indictment on August 17. Typical of the coverage during this period is a front-page interview entitled: "DR. SAM: 'I Wish There Was Something I Could Get Off My Chest—but There Isn't.' " Unfavorable publicity included items such as a cartoon of the body of a sphinx with Sheppard's head and the legend below: " 'I Will Do Everything In My Power to Help Solve This Terrible Murder.'—Dr. Sam Sheppard.". . . We do not detail the coverage further. There are five volumes filled with similar clippings from each of the three Cleveland newspapers covering the period from the murder until Sheppard's conviction in December 1954. The record includes no excerpts from newscasts on radio and television but since space was reserved in the courtroom for these media we assume that their coverage was equally large.

With this background the case came on for trial two weeks before the November general election at which the chief prosecutor was a candidate for common pleas judge and the trial judge, Judge Blythin, was a candidate to succeed himself. Twenty-five days before the case was set, seventy-five veniremen were called as prospective jurors. All three Cleveland newspapers published the names and addresses of the veniremen. As a consequence, anonymous letters and telephone calls, as well as calls from friends, regarding the impending prosecution were received by all of the prospective jurors. The selection of the jury began on October 18, 1954.

The courtroom in which the trial was held measured 26 by 48 feet. A long temporary table was set up inside the bar, in back of the single counsel table. It ran the width of the courtroom, parallel to the bar railing, with one end less than three feet from the jury box. Approximately twenty representatives of newspapers and wire services were assigned seats at this table by the court. Behind the bar railing there were four rows of benches. These seats were likewise assigned by the court for the entire trial. The first row was occupied by representatives of television and radio stations, and the second and third rows by reporters from out-of-town newspapers and magazines. One side of the last row, which accommodated fourteen people, was assigned to Sheppard's family and the other to

Marilyn's. The public was permitted to fill vacancies in this row on special passes only. Representatives of the news media also used all the rooms on the courtroom floor, including the room where cases were ordinarily called and assigned for trial. Private telephone lines and telegraphic equipment were installed in these rooms so that reports from the trial could be speeded to the papers. . . .

On the sidewalk and steps in front of the courthouse, television and newsreel cameras were occasionally used to take motion pictures of the participants in the trial, including the jury and the judge. Indeed, one television broadcast carried a staged interview of the judge as he entered the courthouse. In the corridors outside the courtroom there was a host of photographers and television personnel with flash cameras, portable lights and motion picture cameras. This group photographed the prospective jurors during selection of the jury. After the trial opened, the witnesses, counsel, and jurors were photographed and televised whenever they entered or left the courtroom. Sheppard was brought to the courtroom about ten minutes before each session began; he was surrounded by reporters and extensively photographed for the newspapers and television. A rule of court prohibited picture-taking in the courtroom during the actual sessions of the court, but no restraints were put on photographers during recesses, which were taken once each morning and afternoon, with a longer period for lunch.

All of these arrangements with the news media and their massive coverage of the trial continued during the entire nine weeks of the trial. The courtroom remained crowded to capacity with representatives of news media. Their movement in and out of the courtroom often caused so much confusion that, despite the loud-speaker system installed in the courtroom, it was difficult for the witnesses and counsel to be heard. Furthermore, the reporters clustered within the bar of the small courtroom made confidential talk among Sheppard and his counsel almost impossible during the proceedings. They frequently had to leave the courtroom to obtain privacy. And many times when counsel wished to raise a point with the judge out of the hearing of the jury it was necessary to move to the judge's chambers. Even then, news media representatives so packed the judge's anteroom that counsel could hardly return from the chambers to the courtroom. The reporters vied with each other to find out what counsel and the judge had discussed, and often these matters later appeared in newspapers accessible to the jury.

The daily record of the proceedings was made available to the newspapers and the testimony of each witness was printed verbatim in the local editions, along with objections of counsel, and rulings by the judge. Pictures of Sheppard, the judge, counsel, pertinent witnesses, and the jury often accompanied the daily newspaper and television accounts. At times the newspapers published photographs of exhibits introduced at the trial, and the rooms of Sheppard's house were featured along with relevant testimony.

The jurors themselves were constantly exposed to the news media. Every juror, except one, testified at *voir dire* to reading about the case in the Cleveland papers or to having heard broadcasts about it. Seven of the twelve jurors who rendered the verdict had one or more Cleveland papers delivered in their home; the remaining jurors were not interrogated on the point. Nor were there questions as to radios or television sets in the jurors' homes, but we must assume that most of them owned such conveniences. As the selection of the jury progressed, individual pictures of prospective members appeared daily. During the trial, pictures of the jury appeared over forty times in the Cleveland papers alone. The court permitted photographers to take pictures of the jury in the box, and individual pictures of the members in the jury room. One newspaper ran pictures of the jurors at the Sheppard home when they went there to view the scene of the murder. Another paper featured the home life of an alternate juror. The day before the verdict was rendered—while the jurors were at lunch and sequestered by two bailiffs—the jury was separated into two groups to pose for photographs which appeared in the newspapers.

We now reach the conduct of the trial. While the intense publicity continued unabated, it is sufficient to relate only the more flagrant episodes:

1. On October 9, 1954, nine days before the case went to trial, an editorial in one of the newspapers criticized defense counsel's random poll of people on the streets as to their opinion of Sheppard's guilt or innocence in an effort to use the resulting statistics to show the necessity for change of venue. The article said the survey "smacks of mass jury tampering." . . .

2. On the second day of *voir dire* examination a debate was staged and broadcast live over WHK radio. The participants, newspaper reporters, accused Sheppard's counsel of throwing roadblocks in the way of the prosecution and asserted that Sheppard conceded his guilt by hiring a prominent criminal lawyer. Sheppard's counsel objected to this broadcast and requested a continuance, but the judge denied the motion. . . .

3. As has been mentioned, the jury viewed the scene of the murder on the first day of the trial. Hundreds of reporters, cameramen and onlookers were there, and one representative of the news media was permitted to accompany the jury while it inspected the Sheppard home. . . .

The principle that justice cannot survive behind walls of silence has long been reflected in the "Anglo-American distrust for secret trials." A

responsible press has always been regarded as the handmaiden of effective judicial administration, especially in the criminal field. Its function in
this regard is documented by an impressive record of service over several
centuries. The press does not simply publish information about trials but
guards against the miscarriage of justice by subjecting the police, prosecutors, and judicial processes to extensive public scrutiny and criticism.
This Court has, therefore, been unwilling to place any direct limitations
on the freedom traditionally exercised by the news media for "[w]hat
transpires in the court room is public property.". . .

But the Court has also pointed out that "[l]egal trials are not like
elections, to be won through the use of the meeting-hall, the radio, and the
newspaper." And the Court has insisted that no one be punished for a
crime without "a charge fairly made and fairly tried in a public tribunal
free of prejudice, passion, excitement, and tyrannical power.". . .

Only last Term in *Estes* v. *State of Texas* (1965), we set aside a
conviction despite the absence of any showing of prejudice. We said there:

> "It is true that in most cases involving claims of due process depri-
> vations we require a showing of identifiable prejudice to the ac-
> cused. Nevertheless, at times a procedure employed by the State
> involves such a probability that prejudice will result that it is
> deemed inherently lacking in due process."

And we cited with approval the language of Mr. Justice Black . . . that
"our system of law has always endeavored to prevent even the probability
of unfairness."

It is clear that the totality of circumstances in this case also warrants
such an approach. Unlike *Estes,* Sheppard was not granted a change of
venue to a locale away from where the publicity originated; nor was his
jury sequestered. . . . [T]he Sheppard jurors were subjected to newspaper,
radio and television coverage of the trial while not taking part in the
proceedings. They were allowed to go their separate ways outside of the
courtroom, without adequate directions not to read or listen to anything
concerning the case. . . .

. . . Moreover, the jurors were thrust into the role of celebrities by the
judge's failure to insulate them from reporters and photographers. The
numerous pictures of the jurors, with their addresses, which appeared in
the newspapers before and during the trial itself exposed them to expressions of opinion from both cranks and friends. The fact that anonymous
letters had been received by prospective jurors should have made the
judge aware that this publicity seriously threatened the jurors' privacy.

The press coverage of the Estes trial was not nearly as massive and
pervasive as the attention given by the Cleveland newspapers and broadcasting stations to Sheppard's prosecution. Sheppard stood indicted for
the murder of his wife; the State was demanding the death penalty. For

months the virulent publicity about Sheppard and the murder had made the case notorious. Charges and counthercharges were aired in the news media besides those for which Sheppard was called to trial. . . . The inquest was televised live from a high school gymnasium seating hundreds of people. Furthermore, the trial began two weeks before a hotly contested election at which both Chief Prosecutor Mahon and Judge Blythin were candidates for judgeships.

While we cannot say that Sheppard was denied due process by the judge's refusal to take precautions against the influence of pretrial publicity alone, the court's later rulings must be considered against the setting in which the trial was held. In light of this background, we believe that the arrangements made by the judge with the news media caused Sheppard to be deprived of that "judicial serenity and calm to which [he] was entitled." The fact is that bedlam reigned at the courthouse during the trial and newsmen took over practically the entire courtroom, hounding most of the participants in the trial, especially Sheppard. . . .

From the cases coming here we note that unfair and prejudicial news comment on pending trials has become increasingly prevalent. Due process requires that the accused receive a trial by an impartial jury free from outside influences. Given the pervasiveness of modern communications and the difficulty of effacing prejudicial publicity from the minds of the jurors, the trial courts must take strong measures to ensure that the balance is never weighed against the accused. And appellate tribunals have the duty to make an independent evaluation of the circumstances. Of course, there is nothing that proscribes the press from reporting events that transpire in the courtroom. But where there is a reasonable likelihood that prejudicial news prior to trial will prevent a fair trial, the judge should continue the case until the threat abates, or transfer it to another county not so permeated with publicity. In addition, sequestration of the jury was something the judge should have raised *sua sponte* with counsel. If publicity during the proceedings threatens the fairness of the trial, a new trial should be ordered. But we must remember that reversals are but palliatives; the cure lies in those remedial measures that will prevent the prejudice at its inception. The courts must take such steps by rule and regulation that will protect their processes from prejudicial outside interferences. Neither prosecutors, counsel for defense, the accused, witnesses, court staff nor enforcement officers coming under the jurisdiction of the court should be permitted to frustrate its function. Collaboration between counsel and the press as to information affecting the fairness of a criminal trial is not only subject to regulation, but is highly censurable and worthy of disciplinary measures.

Since the state trial judge did not fulfill his duty to protect Sheppard from the inherently prejudicial publicity which saturated the community and to control disruptive influences in the courtroom, we must reverse the denial of the habeas petition. The case is remanded to the District Court with instructions to issue a writ and order that Sheppard be released from custody unless the State puts him to its charges again within a reasonable time.

It is so ordered.

TOWARD CRITICAL THINKING

1. After *Sheppard,* trial courts increasingly came to rely on gag orders to limit prejudicial pretrial publicity. But in 1976, the Supreme Court made such orders more difficult to defend against First Amendment challenges. How can the rights of criminal defendants be reconciled with the media's right (and some people might argue) obligation to report the news?

2. Noted lawyer F. Lee Bailey, who represented Sheppard successfully on this appeal (Sheppard was acquitted in his new trial), credits the case with launching his career. In 1994, he was called in to be part of O. J. Simpson's legal team. Given the "media circus" that surrounded Simpson's arrest, could he, or someone else in similar circumstances, be given a fair trial? If defendants cannot be given fair trials and must be let free, is this the price Americans pay for a media with few restraints?

THINKING ABOUT THE MEDIA

1. When Alexander Hamilton wrote about the press, he clearly was not envisioning international, instantaneous news media. Do you think if he had, he might have seen the need for national free press protections?

2. Personal privacy is not explicitly protected in the Constitution, yet the Supreme Court has given it fairly sweeping constitutional protections. In today's media age, has the personal privacy of elected officials taken a back seat to the right of the media to report whatever they want? Should there be limits on what the media can report about public officials or candidates? Should the standards be different for elected officials or nongovernmental officials accused of crimes?

3. Think about the other subjects covered in Part III: "Public Opinion," "Political Parties and Interest Groups," and "Campaigns, Elections, and Voting." How have the media affected and changed each subject over time?

❖ PART FOUR ❖

Public Policy

As we have seen in other parts of this volume, the role of the national government and its power and authority have expanded enormously over time. When the Framers met in Philadelphia, they were concerned with creating a new government that could function for the ages—although their most immediate concern was to alleviate the problems that quickly emerged in the economy and foreign policy after the Revolutionary War ended. In fact, ensuring "domestic Tranquility, provid[ing] for the common defence, [and] promot[ing] the General Welfare" were major reasons offered by the Framers for the writing of a new Constitution.

The nature of the national government's role in the promotion of the general welfare and the defense of the nation is quite different today from the 1780s. Not only does the national government play a seemingly ever increasingly important role in setting domestic policies, but the United States also is a world superpower that is ready to respond to international crises at a moment's notice.

All of the institutions of government discussed in Part II—the Congress, the President, the Bureaucracy, and the Judiciary—*and* all of the key actors in the political process discussed in Part III—Political Parties and Interest Groups; Campaigns, Elections, and Voting; and the Media—interact with each other to make domestic and foreign policy. Public policies are the results of purposive actions followed by government in dealing with some problem or matter of concern.*

As such, they represent the collective efforts of varying combinations of institutions and actors. In the case of the proposed changes in the U.S. health care system, for example, the president, various members of his administration, Congress, interest groups, public opinion, and the media all played key roles as reform was debated. Just how issues come to be perceived as issues and addressed by policy makers are questions addressed by readings in Chapters 14 and 15. As you read these chapters, keep in mind the following questions:

---

* James E. Anderson, *Public Policymaking: An Introduction,* 2nd ed. (Boston: Houghton Mifflin, 1994), p. 5.

1. What should the national government's role be in domestic and foreign policy? Should its role be greater in one than the other?

2. How has the nature of the policy-making process been changed by technological advances? Has this made policy making more difficult?

"Domestic Policy" is the focus of Chapter 14. What kind of policy-making role did the Framers intend the national government to have? How do problems get on the policy issue agenda and what does it need to keep them there are questions addressed by the readings in Chapter 14.

Chapter 15 explores some aspects of "Foreign and Military Policy." Of particular interest is the role of Congress and the President as they share powers in making and setting foreign policy in a media age.

CHAPTER 14

◆ ◆ ◆

Domestic Policy

Domestic policy has many facets. It includes issues of health, education, and welfare—all issues that most of the Framers considered to be within the province of the states. But over the years, as the nature of the times changed, so did the national government's role in domestic policy-making. Presidents today are frequently rated on both the "domestic" or "foreign" policy fronts, and Americans expect their national government to take the lead in a variety of domestic policy areas, including civil rights, social welfare programs, and health policy.

Franklin D. Roosevelt's New Deal triggered a change in the role of the national government in domestic policy-making, and it was accompanied by a burgeoning federal bureaucracy created to solve the many public problems needing national solutions. In Anthony Downs's terms (Reading 71), the Great Depression brought many social problems to the fore of what he terms the "issue-attention cycle." Downs uses the environment as his example; you can probably think of many other issues to illustrate his point. Health care policy, for example, discussed by Dana Priest in Reading 72, is but one example of the many issues that end up on the public agenda. Appearing on the public agenda, however, does not necessarily mean that the policy problems presented are solved.

· *70* ·

Federalist No. 44

JAMES MADISON

By placing some of the power for making public policy in the hands of the national government, the Constitution protects citizens from arbitrary fluctuations in public policies. Without the power to make laws, Madison argues, "the whole Constitution would be a dead letter." Therefore, the Framers chose not only to enumerate the law-making powers of Congress, but also to allow it the authority to make "all laws necessary and proper" to carry out those powers. Nevertheless, the power of Congress was to be checked by the other branches of government and also by the electorate, making Congress unlikely to overextend its law-making function.

The sober people of America are weary of the fluctuating policy which has directed the public councils. They have seen with regret and indignation that sudden changes and legislative interferences, in cases affecting personal rights, become jobs in the hands of enterprising and influential speculators, and snares to the more-industrious and less-informed part of the community. They have seen, too, that one legislative interference is but the first link of a long chain of repetitions, every subsequent interference being naturally produced by the effects of the preceding. They very rightly infer, therefore, that some thorough reform is wanting, which will banish speculations on public measures, inspire a general prudence and industry, and give a regular course to the business of society. . . .

The *sixth* and last class consists of the several powers and provisions by which efficacy is given to all the rest.

1. Of these the first is, the . . . power "To make all laws which shall be necessary and proper for carrying into execution the foregoing powers, and all other powers vested by this Constitution in the Government of the United States, or in any department or office thereof."

. . . Without the *substance* of this power the whole Constitution would be a dead letter. . . .

There are four other possible methods which the Constitution might have taken on this subject. They might have copied the second article of the existing Confederation, which would have prohibited the exercise of any power not *expressly* delegated; they might have attempted a positive enumeration of the powers comprehended under the general terms "necessary and proper"; they might have attempted a negative enumeration of them by specifying the powers excepted from the general definition; they might have been altogether silent on the subject, leaving these necessary and proper powers to construction and inference.

Had the convention taken the first method of adopting the second article of Confederation, it is evident that the new Congress would be continually exposed, as their predecessors have been, to the alternative of construing the term *"expressly"* with so much rigor as to disarm the government of all real authority whatever, or with so much latitude as to destroy altogether the force of the restriction. It would be easy to show . . . that no important power delegated by the articles of Confederation has been or can be executed by Congress without recurring more or less to the doctrine of *construction* or *implication.* As the powers delegated under the new system are more extensive, the government which is to administer it would find itself still more distressed with the alternative of betraying the public interests by doing nothing, or of violating the Constitution by exercising powers indispensably necessary and proper, but, at the same time, not *expressly* granted.

Had the convention attempted a positive enumeration of the powers necessary and proper for carrying their other powers into effect, the attempt would have involved a complete digest of laws on every subject to which the Constitution relates; accommodated too, not only to the existing state of things, but to all the possible changes which futurity may produce; for in every new application of a general power, the *particular powers,* which are the means of attaining the *object* of the general power, must always necessarily vary with that object and be often properly varied whilst the object remains the same.

Had they attempted to enumerate the particular powers or means not necessary or proper for carrying the general powers into execution, the task would have been no less chimerical; and would have been liable to this further objection, that every defect in the enumeration would have been equivalent to a positive grant of authority. If, to avoid this consequence, they had attempted a partial enumeration of the exceptions and described the residue by the general terms, *not necessary or proper,* it must have happened that the enumeration would comprehend a few of the excepted powers only; that these would be such as would be least likely to be assumed or tolerated, because the enumeration would of course select such as would be least necessary or proper; and that the unnecessary and improper powers included in the residuum, would be less forcibly excepted, than if no partial enumeration had been made.

Had the Constitution been silent on this head, there can be no doubt that all the particular powers requisite as means of executing the general powers would have resulted to the government by unavoidable implication. No axiom is more clearly established in law or in reason, than that wherever the end is required, the means are authorized; wherever a general power to do a thing is given, every particular power necessary for doing it is included. Had this last method, therefore, been pursued by the convention, every objection now urged against their plan would remain in all its plausibility; and the real inconveniency would be incurred of not removing a pretext which may be seized on critical occasions for drawing into question the essential powers of the Union.

If it be asked what is to be the consequence, in case the Congress shall misconstrue this part of the Constitution and exercise powers not warranted by its true meaning, I answer, the same as if they should misconstrue or enlarge any other power vested in them; as if the general power had been reduced to particulars, and any one of these were to be violated; the same, in short, as if the State legislatures should violate their respective constitutional authorities. In the first instance, the success of the usurpation will depend on the executive and judiciary departments, which are to expound and give effect to the legislative acts; and in the last resort a remedy must be obtained from the people, who can, by the election of more faithful representatives, annul the acts of the usurpers. The truth is that this ultimate redress may be more confided in against unconstitutional acts of the federal than of the State legislatures for this plain reason, that as every such act of the former will be an invasion of the rights of the latter, these will be ever ready to mark the innovation, to sound the alarm to the people, and to exert their local influence in effecting a change of federal representatives. There being no such intermediate body between the State legislatures and the people interested in watching the conduct of the former, violations of the State constitutions are more likely to remain unnoticed and unredressed.

TOWARD CRITICAL THINKING

1. Have constituents and the judicial and executive branches been a check on the law-making activities of Congress as suggested by James Madison? Or, rather, have they been its accomplices in expanding the scope of law making and therefore national policy making?

2. How has the national government's role in setting public policies changed from that envisioned by the Framers? Would Anti-Federalist arguments have won the day if the role of the national government in today's policy making was foreseen at the time the Constitution was ratified?

· 71 ·

Up and Down with Ecology—the "Issue-Attention Cycle"

ANTHONY DOWNS

Downs argues that the U.S. public is unable to focus for long periods of time, even on issues of great public importance. This waxing and waning of interest in issues produce a predictable issue-attention cycle. Using the issue of the environment as an example, Downs forwards the sequences of the cycle. Although issues are regularly replaced on the national agenda before solutions to their problems are found, Downs contends that some issues, like the environment, have characteristics that keep them from leaving the public consciousness for long.

American public attention rarely remains sharply focused upon any one domestic issue for very long—even if it involves a continuing problem of crucial importance to society. Instead, a systematic "issue-attention cycle" seems strongly to influence public attitudes and behavior concerning most key domestic problems. Each of these problems suddenly leaps into prominence, remains there for a short time, and then—though still largely unresolved—gradually fades from the center of public attention. A study of the way this cycle operates provides insights into how long public attention is likely to remain sufficiently focused upon any given issue to generate enough political pressure to cause effective change.

The shaping of American attitudes toward improving the quality of our environment provides both an example and a potential test of this "issue-attention cycle." In the past few years, there has been a remarkably widespread upsurge of interest in the quality of our environment. This change in public attitudes has been much faster than any changes in the environment itself. What has caused this shift in public attention? Why did this issue suddenly assume so high a priority among our domestic concerns? And how long will the American public sustain high-intensity interest in ecological matters? I believe that answers to these questions can be derived from analyzing the "issue-attention cycle."

SOURCE: Anthony Downs, "Up and Down with Ecology—the 'Issue-Attention Cycle,' " *The Public Interest,* 28 (Summer 1972):8–50. Reprinted by permission.

◆ The Dynamics of the "Issue-Attention Cycle"

Public perception of most "crises" in American domestic life does not reflect changes in real conditions as much as it reflects the operation of a systematic cycle of heightening public interest and then increasing boredom with major issues. This "issue-attention cycle" is rooted both in the nature of certain domestic problems and in the way major communications media interact with the public. The cycle itself has five stages, which may vary in duration depending upon the particular issue involved, but which almost always occur in the following sequence:

1. **The pre-problem stage.** This prevails when some highly undesirable social condition exists but has not yet captured much public attention, even though some experts or interest groups may already be alarmed by it. *Usually, objective conditions regarding the problem are far worse during the pre-problem stage than they are by the time the public becomes interested in it.* For example, this was true of racism, poverty, and malnutrition in the United States.

2. **Alarmed discovery and euphoric enthusiasm.** As a result of some dramatic series of events (like the ghetto riots in 1965 to 1967), or for other reasons, the public suddenly becomes both aware of and alarmed about the evils of a particular problem. This alarmed discovery is invariably accompanied by euphoric enthusiasm about society's ability to "solve this problem" or "do something effective" within a relatively short time. The combination of alarm and confidence results in part from the strong public pressure in America for political leaders to claim that every problem can be "solved." This outlook is rooted in the great American tradition of optimistically viewing most obstacles to social progress as *external* to the structure of society itself. The implication is that every obstacle can be eliminated and every problem solved *without any fundamental reordering of society itself,* if only we devote sufficient effort to it. In older and perhaps wiser cultures, there is an underlying sense of irony or even pessimism which springs from a widespread and often confirmed belief that many problems cannot be "solved" *at all* in any complete sense. Only recently has this more pessimistic view begun to develop in our culture.

3. **Realizing the cost of significant progress.** The third stage consists of a gradually spreading realization that the cost of "solving" the problem is very high indeed. Really doing so would not only take a great deal of money but would also require major sacrifices by large groups in the population. The public thus begins to realize that part of the problem results from arrangements that are providing significant benefits to someone—often to millions. For example, traffic congestion and a great deal of smog are caused by increasing automobile usage. Yet this also enhances

the mobility of millions of Americans who continue to purchase more vehicles to obtain these advantages.

In certain cases, technological progress can eliminate some of the undesirable results of a problem without causing any major restructuring of society or any loss of present benefits by others (except for higher money costs). In the optimistic American tradition, such a technological solution is initially assumed to be possible in the case of nearly every problem. Our most pressing social problems, however, usually involve either deliberate or unconscious exploitation of one group in society by another, or the prevention of one group from enjoying something that others want to keep for themselves. For example, most upper-middle-class whites value geographic separation from poor people and blacks. Hence any equality of access to the advantages of suburban living for the poor and for blacks cannot be achieved without some sacrifice by middle-class whites of the "benefits" of separation. The increasing recognition that there is this type of relationship between the problem and its "solution" constitutes a key part of the third stage.

4. **Gradual decline of intense public interest.** The previous stage becomes almost imperceptibly transformed into the fourth stage: a gradual decline in the intensity of public interest in the problem. As more and more people realize how difficult, and how costly to themselves, a solution to the problem would be, three reactions set in. Some people just get discouraged. Others feel positively threatened by thinking about the problem; so they suppress such thoughts. Still others become bored by the issue. Most people experience some combination of these feelings. Consequently, public desire to keep attention focused on the issue wanes. And by this time, some other issue is usually entering Stage Two; so it exerts a more novel and thus more powerful claim upon public attention.

5. **The post-problem stage.** In the final stage, an issue that has been replaced at the center of public concern moves into a prolonged limbo—a twilight realm of lesser attention or spasmodic recurrences of interest. However, the issue now has a different relation to public attention than that which prevailed in the "pre-problem" stage. For one thing, during the time that interest was sharply focused on this problem, new institutions, programs, and policies may have been created to help solve it. These entities almost always persist and often have some impact even after public attention has shifted elsewhere. For example, during the early stages of the "War on Poverty," the Office of Economic Opportunity (OEO) was established, and it initiated many new programs. Although poverty has now faded as a central public issue, OEO still exists. Moreover, many of its programs have experienced significant success, even though funded at a far lower level than would be necessary to reduce poverty decisively.

Any major problem that once was elevated to national prominence may sporadically recapture public interest; or important aspects of it may become attached to some other problem that subsequently dominates center stage. Therefore, problems that have gone through the cycle almost always receive a higher average level of attention, public effort, and general concern than those still in the pre-discovery stage.

◆ Which Problems Are Likely to Go through the Cycle?

Not all major social problems go through this "issue-attention cycle." Those which do generally possess to some degree three specific characteristics. First, the majority of persons in society are not suffering from the problem nearly as much as some minority (a *numerical* minority, not necessarily an *ethnic* one). This is true of many pressing social problems in America today—poverty, racism, poor public transportation, low-quality education, crime, drug addiction, and unemployment, among others. The number of persons suffering from each of these ills is very large *absolutely*—in the millions. But the numbers are small *relatively*—usually less than 15 percent of the entire population. Therefore, most people do not suffer directly enough from such problems to keep their attention riveted on them.

Second, the sufferings caused by the problem are generated by social arrangements that provide significant benefits to a majority or a powerful minority of the population. For example, Americans who own cars—plus the powerful automobile and highway lobbies—receive short-run benefits from the prohibition of using motor-fuel tax revenues for financing public transportation systems, even though such systems are desperately needed by the urban poor.

Third, the problem has no intrinsically exciting qualities—or no longer has them. When big-city racial riots were being shown nightly on the nation's television screens, public attention naturally focused upon their causes and consequences. But when they ceased (or at least the media stopped reporting them so intensively), public interest in the problems related to them declined sharply. Similarly, as long as the National Aeronautics and Space Administration (NASA) was able to stage a series of ever more thrilling space shots, culminating in the worldwide television spectacular of Americans walking on the moon, it generated sufficient public support to sustain high-level Congressional appropriations. But NASA had nothing half so dramatic for an encore, and repetition of the same feat proved less and less exciting (though a near disaster on the third try did revive audience interest). So NASA's Congressional appropriations plummeted.

A problem must be dramatic and exciting to maintain public interest because news is "consumed" by much of the American public (and by publics everywhere) largely as a form of entertainment. As such, it competes with other types of entertainment for a share of each person's time. Every day, there is a fierce struggle for space in the highly limited universe of newsprint and television viewing time. Each issue vies not only with all other social problems and public events, but also with a multitude of "non-news" items that are often far more pleasant to contemplate. These include sporting news, weather reports, crossword puzzles, fashion accounts, comics, and daily horoscopes. In fact, the amount of television time and newspaper space devoted to sports coverage, as compared to international events, is a striking commentary on the relative value that the public places on knowing about these two subjects.

When all three of the above conditions exist concerning a given problem that has somehow captured public attention, the odds are great that it will soon move through the entire "issue-attention cycle"—and therefore will gradually fade from the center of the stage. The first condition means that most people will not be continually reminded of the problem by their own suffering from it. The second condition means that solving the problem requires sustained attention and effort, plus fundamental changes in social institutions or behavior. This in turn means that significant attempts to solve it are threatening to important groups in society. The third condition means that the media's sustained focus on this problem soon bores a majority of the public. As soon as the media realize that their emphasis on this problem is threatening many people and boring even more, they will shift their focus to some "new" problem. This is particularly likely in America because nearly all the media are run for profit, and they make the most money by appealing to the largest possible audiences. Thus, as Marshall McLuhan has pointed out, it is largely the audience itself—the American public—that "manages the news" by maintaining or losing interest in a given subject. As long as this pattern persists, we will continue to be confronted by a stream of "crises" involving particular social problems. Each will rise into public view, capture center stage for a while, and then gradually fade away as it is replaced by more fashionable issues moving into their "crisis" phases.

♦ The Rise of Environmental Concern

Public interest in the quality of the environment now appears to be about midway through the "issue-attention cycle." Gradually, more and more people are beginning to realize the immensity of the social and financial costs of cleaning up our air and water and of preserving and restoring open spaces. Hence much of the enthusiasm about prompt, dramatic improvement in the environment is fading. There is still a great deal of public interest, however, so it cannot be said that the "post-problem stage" has been reached. In fact, as will be discussed later, the environmental issue may well retain more attention than social problems that affect smaller proportions of the population. Before evaluating the prospects of long-term interest in the environment, though, it is helpful to analyze how environmental concern passed through the earlier stages in the "issue-attention cycle."

The most obvious reason for the initial rise in concern about the environment is the recent deterioration of certain easily perceived environmental conditions. A whole catalogue of symptoms can be arrayed, including ubiquitous urban smog, greater proliferation of solid waste, oceanic oil spills, greater pollution of water supplies by DDT and other poisons, the threatened disappearance of many wildlife species, and the overcrowding of a variety of facilities from commuter expressways to National Parks. Millions of citizens observing these worsening conditions became convinced that *someone* ought to "do something" about them. But "doing something" to reduce environmental deterioration is not easy. For many of our environmental problems have been caused by developments which are highly valued by most Americans.

The very abundance of our production and consumption of material goods is responsible for an immense amount of environmental pollution. For example, electric power generation, if based on fossil fuels, creates smoke and air pollution or, if based on nuclear fuels, causes rising water temperatures. Yet a key foundation for rising living standards in the United States during this century has been the doubling of electric power consumption every ten years. So more pollution is the price we have paid for the tremendous advantages of being able to use more and more electricity. Similarly, much of the litter blighting even our remotest landscapes stems from the convenience of using "throwaway packages." Thus, to regard environmental pollution as a purely external negative factor would be to ignore its direct linkage with material advantages most citizens enjoy.

Another otherwise favorable development that has led to rising environmental pollution is what I would call the democratization of privilege. Many more Americans are now able to participate in certain activities that were formerly available only to a small, wealthy minority. Some members of that minority are incensed by the consequences of having their formerly esoteric advantages spread to "the common man." The most frequent irritant caused by the democratization of privilege is congestion. Rising highway congestion, for example, is denounced almost everywhere. Yet its main cause is the rapid spread of automobile ownership and usage. In 1950, about 59 percent of all families had at least one automobile, and 7 percent owned two or more. By 1968, the proportion of families owning at least one automobile had climbed to 79 percent, and 26 percent had two or more cars. In the ten years from 1960 to 1970, the total number of registered automotive vehicles rose by 35 million (or 47 percent), as compared to a rise in human population of 23 million (or only 13 percent). Moreover, it has been estimated that motor vehicles cause approximately 60 percent of all air pollution. So the tremendous increase in smog does not result primarily from larger population, but rather from the democratization of automobile ownership.

The democratization of privilege also causes crowding in National Parks, rising suburban housing density, the expansion of new subdivisions into formerly picturesque farms and orchards, and the transformation of once tranquil resort areas like Waikiki Beach into forests of high-rise buildings. It is now difficult for the wealthy to flee from busy urban areas to places of quiet seclusion, because so many more people can afford to go with them. *The elite's environmental deterioration is often the common man's improved standard of living.*

◆ Our Soaring Aspirations

A somewhat different factor which has contributed to greater concern with environmental quality is a marked increase in our aspirations and standards concerning what our environment ought to be like. In my opinion, rising dissatisfaction with the "system" in the United States does not result primarily from poorer performance by that system. Rather, it stems mainly from a rapid escalation of our aspiration as to what the system's performance ought to be. Nowhere is this phenomenon more striking than in regard to the quality of the environment. One hundred years ago, white Americans were eliminating whole Indian tribes without a qualm. Today, many serious-minded citizens seek to make important issues out of the potential disappearance of the whooping crane, the timber wolf, and other exotic creatures. Meanwhile, thousands of Indians in Brazil are still being murdered each year—but American conservationists are not focusing on that human massacre. Similarly, some aesthetes decry "galloping sprawl" in metropolitan fringe areas, while they ignore acres of rat infested housing a few miles away. Hence the escalation of our environmental aspirations is more selective than might at first appear.

Yet regarding many forms of pollution, we are now rightly upset over practices and conditions that have largely been ignored for decades. An example is our alarm about the dumping of industrial wastes and sewage into rivers and lakes. This increase in our environmental aspirations is part of a general cultural phenomenon stimulated both by our success in raising living standards and by the recent emphases of the communications media. Another cause of the rapid rise in interest in environmental pollution is the "explosion" of alarmist rhetoric on this subject. According to some well-publicized experts, all life on earth is threatened by an "environmental crisis." Some claim human life will end within three decades or less if we do not do something drastic about current behavior patterns.

Are things really that bad? Frankly, I am not enough of an ecological expert to know. But I am skeptical concerning all highly alarmist views because so many previous prophets of doom and disaster have been so wrong concerning many other so-called "crises" in our society.

There are two reasonable definitions of "crisis." One kind of crisis consists of a rapidly deteriorating situation moving towards a single disastrous event at some future moment. The second kind consists of a more gradually deteriorating situation that will eventually pass some subtle "point of no return." At present, I do not believe either of these definitions applies to most American domestic problems. Although many social critics hate to admit it, the American "system" actually serves the majority of citizens rather well in terms of most indicators of well-being. Concerning such things as real income, personal mobility, variety and choice of consumption patterns, longevity, health, leisure time, and quality of housing, most Americans are better off today than they have ever been and extraordinarily better off than most of mankind. What is *not* improving is the gap between society's performance and what most people—or at least highly vocal minorities—believe society *ought* to be doing to solve these problems. Our aspirations and standards have risen far faster than the beneficial outputs of our social system. Therefore, although most Americans, including most of the poor, are receiving more now, they are enjoying it less.

This conclusion should not be confused with the complacency of some super-patriots. It would be unrealistic to deny certain important negative trends in American life. Some conditions are indeed getting worse for nearly everyone. Examples are air quality and freedom from thievery. Moreover, congestion and environmental deterioration might forever destroy certain valuable national amenities if they are not checked. Finally, there has probably been a general rise in personal and social anxiety in recent years. I believe this is due to increased tensions caused by our rapid rate of technical and social change, plus the increase in worldwide communication through the media. These developments rightly cause serious and genuine concern among millions of Americans.

◆ The Future of the Environmental Issue

Concern about the environment has passed through the first two stages of the "issue-attention cycle" and is by now well into the third. In fact, we have already begun to move toward the fourth stage, in which the intensity of public interest in environmental improvement must inexorably decline. And this raises an interesting question: Will the issue of environmental quality then move on into the "postproblem" stage of the cycle?

My answer to this question is: Yes, but not soon, because certain characteristics of this issue will protect it from the rapid decline in public interest typical of many other recent issues. First of all, many kinds of environmental pollution are much more visible and more clearly threatening than most other social problems. This is particularly true of air pollution. The greater the apparent threat from visible forms of pollution and the more vividly this can be dramatized, the more public support environmental improvement will receive and the longer it will sustain public interest. Ironically, the cause of ecologists would therefore benefit from an environmental disaster like a "killer smog" that would choke thousands to death in a few days. Actually, this is nothing new; every cause from early Christianity to the Black Panthers has benefited from martyrs. Yet even the most powerful symbols lose their impact if they are constantly repeated. The piteous sight of an oil-soaked seagull or a dead soldier pales after it has been viewed even a dozen times. Moreover, some of the worst environmental threats come from forms of pollution that are invisible. Thus, our propensity to focus attention on what is most visible may cause us to clean up the pollution we can easily perceive while ignoring even more dangerous but hidden threats.

Pollution is also likely to be kept in the public eye because it is an issue that threatens almost everyone, not just a small percentage of the population. Since it is not politically divisive, politicians can safely pursue it without fearing adverse repercussions. Attacking environmental pollution is therefore much safer than attacking racism or poverty. For an attack upon the latter antagonizes important blocs of voters who benefit from the sufferings of others or at least are not threatened enough by such suffering to favor spending substantial amounts of their money to reduce it.

A third strength of the environmental issue is that much of the "blame" for pollution can be attributed to a small group of "villains" whose wealth and power make them excellent scapegoats. Environmental defenders can therefore "courageously" attack these scapegoats without antagonizing most citizens. Moreover, at least in regard to air pollution, that small group actually has enough power greatly to reduce pollution if it really tries. If leaders of the nation's top auto-producing, power-generating, and fuel-supplying firms would change their behavior significantly, a drastic decline in air pollution could be achieved very quickly, This has been demonstrated at many locations already.

Gathering support for attacking any problem is always easier if its ills can be blamed on a small number of "public enemies"—as is shown by the success of Ralph Nader. This tactic is especially effective if the "enemies" exhibit extreme wealth and power, eccentric dress and manners, obscene language, or some other uncommon traits. Then society can aim its outrage at a small, alien group without having to face up to the need to alter its own behavior. It is easier to find such scapegoats for almost all forms of pollution than for other major problems like poverty, poor housing, or racism. Solutions to those problems would require millions of Americans to change their own behavior patterns, to accept higher taxes, or both.

The possibility that technological solutions can be devised for most pollution problems may also lengthen the public prominence of this issue. To the extent that pollution can be reduced through technological change, most people's basic attitudes, expectations, and behavior patterns will not have to be altered. The traumatic difficulties of achieving major institutional change could thus be escaped through the "magic" of purely technical improvements in automobile engines, water purification devices, fuel composition, and sewage treatment facilities.

◆ Financing the Fight against Pollution

Another aspect of anti-pollution efforts that will strengthen their political support is that most of the costs can be passed on to the public through higher product prices rather than higher taxes. Therefore, politicians can demand enforcement of costly environmental quality standards without paying the high political price of raising the required funds through taxes. True, water pollution is caused mainly by the actions of public bodies, especially municipal sewer systems, and effective remedies for this form of pollution require higher taxes or at least higher prices for public services. But the major costs of reducing most kinds of pollution can be added to product prices and thereby quietly shifted to the ultimate consumers of the outputs concerned. This is a politically painless way to pay for attacking a major social problem. In contrast, effectively combatting most social problems requires large-scale income redistribution attainable only through both higher taxes and higher transfer payments or subsidies. Examples of such politically costly problems are poverty, slum housing, low-quality health care for the poor, and inadequate public transportation.

Many ecologists oppose paying for a cleaner environment through higher product prices. They would rather force the polluting firms to bear the required costs through lower profits. In a few oligopolistic industries, like petroleum and automobile production, this might work. But in the long run, not much of the total cost could be paid this way without driving capital out of the industries concerned and thereby eventually forcing product prices upwards. Furthermore, it is just that those who use any given product should pay the full cost of making it—including the cost of avoiding excessive pollution in its production. Such payment is best made through higher product prices. In my opinion, it would be unwise in most cases to try to pay these costs by means of government subsidies in order to avoid shifting the load onto consumers. . . .

Some proponents of improving the environment are relying on the support of students and other young people to keep this issue at the center of public attention. Such support, however, is not adequate as a long-term foundation. Young people form a highly unstable base for the support of any policy because they have such short-lived "staying power." For one thing, they do not long enjoy the large amount of free time they possess while in college. Also, as new individuals enter the category of "young people" and older ones leave it, different issues are stressed and accumulated skills in marshaling opinion are dissipated. Moreover, the radicalism of the young has been immensely exaggerated by the media's tendency to focus attention upon those with extremist views. In their attitudes toward political issues, most young people are not very different from their parents.

There is good reason, then, to believe that the bundle of issues called "improving the environment" will also suffer the gradual loss of public attention characteristic of the later stages of the "issue-attention cycle." However, it will be eclipsed at a much slower rate than other recent domestic issues. So it may be possible to accomplish some significant improvements in environmental quality—if those seeking them work fast.

TOWARD CRITICAL THINKING

1. What is the impact of the issue-attention cycle as described by Downs for public policy? Should legislators abandon interest in an issue because the public has?

2. Downs argues that issues that affect a minority of the population are likely to conform to the issue-attention cycle. If the public at large shifts its attention to other issues, how do such issues affecting minorities get addressed?

• 72 •

Health Care Reform in 1,100 Easy Steps

DANA PRIEST

Priest chronicles the enormousness of the policy-making process as illustrated by health care reform. During his campaign for president, Bill Clinton promised the country universal health care coverage. Upon taking office, Clinton established a health care task force with Hillary Rodham Clinton at its head. In seeking answers to the nation's health care problems, hundreds of experts and dozens of panels worked daily to provide the president with a bill to present to Congress. Priest notes that in the process, a minor bureaucratic structure was erected to channel proposals. And, in spite of the administration's efforts, the 103rd Congress failed to pass any health care reform.

Nearly every day for the past two months, about 500 health care experts have pushed through the turnstiles at the Old Executive Office Building and camped, sixteen hours a day, in offices where phones are as scarce as desks, chairs and privacy. There the eclectic staff of the president's health care task force—economists, administrators, physicians, ethicists, nurses, sociologists—has churned out thousands of pages of health policy minutiae for the president and First Lady.

A month ago, senior White House adviser Ira Magaziner, who masterminded the unprecedented process, handed Hillary Rodham Clinton an "initial" memo of 1,100 decisions that would have to be made. "Good bedtime reading," she joked as she thumbed through the tome.

The memo was distilled from the contents of thirty-four ever-expanding, large-ringed notebooks kept in a second-floor reading room. The public can't read them, and the staff can't even photocopy them for fear the copies might be leaked to the news media or some interest group.

The first phase of the task force's work ended two weeks ago, when the staff handed over detailed options on everything from how to cover farmers in rural areas to how to make insurance companies play fair. Administration officials outlined for the press the broad parameters of the

SOURCE: Dana Priest, "Health Care Reform in 1,100 Easy Steps," *The Washington Post National Weekly Edition* (April 26–May 2, 1993):31. © 1993 The Washington Post. Reprinted with permission.

plan, but its precise features and how it will be financed have yet to be decided.

The Clintons are completing a series of briefings, and will review the material. Although the schedule has slipped two weeks after the death of Hillary Clinton's father, the president expects to have a near-final version of the plan May 17 and to submit formal legislation to Congress by the end of May, administration officials say.

"You can never get 100 percent of what you want from the policy process," Magaziner says. "But if you get 70 percent, you can get the other 30 percent [later] if you build in the right kind of mechanisms."

On the door to Room 213 in the Old Executive Office Building are the following instructions: The "Cross Cutting Group on Issues Concerning Persons With Disabilities" meets down the hall. The "Managed Care and Low Income Providers" discussion will take place in rooms 211, 100, 400, 412 and 488. A daily calendar is broken down into fifteen-minute intervals. The first meeting starts at 7:30 A.M. Some meetings go through the night.

While Hillary Clinton is in charge of the task force's mission, Magaziner is in charge of the process by which it has assembled and processed vast quantities of information. A forty-five-year-old workaholic business consultant, he brought with him from Rhode Island the tools and jargon of his trade—flowcharts, "tollgates" and schedules.

To overhaul the nation's $930 billion-a-year health industry, Magaziner, a frizzy-haired, self-decribed mumbler, created fifteen committees and then broke them down into thirty-four working groups.

"He starts out each group's meetings by saying he wants to let us know there's talk of a back room with five people in it who are making decisions," says one staff member. "If that room exists, he says, 'I sure don't know about it.' "

For each working group, the policy-making process began with a set of questions. For instance, Clinton has said he wants to require all employers to pay a portion of their employees' health premiums. So the working group on "employer mandates" began with dozens of questions, among them:

How would a mandate be enforced? Would companies be required to cover part-time or seasonal workers? If the government were to require coverage for employees who work at least thirty hours a week, would many employers, to escape the mandate, hire more people at twenty-nine hours a week?

By the end of the process, the working group had narrowed the decision to two options: employers' contribution would be either a percentage of their total payroll or a certain amount per hour for each worker. That's a decision the Clintons will have to make.

Other working groups, however, did not have such an easy time winnowing down the questions. In the group that studied malpractice reform, for example, the discussion often veered from specific ways to prevent malpractice and reduce costs associated with negligence and litigation to whether reform of malpractice laws was necessary at all.

For all working groups, the most critical point in the process has taken place in the ornate Indian Treaty Room. There, Magaziner, health policy analyst Judith Feder from the Department of Health and Human Services, envoys of Cabinet secretaries and the heads of the fifteen committees have quizzed members of the working groups on their conclusions and how they reached them. Magaziner calls these meetings "tollgates"; each working group has seven tollgate reviews to pass through.

About 200 people attend tollgate meetings, which are described variously as "subdued," "restrained," "very professional." The group's leader presents its analysis of options. Often, the meetings have been so long and inconclusive they have taxed the patience of even the most avid policy aficionados. One series of tollgates lasted two days—from 8 A.M. to 11 P.M., Saturday and Sunday.

Sometimes it's all been too much, and staffers have found themselves pushed to unexpected lengths to survive.

"There's a Fanny Farmer [candy store] across from the OEOB and I walked out of one tollgate meeting and walked right over to the store and said, 'I want a pound of fudge, right now,' " says one participant. "I've never eaten a pound of fudge in my life. I just wanted something that was gratifying."

But driving the staff is Magaziner's *modus operandi.* "People work best when they work for deadlines," he explains. "It forces discipline."

Deadlines also keep everyone up late. After Magaziner helped moderate the first and only public meeting of the formal task force, which lasted thirteen hours, he returned to his office for a session with twenty-nine quantitative analysts, all number crunchers. The purpose was to determine the methodology two HHS agencies had used to estimate the annual cost to them of a standard benefit package that the overhaul plan would provide each American. The estimates came in at $1,600 and $1,150. At 1 A.M. they had settled their differences.

"I know this can sound dull to people, but it can make the difference between policy that works and policy that doesn't," says Magaziner.

The administration tapped an unusual mix of people to do this work. Of the 511 staff members, about 400 are either Capitol Hill aides or employees of federal agencies. The others come from universities or business.

Some are advocates of a government-financed, Canadian-style national health system approach. Others favor heavy government regulation.

Still others believe private sector competition should be the driving force in reform.

There also are differences at the top. Magaziner who was instrumental in convincing President Clinton to embrace the "managed competition" approach, which relies in large measure on the private sector, chairs most meetings alongside HHS's Feder, who is closely identified with a strong government role in regulating health care.

"We wanted a broad array of ideologies because ultimately what we need to do is fuse together support from people in Congress and around the country," Magaziner says. "I like processes where people really get agitated and yell and shout. You get people really going. We have lots of heated debates."

Some staffers believe the diversity slowed the groups down. "I don't know that it's a terribly efficient process once you establish that you disagree," one says.

◆

The initial refusal of the White House to name members of the task force publicly, or to describe their work, rattled many on the outside. A physicians' group filed a lawsuit, largely unsuccessful so far, to force it to hold its meetings in public. The case is on appeal.

Task force spokesman Robert Boorstin says the blackout was meant to stop reporters from badgering the staff. But in late March, after several publications printed pirated lists, Boorstin released names. None of the task force staff members interviewed for this article said he or she had been subsequently bothered by reporters or lobbyists. But most would not allow their names to be used.

The secrecy prompted some interest groups to charge they had been left out. Magaziner and others counter that the task force has met with 400 interest groups, including the major professional, consumer and trade organizations. Some, like the American Medical Association, have held numerous meetings with Magaziner and his technical staff. State public health officials were in the other day, as was a group of state insurance auditors.

Meanwhile, the public has insisted on being heard. About 2,000 people have requested an audience and 75,000 more have written to share personal tales or to offer help and home-made health reform plans. "Dear Second White House Chef," began a letter from the financial planner seeking a meeting so he could share his proposal. "Even though I haven't met you, I have a favor to ask of you. . . . "

The letter was forwarded to Alan Hoffman, a twenty-six-year-old lawyer who is now commander-in-chief of Room 205, Central Scheduling, and who receives all requests for visits. On a "hot day," he says, about 100 phone calls come in to his disheveled office.

The president and the First Lady will not be alone in working on the next phase of the health care overhaul project. The working groups' options, and the decisions made by President Clinton, must go to financial auditors and lawyers to assess the economic and legal implications of the plan. Meanwhile, the official task force, made up of six Cabinet secretaries, several White House aides and the director of the Office of Management and Budget, will be asked to weigh in on different aspects of the plan; so will the Council of Economic Advisors.

And the working group on ethics is just getting started. It is the team of academic and religious ethicists who will write a preamble and review all elements of the plan for their moral and philosophical implications. For example:

"Should the value of universal access and fairness take precedence over personal choice [of physician]?" asks Arthur L. Caplan, a University of Minnesota professor in the departments of philosophy and surgery.

It's not exactly a simple question, and Caplan seems to understand the work ahead of him. "This is a hard-sell audience of bureaucrats and practical, hard-nosed folks," he says.

TOWARD CRITICAL THINKING

1. Is the process outlined by Priest the best way to propose public policy? Is this process likely to produce compromises that promise little actual change? In light of the fate of Clinton's health care proposals, was the task force's effort worthwhile?

2. Priest notes the intricate nature of the details with which the task force struggled. Is it possible for "average Americans" to sift through proposals that are of such a technical nature?

THINKING ABOUT DOMESTIC POLICY

1. How does the issue of health care illustrate points made by Downs concerning the "issue-attention cycle"? Is reform short of universal health care a "win" for President Clinton on the domestic policy front?

2. What should the role be for the national government in the setting of domestic policies? Are some issues particularly in need of uniform, national policies? Which ones?

CHAPTER 15

◆ ◆ ◆

Foreign and Military Policy

After more than forty years of relative stability, the United States must identify its new role in the world. The Soviet Union and its communist partners in Eastern Europe no longer exist. Without the threat of Soviet communism, the fundamental principle of post-World War II U.S. foreign policy—anti-communism—no longer exists, either. So far, the Clinton administration has advocated a foreign policy of engagement and enlargement, designed to bring Russia and other countries into an economically liberal, politically democratic community of nations.

These circumstances are much different from those facing the people of the United States as they deliberated ratifying the Constitution. When the states gained independence from Great Britain, it was in no small part because France and other European powers were willing to provide the colonies with assistance.

In its early years, the United States was a relatively weak nation, with a radically new form of government, in a world overshadowed both economically and militarily by monarchies. In response to these conditions, U.S. foreign policy makers tried to remain neutral in European political affairs, while maintaining profitable economic ties with those same countries.

For all nations, foreign policy embraces the objectives that a national government seeks to achieve in its relations with people outside its borders, as well as the means by which the government attempts to achieve those goals. Despite the rapid pace of change in international affairs in recent years, a few basic principles continue to guide U.S. foreign policy. This chapter examines three of these principles. In Reading 73, *Federalist No. 75,* Alexander Hamilton considers why treaties, one of the key tools of foreign policy, should be a joint activity of the executive and legislative branches. Next, given the value placed on divided and limited government in the United States, Jay Rosen considers the participation of a private sector actor, CNN, in foreign policy (Reading 74). Finally, Richard M. Pious explores how the constitutional division of the war-making power continues to create rifts between the Congress and the president over their respective spheres of authority.

73

Federalist No. 75

ALEXANDER HAMILTON

Treaties, which are formal agreements negotiated and ratified between governments, were the primary means of creating rules to govern the relations between countries in the late eighteenth century. Though the Framers believed that the executive branch was better suited to conduct foreign policy than was the legislative branch, they also sought to keep the power to make rules in the hands of the legislature. Treaties, like contracts, created rules with the force of law. The Framers resolved this dilemma by giving the power to negotiate treaties to the President and the power to ratify treaties to the Senate.

. . .

The President is to have power, "by and with the advice and consent of the Senate, to make treaties, provided two thirds of the senators present concur."

Though this provision has been assailed on different grounds. . . . One ground of objection is the . . . intermixture of powers: some contending that the President ought alone to possess the power of making treaties; others, that it ought to have been exclusively deposited in the Senate. Another source of objection is derived from the small number of persons by whom a treaty may be made. Of those who espouse this objection, a part are of opinion that the House of Representatives ought to have been associated in the business. . . .

. . . The essence of the legislative authority is to enact laws, or, in other words, to prescribe rules for the regulation of the society; while the execution of the laws, and the employment of the common strength, either for this purpose or for the common defence, seem to comprise all the functions of the executive magistrate. The power of making treaties is, plainly, neither the one nor the other. It relates neither to the execution of the subsisting laws nor to the enaction of new ones; and still less to an exertion of the common strength. Its objects are CONTRACTS with foreign nations, which have the force of law but derive it from the obligations of good faith. They are not rules prescribed by the sovereign to the subject, but agreements between sovereign and sovereign. The power in question seems therefore to form a distinct department, and to belong, properly, neither to the legislative nor to the executive. The qualities elsewhere detailed as indispensable in the management of foreign negotiations, point out the Executive as the most fit agent in those transactions; while the vast importance of the trust, and the operation of treaties as laws, plead strongly for the participation of the whole or a portion of the legislative body in the office of making them. . . .

. . . It must indeed be clear to a demonstration that the joint possession of the power in question, by the President and Senate, would afford a greater prospect of security than the separate possession of it by either of them.

TOWARD CRITICAL THINKING

1. What advantages does the executive have in managing foreign policy compared with the House and Senate? Why are these advantages particularly important to the conduct of foreign policy?

2. Are these advantages more important today than in the late eighteenth century? Would greater oversight or control of foreign policy by the legislature improve the quality of U.S. foreign policy?

74

Glitz! Visuals! Action! The Whole World Is Watching CNN

JAY ROSEN

Cable News Network (CNN) not only changed the market for major network news shows in the United States, but it also changed viewing habits around the world. Political leaders, foreign policy experts, and international business executives turn to CNN or to CNN's emerging international competitors to watch live events uncensored, often providing crucial information unmatched by other sources for its speed.

As with most new technologies, however, the capacity of CNN to spread information worldwide has mixed consequences. Important global topics with little visual impact, from foreign trade to nuclear safety, may receive less coverage than do attention-grabbing car chases or child rescues. At the same time, global news organizations can provide the audience with more choice, breaking government news media monopolies. In some instances, governments may even be less oppressive, knowing that the whole world really is watching.

The bus shelter ads say, "CNN: NOW MORE THAN EVER." They have a point. Indispensable and omnipresent during the gulf war, Ted Turner's Cable News Network now looks to be the future of TV news. But what kind of future will it be? The answer depends on which of its many identities CNN is inhabiting at a given time (or place). . . .

Any reckoning with CNN must begin with the reasons for its rise, first in the United States and then internationally. The essence of CNN is that it is a twenty-four-hour *news* network, meaning that within the organization there is no other competing programming. By giving its undivided attention to news, CNN gains a large advantage over the news divisions of the three major networks, which are just that—divisions within an increasingly hostile corporate climate, where there's constant pressure to cut costs. . . .

As a global news service CNN will soon have competition—from the BBC, for example,—but none of its international rivals will be able to

SOURCE: Jay Rosen, "Glitz! Visuals! Action! The Whole World Is Watching CNN," *The Nation* (May 13, 1991):622–625. This article is reprinted from *The Nation* magazine. © The Nation Company.

count on the two income streams CNN enjoys in the United States: cable fees and advertising revenues. . . . CNN is here to stay, and not only here but abroad as well. In one form or another, it reaches more than 100 countries; it has agreements to share footage with broadcasting agencies all over the world. . . .

During the gulf war, CNN's triumph became clear to everyone. It achieved its highest-ever U.S. ratings, ranging from 4.7 million to 10.9 million homes in prime-time hours (compared with fewer than 930,000 before the crisis). The networks also saw their ratings jump during the war, but not their revenues. For them, war coverage cut into prime-time hours normally reserved for entertainment shows; the advertisers didn't like it and refused to buy ads. War news, they said, was not the right "environment.". . .

CNN, meanwhile, was not only keeping advertisers but raising its rates, from $3,500 before the war to more than $20,000 for a thirty-second spot. This underlines the essential advantage the network enjoys: Those who watch are watching specifically for news; those who advertise on CNN have already decided they are willing to advertise on the news. The result is that CNN, despite its lower ratings, can invest more in news gathering than any of its competitors, a gap that is certain to grow given the networks' financial losses during the war. ABC now has twelve foreign bureaus, NBC thirteen and CBS seven. CNN has fifteen, with more to come. . . .

On the first night of the war, CNN stunned the rest of the news business by maintaining a phone link to Baghdad as the bombs began dropping. While CNN's correspondents gave us their version of the U.S. bombing raid, the networks witnessed a vivid sign of their own demise. About 200 local stations that had agreements with CNN switched to the cable network's war coverage, including many network affiliates that would ordinarily be carrying Dan Rather, Tom Brokaw, or Peter Jennings. In Los Angeles CNN was on all four independent stations, in New York it was on three. We got a sudden glimpse of the future: Local stations will retain their own highly profitable news operations and rely on CNN for national or international news. . . .

. . . In comparison with the toned-down atmosphere of TV news in other countries, CNN looks rich, glitzy, exciting, "American." The pricey anchors may be absent, but the zooming graphics, high-tech feel and picture-driven pace of a network newscast are important features of CNN. This makes it another vehicle for the spread of American values, disguised this time as production values.

. . . Against the calculated slickness and thrill-a-minute action of the big-budget Hollywood feature, the filmmakers of other nations have a hard time competing. The same kind of competition is already occurring in news, as the polished look and up-tempo pace of CNN force home-grown broadcasters in Europe to adopt similar techniques. . . .

The ethic of "get them watching and keep them watching" is born of the American experience of competing for ratings in a multichannel commercial system. It is an attitude toward the audience, a manipulative way of viewing others, that is highly developed in the U.S. media but still underdeveloped abroad. . . . The one world implied by the production values of CNN is one in which the viewer's attention can be held in the same manner everywhere: with dramatic visuals deployed for their oomph value rather than their importance in any explanatory scheme.

This frenzy of the visual, in which U.S. television has long specialized, has political consequences, but no politics per se. In the gulf war, for example, it worked to the advantage of the U.S. military in favoring repeated showings of laser-guided missiles hitting their targets squarely and spectacularly. But it also dictated that CNN would show scenes of what Iraq said was a civilian shelter destroyed by allied bombs. It would be wrong to suggest that CNN has no politics: It acts in an explicitly political manner when it shows defiance in the face of any attempt to prevent it from airing the footage it wants to broadcast. Thus the live coverage it sent from Beijing in the spring of 1989, when Chinese officials were seen ordering the network to shut down its signal.

We can also expect more arresting irrelevance, like the coverage via satellite of American crews extinguishing oil fires in Kuwait. . . . It's significant that prior to the gulf war, CNN's biggest ratings included its live coverage of the 1987 rescue of a baby trapped in a Texas well and the 1989 San Francisco earthquake. . . .

. . . Of course, the same power can (and no doubt will) be used to focus worldwide attention on various government atrocities and political crimes, as long as they are highly visual and available to the cameras. Any rumbling of tanks into city streets, as in Tiananmen Square, will be costly to the government involved.

As CNN begins to constitute—rather than merely inform—the global public sphere, its limitations will become global as well. Political deeds that lack a visual dimension may tend to escape world notice because they bore the image-hungry producers at CNN (or its competitors). Consider in this connection the savings and loan scandal and other complex maneuvers of finance; they occur in a political field that is fundamentally nonvisual and this of negligible interest to those whose task is to "get them watching and keep them watching." It's not that the facts of such scandals are suppressed, but they are relegated to financial news segments and therefore escape the continuous cycles of repetition that are the essence of the CNN style.

Still, it would be wrong to assume that CNN is entirely or even predominantly a malignant influence. There are several ways in which its approach to news is a progressive one. For example, its preference for live coverage means that it will often carry important news conferences, announcements and hearings in their entirety, avoiding the tyranny of the soundbite and the TV reporter's breezy, overly facile wrap-up. Granted, what CNN considers "important" is likely to involve government officials, but there's still a net gain for viewers, who can watch, listen and decide for themselves what they think. Similarly, the refusal to build up the on-air people as stars has a welcome effect: They're not tempted to appoint themselves Secretary of State, as Ted Koppel is inclined to do.

In general, the fact that CNN is on all the time reduces the pressure on any particular half-hour to perform in the ratings, which means that the people on air don't have to blow-dry themselves to perfection or edit out every trace of reality's messiness. Among network news traditionalists, CNN is often said to lack "depth." But in a tradition where "depth" means five minutes for a complex subject rather than two, the charge is hard to take seriously. For a standard thirty-minute newscast, CNN is similar enough to the networks to substitute for them, which it is doing and will continue to do.

CNN's shrewdest move to date has been to target the international elite, those who are involved in the news as actors more than audiences. In newsrooms, international airports, foreign ministries and financial houses around the world, CNN is left on all the time, becoming the medium of record for people whose business it is to monitor the globe. For hotels that cater to international elites, CNN is also a must. It is this elite viewer, more than any mass audience in foreign countries, who gives CNN a potent international presence. In Iraq during the war, CNN was received by satellite, but only by a handful of government offices that could bear the expense of rooftop dishes. Saddam Hussein could watch, but not most Iraqis. This international presence gives CNN the cachet it needs to capture interviews with world leaders and key announcements from the players in a crisis. These can be aired in real time, making the network even more valuable to political actors. That is why desk officers at foreign ministries assign someone to watch CNN around the clock.

In countries where television and the press have been rigidly controlled, there is little doubt that the arrival of CNN means a freeing-up of the media system. Solidarity knew what it was doing in the mid-1980's when it got the Polish authorities to concede a half-hour of CNN on the nightly government newscast. Similarly, opponents of the ruling party in Mexico credit CNN's presence with making it harder for the government to manipulate voting results. For U.S. viewers, there's the fact that CNN is more likely to give "outlaw" leaders like Saddam [Hussein] and Col. Muammar el-Qaddafi a chance to be heard. . . .

In its often sloppy, seat-of-the-pants reporting during the gulf war, and in presenting Peter Arnett's censored reports from Baghdad, CNN showed a tendency to shift the editing function toward the audience. The right to sort through information and discount what some people say was removed from TV producers and given to viewers. That's progress, at least on my ledger. What isn't progressive about CNN is the implicit nihilism of picture-driven news and the "keep 'em watching" mentality. In these respects, Turner's triumph will do more for the spread of TV culture than for the cultivation of intelligent citizenship around the globe. But CNN bears watching, if for no other reason than that a good portion of the world is likely to be watching too.

TOWARD CRITICAL THINKING

1. Why do many governments try to keep tight control on the information on television and radio stations, especially news? CNN or other global news stations are now available in many of these countries. Why have they been allowed in, even on a limited basis?

2. What advantages does CNN have over foreign competitors? What does this say about the advantages that companies and people in the large, rich countries such as the United States have in the global economy?

· 75 ·

Presidential War Powers, the War Powers Resolution, and the Persian Gulf*

RICHARD M. PIOUS

Congress has declared war only eight times since 1789. In the same span of time, presidents have dispatched troops to more than two hundred international conflicts without a congressional declaration of war. The ambiguous nature of the distribution of war powers in the Constitution has often created controversy between presidents and Congress.

In the wake of the distortion and loss surrounding the Vietnam War, Congress attempted to impose more control on the war-making authority of the president by passing the War Powers Resolution of 1973. In many cases, presidents, however, have ignored, evaded, or manipulated the requirements of the Resolution. So far, despite protests by many members, Congress has been unwilling to take further action that would require presidents to work more closely with the congressional majority.

Since 1789, when the national government began operating under the Constitution, Congress has passed eight declarations of war involving five hostilities (the War of 1812, the Mexican-American War, the Spanish-American War, and the First and Second World Wars). Yet as early as 1798 President John Adams used the navy against French ships in an undeclared naval war, an action which the Supreme Court . . . upheld, holding that there could be "perfect" wars declared by Congress as well as "imperfect" undeclared wars.

Since then, our armed forces have been used more than two hundred times without declarations of war. Many of these involved small operations: anti-terrorist actions, protection of American lives and property in civil disturbance, evacuations of Americans and third-party nationals, participation in international policing or peacekeeping efforts, covert operations designed to destabilize or overthrow foreign governments, airlifts

SOURCE: Reprinted from "Presidential War Powers, the War Powers Resolution, and the Persian Gulf" by Richard M. Pious, in *The Constitution and the American Presidency* by Martin Fausold and Alan Shank by permission of the State University of New York Press.

*Footnotes deleted.

or sealifts of supplies to neutral or friendly nations involved in hostilities, convoying ships of neutral or friendly nations, convoying in disputed waters to assert freedom of navigation, and the imposition of blockades and quarantines. Even though these operations usually risked few American lives, some have involved us in direct or indirect confrontation with important regional powers or with the Soviet Union, risking much wider hostilities. In addition, since World War II presidents have involved our nation in two undeclared wars (in Korea and Indochina), in which more than one hundred thousand American servicemen and servicewomen were killed, more than half a million were injured, and hundreds of billions of dollars were expended. . . .

Debates over the reach of presidential war powers cannot be settled conclusively by analyzing the intentions of the Framers of the Constitution of 1787. Neither presidents nor members of Congress limit themselves to these intentions: presidential warmaking remains entangled in constitutional and legal thickets, and debates over war powers have not been settled by the judiciary. Thus, warmaking abroad is paralleled by constitutional warmaking at home: a two-pronged attack against both the viability of the White House policy making and its legitimacy.

◆ Warmaking: Who Decides?

Who should decide when and how the United States would use force in its relations with other nations was one of the most contentious issues debated at the Constitutional Convention. Pierce Butler argued for a powerful president who would have the power to make war. James Madison and James Wilson, fearful of executive tyranny, opposed giving the president the prerogatives exercised by the British Crown. They wanted Congress to continue to exercise war powers, just as it had during the revolutionary war under the Articles of Confederation.

The result was an uneasy compromise. At first glance, the plain meaning of the Constitution seems to divide war powers. Article I, Section 8, grants Congress the power "to declare war," raise the Armed Forces, organize and regulate them, grant letters of marque and reprisal, and punish piracy and other offenses against the law of nations. . . . The appropriations power funds the military, and the "necessary and proper" clause gives Congress broad legislative powers for war waging. Article II names the president commander in chief of the armed forces (and of the state militias when called into national service). He has the executive power of the United States. . . . By and with the advice and consent of the Senate, the president appoints military officers. . . .

These grants of power are ambiguous, underdefined, or incomplete. They do not cover the entire field of war powers, and their loose construction virtually invites the president and Congress into boundary disputes. . . . For example, the Constitution makes no mention of aggressive war, acquisition of territory, interventions and interpositions, police actions, truces, armistices, proclamations of neutrality, convoying in sea lanes, undeclared naval wars, or covert operations. Nonetheless, all these are acts of sovereign nations, and presidents have engaged in all of these activities.

Consider the powers of Congress, which are also loose and ambiguous and provide ample opportunity for expansion. The early Convention drafts gave it the power "to make war," but this was changed to "declare" because some delegates argued that the original wording would have prevented the government from repelling an invasion unless and until Congress assembled (which might not be possible if an enemy launched a surprise attack which cut off north from south). Does this imply that the power "to make war" goes to the president? . . . Justice William Paterson (a delegate to the Convention) later held in a case that "there is a manifest distinction between our going to war with a nation at peace, and a war being made against us by an actual invasion. . . . In the former case, it is the exclusive province of Congress to change a state of peace into a state of war." May the declaration itself become more than a simple statement "changing a state of peace into a state of war"? Can it be used to define war aims? To prescribe how a war is to be conducted? To limit the president's discretion in using force? . . .

Constitutional ambiguities continue to provoke commentators into disparate interpretations of executive and legislative war powers, which have led to fierce debates over the legitimacy of presidential warmaking. During the Mexican-American War, President Polk's actions in sending troops into disputed territories to provoke a Mexican response were roundly condemned in his maiden speech to the House of Representatives by an obscure first-term member of the Whig party named Abraham Lincoln. The Whigs even managed to pass a resolution in Congress which condemned that war as "illegally and unconstitutionally begun." Later, Lincoln was on the receiving end of this kind of criticism, as northern Democrats attacked his conduct in provoking and prosecuting the Civil War in much the same terms. Indeed, much of the 1864 Democratic party platform involved an attack on the prerogatives asserted by Lincoln. Today the debates over war powers are carried on in much the same terms as these nineteenth-century disputes: those who worry chiefly about how effectively our nation can use its armed forces to project its power abroad tend to advocate presidential war powers; those concerned about constitutional balance, or about the arrogance of presidential power at home and abroad, seek to expand the congressional role. . . .

Proponents of presidential power argue that each power granted to Congress can be treated as a limited exception to the war powers confided by the Constitution in the commander in chief. The president, the argument goes, can unilaterally send American forces into combat as part of his duty to see laws faithfully executed—in this case international law. He may use the armed forces to uphold treaty commitments of the United States without obtaining further congressional approval. He may use the military in a nuclear crisis as part of the understanding that he "preserves, protects, and defends" the constitution. Alternatively, partisans of Congress argue that legislative powers add up to a war-waging power to be exercised by a sovereign Congress over a compliant president. They can also be considered a set of checks that the president must surmount, a form of political constraint that requires him to seek support in Congress in order to gain a national consensus for his war aims. Even presidential orders for the use of nuclear weapons, from this perspective, must be preceded by consultation with congressional leaders.

Consider the impact which these formal powers have on the way we wage war. Congressional powers have a discrete "stop-go" quality to them: either the legislature chooses to declare war, or it does not; either it grants legislative and budgetary authority to draft troops and pay them to fight, or it does not; either it insists that hostilities be ended, or it does not; either it consents to a peace treaty, or it does not. These constitutional powers provide Congress with only an intermittent and sporadic influence over war-waging. . . .

In contrast, the president's constitutional war-waging powers permit him to exercise continuous direction and supervision over the armed forces. He may deploy forces to "signal" other nations, he may engage in total war, or he may do anything in between in his attempt to calibrate means and ends and comply with the international law of proportionality in the use of armed force, as well as with strategic and tactical doctrines.

◆ The War Powers Resolution

To see how the intermittent exercise of legislative power intersects with the continuous obligations of executive power, let us consider how presidents have used the armed forces in hostilities since passage of the War Powers Resolution in 1973 over President Nixon's veto. "At long last," proclaimed its sponsor, Senator Jacob Javits, "Congress is determined to recapture the awesome power to make war." But did it?

The purpose of the WPR is to "insure that the collective judgment of both the Congress and the president will apply to the introduction of United States armed forces into hostilities" or into situations in which hostilities might be imminent. Section 2(c) restricted presidential war-making to situations in which Congress had declared war or given specific statutory authorization, or in which the United States, its territories or possessions or armed forces, had been attacked. . . . Section 3 required the president "in every possible instance" to consult with Congress before introducing American forces into hostilities. And after every such introduction he was to "consult regularly with the Congress until United States Armed Forces are no longer engaged in hostilities or have been removed from such situations." Section 4 required the president to report to Congress within forty-eight hours of such introduction of forces, and every six months thereafter. . . .

Presidential use of force in hostilities triggered a sixty-day period, (under Section 5 of the WPR), at the end of which time the president would have to remove troops unless he obtained one of the following from Congress: a declaration of war; specific statutory authorization to continue fighting; or an extension of the time limit. Unless the president obtained congressional approval, he would have thirty days to remove the forces. Moreover, at any time that the president used force without a declaration of war or specific statutory authorization, Congress could by concurrent resolution (not subject to presidential veto) order him to withdraw within thirty days.

The WPR has had limited impact. Presidents from Ford (the Mayaguez rescue attempt of 1975) through Bush (troop movements to Panama during a 1989 coup attempt against Noriega) have routinely minimized, evaded or ignored its provisions, arguing that it is an unconstitutional infringement on their powers as commander in chief, that it weakens the certainty of collective security arrangements, and that it fails to consider important security interests of the nation. They ignore the prior consultation clause. The WPR did not specify with whom the president should consult. . . . Consultation was not required in all cases, but only if the president thought it "feasible." Nor did the language define "consult." Presidents assume that they are complying with the WPR if they simply brief several senior members of Congress after the fact, not while decision is pending on the use of force.

Presidents sometimes ignore the reporting requirements. Congress, after all, cannot compel a president to issue a report within forty-eight hours of using force, particularly if the president denies that the use of force constitutes "hostilities.". . . Even when presidents do issue reports, it is in the form of a two-page letter, with less information about the incident than can be found in the evening's network news. Presidential reports are not issued "under" the WPR, and do not refer to it, nor to the sixty-day "clock" which is supposed to limit their use of the armed forces without subsequent legislative approval. Thus, if Congress wishes to set a time limit, it must do so itself, just when the crisis is heating up and the American people are likely to "rally round the flag" and support the administration and its version of events—making it extremely unlikely it will oppose the presidential decision.

Presidents can ignore the WPR's congressional sanctions with impunity. The provision allowing Congress to end presidential war-making by concurrent resolution is probably unconstitutional, given the Supreme Court holding in the *INS* v. *Chadha* case that such "legislative veto" resolutions which are not in turn presented to the president for *his* signature or veto are unconstitutional. Thus, the only way Congress could check the president would be by a *joint* resolution which is subject to presidential veto—and Congress has yet to amend the WPR to provide for such a mechanism. . . .

Presidents have no incentive to make the WPR work. On the contrary, they have every incentive to sabotage or ignore it. Consider the *Mayaguez* crisis during the Ford administration. In 1975 the Khmer Rouge government in Cambodia seized the American merchant ship *U.S.S. Mayaguez* in international waters. It was taken to the island of Kho Tang. President Ford demanded that the ship be released, but the message, relayed through Peking, was slow in getting to Cambodia. Two days later, without consulting members of Congress in advance, Ford ordered U.S. planes to attack Cambodian patrol boats. The next day, again without advance consultation, the president ordered [the] marines to rescue the crew. They stormed onto the wrong island, ran into an ambush, and suffered heavy casualties before withdrawing. Yet shortly before the operation was launched, Cambodians in another sector had released the crew in a boat which was picked up by the navy, which also retrieved their abandoned ship. Had Ford taken the extra time to consult members of Congress, the operation would have been delayed, the news of the crew's release would have reached Washington—and forty-one marines might not have died, nor fifty have been wounded.

. . . President Carter did not consult with Congress prior to attempting the rescue of American hostages in Iran, which prompted the resignation of Secretary of State Cyrus Vance, who had promised the Senate at his confirmation hearing that the administration would consult Congress before committing American armed forces in a rescue attempt.

President Reagan also ignored key provisions of the WPR, delayed complying with others, and narrowed the reach of the act. The invasion of Grenada provides an illustration. The administration sent 1,900 marines and 4,000 airborne rangers into Grenada in 1983 in the midst of a civil war involving rival Marxist factions of the government, with instructions to evacuate American medical students, "forestall further chaos," and "help in the restoration of democratic institutions in Grenada." Reagan did not consult Congress or obtain its prior approval. His final orders for the invasion were issued three hours before five leaders of Congress were given a briefing. Twelve hours after the invasion, Reagan sent a letter to Congress in lieu of a formal report, but did not activate the sixty-day clock—although in putting down the resistance eighteen American soldiers were killed and thirty-nine wounded. Congress thereupon decided to start the sixty-day clock itself: by a vote of 403 to 23 in the House and 64 to 20 in the Senate, with a majority of both houses voting in favor—but did so in separate legislative vehicles which did not trigger the clock. The popularity of the invasion with the American people, as well as the quick victory which made withdrawal of most American forces possible within the week, forestalled any conflict between president and Congress. . . .

For a time in Reagan's second term, the WPR became completely inoperative. The administration decided to punish the regime of Colonel Muammar Khadaffi for its support of international terrorism. On March 25, 1986, in operation Prairie Fire, A–7 and A–6 naval attack planes armed with Harm and Harpoon missiles hit a Libyan missile site and two patrol boats after six Sam–5 missiles were launched at American aircraft on routine patrol over the Gulf of Sidra. Although the operation had been decided upon on March 14, Congress was never briefed—even though the Soviet Union was given advance warning so it could evacuate its technicians from Libyan missile sites to avoid a great power confrontation. State Department legal advisor Abraham Sofaer argued that no consultation was required if American forces were operating in international waters or airspace—even if their location might expose them to hostile fire, further restricting the reach of the WPR. . . .

◆ Case Study: War Powers in the Persian Gulf, 1987–1988

American naval convoying in the Persian Gulf in the late 1980s demonstrates continued congressional impotence and judicial evasion in dealing with presidential war powers. Our nation's regional interests in the Persian Gulf are to ensure the stability of friendly oil-producing countries, maintain freedom of navigation in international waters, and promote a balanced settlement of the Iran-Iraq conflict. Our strategic interests are to increase our influence in the region at the expense of the Soviet Union, for as President Carter put it in his address of January 23, 1980, "any attempt by any outside force to gain control of the Persian Gulf region will be regarded as an assault on the vital interests of the United States, and such an assault will be repelled by any means necessary, including military force."

. . . In May 1984 U.S. warships in the gulf began escorting oil tankers chartered by the navy's Military Sealift Command to provide fuel for our naval forces in the area. And in late May 1987, the Defense Department announced that President Reagan had acceded to a Kuwaiti request to reflag eleven of its tankers and provide naval protection for them, a move directed against Iran, which had been attacking ships heading toward Kuwait and other gulf nations, and designed to preempt an offer by the Soviet Union to provide such protection for supertankers in the Gulf. This decision was made in late February without congressional collaboration, and communicated to the Kuwaitis on March 7. It was not until March 19 that the Senate Foreign Relations Committee received its first word of the decision.

American warships sailed in dangerous waters. On May 17, while on routine patrol, the destroyer *U.S.S. Stark* was severely damaged by an Iraqi missile, and thirty-seven sailors were killed. Three days later, the Pentagon announced new rules of engagement which put American warships on a high state of alert, with permission to shoot at Iraqi or Iranian aircraft approaching in a threatening manner (an action taken that August against an Iranian aircraft). Through 1987 and into early 1988, American warships convoyed the reflagged Kuwaiti tankers and other American flagships through the Gulf with great success. Our ships were rarely attacked, and the only damage sustained came from mines, most of which were neutralized by minesweepers. Meanwhile, ships of other nations not protected by American and European convoying operations had to brave magnetic mines, silkworm missiles, bombing and strafing by airplanes, and rocket-propelled grenades launched from speedboats. Most observers gave the administration high marks for its tactical successes, and the convoying no doubt contributed to Iran's decision to enter into negotiations with Iraq in 1988. . . .

After the president announced the decision to convoy the reflagged vessels, some officials (Defense Secretary Weinberger, Secretary of State Schultz, NSC advisor Carlucci) claimed that the War Powers Resolution did not apply since their intention was to deter further military action. They held to that position even after the *Stark* was damaged by the Iraqis. Yet a military convoy operation (complete with minesweeping) is clearly a risky venture, in which fighting may occur. Shouldn't Congress have been in on that decision? Other officials in the Reagan administration (Chief of Staff Howard Baker, Attorney General Edwin Meese, and Treasury Secretary James Baker), argued that Congress should be brought in under the War Powers Act, but they were overruled. . . . Democrats in the House (110 of them) thereupon brought suit in federal court to direct the president to obey the WPR requirements, a suit which was dismissed immediately by the federal district court in which it was filed on the grounds that compliance with this law involved "a political question.". . .

The administration held a strong hand. It had enough supporters in the Senate to prevent Congress from taking any action against its policy. . . .

Eventually the administration decided on limited consultation. When the U.S. frigate *Samuel B. Roberts* suffered extensive damage and casualties after hitting a mine laid by the Iranian navy, congressional leaders were summoned to the White House for consultations on a possible American reprisal. "For the first time, we were consulted before the 'executive' order was sent out and before it was decided," said Senate Majority Leader Robert Byrd, agreeing that a reprisal would be "a legitimate response." The U.S. cruiser *Wainwright* and frigate *Simpson* and destroyer *Joseph Strauss* and A–6 jets from the carrier *Enterprise* thereupon sank or damaged three Iranian warships (the *Joshan, Sahand,* and *Sabalan*), and three motor boats, and damaged the Sassan and Sirri oil platforms. On April 20 Reagan sent a report to Congress, "consistent with" provisions of the WPR.

Because congressional leaders had been in on the decision, there was no discussion on the floor of Congress in the days immediately following the attack. On April 19, Senator Robert Dole observed: "Having attended a number of 'consultations,' I have found over the years that they primarily have been notifications, not consultations, but I think that in this instance, to the credit of the administration, there were consultations." "There won't be a fight, so long as they keep consulting," Democratic House Whip Tony Coelho promised. On June 7, a majority of the Senate (by a 51–31 vote) upheld a parliamentary maneuver to block a vote on keeping forces in the Gulf, further acquiescing in (or legitimizing, depending on your point of view) the president's policy.

Congressional reactions to the administration policy are perhaps best understood in the context of American public opinion. Americans don't like the armed forces being sent to faraway places to act as the world's police force. They don't want casualties in small scale military operations. But they also rally round the president and the military when it is perceived to be under attack. Thus, after the navy attacked and captured an Iranian minesweeper in the Gulf, a NYT/CBS news poll found that 78 percent of the public approved while only 8 percent disapproved. Moreover, 64 percent favored an attack on Iran if it attacked U.S. ships, only 24 percent were opposed. Yet, as public opinion in the Vietnam War and in the Lebanon peacekeeping operation demonstrates, the public mood is volatile. Support can drop sharply if casualties are high.

For the most part in the convoying operation, the president missed an opportunity to use the WPR. As Alan Cranston put it, "Like his Democratic and Republican predecessors, Reagan has failed to strengthen his hand by seizing the opportunity that war powers requirements can offer for enlisting congressional support." Instead, by ignoring the War Powers Resolution, the president simply alienated members of Congress, gave opponents of his policy leverage by allowing them to raise constitutional and legal issues and fault the legitimacy of his actions.

On all counts, the WPR has been a failure. Presidents have ignored its requirements with impunity, confident that its provisions would never stand up in court. Members of Congress have used it as a convenient way to distance themselves from the administration—unless it turns out that the operations are successful, in which case they drop their objections and ignore the WPR. Congress has not insisted that the administration adhere to the terms of the WPR, and there is no reason to think it will be anything more than a dead letter in the future.

"It is not a lack of power which has prevented the Congress from ending the war in Indochina," Senator William J. Fulbright observed in 1972, "But a lack of will." The same could well be said of the reason why Congress cannot get presidents to collaborate effectively on decisions involving peace and war. Given the ambiguities and silences of the Constitution of 1787, the realities of constitutional interpretation are created "on the ground," when presidents and Congress interact. The only way for Congress to play an important role in decisions about peace or war is to insist on it, and then to do so. The record to date gives little indication that Congress will defend either its constitutional prerogatives or its statutory powers under the WPR. And if Congress will not stand up for itself, is there any reason to suppose that either the president or the judiciary will stand up for it?

TOWARD CRITICAL THINKING

1. How does the War Powers Resolution provide "cover" for Congress if a war becomes unpopular? What could Congress do if it really wants to end U.S. participation in a war? What authority did President Clinton have to send troops to the Gulf again in late 1994?

2. Why are presidents reluctant to abide by the demands of the War Powers Resolution? Could Congress manage a war itself?

THINKING ABOUT FOREIGN AND MILITARY POLICY

1. What should the role of the United States be in foreign affairs today? Should the United States intervene to protect human rights violations in other nations, for example?

2. How has Congress's role in foreign affairs diminished since the late 1700s? Do new technologies point to the need to give the president expanded formal powers to conduct foreign affairs?

The Constitution of the United States of America

We the People of the United States, in Order to form a more perfect Union, establish Justice, insure domestic Tranquility, provide for the common defence, promote the general Welfare, and secure the Blessings of Liberty to ourselves and our Posterity, do ordain and establish this Constitution for the United States of America.

ARTICLE I

SECTION 1. All legislative Powers herein granted shall be vested in a Congress of the United States, which shall consist of a Senate and House of Representatives.

SECTION 2. The House of Representatives shall be composed of Members chosen every second Year by the People of the several States, and the Electors in each State shall have the Qualifications requisite for Electors of the most numerous Branch of the State Legislature.

No person shall be a Representative who shall not have attained to the Age of twenty five Years, and been seven Years a Citizen of the United States, and who shall not, when elected, be an Inhabitant of that State in which he shall be chosen.

Representatives and direct Taxes shall be apportioned among the several States which may be included within this Union, according to their respective Numbers which shall be determined by adding to the whole Number of free Persons, including those bound to Service for a Term of Years, and excluding Indians not taxed, three fifths of all other Persons. The actual Enumeration shall be made within three Years after the first Meeting of the Congress of the United States, and within every subsequent Term ten Years, in such Manner as they shall by Law direct. The Number of Representatives shall not exceed one for every thirty Thousand, but each State shall have at Least one Representative; and until such enumeration shall be made, the State of New Hampshire shall be entitled to chuse three, Massachusetts eight, Rhode-Island and Providence Plantations one, Connecticut five, New-York six, New Jersey four, Pennsylvania eight, Delaware one, Maryland six, Virginia ten, North Carolina five, South Carolina five, and Georgia three.

When vacancies happen in the Representation from any State, the Executive Authority thereof shall issue Writs of Election to fill such Vacancies.

The House of Representatives shall chuse their speaker and other Officers; and shall have the sole Power of Impeachment.

SECTION 3. The Senate of the United States shall be composed of two Senators from each State chosen by the Legislature thereof, for six Years; and each Senator shall have one Vote.

Immediately after they shall be assembled in Consequence of the first Election, they shall be divided as equally as may be into three Classes. The Seats of the Senators of the first Class shall be vacated at the Expiration of the second year, of the second Class at the Expiration of the fourth Year, and of the third Class at the Expiration of the sixth Year, so that one third may be chosen every second Year and if Vacancies happen by Resignation, or otherwise, during the Recess of the Legislature of any State, the Executive thereof may make temporary Appointments until the next Meeting of the Legislature, which shall then fill such Vacancies.

No Person shall be a Senator who shall not have attained to the Age of thirty Years, and been nine Years a Citizen of the United States, and who shall not, when elected, be an Inhabitant of that State for which he shall be chosen.

The Vice President of the United States shall be President of the Senate, but shall have no Vote, unless they be equally divided.

The Senate shall chuse their other Officers, and also a President pro tempore, in the Absence of the Vice President, or when he shall exercise the Office of President of the United States.

The Senate shall have the sole Power to try all Impeachments. When sitting for that Purpose, they shall be on Oath or Affirmation. When the President of the United States is tried, the Chief Justice shall preside: And no Person shall be convicted without the Concurrence of two thirds of the Members present.

Judgment in Cases of Impeachment shall not extend further than to removal from Office, and disqualification to hold and enjoy any Office of honor, Trust or Profit under the United States; but the Party convicted shall nevertheless be liable and subject to Indictment, Trial, Judgment and Punishment, according to Law.

SECTION 4. The Times, Places and Manner of holding Elections for Senators and Representatives, shall be prescribed in each State by the Legislature thereof; but the Congress may at any time by law make or alter such Regulations, except as to the Places of chusing Senators.

The Congress shall assemble at least once in every Year, and such Meeting shall be on the first Monday in December, unless they shall by Law appoint a different Day.

SECTION 5. Each House shall be the Judge of the Elections, Returns and Qualifications of its own Members, and a Majority of each shall constitute a Quorum to do Business; but a smaller Number may adjourn from day to day, and may be authorized to compel the Attendance of absent Members, in such Manner, and under such Penalties as each House may provide.

Each House may determine the Rules of its Proceedings, punish its Members for disorderly Behaviour, and with the Concurrence of two thirds, expel a Member.

Each House shall keep a journal of its Proceedings, and from time to time publish the same, excepting such Parts as may in their judgment require Secrecy; and the Yeas and Nays of the Members of either House on any question shall, at the Desire of one fifth of those present, be entered on the Journal.

Neither House, during the Session of Congress, shall, without the Consent of the other, adjourn for more than three days, nor to any other Place than that in which the two Houses shall be sitting.

SECTION 6. The Senators and Representatives shall receive a Compensation for their Services, to be ascertained by Law, and paid out of the Treasury of the United States. They shall in all Cases, except Treason, Felony and Breach of the

Peace, be privileged from Arrest during their Attendance at the Session of their respective Houses, and in going to and returning from the same; and for any Speech or Debate in either House, they shall not be questioned in any other Place.

No Senator or Representative shall, during the Time for which he was elected, be appointed to any civil Office under the Authority of the United States, which shall have been created, or the Emoluments whereof shall have been encreased during such time; and no Person holding any Office under the United States, shall be a Member of either House during his Continuance in Office.

SECTION 7. All Bills for raising Revenue shall originate in the House of Representatives; but the Senate may propose or concur with Amendments as on other Bills.

Every Bill which shall have passed the House of Representatives and the Senate, shall, before it become a Law, be presented to the President of the United States; If he approves he shall sign it, but if not he shall return it, with his Objections to that House in which it shall have originated, who shall enter the Objections at large on their journal, and proceed to reconsider it. If after such Reconsideration two thirds of that House shall agree to pass the Bill, it shall be sent, together with the Objections, to the other House, by which it shall likewise be reconsidered, and if approved by two thirds of that House, it shall become a Law. But in all such Cases the Votes of both Houses shall be determined by yeas and Nays, and the Names of the Persons voting for and against the Bill shall be entered on the Journal of each House respectively. If any Bill shall not be returned by the President within ten Days (Sundays excepted) after it shall have been presented to him, the Same shall be a Law, in like Manner as if he had signed it, unless the Congress by their Adjournment prevent its Return, in which Case it shall not be a Law.

Every Order, Resolution, or Vote to which the Concurrence of the Senate and House of Representatives may be necessary (except on a question of Adjournment) shall be presented to the President of the United States; and before the Same shall take Effect, shall be approved by him, or being disapproved by him, shall be repassed by two thirds of the Senate and House of Representatives, according to the Rules and Limitations prescribed in the Case of a Bill.

SECTION 8. The Congress shall have Power To lay and collect Taxes, Duties, Imposts and Excises, to pay the Debts and provide for the common Defence and general Welfare of the United States; but all Duties, Imposts and Excises shall be uniform throughout the United States;

To borrow Money on the credit of the United States;

To regulate Commerce with foreign Nations, and among the several States, and with the Indian Tribes;

To establish a uniform Rule of Naturalization, and uniform Laws on the subject of Bankruptcies throughout the United States;

To coin Money, regulate the Value thereof, and of foreign Coin, and fix the Standard of Weights and Measures;

To provide for the Punishment of counterfeiting the Securities and current Coin of the United States;

To establish Post Offices and post Roads;

To promote the Progress of Science and useful Arts, by securing for limited Times to Authors and Inventors the exclusive Right to their respective Writings and Discoveries;

To constitute Tribunals inferior to the supreme Court;

To define and punish Piracies and Felonies committed on the high Seas, and Offences against the Law of Nations;

To declare War, grant Letters of Marque and Reprisal, and make Rules concerning Captures on Land and Water;

To raise and support Armies, but no Appropriation of Money to that Use shall be for a longer Term than two Years;

To provide and maintain a Navy;

To make Rules for the Government and Regulation of the land and naval Forces;

To provide for calling forth the Militia to execute the Laws of the Union, suppress Insurrections and repel Invasions;

To provide for organizing, arming, and disciplining, the Militia, and for governing such Part of them as may be employed in the Service of the United States, reserving to the States respectively, the Appointment of the Officers, and the Authority of training the Militia according to the discipline prescribed by Congress;

To exercise exclusive Legislation in all Cases whatsoever, over such District (not exceeding ten Miles square) as may, by Cession of particular States, and the Acceptance of Congress, become the Seat of the Government of the United States, and to exercise like Authority over all Places purchased by the Consent of the Legislature of the State in which the Same shall be for the Erection of Forts, Magazines, Arsenals, dock-Yards, and other needful Buildings;—And

To make all Laws which shall be necessary and proper for carrying into Execution the foregoing Powers, and all other Powers vested by this Constitution in the Government of the United States, or in any Department or Officer thereof.

SECTION 9. The Migration or Importation of such Persons as any of the States now existing shall think proper to admit, shall not be prohibited by the Congress prior to the Year one thousand eight hundred and eight, but a Tax or duty may be imposed on such Importation, not exceeding ten dollars for each Person.

The Privilege of the Writ of Habeas Corpus shall not be suspended, unless when in Cases of Rebellion or Invasion the public Safety may require it.

No Bill of Attainder or ex post facto Law shall be passed.

No Capitation, or other direct, Tax shall be laid, unless in Proportion to the Census or Enumeration herein before directed to be taken.

No Tax or Duty shall be laid on Articles exported from any State.

No Preference shall be given by any Regulation of Commerce or Revenue to the Ports of one State over those of another; nor shall Vessels bound to, or from, one State, be obliged to enter, clear, or pay Duties in another.

No Money shall be drawn from the Treasury, but in Consequence of Appropriations made by Law; and a regular Statement and Account of the Receipts and Expenditures of all public Money shall be published from time to time.

No Title of Nobility shall be granted by the United States: And no Person holding any Office of Profit or Trust under them, shall, without the Consent of the Congress, accept of any present, Emolument, Office, or Title, of any kind whatever, from any King, Prince, or foreign State.

SECTION 10. No state shall enter into any Treaty, Alliance, or Confederation; grant Letters of Marque and Reprisal; coin Money; emit Bills of Credit; make any Thing but gold and silver Coin a Tender in Payment of Debts; pass any Bill of Attainder, ex post facto Law, or Law impairing the Obligation of Contracts, or grant any Title of Nobility.

No State shall, without the Consent of the Congress, lay any Imposts or Duties on Imports or Exports, except what may be absolutely necessary for executing its inspection Laws: and the net Produce of all Duties and Imposts, laid by any State on Imports or Exports, shall be for the Use of the Treasury of the United States, and all such Laws shall be subject to the Revision and Controul of the Congress.

No State shall, without the Consent of Congress, lay any Duty of Tonnage, keep Troops, or Ships of War in time of Peace, enter into any Agreement or Compact with another State, or with a foreign Power, or engage in War, unless actually invaded, or in such imminent Danger as will not admit of delay.

ARTICLE II

SECTION 1. The executive Power shall be vested in a President of the United States of America. He shall hold his Office during the Term of four Years, and, together with the Vice President, chosen for the same Term, be elected as follows.

Each State shall appoint, in such Manner as the Legislature thereof may direct, a Number of Electors, equal to the whole Number of Senators and Representatives to which the State may be entitled in the Congress; but no Senator or Representative, or Person holding an Office of Trust of Profit under the United States, shall be appointed an Elector.

The Electors shall meet in their respective States, and vote by Ballot for two Persons, of whom one at least shall not be an Inhabitant of the same State with themselves. And they shall make a List of all the Persons voted for, and, of the Number of Votes for each; which List they shall sign and certify, and transmit sealed to the Seat of the Government of the United States, directed to the President of the Senate. The President of the Senate shall, in the Presence of the Senate and House of Representatives, open all the Certificates, and the Votes shall then be counted. The Person having the greatest Number of Votes shall be the President, if such Number be a Majority of the whole Number of Electors appointed; and if there be more than one who have such Majority, and have an equal Number of Votes, then the House of Representatives shall immediately chuse by Ballot one of them for President; and if no Person have a Majority, then from the five highest on the List the said House shall in like Manner chuse the President. But in chusing the President, the Votes shall be taken by States, the Representation from each State having one Vote; A quorum for this Purpose shall consist of a Member or Members from two thirds of the States, and a Majority of all the States shall be necessary to a Choice. In every Case, after the Choice of the President, the Person having the greatest Number of Votes of the Electors shall be the Vice President. But if there should remain two or more who have equal Votes, the Senate shall chuse from them by Ballot the Vice President.

The Congress may determine the Time of chusing the Electors, and the Day on which they shall give their Votes; which Day shall be the same throughout the United States.

No Person except a natural born Citizen, or a Citizen of the United States, at the time of the Adoption of this Constitution, shall be eligible to the Office of President; neither shall any Person be eligible to that Office who shall not have attained to the Age of thirty five Years, and been fourteen Years a Resident within the United States.

In Case of the Removal of the President from Office, or of his Death, Resignation, or Inability to discharge the Powers and Duties of the said Office, the Same shall devolve on the Vice President, and the Congress may by Law provide for the Case of Removal, Death, Resignation or Inability, both of the President and Vice President, declaring what Officer shall then act as President, and such Officer shall act accordingly, until the Disability be removed, or a President shall be elected.

The President shall, at stated Times, receive for his Services, a Compensation, which shall neither be encreased nor diminished during the Period for which he shall have been elected, and he shall not receive within that Period any other Emolument from the United States, or any of them.

Before he enter on the Execution of his Office, he shall take the following Oath or Affirmation—"I do solemnly swear (or affirm) that I will faithfully execute the Office of President of the United States, and will to the best of my Ability, preserve, protect and defend the Constitution of the United States."

SECTION 2. The President shall be Commander in Chief of the Army, and Navy of the United States, and of the Militia of the several States, when called into the actual Service of the United States; he may require the Opinion, in writing, of the principal Officer in each of the executive Departments, upon any Subject relating to the Duties of their respective Offices, and he shall have Power to grant Reprieves and Pardons for Offences against the United States, except in Cases of Impeachment.

He shall have Power, by and with the Advice and Consent of the Senate, to make Treaties, provided two thirds of the Senators present concur; and he shall nominate, and by and with the Advice and Consent of the Senate, shall appoint Ambassadors, other public Ministers and Consuls, Judges of the supreme Court, and all other Officers of the United States, whose Appointments are not herein otherwise provided for, and which shall be established by Law: but the Congress may by Law vest the Appointment of such inferior Officers, as they think proper, in the President alone, in the Courts of Law, or in the Heads of Departments.

The President shall have Power to fill up all Vacancies that may happen during the Recess of the Senate, by granting Commissions which shall expire at the end of their next Session.

SECTION 3. He shall from time to time give to the Congress Information of the State of the Union, and recommend to their Consideration such Measures as he shall judge necessary and expedient; he may, on extraordinary Occasions, convene both Houses, or either of them, and in Case of Disagreement between them, with Respect to the Time of Adjournment, he may adjourn them to such Time as he shall think proper; he shall receive Ambassadors and other public Ministers; he shall take Care that the Laws be faithfully executed, and shall Commission all the Officers of the United States.

SECTION 4. The President, Vice President and all civil Officers of the United States, shall be removed from Office on Impeachment for, and Conviction of, Treason, Bribery, or other high Crimes and Misdemeanors.

ARTICLE III

SECTION 1. The judicial Power of the United States, shall be vested in one supreme Court, and in such inferior Courts as the Congress may from time to time ordain and establish. The Judges, both of the supreme and inferior Courts, shall hold their Offices during good Behaviour, and shall, at stated Times, receive for their Services, a Compensation, which shall not be diminished during their Continuance in Office.

SECTION 2. The judicial Power shall extend to all Cases, in Law and Equity, arising under this Constitution, the Laws of the United States, and Treaties made, or which shall be made, under their Authority;—to all Cases affecting Ambassadors, other public Ministers and Consuls;—to all Cases of admiralty and maritime Jurisdiction;—to Controversies to which the United States shall be a Party;—to Controversies between two or more States;—between a State and Citizens of another State;—between Citizens of different States,—between Citizens of the same State claiming Lands under Grants of different States,—and between a State, or the Citizens thereof, and foreign States, Citizens of Subjects.

In all Cases affecting Ambassadors, other public Ministers and Consuls, and those in which a State shall be Party, the supreme Court shall have original Jurisdiction. In all the other Cases before mentioned, the supreme Court shall have appellate Jurisdiction, both as to Law and Fact, with such Exceptions, and under such Regulations as the Congress shall make.

The Trial of all Crimes, except in Cases of Impeachment, shall be by Jury; and such Trial shall be held in the State where the said Crimes shall have been committed; but when not committed within any State, the Trial shall be at such Place or Places as the Congress may by Law have directed.

SECTION 3. Treason against the United States, shall consist only in levying War against them, or in adhering to their Enemies, giving them Aid and Comfort. No Person shall be convicted of Treason unless on the Testimony of two Witnesses to the same overt Act, or on Confession in open Court.

The Congress shall have Power to declare the Punishment of Treason, but no Attainder of Treason shall work Corruption of Blood, or Forfeiture except during the Life of the Person attainted.

ARTICLE IV

SECTION 1. Full Faith and Credit shall be given in each State to the public Acts, Records, and judicial Proceedings of every other State. And the Congress may by general Laws prescribe the Manner in which such Acts, Records and Proceedings shall be proved, and the Effect thereof.

SECTION 2. The Citizens of each State shall be entitled to all Privileges and Immunities of Citizens in the several States.

A Person charged in any State with Treason, Felony, or other Crime, who shall flee from Justice, and be found in another State, shall on Demand of the executive Authority of the State from which he fled, be delivered up, to be removed to the State having Jurisdiction of the Crime.

No Person held to Service or Labour in one State under the Laws thereof, escaping into another, shall, in Consequence of any Law or Regulation therein, be discharged from such Service or Labour, but shall be delivered up on Claim of the Party to whom such Service or Labour may be due.

SECTION 3. New States may be admitted by the Congress into this Union; but no new State shall be formed or erected within the Jurisdiction of any other State; nor any State be formed by the Junction of two or more States, or Parts of States, without the Consent of the Legislatures of the States concerned as well as of the Congress.

The Congress shall have Power to dispose of and make all needful Rules and Regulations respecting the Territory or other Property belonging to the United States; and nothing in this Constitution shall be so construed as to Prejudice any Claims of the United States, or of any particular State.

SECTION 4. The United States shall guarantee to every State in this Union a Republican Form of Government, and shall protect each of them against Invasion, and on Application of the Legislature, or of the Executive (when the Legislature cannot be convened) against domestic Violence.

ARTICLE V

The Congress, whenever two thirds of both Houses shall deem it necessary, shall propose Amendments to this Constitution, or, on the Application of the Legislatures of two thirds of the several States, shall call a Convention for proposing Amendments, which, in either Case, shall be valid to all Intents and Purposes, as Part of this Constitution, when ratified by the Legislatures of three fourths of the several States, or by Conventions in three fourths thereof, as the one or the other Mode of Ratification may be proposed by the Congress; Provided that no Amendment which may be made prior to the Year One thousand eight hundred and eight shall in any Manner affect the first and fourth Clauses in the Ninth Section of the first Article; and that no State, without its Consent, shall be deprived of its equal Suffrage in the Senate.

ARTICLE VI

All Debts contracted and Engagements entered into, before the Adoption of this Constitution, shall be as valid against the United States under this Constitution, as under the Confederation.

This Constitution, and the laws of the United States which shall be made in Pursuance thereof; and all Treaties made, or which shall be made, under the Authority of the United States, shall be the supreme Law of the Land; and the Judges in every State shall be bound thereby, any Thing in the Constitution or Laws of any State to the Contrary notwithstanding.

The Senators and Representatives before mentioned, and the Members of the several State Legislatures, and all executive and judicial Officers, both of the United States and of the several States, shall be bound by Oath or Affirmation, to support this Constitution; but no religious Test shall ever be required as a Qualification to any Office or public Trust under the United States.

ARTICLE VII

The Ratification of the Conventions of nine States, shall be sufficient for the Establishment of this Constitution between the States so ratifying the Same.

Done in Convention by the Unanimous Consent of the States present the Seventeenth Day of September in the Year of our Lord one thousand seven hundred and Eighty seven and of the Independence of the United States of America the Twelfth. In WITNESS whereof we have hereunto subscribed our Names,

Go. WASHINGTON
Presid't. and deputy from Virginia

Attest
WILLIAM JACKSON
Secretary

DELAWARE
Geo. Read
Gunning Bedford jun
John Dickinson
Richard Basset
Jaco. Brown

MASSACHUSETTS
Nathaniel Gorham
Rufus King

CONNECTICUT
Wm. Saml Johnson
Roger Sherman

NEW YORK
Alexander Hamilton

NEW JERSEY
Wh. Livingston
David Brearley

Wm. Paterson
Jona. Dayton

PENNSYLVANIA
B. Franklin
Thomas Mifflin
Robt. Morris
Geo. Clymer
Thos. FitzSimons
Jared Ingersoll
James Wilson
Gouv. Morris

NEW HAMPSHIRE
John Langdon
Nicholas Gilman

MARYLAND
James McHenry
Dan of St. Thos. Jenifer
Danl. Carroll

VIRGINIA
John Blair
James Madison, Jr.

NORTH CAROLINA
Wm. Blount
Richd. Dobbs Spaight
Hu. Williamson

SOUTH CAROLINA
J. Rutledge
Charles Cotesworth
  Pinckney
Charles Pinckney
Pierce Butler

GEORGIA
William Few
Abr. Baldwin

Articles in addition to, and amendment of the Constitution of the United States of America, proposed by Congress and ratified by the Legislatures of the several states, pursuant to the Fifth Article of the original Constitution.

(The first ten amendments were passed by Congress on September 25, 1789, and were ratified on December 15, 1791.)

Amendment I

Congress shall make no law respecting an establishment of religion, or prohibiting the free exercise thereof; or abridging the freedom of speech, or of the press; or the right of the people peaceably to assemble, and to petition the Government for a redress of grievances.

Amendment II

A well regulated Militia, being necessary to the security of a free State, the right of the people to keep and bear Arms, shall not be infringed.

Amendment III

No Soldier shall, in time of peace be quartered in any house, without the consent of the Owner, nor in time of war, but in a manner to be prescribed by law.

Amendment IV

The right of the people to be secure in their persons, houses, papers, and effects, against unreasonable searches and seizures, shall not be violated, and no warrants shall issue, but upon probable cause, supported by Oath or affirmation, and particularly describing the place to be searched, and the persons or things to be seized.

Amendment V

No person shall be held to answer for a capital, or otherwise infamous crime, unless on a presentment or indictment of a Grand Jury, except in cases arising in the land or naval forces, or in the Militia, when in actual service in time of War or public danger; nor shall any person be subject for the same offence to be twice put in jeopardy of life or limb; nor shall be compelled in any criminal case to be a witness against himself, nor be deprived of life, liberty, or property, without due process of law; nor shall private property be taken for public use, without just compensation.

Amendment VI

In all criminal prosecutions, the accused shall enjoy the right to a speedy and public trial, by an impartial jury of the State and district wherein the crime shall have been committed, which district shall have been previously ascertained by law, and to be informed of the nature and cause of the accusation; to be confronted with the witnesses against him; to have compulsory process for obtaining witnesses in his favor, and to have the assistance of counsel for his defence.

Amendment VII

In Suits at common law, where the value in controversy shall exceed twenty dollars, the right of trial by jury shall be preserved, and no fact tried by a jury, shall be otherwise re-examined in any Court of the United States, than according to the rules of the common law.

Amendment VIII

Excessive bail shall not be required, nor excessive fines imposed, nor cruel and unusual punishments inflicted.

Amendment IX

The enumeration in the Constitution, of certain rights, shall not be construed to deny or disparage others retained by the people.

Amendment X

The powers not delegated to the United States by the Constitution, nor prohibited by it to the States, are reserved to the States respectively, or to the people.

Amendment XI *(Ratified on February 7, 1795)*

The Judicial power of the United States shall not be construed to extend to any suit in law or equity, commenced or prosecuted against one of the United States by Citizens of another State, or by Citizens or Subjects of any Foreign State.

Amendment XII *(Ratified on June 15, 1804)*

The Electors shall meet in their respective states, and vote by ballot for President and Vice-President, one of whom, at least, shall not be an inhabitant of the same state with themselves; they shall name in their ballots the person voted for as President, and in distinct ballots the person voted for as Vice-President, and they shall make distinct lists of all persons voted for as President, and of all persons voted for as Vice-President, and of the number of votes for each, which lists they shall sign and certify, and transmit sealed to the seat of the government of the United States, directed to the President of the Senate;—The President of the Senate shall, in the presence of the Senate and House of Representatives, open all the certificates and the votes shall then be counted;—The person having the greatest number of votes for President, shall be the President, if such number be a majority of the whole number of Electors appointed; and if no person have such majority; then from the persons having the highest numbers not exceeding three on the list of those voted for as President, the House of Representatives shall choose immediately, by ballot, the President. But in choosing the President, the votes shall be taken by states, the representation from each state having one vote; a quorum for this purpose shall consist of a member or members from two-thirds of the states, and a majority of all the states shall be necessary to a choice. And if the House of Representatives shall not choose a President whenever the right of choice shall devolve upon them, before the fourth day of March next following, then the Vice-President shall act as President, as in the case of the death or other constitutional disability of the President.—The person having the greatest number of votes as Vice-President, shall be the Vice-President, if such number be a majority of the whole number of Electors appointed, and if no person have a majority, then from the two highest numbers on the list, the Senate shall choose the Vice-President; a quorum for the purpose shall consist of two-thirds of the whole number of Senators, and a majority of the whole number shall be necessary to a choice. But no person constitutionally ineligible to the office of President shall be eligible to that of Vice-President of the United States.

Amendment XIII   *(Ratified on December 6, 1865)*

SECTION 1. Neither slavery nor involuntary servitude, except as a punishment for crime whereof the party shall have been duly convicted, shall exist within the United States, or any place subject to their jurisdiction.

SECTION 2. Congress shall have power to enforce this article by appropriate legislation.

Amendment XIV   *(Ratified on July 9, 1868)*

SECTION 1. All persons born or naturalized in the United States, and subject to the jurisdiction thereof, are citizens of the United States and of the State wherein they reside. No State shall make or enforce any law which shall abridge the privileges or immunities of citizens of the United States; nor shall any State deprive any person of life, liberty, or property, without due process of law; nor deny to any person within its jurisdiction the equal protection of the laws.

SECTION 2. Representatives shall be apportioned among the several States according to their respective numbers, counting the whole number of persons in each State, excluding Indians not taxed. But when the right to vote at any election for the choice of electors for President and Vice President of the United States, Representatives in Congress, the Executive and Judicial officers of a State, or the members of the Legislature thereof, is denied to any of the male inhabitants of such State, being twenty-one years of age, and citizens of the United States, or in any way abridged, except for participation in rebellion, or other crime, the basis of representation therein shall be reduced in the proportion which the number of such male citizens shall bear to the whole number of male citizens twenty-one years of age in such State.

SECTION 3. No person shall be a Senator or Representative in Congress, or elector of President and Vice President, or hold any office, civil or military, under the United States, or under any State, who, having previously taken an oath, as a member of Congress, or as an officer of the United States, or as a member of any State legislature, or as an executive or judicial officer of any State, to support the Constitution of the United States, shall have engaged in insurrection or rebellion against the same, or given aid or comfort to the enemies thereof. But Congress may by a vote of two-thirds of each House, remove such diability.

SECTION 4. The validity of the public debt of the United States, authorized by law, including debts incurred for payment of pensions and bounties for services in suppressing insurrection or rebellion, shall not be questioned. But neither the United States nor any State shall assume or pay any debt or obligation incurred in aid of insurrection or rebellion against the United States, or any claim for the loss or emancipation of any slave, but all such debts, obligations and claims shall be held illegal and void.

SECTION 5. The Congress shall have power to enforce, by appropriate legislation, the provisions of this article.

Amendment XV   (Ratified on February 3, 1870)

SECTION 1. The right of citizens of the United States to vote shall not be denied or abridged by the United States or by any State on account of race, color, or previous condition of servitude.

SECTION 2. The Congress shall have power to enforce this article by appropriate legislation.

Amendment XVI   (Ratified on February 3, 1913)

The Congress shall have power to lay and collect taxes on incomes, from whatever source derived, without apportionment among the several States, and without regard to any census or enumeration.

Amendment XVII   (Ratified on April 8, 1913)

The Senate of the United States shall be composed of two Senators from each State, elected by the people thereof, for six years; and each Senator shall have one vote. The electors in each State shall have the qualifications requisite for electors of the most numerous branch of the State legislatures.

When vacancies happen in the representation of any State in the Senate, the executive authority of such State shall issue writs of election to fill such vacancies: Provided, That the legislature of any State may empower the executive thereof to make temporary appointments until the people fill the vacancies by election as the legislature may direct.

This amendment shall not be so construed as to affect the election or term of any Senator chosen before it becomes valid as part of the Constitution.

Amendment XVIII   (Ratified on January 16, 1919)

SECTION 1. After one year from the ratification of this article the manufacture, sale, or transportation of intoxicating liquors within, the importation thereof into, or the exportation thereof from the United States and all territory subject to the jurisdiction thereof for beverage purposes is hereby prohibited.

SECTION 2. The Congress and the several States shall have concurrent power to enforce this article by appropriate legislation.

SECTION 3. This article shall be inoperative unless it shall have been ratified as an amendment to the Constitution by the legislatures of the several States, as provided in the Constitution, within seven years from the date of the submission hereof to the States by the Congress.

Amendment XIX   *(Ratified on August 18, 1920)*

The right of citizens of the United States to vote shall not be denied or abridged by the United States or by any State on account of sex.

Congress shall have power to enforce this article by appropriate legislation.

Amendment XX   *(Ratified on February 6, 1933)*

SECTION 1. The terms of the President and Vice President shall end at noon on the 20th day of January, and the terms of Senators and Representatives at noon on the 3d day of January, of the years in which such terms would have ended if this article had not been ratified; and the terms of their successors shall then begin.

SECTION 2. The Congress shall assemble at least once in every year, and such meeting shall begin at noon on the 3d day of January, unless they shall by law appoint a different day.

SECTION 3. If, at the time fixed for the beginning of the term of the President, the President elect shall have died, the Vice President elect shall become President. If a President shall not have been chosen before the time fixed for the beginning of his term, or if the President elect shall have failed to qualify, then the Vice President elect shall act as President until a President shall have qualified; and the Congress may by law provide for the case wherein neither a President elect nor a Vice President elect shall have qualified, declaring who shall then act as President, or the manner in which one who is to act shall be selected, and such person shall act accordingly until a President or Vice President shall have qualified.

SECTION 4. The Congress may by law provide for the case of the death of any of the persons from whom the House of Representatives may choose a President whenever the rights of choice shall have devolved upon them, and for the case of the death of any of the persons from whom the Senate may choose a Vice President whenever the right of choice shall have devolved upon them.

SECTION 5. Sections 1 and 2 shall take effect on the 15th day of October following the ratification of this article.

SECTION 6. This article shall be inoperative unless it shall have been ratified as an amendment to the Constitution by the legislatures of three-fourths of the several States within seven years from the date of its submission.

Amendment XXI   *(Ratified on December 5, 1933)*

SECTION 1. The eighteenth article of amendment to the Constitution of the United States is hereby repealed.

SECTION 2. The transportation or importation into any State, Territory, or possession of the United States for delivery or use therein of intoxicating liquors, in violation of the laws thereof, is hereby prohibited.

SECTION 3. This article shall be inoperative unless it shall have been ratified as an amendment to the Constitution by conventions in the several States, as provided in the Constitution, within seven years from the date of the submission hereof to the States by the Congress.

Amendment XXII   *(Ratified on February 27, 1951)*

No person shall be elected to the office of the President more than twice, and no person who has held the office of President, or acted as President, for more than two years of a term to which some other person was elected President shall be elected to the office of the President more than once. But this Article shall not apply to any person holding the office of President when this Article was proposed by the Congress, and shall not prevent any person who may be holding the office of President, or acting as President, during the term within which this Article becomes operative from holding the office of President or acting as President during the remainder of such term.

Amendment XXIII   *(Ratified on March 29, 1961)*

SECTION 1. The District constituting the seat of Government of the United States shall appoint in such manner as the Congress may direct:

A number of electors of President and Vice President equal to the whole number of Senators and Representatives in Congress to which the District would be entitled if it were a State, but in no event more than the least populous State; they shall be in addition to those appointed by the States, but they shall be considered, for the purposes of the election of President and Vice President, to be electors appointed by a State; and they shall meet in the District and perform such duties as provided by the twelfth article of amendment.

SECTION 2. The Congress shall have power to enforce this article by appropriate legislation.

Amendment XXIV   *(Ratified on January 23, 1964)*

SECTION 1. The right of citizens of the United States to vote in any primary or other election for President or Vice President, for electors for President or Vice President, or for Senator or Representative in Congress, shall not be denied or abridged by the United States or any State by reason of failure to pay any poll tax or other tax.

SECTION 2. The Congress shall have power to enforce this article by appropriate legislation.

Amendment XXV   *(Ratified on February 10, 1967)*

SECTION 1. In case of the removal of the President from office or of his death or resignation, the Vice President shall become President.

SECTION 2. Whenever there is a vacancy in the office of the Vice President, the President shall nominate a Vice President who shall take office upon confirmation by a majority vote of both Houses of Congress.

SECTION 3. Whenever the President transmits to the President pro tempore of the Senate and the Speaker of the House of Representatives his written declaration that he is unable to discharge the powers and duties of his office, and until he transmits to them a written declaration to the contrary, such powers and duties shall be discharged by the Vice President as Acting President.

SECTION 4. Whenever the Vice President and a majority of either the principal officers of the executive departments or of such other body as Congress may by law provide, transmit to the President pro tempore of the Senate and the Speaker of the House of Representatives their written declaration that the President is unable to discharge the powers and duties of his office, the Vice President shall immediately assume the powers and duties of the office as Acting President.

Thereafter, when the President transmits to the President pro tempore of the Senate and the Speaker of the House of Representatives his written declaration that no inability exists, he shall resume the powers and duties of his office unless the Vice President and a majority of either the principal officers of the executive department or of such other body as Congress may by law provide, transmit within four days to the President pro tempore of the Senate and the Speaker of the House of Representatives their written declaration that the President is unable to discharge the powers and duties of his office. Thereupon Congress shall decide the issue, assembling within forty-eight hours for that purpose if not in session. If the Congress, within twenty-one days after receipt of the latter written declaration, or, if Congress is not in session, within twenty-one days after Congress is required to assemble, determines by two-thirds vote of both Houses that the President is unable to discharge the powers and duties of his office, the Vice President shall continue to discharge the same as Acting President; otherwise, the President shall resume the powers and duties of his office.

Amendment XXVI   *(Ratified on July 1, 1971)*

SECTION 1. The right of citizens of the United States, who are eighteen years of age or older, to vote shall not be denied or abridged by the United States or by any State on account of age.

SECTION 2. The Congress shall have power to enforce this article by appropriate legislation.

Amendment XXVII   *(Ratified on May 7, 1992)*

No law varying the compensation for the services of Senators and Representatives shall take effect until an election of Representatives shall have intervened.